THE PSYCHOLOGY OF
CHRISTIAN PERSONALITY

THE MACMILLAN COMPANY
NEW YORK · CHICAGO
DALLAS · ATLANTA · SAN FRANCISCO

**THE MACMILLAN COMPANY
OF CANADA, LIMITED**
TORONTO

The Psychology of Christian Personality

by
Ernest M. Ligon, Ph.D.
*Department of Psychology, Union College,
Schenectady, New York*

New York
The Macmillan Company
1957

Copyright, 1935, by
THE MACMILLAN COMPANY.

All rights reserved—no part of this book may be reproduced in any form without permission in writing from the publisher, except by a reviewer who wishes to quote brief passages in connection with a review written for inclusion in magazine or newspaper.

Twentieth Printing, 1957

PRINTED IN THE UNITED STATES OF AMERICA

TO MY PARENTS,
ALICE WAGGONER LIGON AND ROBERT LEONARD LIGON,
IN GRATEFUL APPRECIATION FOR THE INSPIRATION
OF THEIR UNFAILING FAITH AND LOVE,
I AFFECTIONATELY DEDICATE
THIS BOOK.

PREFACE

It is the aim of this book to interpret the teachings of Jesus in terms of modern psychology. Religion should play an important part in every phase of the life of its adherents. Furthermore, this rôle should be toward the increased happiness and wholesome personality of men and women. But these attributes also constitute an important part of the problems of psychology. It is manifestly evident that religion has not always led to mental health. It follows, therefore, that psychology may contribute toward an interpretation of religion which will make it the great power that it ought to be in human life. Therefore, I have taken the teachings of Jesus and pointed out the psychological significance of each from the point of view of mental health.

This book has been written with three groups especially in mind. It is hoped that Christian parents will find in it some help toward bringing up their children with such a religious training as will make them not only men and women of integrity and moral character, but also personalities of wholesomeness and power. Ministers who are faced with the task of interpreting the teachings of Jesus to their people, on the one hand, and understanding their sorrows and troubles, on the other, often find no very high correlation between the two. In this interpretation of the teachings of the Sermon on the Mount in terms of psychology, it is hoped that they may find help in unifying these two phases of their ministry. Finally, Christian men and women everywhere and, for that matter, men and women who discern no sources of strength in religion and therefore question its value, may find in these pages an interpretation of religion which will show them both the validity of religion for life and the methods of gaining from it the power that is there.

Since this book is written especially for these three groups, certain features of it have necessarily been determined. In the first place, it is not a scientific monograph. As far as possible technical scientific terminology has been avoided. In the second place, a liberal use of ordinary religious terminology has been employed. In the third place, it contains a much greater measure of apparent dogmatism than accurately represents the attitude of the author toward its various hypotheses. The author is well aware of the tentative nature of many of these hypotheses, and the probability of a great deal of refinement and modification as psychology progresses. The psychological principles presented in the book do represent, however, as far as I am able to judge, the best opinion of psychology at the present time.

The book is based upon the Sermon on the Mount as found in Matthew. I am not unaware of or indifferent to the work of historical criticism in its careful analysis and evaluation of this sermon. The results of a large portion of this work have been examined and have been kept constantly in mind in making an estimate of the reliability of the passages studied. In a very few cases, the evidence that certain passages in the sermon are spurious additions.is so unanimously agreed upon that they have been stricken from the version used in this book. On the other hand, the best attested passages have been studied with more than usual care in an effort to determine whether or not the most certain teachings of Jesus are in accord with the results of research in the field of psychology. The Sermon on the Mount, as found in Matthew, is the basis for most of the Christian preaching and thinking of today.

It has been my aim throughout the book to use as objective an attitude as possible. It may seem that I have been prejudiced toward finding a favorable interpretation of Jesus' teachings. Realizing that this was inevitable, I have endeavored deliberately to see if I could so interpret Jesus' teachings that they would be in accord with all we know of the psychology of personality. Thus, if there were two possible interpretations of a passage, neither of which was impossible because of critical or historical evidence, the one in agreement with my theory was chosen. I have erred, then, only if this interpretation has been pushed beyond the possibilities of honest exegesis. The same may be said on the psychological side. It is obvious that psychology is far from having completely solved the problems of personality. Where two theories stand side by side, with equally good evidence for both, the one in line with my theory has been chosen. The book has been prepared frankly with the desire that it may prove an inspiration to those who follow Jesus to grasp a deeper understanding of him and of the significance of his teachings for their lives. With respect to the psychological hypotheses presented in the book, I have endeavored as far as possible to avoid those theories which constitute debatable interpretations of experimental and clinical data, but at the same time to make full use of all of that data. For example, with respect to Freud's theory of the psychosexual development, there are many scholars who are very doubtful as to the genetic relationship of the various so-called stages of development. No one will deny, however, that there are five distinct forms of love which appear naturally in the life of every normal individual. One term which will be found frequently in the text should be defined; namely, *instinct*. Strictly speaking, an instinct is defined as a definite complex response mechanism which appears without learning when the organism meets a definite situation. Psychologists are pretty well agreed that in the human organism few if any such mechanisms exist. I am in perfect accord with this position. Therefore, when the term *instinct* or *instinctive* is used, it is implied simply that there is an inherited urge or impulse behind the behavior, and that the modes of behavior have inherited backgrounds. In this book, then, the term *instinctive* is almost synonymous with *inherited*.

It is impossible to list all of those to whom I am indebted in the preparation of the book. In the first place, there are a great many of my teachers to whom I owe much of my in-

PREFACE

spiration and information. Some of them have been so deeply influential that they will find many of their ideas in these pages, for which no credit is given, because their ideas have become an integral part of my own thinking. These include: Professor E. W. McDairmid, of Texas Christian University; Professors Charles R. Brown, Luther A. Weigle, and Douglas Clyde Macintosh, of Yale Divinity School; Professors Roswell P. Angier, Raymond Dodge, and Robert M. Yerkes, of the Yale Graduate School of Psychology; John E. Anderson, formerly of the Yale Graduate School of Psychology; and the late Professor John C. Chapman, also of Yale University. To this list should be added two who, while not among my teachers, have deeply influenced my thinking: Dr. Harry Emerson Fosdick, whose writings and lectures have been among the strongest influences of my life; and Professor John L. March, my present colleague and most honored superior in the Department of Psychology at Union College, whose encouragement and constructive criticism have been invaluable. Among those who have been most kind in their encouragement and advice are Dr. Edward Ellery, Dr. Harry Lathrop Reed, and Rev. Kenneth B. Welles. The many groups to whom much of this material has been given as lectures have been very encouraging and stimulating, especially those of the Westminster Presbyterian Church of Albany, New York, and the Auburn Theological Seminary. The contribution of my wife, Lois Wood Ligon, has been so great that her name might well have been included as co-author. In every phase of the work, her assistance has been invaluable.

ERNEST M. LIGON.

CONTENTS

	PAGE
PREFACE	vii
INTRODUCTION	1

CHAPTER

		PAGE
I.	THE PSYCHOLOGY OF PERSONALITY AND THE SERMON ON THE MOUNT	5
II.	AN EXPERIMENTAL FAITH	24
III.	THE DYNAMIC OF FATHERLY LOVE	63
IV.	THE SALT OF THE EARTH	92
V.	THE INTEGRATION OF CHARACTER	106
VI.	SOURCES OF POWER	152
VII.	CREATIVE THINKING	191
VIII.	THE CHAOS OF FEAR	221
IX.	THE MEASURE OF A MAN	253
X.	THE RÔLE OF INFERIORITY IN HUMAN BEHAVIOR	295
XI.	THE CHRISTIAN PERSONALITY	334
	BIBLIOGRAPHY	373
	INDEX	379

THE PSYCHOLOGY OF
CHRISTIAN PERSONALITY

INTRODUCTION

CHRISTIANITY once showed an amazing power to transform the lives of men. Whatever emphasis may have been placed on its theological doctrines and its other-world salvation, it gained most of its influence, because of its ability to make men better men. The apparent decline in the power of the church within the last half-century is in no small measure due to the fact that its unique ability to develop strength of personality and character is no longer obvious. Consider the citizenry of any community. It is difficult to distinguish between church members and non-church members on the basis of their outstanding qualities of character, personality, and leadership. There are many who offer evidence that the value of religion in the life of a man is negligible. The friends and adherents of Christianity will do well to consider thoughtfully this evidence. If it is true that the church does not change men nor develop character, it may be because religion has no such capacity; in which case the religious education program of the church may as well be abandoned. On the other hand, it may be that there are latent powers in the religion of Jesus which have never been tapped, which can be utilized to make the church the greatest builder of character in the world.

It is the purpose of this book to consider the teachings of Jesus in the light of the psychology of personality. To do this will require the setting forth of three sets of facts.

In the first place, it will be necessary to describe, as accurately as possible, the Christian personality. This means that the various teachings of the Sermon on the Mount, which will be used as the basis of Jesus' teachings, will have to be interpreted. These interpretations are based upon a study of most of the existing exegetical and expository material on these passages. Where New Testament students are not agreed upon the meaning of certain teachings, the psychological validity has often been the deciding factor.

In the second place, these teachings will be examined psychologically. That is, the Christian personality will be evaluated in terms of mental health and strong personality, using the principles of mental hygiene, psychiatry, and psychology. Religion has not always produced healthy minds. Religious people have frequently been morbid and unwholesome, with weak and futile personalities. If children were trained exactly along the lines of Jesus' teaching, would they be mentally healthy or unhealthy?

Finally, assuming that the Christian personality is mentally healthy and strong, how can it be developed? Child psychology is easily the most important branch of the subject. Parents want to know how to bring up mentally sound children. If the Christian personality is to be created, it must be done by methods which are psychologically sound.

Every section of the Sermon on the Mount will be dealt with according to each of these three problems.

A brief survey of the problems of personality that face men and women everywhere will convince anyone of the vital importance of finding solutions to them.

In the bewildering complexity of modern life, parents are looking eagerly for help in bringing up their children to be happy and successful. Has Christianity the adequate resources for such training? Can it give children the opportunity to make the most of their lives, to be strong, healthy characters, to be respected and influential in their communities? Can it prevent some of the tragedies of modern youth? It is the province of psychology to study these questions. With its knowledge of the factors that constitute human personality, what has it to say about the teachings of Jesus, so far as their psychological validity is concerned?

INTRODUCTION

Men and women of adult years find that their lives are far from satisfactory. They are filled with fears, angers, hates, suspicions, littlenesses, and failures. They too, plead for relief from this mental suffering. These people come in great numbers to the psychological clinic. Ministers and teachers daily hear their tales of woe. Psychology has studied the causes of these failures and searched for the sources of cure. Is there anything in Christianity which makes it especially able to solve these problems? The psychologist can answer not only this question, but also contribute to a deeper understanding of the teachings of Jesus with respect to its applicability to such problems.

Above all is youth, ever modern, searching for the abundant life. They want to Live, with a capital "L." They follow anyone who calls himself a prophet, whether his program is greed, intrigue, crime, revolution, murder, war, or violence; so long as he promises a pot of gold at the foot of the rainbow. Has Jesus a challenge for youth which will satisfy its craving for action, adventure, achievement, and happiness?

Leaders in every walk of life find their most difficult problem that of influencing human behavior. Ministers are distraught in their efforts to achieve some change in their parishioners. Teachers wonder how they can leave some permanent impression in the minds of their students. Statesmen are concerned with the methods of securing the coöperation of the people in building better nations. All sorts of motivations have been employed; fear, threat, emotional appeal, high-powered salesmanship, propaganda, evangelism, promises, and external rewards. Is there in Christianity the secret of influencing human behavior, without the evils that so commonly accompany these other methods?

There are many who will say that such hopes are impossible of fulfillment, because these evils of fear, anger, hate, and greed are simply a part of human nature, and "human nature cannot be changed." On the other hand, there are others who remember the "impossibilities" which science has overcome within the last few decades. These people wonder if there may not be potential miracles in the fields of the mental and spiritual forces as well as in the physical world. It is the conviction of the author that the solution of all of these problems is to be found in the teachings of Jesus.

Chapter I

THE PSYCHOLOGY OF PERSONALITY AND THE SERMON ON THE MOUNT

A HALF-CENTURY ago the most popular act on any vaudeville bill was that of the magician. Audiences were thrilled when he mysteriously pulled rabbits from hats and caused even elephants to disappear by a wave of his magic wand. The same act is received today with the coolest of tolerant amusement. Why? The answer is, that science has produced wonders which make the best efforts of the magician dwindle into insignificance. What is more interesting is the fact that these wonders are not tricks at all, but veritable miracles performed by the men who have mastered the natural laws.

The advances that have been made in the physical sciences have come about because the phenomena of the physical world have been described and measured carefully and accurately. The spirit of science can be found in this assertion of a great scientist, "Whatever exists, exists in some amount, and can be measured." Vague and inaccurate generalizations are taboo in all fields of scientific research. Some people wonder about the value of measuring to thousandths of an inch, or calculating the error to three decimal places. The achievements of modern science furnish an overwhelmingly convincing answer. Our forefathers made ingenious uses of some of the forces of nature, such as gravitation. We cannot help being impressed with their shrewdness and cleverness. It was, however, only when exact measurements were made that the natural laws were truly known, and such wonders as the railroad, telephone, electric light and power, aëroplane, skyscraper, and radio came into being.

Every age has made its contribution to the understanding of the teachings of Jesus. It is quite natural that the contribution of our own time should come from psychology. This is the age of science. Almost every important advance in man's knowledge in the last century has come as a result of the application of the scientific method. In psychology the scientific method is rigorously applied, and is beginning to yield its usual amazing crop. It is through psychology that the scientific method can contribute most to a healthy religious life.

The problems of science have always intrigued those who have tried to solve them. As the various bits of data are wrested from mother nature and fitted together like the pieces of a puzzle, the scientist watches the growing picture with eager interest. Sometimes the results are as totally unexpected and marvelous to him as to those who only see the miracles which have been performed. One problem which has attracted men perhaps more than any other, but whose solution has proved most baffling, is the enigma of personality. Indeed, it is so difficult that until very recent years science has not even attempted its mastery. This, unfortunately, has left it the prey of the fakir and armchair philosopher. Its very definition has been shrouded with mystery. For many years it was thought to be a kind of mysterious magnetism which certain fortunate individuals possess and all others covet. Our pseudo-psychologists promise to give it to anyone for a cash consideration. The youthful science of psychology had much of its foundation work to do before it could tackle the problem seriously. Within the last few years, however, due to important advances, especially in child psychology and abnormal psychology, sufficient accurate experimental and clinical data have been accumulated to make possible considerable insight into its nature. Many of its problems still remain unsolved, but some significant principles are now discernible.

Like the other sciences, the psychology of personality can yield reliable and useful laws only when it can measure its phenomena quantitatively. To be sure, "common sense" has had a certain measure of success in dealing with human nature. Parents, using a minimum of information and a maximum of good intention, manage to produce men who make a fair adjustment to their environments. However, when one observes that there comes from so highly selected a group as a college class only a handful of outstanding men; it is evident that common sense falls far short of being able to master all of the secrets that make strong personality. That even uncommon sense cannot solve the problem of personality, by theory alone, is evident when the names of those who have tried are listed. Socrates, Plato, Aristotle, Descartes, and Kant are only a few of the host of wise men who have wrestled with this fascinating problem. Such great and keen minds were certain to make many ingenious observations. However, in every case, the basic theories advanced by them have proved untenable in the light of modern research. It is only on conclusions based upon quantitative studies that dependable theories can be constructed. A considerable body of such data exists in the psychology of personality, which can be examined in the growing number of summary volumes describing many hundreds of quantitative studies.[1] The theories proposed in this work are based entirely upon such studies.

Religion has usually been considered outside the scope of science, but it is a growing belief that the methods of science can, will, and should be brought into religion. For ages religious teachers have proposed their widely divergent theologies. Each has been developed largely by logical reasoning. The system of ethics proposed by any one of the great religions has been taught as one's duty, to be performed because of the command of God, and enforced by threat of some punishment to be met with in a future life. It has often been supposed that if fear of hell were withdrawn,

[1] Symonds, P. M., *Diagnosing Personality and Conduct*, The Century Company, 1931, is the most complete of those summary volumes.

there would be no strong motivation for moral behavior in life. Yet no one imagines that he would be free to break the laws of gravitation, if the existence of God were disproved, because the laws of gravitation seem to be in the very nature of things. To love one's neighbors or one's enemies, however, seems to be only a duty, for the neglect of which one would suffer no immediate consequences. The realization that there are spiritual laws, which are just as much a part of the universe as the laws of physics, is as yet fairly rare. Thus, critics of religion often insist that no one system of ethics has any advantage over the others. They point out, and justly, that the religion embraced by an individual is usually an accident of the time and place of his birth. Jesus, Buddha, Confucius, Zoroaster, Mohammed, and others, each demanded forms of conduct which are of the greatest significance in the development of personality. Is there no method by which we can distinguish the ultimate truth in religion? It may be well to consider the basic assumptions of the scientific method, and the implications of applying them to religion.

The first assumption made by science is that the universe is orderly. If the phenomena of nature behaved in such inconsistent fashion that prediction were impossible, science could never have been born. The motion of the planets is so ordered that astronomers consider a fraction of a minute a large error in predicting an eclipse of the sun. The laws of gravitation are so exact that physicists can rely upon them to behave with the greatest precision. What would this imply in connection with religion? It would imply the existence of a God who governs the spiritual world by certain great spiritual principles, which are just as universal and as consistent as these physical laws. For example, if the teachings of Jesus are correct, the law of vicarious sacrifice is as much a part of the very nature of things as the laws of gravitation. This whole study is based on the assumption that there are such spiritual laws. It has grown out of the expectation that a careful study of such qualities as faith and love will reveal them to be forces as great as any ever found by the natural sciences.

The second assumption of science is the philosophy of pragmatism. How shall we know when we have found the correct statement of universal laws? Theology has commonly appealed to authority, philosophy to reason and the rules of logic. Science has depended upon induction. That is, science gathers carefully observed data and tries to see in them the principles governing their behavior. Differences of opinion are tested by experiment. For example, a few years ago the various schools of psychology were in wide disagreement; but each went into its laboratory to test its hypotheses, and often found as many errors in itself as in the other systems. As a result, today the differences between them are insignificant when compared to their similarities. Theologists have usually used authority or logic to settle their disputes. Ordinarily both parties to a religious quarrel come out with the same opinion still. Our numerous sects and isms bear unquestioned testimony to this fact. Science, then, has abandoned the treacherous dangers of the syllogism for the more definite and refinable methods of induction and experiment.

Can pragmatism become the determiner of truth in religion? Fundamentally, it is the unconscious criterion that always has been used. Theologians have offered logical arguments for belief in the existence of God. Actually, men have believed in God because they could not explain the phenomena of the universe in any other way. This is a crude form of induction. Science, with more refined methods, employs much the same sort of reasoning. For example, no one ever saw an atom. Yet every physicist believes in atoms. Why? Because such an assumption is necessary to explain the phenomena he can see. No one ever saw electricity. Yet everyone believes in electricity, because there is no other way to explain the great number of electrical manifestations. If then, the hypothesis of a personal God or of immortality is necessary to explain the other phenomena of the universe, that is the same kind of an assumption as any scientific hypothesis. It is probable that logical argument would never find a common ground for religious belief. Appeal to authority does not carry conviction outside the scope of that authority. Let us then turn to induction, scientific reasoning, to solve religious differences. This was the method taught by Jesus. "By their fruits, ye shall know them."

But, how shall we experiment? Religious phenomena seem to be spiritual and infinite in their scope. They do not seem to lend themselves readily to measurement. The truth is, science seldom measures the forces of nature directly. Usually, certain minute portions or manifestations of those forces are isolated and measured. Scientific laws are based on the assumption that the rest of the force will behave like this sample which has been measured. Is there a portion of the spiritual forces or a manifestation of them which can be measured, and act as a criterion for the rest? The development of personality offers such a criterion. Symptoms of a disease do not constitute the disease. The doctor must depend upon these symptoms, however, for his diagnosis and for evidence of the value of his treatment. Likewise, the healthiness of one's personality does not constitute the whole of his religious life. However, it seems probable that if he is in tune with the infinite, his mental life will be healthy. Certainly, if the universe is orderly, mental health will be evidence of conformity to its spiritual laws. Furthermore, if God is good, mental health will be one of the results of obeying his laws. It is unbelievable that God would so order the universe that godliness would produce unhappiness and mental disorder. Jesus insisted that happiness is an accompaniment of the Christian life. Moreover, personality is more intimately related to the life of the soul than any other part of man. May we not, then, test the correctness of our theological concepts, of our methods in religious education, and of our systems of ethics, by measuring their results in terms of strong character and wholesome personality? Mental health, powerful character, and attractive personality are at least a measure of spiritual law, if not identical with it.

Mighty things have been done by faith and the power of love, even though these forces have been used ignorantly and inaccurately. What may we not expect, if we master them? We may discover that they are the latent sources of power in religion, which will make it the only source of true greatness in human personality.

Religious education has for its purpose the development of character and personality. It is here that we can determine the effectiveness of religion in human life. Not all religious education is healthy. Some perfectly sincere and energetic religious educators have produced warped and pathetically ill personalities. Repression is the characteristic result of one very common trend in religious education. This is the philosophy of negative morality. "Thou shalt not" is the one thing which most people connect with religion. What is even more significant psychologically is the fact that the chief motivation used for securing this morality is shame; and shame regularly seems to be mentally unhealthy. Many people think the job of the church school is the dissemination of religious knowledge. This theory is based on the assumption that knowledge of the Bible and of moral principles will result in moral and religious behavior. There is considerable evidence that this is not true. There is still a third type of religious education. The Rally-day method is symptomatic of a different motivation entirely. Religious education cannot consist only in the mobilizing of large numbers by an emotional loyalty motivated fundamentally by anger. That destroys character. Another type of religious education teaches an unreal and impossible approach to life. The educational program of the church cannot consist in the use of high-sounding phrases to meet the problems of men, because this contradicts the practical demands of life. True religious education must produce men and women of courage and magnanimity; men and women who have found a purpose in life in the service of mankind, which challenges the best that is in them.

The potential personality strength of a man is determined by his inherited characteristics. Men are not born free and equal. Each man inherits a certain degree of intelligence, which no amount of education can appreciably increase. He also has certain special capacities in addition. For example, he may have some musical aptitude, which probably consists in a finely sensitive auditory mechanism. He may have other abilities which will later make it easy for him to succeed in mathematics, rote memorizing, athletics, the fine arts, and the like. He will possess these in varying amounts. Furthermore, he will have the various instinctive urges, also in varying amounts. Finally, there are his physical attributes: size, form, color, eye color, hair color, and so forth. Some of these, such as his glandular constitution, his nervous mechanism, and his muscular equipment play an important part in his mental functioning.

The interplay between the functions of these inherited mechanisms and the environment constitutes the stimulus-response behavior characteristic of all animal life. All of the mechanisms inherited by the individual tend to express themselves.

The truth is, that, having native capacity for performing certain acts and dealing with certain classes of material, we are interested in performing those acts and handling this material. . . . The social motive is inherent in social activity. Possessing, as he eminently does, the capacity for group activity, man is interested in such activity.[2]

Thus, not only do the appetites and urges call for satisfaction, but the intelligent child tends to use his intelligence, and the child with special aptitudes is motivated to use these abilities. These characteristics and their inherited modes of expression constitute the man's instinctive equipment. When an urge arises, the child responds with one of these patterns or modes of behavior. The world into which the child is born, however, is not always friendly to these inherited responses. Therefore, very early in his life the child discovers that his innate modes of behavior have to be modified,

[2] Reprinted from Woodworth: *Dynamic Psychology*, by permission of the Columbia University Press.

if they are to find satisfaction for his appetites in his environment. This modification constitutes learning.

All behavior is fundamentally an effort to discover satisfaction for one's appetites and urges, and expression for his abilities. He will adopt those forms of behavior which furnish such satisfaction. To them he will attach a feeling tone of pleasure. Thus, his world will gradually be classified and evaluated according to its satisfactions. His system of values, likes and dislikes, fears, angers, and loves will grow out of this process. If, in the process of activity, an urge finds no immediate satisfaction, an emotion arises. Thus, if he is hungry, and it appears that no food will ever be available, he is likely to experience an emotion of fear. On the other hand, if there is food, and someone is simply withholding it from him, the emotion will probably be anger. Finally, if someone consistently satisfies his urges, the emotion may be love. Thus, he may respond to people or things habitually with fear, anger, hate, love, and the like, depending on their contributions to his desires. Likewise, he will find certain types of behavior adequate or not, and he will classify them as fearful, or desirable. Thus, he may love or hate an individual, like or dislike a food, fear or like to swim. The sum total of all these emotional reactions to his environment is his real philosophy of life. We call these reactions emotional attitudes. We are not always experiencing a conscious emotion when these attitudes are a part of our personality, but they will produce such an emotion when a stimulus occurs. For example, one may have an emotional attitude of fear for dogs. He is not always experiencing a conscious emotion of fear. He only has such conscious fear when a dog appears.

The emotional attitude is the functional unit of personality. The type of personality, the kind of character, the health of mind of the individual will depend upon the emotional attitudes developed. Some emotional attitudes are fundamentally unhealthy; some are decidedly wholesome. If the psychologist were required to form a system of ethics, he might classify those forms of behavior as wrong, which lead to mental failures; those forms of behavior as right, which lead to strong healthy personality. The emotional attitude is not in itself inherited. It is a learned response adopted to satisfy inherited urges. It can be changed if other means of satisfying these urges can be found. It is the instinctive urges that constitute the "human nature that cannot be changed." The emotional attitudes of fear, anger, hate, and the like, can be changed. It is vitally important which attitudes we develop. Two individuals with identical natures could develop totally different types of personality. Notice some of the more conspicuous attitudes which men learn.

There are one's attitudes toward one's self, conceited or depreciatory; toward others, helpful or selfish; toward one's work, interested or bored; toward life and the world, aggressive or shrinking; toward the present, attentive or indifferent; toward the past, absorbed in it or forgetful; toward the future, optimistic or pessimistic; toward society, seeking it or shunning it; toward authority, yielding or antagonistic; toward nature, following it or fighting it; toward convention, obeying it, or ignoring it. Involved in these general attitudes toward life are the distinctly affective attitudes, such as enthusiasm, depression, hopelessness, fear, courage, indignation, approval, affection, jealousy, amusement, curiosity, disgust, relaxation, strain, worry, confusion, etc.[3]

We can measure the healthiness and unhealthiness of various emotional habits. The mentally ill are studied to discover what attitudes constitute the various mental diseases. A great number of such studies have been made. From this data certain principles of health have emerged. The most important one is the concept of integration.

Briefly, integration is the condition of a personality in which all of the emotional attitudes are harmonious and mutually helpful, thus permitting all of one's natural energy to be directed toward one end. Thus, integrated action is coördinated action in an organism or machine. Each part

[3] Burnham, W. H., *The Normal Mind*, 288. D. Appleton and Company, 1929. By permission of D. Appleton-Century Company.

contributes its portion to the whole, and all the parts are mutually interdependent upon one another. Integration, then, is the natural form of activity.

It is the exception to find disintegrated activity in the physical organism. When such disintegration does occur, the resultant inefficiency is quite obvious. Fatigue, when it is extreme, produces poorly coördinated activity. We are awkward in all of our behavior. This is an example of physical disintegration.

In the mental field disintegration is more common, but we do not notice it so easily. However, it is quite as important in the production of inefficiency as in the physical realm. Concentration is a form of integration. Distractibility is disintegration. Every student knows its inefficiency. If an individual can organize his emotional attitudes in such harmony with one another, that he can direct all of his urges and appetites about one central purpose, which is always the focus of his interest and of his attention, we find the peak of efficiency, and the perfect integration.

In a rather rough way, we may classify personalities into three groups, according to the extent and nature of their integration. In the first place, there is the so-called psychopathic personality. This individual tries to satisfy each instinctive urge immediately upon its appearance, and in a totally infantile and primitive fashion. His motto might read, "I want what I want, when I want it." When any one urge is potent, it dominates his whole personality. Such a personality has no purpose, with the result that the desire for achievement is never satisfied. This results in unhappiness, and soon the individual finds that the various appetites conflict with one another and pull in opposite directions. Finally, he comes into constant conflict with society, winning no social approval.

At the other extreme is the inhibited personality often developed by a negative morality type of religious education. The inhibited personality results from the child being taught that some of his instinctive urges are sinful. He becomes ashamed of them, and refuses to admit them even to himself. This is called repression. Unfortunately, instinctive appetites can be banished from one's consciousness of them, but they cannot be banished from one's personality. They will express themselves in one malignant fashion or another. Furthermore, in the effort to keep them out of consciousness, some other natural energies of the individual must be employed. As a result, important sources of power have been subtracted from the potential strength of the personality; namely, the urges repressed and the energy required to repress them. Hence, the facetious but all too accurate description of many a pious individual, "He is good, but not good for anything."

Finally, there is the individual who succeeds in forming such a harmony of healthy emotional attitudes, that all of his energy is united into one common purpose, moving in one direction. It is he who has developed the strongest personality for which his native endowments fit him. This is the integrated personality.

The most common sources of conflict, and hence of disintegration, are found in the unbridled appetites, especially sex and hunger, and in the violent emotions, especially fear and anger. Indeed, fear and anger, when they occur excessively, are really forms of disintegration. If the psychologist were asked to name the two major sins, from his point of view, he probably would name fear and anger. They form the basis for most of our unhappiness. They are impossible to integrate into a healthy personality. It is significant that Jesus said so much about each of them. His plan for dealing with them will be of the greatest interest to study from the psychological point of view.

The sources of integration also, have been sought. The most universally recognized source of integration, and therefore of mental health, is a dominant purpose in life. Among our college students, those who are the best adjusted and do the finest work are those who know where they are going. Behavior difficulties occur most frequently among those who have no such purpose.

From the time when Adolph Meyer described the shut-in personality as the beginning of dementia præcox, the social life of the individual has been considered vitally important to mental health. An increasing number of the men who are conducting research on personality insist that the dominant purpose must be in the service of mankind, as one of them puts it, in social interest. This, too, is interesting in the light of Jesus' emphasis on love.

Another vitally important principle is that one's purpose must be in line with his capacities. One must find a task which uses all of his natural abilities, but does not require abilities which he does not possess. Many a man is unhappy because he has taken a job which is too small for him. Many others become mentally abnormal because they have attempted tasks that are beyond their abilities.

Finally, there is a certain group of healthy attitudes which should be formed. One must have faith in his ability, faith in the value of his task, and in the worthwhileness of society. He should find real pleasure in his work. Perhaps it may be thought that such attitudes will depend on one's experience. Such is not the case. They are formed in early childhood, and continue throughout life, influenced very little by one's actual experience. For example, there is the fear of failure. Here is a student consistently making the highest grades in his class. Yet, he is always sure that he will flunk the next examination. He has an attitude of failure. No amount of successes seem able to overcome the habit. On the other hand, here is a boy who consistently fails. Yet, he is always going to pass the next examination with flying colors. He has the attitude of success. Failures seem to affect it very little. Consider the man who invests in "get-rich-quick" stocks. He loses on all of them. One would think that he would learn. He usually does not. The next scheme always looks different, and he falls again. Most of the emotional attitudes of adults are formed in this fashion. Some of them are healthy and some unhealthy. Either type can be formed in children.

Here, then, is a very brief picture of personality. Our task is to study carefully the emotional attitudes which are implied in Jesus' teachings, and to ascertain whether they are integrating or disintegrating factors in personality.

The Sermon on the Mount is the best single collection of the teachings of Jesus in the Gospels. It has the advantage of unity and familiarity. Careful studies of the Gospels find it an accurate account of Jesus' words. We can be sure to sense the very spirit of the Master in its remarkable verses. Of course, references will be made freely to other portions of Jesus' teachings, but the Sermon on the Mount will be used as a systematic presentation of Jesus' whole point of view.

And seeing the multitudes, he went up into the Mountain: and when he had sat down, his disciples came unto him: and he opened his mouth and taught them, saying, —Matthew 5:1-2.

With these simple words the author of the First Gospel introduced the most influential document in history. The Sermon on the Mount has had an almost uncanny power over men. Even those who have rejected its teachings have been profoundly impressed by its challenging principles. Men, too commonly, read it like the verses of some beautiful poem, because it pleases their esthetic sensibilities; but they believe it to be entirely impractical and too idealistic. Others interpret it superficially, quite commonly misplacing its emphases and missing its deeper meaning. It has been thought of by some as a system of morals and ethics; a catalogue of the things which we ought to do, but leave undone; and the things we ought to leave undone, but often do. Actually it constitutes a powerful philosophy of life.

Almost every religion emphasizes faith and love. Like any other universal force, they can be used with their greatest efficiency, only when they are accurately known and intelligently applied. Christianity has committed many psychological crimes by its ignorant and superstitious uses of these very forces. However, as Jesus understood them, they can be applied to the production of strong and healthy personalities. Jesus gave precise meanings to faith and love. There was nothing vague about his use of these terms. He did not teach a hazy notion of faith, but a definite type of it. He did not use the term *love* in a loose, vaguely defined fashion. He was specific about the nature of the love one should have toward his neighbor. It seems desirable to make a general statement of Jesus' doctrines of faith and love now, and elaborate them throughout the book.

Jesus believed in an experimental faith. Just what is meant by an experimental faith can be shown best by describing several types of faith. There is a faith which consists largely in intellectual assent. For example, one has faith that the facts of history are accurate accounts of things that have happened. Not infrequently, men hold intellectual philosophies of life which have no effect upon their behavior. They may believe that life is not worth living, but live as if it were. Most commonly, such faith is based upon acceptance of authority. Many theological doctrines command only faith of this sort. People frequently accept teachings with their minds which should apply to their behavior, but do not. Students listen to a professor, accept his teaching intellectually, and wholly ignore it in their behavior. An instructor of psychology asked a student to state the James-Lange theory of emotion. The student did so, perfectly. The instructor then asked him what it meant. The student replied, "Honestly, I haven't a ghost of an idea." Many people, if honest, would have to say the same thing about their religious faith. Some religious teachers have insisted upon this, and only this sort of faith.

Then, there is a type of faith which is credulity. It consists in the uncritical acceptance of some proposition. Often there is not the slightest evidence for its validity, nor does the faithful seek any such evidence. He even ignores the evidence when it is present. Dr. John L. March describes an example of it. One evening, he was walking past the farmhouse of a friend. It had been a beautiful day. Dr. March commented upon this fact to the farmer. That gentleman, however, was depressed, because it was St. Swithin's Day, and it had not rained. He asserted that if it did not rain on St. Swithin's day, it would not rain for forty days. He was sure that it had never failed to work that way. However, it is probable that section of Pennsylvania had never had a drought of forty days. It had never happened that way. Yet, here was a man, who had the most complete faith in such a superstition. Popular cures are examples of this type of faith. When one is afflicted with some ailment, his neighbors can supply him with countless infallible cures. Whole nations accept atrocity stories in war propaganda. An authority in one field is given credulous faith in whatever he says about any field. Here is a recognized authority in the field of physics. He was asked his opinion of the beauty of American girls. It is quite probable that the opinion of any college undergraduate man is better than his on this question. Yet, his word carried weight. One of the most accepted authorities in the world is expressed in the common question, "Can't I believe my own eyes?" Finally, the unquestioned confidence that men have in that mythical entity known as "common sense" is sufficient evidence of the commonness of credulity.

These types of faith have had much influence. Great things have been done by them. But there is another sort of faith based upon the scientific attitude of experimental testing. In the effort to discover the laws of nature, the scientist has observed natural phenomena under controlled conditions; formed hypotheses to explain this data; then performed further experiments to test the accuracy of his hypotheses. This method has been far more fruitful than any other yet devised. A close examination of Jesus' teachings will show that exactly this spirit characterizes his statement of principles. "By their fruits ye shall know them." He rarely appealed to authority. Indeed, one of the things which astonished his hearers was the fact that he did not appeal to older authorities, as the scribes and Pharisees did. Observe the appeal to experience which characterizes his teachings. "Ask, and it shall be given you." "Happy are they that mourn; for they shall be comforted." "Seek ye first His kingdom, and His righteousness; and all these things shall be added unto you." He did not teach that things should be done or not done simply because they are right or wrong, or because they constitute one's duty. It is no accident that science was born under the influence of Christianity and has had almost all of its growth there. The scientific method is inherent in the teachings of Jesus. This method, which has been so useful in the physical sciences, will bring it about that even "greater things than these" shall be done in the spiritual realm. This, then, is a general statement of Jesus' teachings about faith. He taught experimental faith. "Every tree that bringeth not forth good fruit is hewn down, and cast into the fire."

In Jesus' teaching on love, lies an even greater source of spiritual power. No one questions the power of faith, which has been demonstrated time and again. Due to its prominent rôle in the development of science, experimental faith has given dramatic evidence of its value. This is not so true of love. No one doubts that it is a great power. Everyone recognizes its necessity to life and happiness. For two reasons, however, its possibilities have never been fully tested. In the first place, there has been no great institution, such as science in the case of faith, which has demonstrated its influence. In the second place, it has been used with the grossest ignorance and carelessness. It is one aim of this book to make some contribution toward an accurate knowledge of Jesus' teachings about love, and what it can mean in society.

Love is a great dictionary word. It has a wide variety of meanings. Furthermore, there are several possible Greek words that might have been translated love. It is necessary, therefore, to study the teachings of Jesus in the original languages, if we are to understand what he meant by love. The term *Christian love* has been so much misused, it is a wonder any significance at all is still attached to it. To show

how easily it may become a mere formality, Moffatt quotes the argument of a Jesuit in the tenth *Provincial Letter.*

"Suarez says it is enough if we love Him sometime before death, but he does not say when." This in answer to the question as to when a Christian is obliged to show love for God. "Vasquez says it is sufficient to love Him at the point of death; some say, at baptism, others say, at festivals. Hurtado de Mendoza declares that we are obliged to love God once a year, and that we are being indulgently treated in not being obliged to do it more often. Father Conich thinks we are bound to do it once in three or four years; Henriquez, every five years; but Filiutius says it is probable that one is not rigorously obliged to do it every five years." In fact, the Jesuit assures Pascal, by God's goodness we are really not obliged so much to love God as not to hate Him.[4]

The term *brotherly love* has become so inextricably bound up with the name of Jesus, that to most people one is the outstanding characteristic of the other. But just what *brotherly* means is not so commonly agreed upon. The common opinion that Jesus taught brotherly love, sets up many difficulties in his teachings. It is usually explained either as high idealism, not humanly possible, or as nothing more than high-sounding liturgy. "Loving your enemies" has been called the impossible commandment. To "turn the other cheek" is thought by some to be an act of cowardice. "Returning good for evil" and "praying for those who despitefully use you" are pretty generally conceded to be far too difficult for most of us. If Jesus' teachings are to be used very much in everyday life, they must not be so far above the normal abilities of ordinary human beings. Is it possible that we have been mistaken in our understanding of what Jesus taught about love? The scientist forms an hypothesis and tests it by finding out whether or not it will explain his data. What hypothesis, in this case, will bring these teachings from the realm of the impossible to principles which can be utilized in the normal development of personality? Such an hypothesis is the central theme of this book. In this

[4] Moffatt, James, *Love in the New Testament,* 24. Richard R. Smith, Inc., 1930.

hypothesis will be found an understanding of Jesus, which will show his teachings to be psychologically valid. *Jesus did not teach brotherly love; he taught fatherly love.*

Notice what a change this hypothesis makes in the so-called impossible teachings of Jesus. "Love your enemies." It has been thought mighty hard to love one's enemies, but think of a father loving an enemy son. No one thinks David was abnormal or unnatural because he still loved Absalom when that son had become his bitterest enemy. That seemed perfectly natural for a father. What father does not have to "turn the other cheek" to his son hundreds of times? What parents do not pray fervently for the children "who despitefully use them"? How frequently parents "bless" their children, even when the latter are "cursing" them. Fathers are constantly "returning good for evil." This hypothesis, then, makes these great ethical principles, not otherworldly impossibilities, but perfectly normal human behavior.

Then, look at it from the point of view of psychology. Students of personality are almost unanimously agreed that mental health can exist only as an accompaniment of social interest. Certainly, no social interest is greater than that of a father for his son. Parental love has long been recognized as the noblest impulse in mankind. Psychology has shown that fear and anger are the great enemies of personality. Parents lose their fear for themselves in the interests of their children. Anger is not the characteristic response of parents toward their children. What emotional attitude, then, could be formed, which would be so mentally healthy as this attitude of fatherly love toward others? Perhaps it will be asked, how we are to get this fatherly love for others, and how we shall express it after we get it. One cannot go about being "fatherly" to everyone in the ordinary sense of that term. The answer is that fatherliness consists of a group of characteristic attitudes toward others. When all of the Sermon on the Mount has been studied, they will have been described; and it will be shown how these attitudes can be learned, and what their effect on personality will be.

Chapter II

AN EXPERIMENTAL FAITH

The Sermon on the Mount begins with the word *happy*. Into this one word are crowded the deepest longings of the human heart. However, there are almost as many different ideas of happiness as there are people seeking it. Many believe that it is found in the abundance of things possessed, whereas others search for it in fame, and still others believe that it rests in power. Popularity, pleasures, comfort, and adventure rank high in the list of popular satisfactions of the instinctive urges. When a man conceives of heaven in terms of these things, no religion is acceptable to him which does not guarantee these rewards. Yet, in the Beatitudes, which constitute Jesus' theory of happiness, none of these things is found.

In the history of psychology, numerous attempts have been made to list the instincts. No common agreement has ever been reached. Our motives are so interdependent, and even overlapping, that many feel it is hopeless to attempt to give a definite list of instincts. That there is instinctive behavior, namely, behavior which is inherited and expresses itself without learning, no one doubts. For example, the tendency to satisfy one's appetites is instinctive; and there are unlearned modes of behavior by which we try to satisfy them. It also seems to be instinctive to find expression for all of one's inherited abilities. For example, it is natural for an intelligent individual to use his intelligence. Children with a large native endowment of imagination need neither training nor encouragement to use it. Indeed, many a parent has been greatly worried about the terrible "lies" told by his children, when really they were only exercising this capacity of imagination. The child who inherits a strong body, a highly integrated nervous system, fine muscular coördination, and a glandular equipment which produces energy, does not need to be urged or taught to use them. He insists on doing so, often to the distraction of everyone around him, and to the destruction of everything in reach. Finally, there are unquestionably some instinctive tendencies which are social in their nature. Adler has emphasized the universal tendency to seek social approval, in the sense of being recognized as "a complete man." It has been thoroughly demonstrated that social isolation is almost certain to lead to mental disease, and that social interest is essential to mental health. Like the appetites and the abilities, these social tendencies undoubtedly differ from individual to individual in the relative strength of their driving power. We do not know much about these instinctive drives, as such, but their significance in behavior is recognized. It is with their modes of expression that we are primarily concerned, and we are much better informed about these.

A common error in thinking about human nature is to suppose that adult forms of behavior are instinctive. It is quite common to hear someone speak of a gambling instinct. There is no gambling instinct. There is, undoubtedly, some instinctive tendency for which gambling is a very popular type of expression. There is no religious instinct, but religion is a common satisfaction for certain instinctive drives. Adult behavior patterns are reactions performed to satisfy instinctive urges. Every instinct, however, can be expressed in many different ways. For example, hunger is instinctive, but the variety of things sought by different individuals for food is countless. Sex is instinctive, but the forms of sex expression are many. No single form of adult behavior is absolutely necessary to satisfy these urges.

Learning consists in finding satisfactions for instinctive urges. When some method is found which consistently gives expression to a motive, a feeling of pleasantness is attached to it, and it stimulates the emotions of faith or love. Thus, if money seems to satisfy one's urges adequately, the individual comes to love money and to have faith in it. If a belief in God satisfies an instinctive desire for security, the individual develops a love for and a faith in God. It follows, then, that happiness consists in finding an ever attainable group of satisfactions for all of the instinctive urges.

On the other hand, the individual is indifferent to or even unaware of the persons or things or acts which provide no satisfaction for his motives. For example, a number of students had been meeting regularly in a certain classroom, in which there was a large bookcase. One day, as an experiment, the instructor asked if there was a bookcase in the room. Very few of the students were aware of its presence. Try to remember the location of some place of business for which you have never had a need. You may have passed it many times without ever becoming aware of its existence.

If, however, the satisfaction of some motive is inhibited, one will have a feeling tone of unpleasantness toward the inhibiting factors, and these factors will thereafter arouse the emotion either of fear or anger. Thus, if one is restrained from eating when he is hungry, he may become angry at the cause of the restraint. If it happens to be poverty, or something which threatens to inhibit its satisfaction permanently, fear will be the result. Thus, it is obvious that the extent of one's unhappiness will be measured by the number of these fear and anger stimuli in one's environment.

It might seem, then, that the pursuit of happiness would be relatively simple; merely to secure satisfaction for each of the appetites. Unfortunately, the pursuit of happiness is not so simple. Many times the method chosen for satisfying one instinct will at the same time inhibit the satisfaction of some other. For example, the soldier in battle may find that acts of heroism satisfy his desire for social approval, but not his desire for security. Whichever one of these motives is the stronger, will determine his behavior, but obviously it will not be completely satisfactory either way. One who seeks only physical pleasures will inhibit his desire for achievement and social approval.

One may go about the task of seeking happiness, then, in either of two ways. He may search for an environment which will satisfy his every wish. Such a quest is almost universally unsuccessful. Parents often expect their children to be happy, if a sufficient number of material advantages are given to them. If one observes the people who are happy, and those who are unhappy, it will be obvious that those with and those without material advantages are found in both groups. To assert that salaries, comforts, luxuries, and pleasures are of no concern, would be foolish. They are quite desirable, and are often the sources of opportunity. They are not, however, a guarantee of happiness. Many people who have them in great abundance are unhappy. On the other hand, a lack of them is not an insurmountable obstacle to happiness. Many people without them live in supreme happiness. This method, then, of seeking a more favorable environment is not the road to happiness.

The second method is to build such personality traits in an individual that he will be happy in any environment. For example, it is theoretically possible to guard a child from fear by placing him in an environment in which there is no danger. It is much better to develop in him courage with which to face danger. The healthy personality will use material advantages profitably if he has them. On the other hand, he will find meaning and happiness in life, even if he has none of them. To secure happiness, then, one must form the traits and emotional attitudes of the wholesome personality. Material advantages may be desirable, but they are quite secondary to these inner mental habits.

Jesus taught this latter method in the Beatitudes. He laid down principles by which one might learn to adjust himself to his environment, and make the environment better in the process. The Beatitudes consist of a series of eight fundamental emotional attitudes. If a man reacts to his environment in the spirit of them, his life will be a happy one, regardless of what the environment offers, rewards and pleasures or sacrifices and persecution.

To treat the Beatitudes psychologically, it is necessary to discuss them in a different order than that in which they are given in Matthew. Psychologically they fall into two groups. The first group consists of the attitudes of experimental faith. It includes the poor in spirit, those who hunger and thirst after righteousness, the meek, and the pure in heart. The second group gives the characteristics of fatherly love. It includes those who mourn, the merciful, the peacemakers, and those who are persecuted for righteousness' sake. These eight traits constitute the Christian personality.

Whenever one attaches fear or anger to portions of his environment, he is increasing his unhappiness and weakening his personality. When he attaches faith or love to them, he increases his happiness and strengthens his personality. The perfect personality, then, would have faith in everything, and love for everyone. But you say that this is utterly impractical and impossible. There are dangers of which one must be afraid if he is to survive. To give a child a naïve faith in all men would only subject him to the pain of being deceived many times. This is very true. If Jesus had taught such a naïve faith, he would have been guilty of dodging facts, as they actually are. The alternative to this naïve faith, however, is not fear. It is an intelligent faith. It is a faith which is perfectly aware of danger, and adjusts to it, but without fear. Every parent would like his child to grow up unafraid. He does not, however, want him to endanger his life and happiness by a blind faith, which takes no forethought of danger. The faith, which Jesus taught, will be acceptable only if it meets the practical demands of life. It has been pointed out that this intelligent faith is very much like the spirit of science, and is therefore called an experimental faith.

Adjusting to one's environment is not synonymous with being satisfied with it. A scientist loves his field of research,

AN EXPERIMENTAL FAITH

but devotes his whole life to changing it. No progress is made except where the need of progress is felt. If anyone imagines that Jesus taught his followers simply to accept the world as it is, with no vision for making it better, let him read the first verse of the Sermon on the Mount, which is the first characteristic of an experimental faith.

Happy are the poor in spirit: for theirs is the kingdom of heaven.—Matthew 5:3.

To the young child, happiness seems to consist in the satisfaction of whatever appetite or urge happens to be dominant at the moment. Even a minor wish, of the present moment, seems much more desirable than a greater prize in the future. Anyone who has tried to persuade a child to go to bed early, when he does not want to, with the promise of some tempting reward for the morrow, realizes the truthfulness of this statement. The child lives in the present, and if his immediate desires are being satisfied, all is right with the world. If the child has wise parents and teachers, he is taught to look forward to greater rewards, and even to sacrifice something if necessary to secure them. Unfortunately, not all children are taught this. Consequently, we find even adults who still operate on this infantile level of behavior. When Esau sold his birthright for some food to satisfy his immediate physical appetite, he was demonstrating this sort of childishness. To the child this is happiness. He has no greater vision of happiness than his immediate pleasure.

The audience to which Jesus spoke, had much the same general ideas about happiness, that most of us have today. They believed that happiness was highly correlated with wealth. Poverty seemed to them, as to us, the very foundation of misery. While poverty of worldly goods and poverty of spirit are not the same things, nevertheless, it is true that people with wealth do not often learn to be poor in spirit. Too often, families of wealth give their children a feeling of satisfaction in the things money can buy. The very core of poverty of spirit is a vision of higher things, compared with which, the present pleasures are of little value. It was best exemplified by Jesus, when he said, "He that believeth on me, the works that I do shall he do also; and greater works than these shall he do." It is the faith, that however great a man's achievements are, there are greater things to be accomplished in the future. It does not imply that one should not rejoice in what he has done, but that he should make each achievement a challenge to a greater one. In every walk of life, men and women have their victories. To the poor in spirit, there are always greater victories to be won. Progress is likely to make men poor in spirit, because the more we learn about a thing, the more there seems to be still to learn about it. No man can struggle with the complex problems of any field, and not become poor in spirit with respect to them.

There are degrees of poverty of spirit. Some individuals are poor in spirit in some things, and equally rich in spirit in respect to all others. Many a scientist is poor in spirit in his own field of study, while at the same time, he makes sweeping generalizations in other fields, about which he may have little information. One may be poor in spirit in his work and bigoted in his patriotism. He may be poor in spirit in his home life and self-satisfied with respect to religion. It is important that this mental attitude of poverty of spirit be attached to every phase of his life, if it is to become a trait of his personality.

Here is the story of a young scientist in the field of psychology, who failed to obey this spiritual law. He was well trained and a brilliant experimenter. He made important contributions both in data obtained and in experimental method. For a time, he was among the leading psychologists of his day. Then, like many another, he became rich in spirit, and thought he had found the final answer to mental life. It became an obsession with him. He scorned all other theories, and could see no fault in his own. Fifteen years after he had reached the pinnacle of his fame, his teachings had been discarded.

AN EXPERIMENTAL FAITH

Jesus' best illustration of this attitude is found in the parable of the Pharisee and the publican. The Pharisee, in his own mind, was spiritually rich. He is described as praying to himself, not to God. The publican had no doubt as to his own spiritual poverty. He, therefore, prayed to God. When men are satisfied with themselves, their prayers, if any, are likely to be little more than ritual. But, when they feel their own inadequacy, they pray to God. Each prayer was the natural expression of the character of the man. One was humble, the other haughty. Even had their positions in life been reversed, the spirit of each prayer would have been the same. This brings out a psychological point, which it is important to grasp if one is to understand human personality. It is commonly thought that our emotional responses are caused by external circumstances. For example, most people believe that they are depressed when there are depressing circumstances, and are happy when things are going well. This is true less frequently than is supposed. What usually happens is that first we become depressed, and then find something about which to be depressed. When we are happy, the world seems full of happy situations. Of course, we do react emotionally to external circumstances, somewhat depending upon their nature, but most of our emotional behavior is of this other type. The timid soul will find something about which to be afraid, in the same environment to which others react with confidence. Undoubtedly many a Pharisee went to the temple to pray, with all the humility of the publican in the parable. On the other hand, probably a majority of the publicans rarely went to the temple to pray, and felt themselves in little need of spirituality.

Now let us observe a number of typical examples of being rich in spirit, and discover what their effect is upon personality. First, there are the men and women who admit that they know almost everything worth knowing. They can give the final answer to most questions, never mistrusting the accuracy of their judgment. Curiously enough, they seek little or no evidence as a basis for their conclusions. This is the way human nature expresses itself, when it is not trained to the contrary. Being poor in spirit would not come naturally to the child. The experimental method was not widely adopted until a few centuries ago. A large proportion of scientific experiments have been done within the last two hundred years. One who is satisfied with his judgment of things will not experiment to test it. Only the poor in spirit, who always have the hope for better insight, experiment to discover it.

In religion, the man rich in spirit is a common sight. There is the man who is confident that he can distinguish between right and wrong by the use of his conscience or by common sense. He is not easily persuaded to study the Bible or any other religious teaching, because he feels no real need for it. It is often possible to sell him books on contract bridge, because ignorance in this case soon shows itself. In religion, the results of ignorance are not so quickly obvious. The writer of the book of Judges was describing such a person, when he said, "Every man did that which was right in his own eyes." But as he later pointed out, it proved to be "evil in the sight of Jehovah." Consequently, "Jehovah delivered them into the hands of their enemies."

The mental attitude of being rich in spirit, then, results in drawing conclusions quickly, without evidence, and subscribing to them unquestioningly. The attitude of being poor in spirit results in reaching conclusions slowly, after having obtained and weighed all available data; and even then realizing that the conclusions are still not perfect. Such an individual will always have a vision of greater possibilities ahead, and will progress to higher attainments. For the rich in spirit there is no progress.

The rich in spirit respond with uncritical emotion. Such people can be swept off their feet in a political campaign, by an emotional appeal which has no basis in fact. They vote for or against an issue, with an emotional but not an intelligent intensity. Why can men be led into such uncritical judgments? It is not entirely a function of intelligence.

Whether or not one does such thinking, depends upon his mental attitude. If we are rich in spirit, that is, confident of our own infallibility, we will give unquestioned assent to the first conclusion that comes into our minds. The poor in spirit, on the other hand, will be critical of whatever judgment they reach. Unintelligent emotional thinking leads to the disintegration of personality, and to the instability of society.

The advance of science has met with no greater obstacle than this willingness of people to make and accept untested theories. Popular theories, which are incorrect, are numerous in every field of science, and thousands of people give unquestioned assent to them. In psychology they are more common than elsewhere. An enumeration of a few of these false but popular hypotheses will demonstrate the failure of "common sense" to understand mental behavior, and the need for poverty of spirit. "Practice makes perfect." "All work and no play make Jack a dull boy." "Spare the rod and spoil the child."

It has often been stated that the characteristic of the scientific mind is disinterestedness, as opposed to the wish-thinking of the non-scientific mind. A closer observation of the facts shows this statement to be false. Real disinterestedness would result in no behavior at all. Every professor finds a number of disinterested minds in his classes, but he does not expect them to make any important contributions to the present store of knowledge. It is not a question of whether or not one does wish-thinking; his behavior will always be motivated by some wish. The question is, what the wish shall be. The poor in spirit wish for some things; the rich in spirit for entirely different things. The scientific mind is not disinterested, but scientifically interested.

If richness in spirit leads to unhappiness, it is because of the frustration of some native drives. What native drives will not be satisfied if one is rich in spirit? It has been shown that the healthy personality is integrated about some goal or purpose. But the rich in spirit are satisfied with things as they are. It is not likely, that one who is satisfied with things as they are, will be a man of strong purpose. Furthermore, the greatest source of pleasure which comes to a man is a sense of achievement. The rich in spirit are not often ambitious for achievement. Often it has been contended that men and women, who accept the "old time religion" without any question or doubt, are the happiest. It is easy to see that if everyone took this attitude there would be no progress. The reason why those people are not genuinely happy is because they inhibit their native drive toward achievement. Finally, being satisfied with one's judgment is a form of vanity. The faith such a man has in his judgment is comfortable to his sense of self-importance. But since his fellows are not likely to have such faith in his infallibility as he has himself, his vanity will be frequently wounded; and this is the chief cause of anger, conflict, and feelings of inferiority. Parents, who are anxious that their children shall have self-confidence, will not gain this end by teaching them blind conceit. Those who want their children to become men of faith, will accomplish this in a very unhealthy form, if they insist on an unquestioning credulity in certain prescribed authority.

So much for the rich in spirit. Unfortunately, they constitute a majority of the world's population. Their unreflective thinking is the principle factor in the instability of our social institutions.

Now, why are the poor in spirit happy? Quite apart from its ethical quality and its value to social progress, poverty of spirit must have the capacity to make men happy. They are happy, in the first place, because they see the possibility of better things. This vision motivates them to reach for ever greater achievements. Many a scientist has demonstrated this spirit by his life. As a lad in high school he imagines that his high school diploma will represent almost the acme of human knowledge. He eagerly works for it. Having obtained it, instead of being satisfied, he looks forward now to his college degree, certain that this will be the mark of an educated man. When that goal has been reached, graduate degrees beckon to him. They, too, give way to successive dreams of greater achievements. There is no end to the process for these men. It cannot be denied in the light of the past fifty years, that theirs has been the kingdom of heaven. Poverty of spirit, then, stimulates achievement, the greatest single source of happiness.

Secondly, it will be obvious that such a spirit is productive of men with dominant purpose. It has been shown that a dominant purpose is the prime essential of mental health. Certainly, one will not have a very absorbing purpose who does not feel a poverty of spirit with respect to something.

Finally, poverty of spirit brings the healthiest sort of social approval. Not all of our leaders are poor in spirit; but when we meet men who really are, we intuitively stand in admiration of them. In their very manner, which lacks the dogmatism and cocksureness of the rich in spirit, they command our respect. Mere social popularity is a dangerous reward upon which to depend for happiness. This implicit social respect, however, is treasure in heaven.

When Jesus said that the poor in spirit are happy, because "theirs is the kingdom of heaven"; observe that this is not a promise of some future material reward, but a statement of a present condition. Most people think that heaven is some future bliss consisting in peaceful rest and endless pleasure. Psychology teaches that these things carry no certainty of happiness, but that happiness is an attitude of mind, which one has under all conditions or not at all. For example, a man who is unhappy because his income is too small, will find that he is still unhappy when it grows larger. Likewise, a couple who cannot be happy on one hundred dollars a month, probably will not be happy on several times that amount. Let us examine Jesus' teachings on the nature of the kingdom of heaven, in the light of the discoveries of psychology.

Religious people of all times and creeds pray, "Thy kingdom come." Yet, even among Christians, the ideas they have about the nature of this heaven are widely different. The common slang phrase, "that is heavenly," often applied to something which is especially pleasing, has more significance than is regularly supposed. People usually decide what things are "heavenly," and then hope that heaven will contain those things. Most ideas of heaven, then, consist in the material, external rewards to be given for goodness; and goodness is thought of usually as a disagreeable duty. It is surprising that this idea has persisted, because the principle of external rewards never has worked. Yet, heavenly streets are commonly paved with gold; mansions are free for the asking; and work, tears, troubles, and other so-called evils are conspicuous by their absence.[1]

Jesus told of a kingdom in which the great spiritual laws of God can be used to make men able to do great things. He believed that happiness can be achieved by the mastery and intelligent use of these laws. Once, when the Pharisees asked him when the kingdom would come, he answered, "The kingdom of God cometh not with observation: Neither shall they say, Lo here! or, lo there! for, behold, the kingdom of God is within you." To him, the kingdom consisted, not in some outward condition or place, but in human personality.

One feature of heaven is common to all concepts of it: It is a place of perfect happiness. Different concepts of heaven, then, are due to different theories of happiness. Men, whose ideas of happiness make it impossible for them to obtain it in this world, dream of a heaven in a future life, to compensate for the disappointments of this one. This is not a mentally healthy attitude. It is mental surrender. Let us observe psychologically how a man gets his notion of happiness. This will help us explain the wide variety of concepts of heaven, and will show us how to go about giving a child

[1] Sources used most for this material:
Manson, T. W., *The Teachings of Jesus,* Cambridge University Press, 1931.
Scott, E. F., *The Kingdom of God,* The Macmillan Company, 1931.

the right concept, that does lead to a healthy, wholesome happiness.

The most common way in which one's behavior patterns are formed, is by the process known as conditioning. The classic illustration of this process is the experiment of Pavlov. He conditioned dogs to respond to the sound of a bell with an increased flow of saliva. They naturally secrete saliva in abundance at the sight of meat, but not at the sound of a bell. After the bell and the meat were presented simultaneously for a series of trials, the sound of the bell alone produced an increased flow of saliva. The dog had become conditioned to the bell, to make a response which he would not have made naturally.

Let us observe a few common examples of conditioning in everyday life. The desire for money is an example of this conditioning process in man. Money, in itself, has no value. It is simply a means to an end. It is, however, so frequently associated with the end, that it becomes conditioned, and seems to have value in itself; frequently, so much so, that the end is sacrificed in order to obtain the means. Certainly the heaven of money has been tried sufficiently to demonstrate the fact that it is not the source of happiness. During the last thirty years our material comforts have multiplied many times; not only in the invention and development of pleasures of which the past never dreamed, but also in the level of material wealth, which has surpassed anything in the history of man. Prosperity is the watchword of the age. Yet, neither before nor since the beginning of the current financial depression, have we been any happier. "What shall it profit a man if he gain the whole world and lose his own soul?" These years have demonstrated the fallacy of the popular platitude, "Happy are the wealthy." This concept of heaven as wealth, is due to learning the emotional attitude that wealth is an adequate satisfaction for one group of inherited drives: namely, the appetites. One who can see no higher vision than wealth is indeed rich in spirit. He is confident that heaven consists in the abundance of things possessed. He will not look for any other source of happiness. His life will be made up of a search for new ways of obtaining wealth. It never has worked. It is not probable that it ever will.

Another curious form of conditioning is found in the popular notion of fame as heaven. Obviously, fame in itself is pleasant. Usually, however, fame accompanies achievement, which is also instinctively pleasant. Because fame and achievement are so regularly associated, it is easy for fame to become conditioned to give even greater pleasure. Many a man, therefore, seeks short cuts to fame, which do not involve achievement. Having obtained such fame, he finds it less pleasurable than he had expected. Its inevitable accompaniments are suspicions and jealousies. These are forms of fear and anger. The instinctive urge which fame does satisfy, is found in man's inherited social tendencies. Fame, deserved or not, is a satisfaction for some of them. If undeserved, however, it does not satisfy the stronger instinctive desire for achievement.

Children may be brought up to hold any concept of heaven that parents choose to teach them, unless it directly contradicts their original nature. Here, then, is the first task for the parent and the teacher of the child. We may teach him that wealth and fame are the great sources of happiness. If we do, he will spend his life seeking them. On the other hand, he may be taught poverty of spirit, so that it will characterize his behavior throughout life.

Notice how Jesus connected the ideas of poverty of spirit and kingdom of heaven. Poverty of spirit, in itself, is a dissatisfaction with things as they are. This is only possible, however, if he gains a vision of better things. Why should being dissatisfied with things be a source of happiness? Let us quote from a recent text book in child psychology.

Dissatisfaction with the present is one condition for the development of ambition. This element is present in the background of all imagination. In connection with the development of ambition all that needs to be added is that type of situation which the child imagines as a substitute for present difficulties is the all important problem. In other words, if dissatisfaction is to give rise to personal ambition, the dissatisfaction must be with one's present status and must lead to an ambition of self-improvement.

Dissatisfaction with one's present status is not enough to produce ambition. If it stops there we have the so-called inferiority complex. If, as a result of this dissatisfaction, a *vision* appears of a different individual in the future, we have the incentive for a progression to that individuality. In short, we must have a contrast between what we would like to become and what we are.[2]

In developing the attitude of poverty of spirit in children, then, it is important to give the child a vision of heaven which is inspiring to him, and which arouses in him both a dissatisfaction of things as they are and a vision of things as they might be.

Consider an example of the way parents often do go about giving a child a high vision in life. Many a parent decides what his son is to be even before he is born, then tries to force that goal upon him throughout his early life. It may prove to be a goal for the attainment of which the child has no capacity. In this case he suffers untold agony because of his failure to achieve what he has been taught he should achieve. On the other hand, it may be a goal which uses too few of his capacities. In this case, he is likely to find life very uninteresting and perhaps little worth living. If goals too remote are presented to the child, he is likely to do nothing about them. This will develop the mental habit of doing nothing about things. The child must be given goals about which he can do something immediately, and reach relatively soon. As each one is reached, a higher one must be discovered for him. Soon, each attainment will become in itself the stimulus for a new task. New visions will be constantly leading him on to new achievements.

In teaching men about the kingdom of heaven, Jesus did not use high-sounding, abstract phrases to describe it. He used metaphors which were within the experience of his

[2] From J. J. B. Morgan, *Child Psychology,* Revised Edition, New York: Farrar & Rinehart, Inc., 1934.

hearers. Merchants were told that it is a "pearl of great price." Farmers were assured that it is like "good seed which a man sowed." If children are to become poor in spirit, they must have a vision of the kingdom of heaven which stimulates them to action. As the child develops, give him increasing visions of a better social order, to which he can contribute if he becomes wise enough and has sufficient strength of character. Finally, engrain in him the belief that the kingdom of heaven is like a "treasure buried in a field," to be found by him who seeks diligently for it. This is the first and fundamental characteristic of experimental faith. It should be clear that such an attitude is a mark of a strong, healthy mind and a useful life.

An important mark of physical well-being is a good, healthy appetite. Jesus believed that this is also true of spiritual well-being.

Happy are they who hunger and thirst after righteousness: for they shall be filled.—Matthew 5:6.

If one has acquired an appetite for good food, he eats with zest, and health is his compensation. If, however, the time of his eating is irregular, and if the foods he eats are over-rich or unnourishing, he soon finds his appetite reduced to a minimum, and his health at a low ebb. The body may crave indigestible foods, if it has acquired a taste for them. The word translated *filled* in the Beatitude means *to be well nourished*. People often learn to hunger and thirst for foods which have no nourishing value. One can learn to crave almost anything. He will be healthy, only if he is taught to enjoy wholesome foods. If one stops eating, his body ceases to be hungry. After about three days of fasting, he no longer experiences any craving for food. Man should not live to eat, but it is certain that he must eat to live. If he is to live an "abundant" life, his eating must be of the healthy variety which characterizes physical vigor.

These facts which apply to physical hunger are equally applicable to other phases of human behavior. It is obvious that one will not hunger and thirst for anything unless he feels a lack of it. But, while hungering and thirsting presupposes being poor in spirit, it does not necessarily follow it. Even if students are sincerely "poor in spirit" with respect to their knowledge, no instructor can help them much unless they also hunger and thirst for knowledge. Tube feeding is not very healthy in either physical or mental nourishment. This Beatitude is frequently neglected by Christian men and women. It is difficult to persuade many of them that they are poor in spirit, and almost impossible to inspire in them a hunger and thirst for righteousness. But the body does not become more hungry than the soul. It may be that our long period of fasting with respect to righteousness has made us forget how to be hungry for it. Some of us seem to require no mental food at all; others only a sort which is, to say the least, not rich in spiritual vitamines.

It is fairly common for students to come into a course, who are painfully aware of their lack of knowledge of the subject. They are equally convinced of the possibility of more information. To this extent they are poor in spirit. They do not, however, always hunger and thirst for further information. These students seem quite content to remain in the same stage of poverty with respect to their knowledge of the subject. One who does not hunger and thirst after the laws of human nature, is not likely to be filled with understanding.

Men, who have made a healthy adjustment to their vocation, are likely to show this health by a vigorous appetite for their work. To many men, however, work is a necessary evil, to bring in enough money to buy happiness. They do not enjoy their work. To them, the word *work* means the opposite of *pleasure*. But the man who finds a task which challenges the best that is in him, gets his greatest pleasure in his work. He can be said to hunger and thirst after achievement. His happiness is of a quality which the former group can never know or understand. To such a man, striking for shorter hours would seem as ridiculous as to have a family of healthy growing boys demand that their mother give them less food. To find the measure of a man's success, one should not look at his salary, bank account, or home luxuries; but find out how much he enjoys his work.

Some may believe that this concept is too idealistic; that no one loves his work more than his salary. However, here is a group of young science professors who meet together fortnightly to read papers and discuss scientific problems. During the first two years of the group's existence, the meetings were very regularly attended. During these same two years, radical changes in policy were being made in the college in which they were teaching. Furthermore, due to the current financial depression, economies were being put into effect in the college. Almost any member of that group was in danger of losing his position, yet not one minute of the group's time was spent discussing economics or campus politics. The entire time was used to discuss science. Here is one example to prove that men can hunger and thirst after their work more than their pay.

That everyone hungers and thirsts after something, no one will deny. But will righteousness satisfy the instinctive drives which cause hungering and thirsting? To answer this question, we must know exactly what righteousness is.

The scribes and Pharisees were very much interested in righteousness, of a sort. They believed, however, that they possessed all there was of it; and could hardly be described as hungering and thirsting for more.

To Jesus, righteousness consisted of the laws which govern the spiritual and social universe. A study of his teachings will show that his conception of these laws was, that they were based on the positive dynamic of love and not on negative ethics. The negative morality concept of the older Judaism, however, was so widespread that the word *righteousness* still carries to most people the idea, that the righteous man is the man who does no wrong. It is difficult to imagine being hungry and thirsty for learning the things one should not do. Indeed, it is safe to say, that when people do seem to have such an appetite very strongly, there is something unhealthy in their personality. Jesus' righteousness consists of the spiritual laws of God. Since the central motivation of these laws is fatherly love, righteousness is made up of the principles of fatherliness. The eagerness, with which parents search for the secrets by which they may contribute to the happiness of their children, is a good example of hungering and thirsting after righteousness.

Jesus believed that righteousness was the sort of thing which should be hungered for, and not a bitter medicine to be taken at rare intervals. He expected it to dominate men's whole beings; to become the ruling dynamic of their lives. The man who loves his job, or the student who enjoys his course to the fullest, will work and study with an intensity which is like the hunger of a healthy man before a good meal. Hungering and thirsting after righteousness brings its own reward, that of being filled; just as the mastery of a course of study is its own chief compensation. Probably science is the healthiest field of interest in life today. This is largely because men get such keen delight in discovering something new about the laws of nature. The search for more insight into the spiritual laws, which will bring the kingdom of heaven into human personality and society, is just as full of satisfaction.

If we turn to the psychology of personality, we find that one of the essentials to mental health is persistence in the pursuit of one's purpose. The healthy individual does not grow tired of eating his meals. Likewise, persistence in one's purpose in life naturally follows, if he hungers and thirsts for it. This Beatitude, instead of urging men to be righteous because it is their duty, teaches them that happiness will come, only when they have acquired a hunger and thirst for it.

Here, then, is another step in experimental faith. One who has this attitude has the faith that righteousness exists, that it is highly desirable, and that if he wishes for it he will find it and be satisfied with it. The pragmatic test of science was urged by Jesus. He was urging obedience to spiritual laws, not from some arbitrary sense of duty, but because they work to the advantage of the one who masters them.

Like the attitude of poverty of spirit, hungering and thirsting after righteousness is the result of one's emotional education. To be mentally healthy, it, too, must form an adequate expression of instinctive drives. This attitude must be learned in early childhood, and can be taught the child by using his natural tendencies. One of the natural tendencies of any intelligent child is to ask questions. Unfortunately, it does not seem to be the natural tendency of most parents to answer them. To be sure, the queries of the child are sometimes embarrassing, far outreaching our store of knowledge. It is easier to insist that "children should be seen and not heard." But, on the basis of this natural tendency to ask questions can be built a true hunger and thirst for knowledge, which will become a life habit. Never for a moment suggest to the child that learning is anything else than a most enjoyable privilege. He inherits an eagerness to learn, in proportion to his intelligence. If his native tendencies are fully used, he can learn this Beatitude. Actually, it is one of the easiest attitudes to teach him. It is a part of the experimental faith which is essential to great achievement.

The attitudes of poverty of spirit and especially of hungering and thirsting after righteousness are relatively easy to teach the child. The third characteristic of experimental faith is much less common, and is neither easily understood nor mastered. Yet, it is a mark of greatness. It can be learned by the normal individual, and is essential to the strongest type of personality. It is the characteristic described by Jesus in the next Beatitude.

Happy are the meek: for they shall inherit the earth.—Matthew 5:5.

Like poverty of spirit, and righteousness, meekness has acquired a rather undesirable connotation, especially to our

AN EXPERIMENTAL FAITH

American mind. Some people have imagined that meekness is a spineless, groveling attitude. The timid soul has come to be known as the meek man who submits to the wishes of other individuals, because he is afraid to resist them. This notion of meekness is far from the attitude of mind described in Jesus' teaching. It was not Jesus who invented the phrase, "such a worm as I."

The idea is held by some, that it is a surrender attitude. This attitude of surrender is one of the fundamental characteristics of a common mental disease in our hospitals. The patient faces a social situation which is not pleasant to him. Instead of trying to adjust to it, he simply gives up. He becomes indifferent, child-like, obstinate, or suspicious. This is far from being meekness.

Let us observe a few examples of meek behavior. Then we shall be better prepared to interpret this Beatitude.

When Jesus faced the inevitable result of his ministry, as he prayed in the Garden of Gethsemane, he gave a magnificent demonstration of meekness. "If it be possible, let this cup pass from me; but, not my will but Thine be done." Luke records that when he had said this, there appeared an angel strengthening him. This willingness to subordinate his will to the will of God was meekness.

Another example is the case of two parents who give their son all they have of affection, training, and money. Due to their erroneous methods, however, they lose him. They do not blame God. They pray for insight to show how they disobeyed His laws, and to help prevent such tragedies happening in the future.

Moses has frequently been described as the meekest of men. In what did his meekness consist? From the moment he was called to fight an almost impossible battle, he was bowing to what he considered the will of God. Certainly, the people whom he led out of Egypt, still slaves at heart, would be a trial to any man. The moment any trouble arose, they turned on him in fury, demanding to know why he had led them into disaster. Yet, with the exception of one instance, Moses was patient with them, never losing his faith that they were worth saving. His contributions to spiritual progress grew from this meekness.

With these illustrations of meekness before us we are now prepared to define it. Meekness can be defined as the unshakable faith that the universe is lawful. Christian meekness is the faith that the universe is fatherly. When trouble, sorrow, and suffering befall the meek man, he is certain that it is the working of a fatherly universe. He does not always understand why such things happen, but he does believe that if men knew all of the spiritual laws, they would not only understand but be able to prevent these tragedies.

The nature of this trait is implied in the Hebrew derivation of the word *meek*. It carries the connotation of being of that disposition of heart, which has in it the susceptibility of being molded by the spirit of God, as compared with the defiant inflexibility of self-will. A child does not always understand the discipline of his parents. The wise youth, however, gradually comes to have faith in the wisdom of his parents. He will, then, adopt their advice against his own opinion, because he believes that by so doing he will be happier. The man with Christian meekness has this same faith in the fatherliness of the universe. It is reported that when an orator once declared from the platform, "I accept the universe," one of her auditors remarked, "She'd better." This response had more significance than he realized. He was exactly right. Whoever accepts the universe and tries to discover its nature will be much better adjusted than he who tries to fight it. Meekness is faith.

Meekness has come to be the normal attitude toward nature. Scientists have complete faith that the universe is lawful. They stand before the most bewildering chaos, with the certainty that what seems to be chaotic will prove to be orderly, when they have discovered the laws governing its behavior. It has not always been so. Millions have rebelled against the natural laws throughout the ages. Consider what the results would have been, if all the prayers for intervention in the realm of natural law had been answered. If every

AN EXPERIMENTAL FAITH   47

danger about to befall a child had been averted because of the prayer of the terrified mother, what chance would there have been for modern physics to develop? Physicists do not try to fight nature; they use nature. If every case of poisoning had been healed because of the intercession of loved ones, how far could chemistry have progressed? If every disease had been cured by prayer for which a prayer was offered, where would the sciences of biology and medicine be? Under such conditions prediction would be impossible. Consider the heroes who have voluntarily contracted diseases in order that careful studies of them might be made. Suppose God had intervened and saved their lives; their efforts would have been in vain. They expected the laws of nature to work with unfailing regularity, so they could be observed, understood, predicted, and used for the advancement of mankind. Scientists do not lose their faith when their hypotheses fail and their experiments do not come out according to expectation. They seek new hypotheses nearer to an understanding of nature. They believe that a mastery of these natural laws will make possible tremendous achievements. They are willing not only to accept the workings of those laws in their own lives, they would be greatly distressed if they did not work.

This is not yet true in the spiritual realm. Men still pray God not to make them suffer for their violations of His spiritual laws. We shall not bring the kingdom of heaven on earth until we are meek, any more than the achievements of modern science would come before men became meek with respect to the natural laws. Meekness is not an easy attitude to learn. There are many temptations to rebel against the working of the spiritual laws. It is a characteristic of human nature to want laws set aside, when one is facing the consequences of breaking them. Probably the most earnest prayers that have been uttered by man to his God have been petitions for His miraculous intervention in the working of His own laws. Many people have lost their faith in a "good" God because He has not broken His laws for their sakes. To pray, "Thy will be done," when His will involves suffering to him who prays, requires a meekness not common among men.

A few examples of the conflicts men have with their environment will show the various methods by which they seek happiness, why these methods fail, and why meekness is successful.

Here is a teacher who is enthusiastic, well-trained, and brilliant. He is ambitious to reach the top of his profession quickly, but he is not satisfied to win his promotions on the basis of merit. He uses underhand methods. With what result? He reaches what seems to be the top, but he lacks friends and the confidence of his associates. Then, as if that were not sufficient punishment for his crimes, symptoms of mental disease develop which have as their first result the loss of his position. It is frequently true that the man of merit does not receive his just reward in the form of advancement. However, happiness and strength of personality do not depend upon outward circumstances so much as upon certain inner conditions of mental life. To find a career which uses all of one's capacities in the service of mankind; this is the formula for happiness. The meek man can fulfill this formula. He does not have to repress or even suppress his energies. He can throw them all into his task. He does not need to win the plaudits or appreciation of those whom he serves. If he is meek, he will serve them whether they will or not.

We are born with appetites. When they dominate us they seem all-important. When we cannot satisfy them we are unhappy. When circumstances arise which not only prevent their satisfaction, but show clearly that they never can be satisfied, we become obsessed with a desire for their satisfaction. It is difficult for us to see in such conditions anything good. We feel that life is not worth living. Perhaps it will be said that it requires an idealism not humanly possible to be meek in the face of such circumstances as these. Yet there are those who do face these situations with meekness

AN EXPERIMENTAL FAITH 49

and courage. They do not deny the presence of their appetites. They recognize them frankly. Then they throw all of the energy of those unsatisfied drives into their life's work, with the perfect faith that in so doing they are going to find greater happiness than if their appetites had been satisfied in the usual fashion. They have faith that the evils of our present society are not evidence of an unfriendly universe, but of our failure fully to understand and apply its laws.

The testing of meekness occurs in many other walks of life. Here is a young man with a vision of right and justice. He is aflame with the wonder of his vision. He sets forth like a knight of the age of chivalry to right all wrongs, to bring his vision to pass. What happens? He meets indifference on every hand. He finds scorn and resentment to social change. He soon thinks that there is neither justice nor right in the world. Gradually he realizes that even after he has spent a lifetime of effort, he will have touched hardly the surface of his problem. The world probably will not even know that he has lived. He wonders if it is worth the struggle. He grows cynical and hard. He deserts his vision, and is unwilling to pay the price it costs to follow it. He sees humanity: indifferent, dishonest, cruel, unjust, unhappy. He would have liked to cure them, but they would not. The universe does not seem fatherly to him, but totally heartless. He thinks he is facing all of the facts, but what of his own personality? No man will be genuinely happy unless he achieves something in the service of society. This sort of reception by society is very likely to meet him. If he resents this, he is filled with anger. If he gives up, he does not achieve. In either case he is unhappy.

Buddha recognized this problem in humanity and met it with another reaction of resignation. His theory was: Do not want so much; decrease your desires and you will be able to satisfy them. To one who can do this there is a measure of content. Desire is subdued and one goes on, less enthusiastically to be sure, but at least without mental torture. But this is repression, which is the worst reaction one can make to his conflicts. It is followed by weakness of character and often by mental disease.

It is the meek who realize that the men who seem to be dying on a cross are really only beginning to live; that they are the people who will inevitably inherit the earth. We shall grasp the full significance of this inheritance if the rewards of meekness are summarized. Jesus has come nearer inheriting the earth than any one else, and he probably never owned property. The inheritance of which he spoke was of a different sort. In the first place, meekness is a characteristic of the wholesome personality which makes one feel that he possesses the most valuable of all things, happiness. By its very nature meekness implies faith, which in turn inhibits fear and often anger. It disposes him to the choice of the sort of purpose about which integration is possible. It makes him the master of his troubles and disappointments, for he seeks in them for values. In the second place, he gains the deepest respect of his fellow men and serves them. He may be imposed upon, taken advantage of, and laughed at; but in the long run, we stand before the meek man in awe and admiration, as the Roman centurion did at the foot of the cross. Because of his confidence and firmness in time of danger, he commands his fellows. By his steadfastness he stabilizes society.

Here, then, is another fundamental attitude which we must teach our children. This trait seems much more difficult than the others. How shall we go about educating our children in meekness?

In the early years of the child's development the growth in meekness depends upon the types of reward that he learns to expect and enjoy. There are three native tendencies in the child which can be employed in the development of meekness.

In the first place, achievement is the strongest innate source of pleasure. Use the native reward. Let the child get his rewards only from a sense of achievement. Here is a boy who does splendid work throughout three years of his

AN EXPERIMENTAL FAITH

college life. During the first two years honors are heaped upon him. In the third year he meets with one disappointment after another. The result is that he becomes so depressed he goes to pieces. He had learned to expect social approval. There is only one reward which can be depended upon, and that is a sense of having done one's task well. It will be easier to learn meekness, if the child is taught to look for this reward rather than the more fickle one of social approval.

In the second place, it is natural to get more pleasure from an achievement for which one has sacrificed and struggled than from one gained easily. Teach the child to seek achievements which will cost sacrifice and struggle. If this is done gradually, it will be learned easily by every healthy child. He can be taught actually to seek for obstacles to overcome.

The third of the inherited motives which can be utilized in this process is the instinctive love of parents, which matures at a fairly early age in the child. Dr. Weigle illustrates such a possibility in this story.[3]

One morning when Bradley came down to breakfast he put on his mother's plate a little piece of paper neatly folded. His mother opened it. She could hardly believe it, but this is what Bradley had written:

Mother owes Bradley:

For running errands	$0.25
For being good	.10
For taking music lessons	.15
Extras	.05
Total	$0.55

His mother smiled, but did not say anything, and when lunch time came she placed the bill on Bradley's plate with fifty-five cents. Bradley's eyes fairly danced when he saw the money and thought his business ability had been quickly rewarded, but with the money there was another little bill, which read like this:

[3] From *The Training of Children in the Christian Family*, by Luther A. Weigle. Copyright The Pilgrim Press. Used by permission.

Bradley owes mother:

For being good	$0.00
For nursing him through his long illness with scarlet fever	.00
For clothes, shoes, gloves, and playthings..	.00
For all his meals and his beautiful room...	.00
Total that Bradley owes Mother	$0.00

Tears came into Bradley's eyes, and he put his arms around his mother's neck, put his little hand with the fifty-five cents in hers, and said, "Take the money all back, mamma, and let me love you and do things for nothing!"

After these three lessons have been learned, the next step is the foundation of a firm faith in a fatherly God and His laws. The child will adopt any faith he is given, but sometimes with tragic results. The boy who loses his religion in college does so because of the unintelligent things he has been taught about religion in his childhood. A faith in the God described by Jesus will never be in danger of being overthrown by science and philosophy. The hypothesis of a fatherly God has proved a fruitful one in spiritual progress. It is a valuable one for mental health. If you give the child this hypothesis, you assure him of mental health, and probably of worthwhile achievement.

The fourth characteristic of experimental faith is a natural fulfillment of the other three. Into it is crowded all of the meaning that is found in such phrases as singleness of purpose, dedication of self to God, and faith in one's fellow man.

Happy are the pure in heart: for they shall see God.—Matthew 5:8.

Unfortunately, the popular interpretation of this Beatitude has taken on a negative tone. The pure in heart are thought to be those who do no evil. Notice, however, that the word *purity* is more positive than negative. Pure water is not simply the lack of sediment and bacteria. It is good water, which quenches thirst. Pure food is not simply the lack of poison or dirt. It is good food, which feeds the body. Likewise, purity of action is not simply the lack of sin and evil. To have done no wrong may be good, but it cannot be said to be pure. Purity has more significance than this. Pure gold is all gold. The pure in heart are all heart, dominated by a love of mankind.

Purity of heart is first and foremost a faith in the potential goodness of one's fellow men. Suspicion and distrust are the characteristic responses of many people to their social contacts. If they are asked why they have no confidence in their fellows, they reply that they have been deceived and taken advantage of so many times, that they realize if one is to survive in his social environment, he must look out for his own interests. This is not the attitude of the pure in heart.

Consider Jesus' attitude toward others. When he looked at men he saw the best in them. It must have seemed ridiculous to those who knew the impulsiveness and changeability of Simon to call him Peter the Rock. But when Jesus saw the wasted energy in the emotional explosions of Simon, he also perceived the potential, dynamic personality on whom he could build a church. It was this faith that Jesus had in him which gradually transformed Simon into the powerful leader of the early church. Changing personality in adults is a difficult thing to accomplish. Here is an example of one good method by which it can be done.

What man has not felt the power which comes from the faith of his mother? She inspires him to greater effort by her purity of heart. To be sure, parents sometimes bring about serious conflicts in their children when they try to inspire in them some ambition which they have not the capacity to carry out. Not every child can be President. But an intelligent faith, which burns steadily through whatever failures and mistakes a child may make, is an inspiration to any growing man. That faith, however, must be intelligent. To have a blind confidence in a child, which his inherited capacities do not warrant, may cause him much unhappiness. Many a father, anxious for his son to follow in his footsteps, condemns him to failure and unhappiness, when he might have been successful in some other occupation. The fact remains that the pure in heart, who see the best in us, are our greatest inspiration. If it is a perception of our actual capacities, however, it will be a more wholesome inspiration than if it is a blind projection into us of abilities we do not possess.

There are two objections often brought against developing this habit of having faith in all men. The first one is that such a trusting individual will be deceived. The second is that if there is more evil than good in a man, we shall simply be shutting our eyes to the facts, if we fail to acknowledge it.

To the first of these objections, two answers can be made. In the first place, one is deceived a very small percentage of the time. One finds his faith in his fellow men warranted much more often than he is deceived by them. Furthermore, men respond to faith. In the second place, to distrust men has a direct destructive effect on our personality. It involves fear, suspicion, hate, and anger, which are the worst enemies of happiness and strong personality. On the other hand, faith, in itself, whether well-founded or not, builds up and strengthens personality. It is healthy to believe in one's associates. It is morbid to distrust them.

The answer to the second objection is found in the fact that an intelligent faith does not condone evil, but it sees in the forces which produce evil, the potential strength for good. Jesus did not shut his eyes to the sins of those whom he met, not even of his disciples. He found it necessary to rebuke Peter on several occasions, but he never lost his faith in him. Life is largely what one sees in it, and what he sees in it depends much more upon him than upon the outside world. Our sense organs receive stimuli from the external world in a somewhat regular fashion. At any one moment a great many sensory stimuli are affecting one's sense organs. He responds to only a small portion of them, consciously. To which ones he responds, and what response he makes to them, is more a function of his personality than of the nature of the stimuli themselves. For example, the fear-stricken mind can hear strange noises and see ominous shadows to which others are indifferent. Everyone is familiar with the ease with which we discover flaws in those whom we dislike. Fear, anger, worry, sorrow, anxiety, and guilt are largely in the things into which we have learned to put them. The pure in heart find them in very few things. This is not a philosophy of closing one's eyes to the ugly things in life. It is a matter of interpreting, even the ugly things in life, in terms of their highest potentialities. Jesus was not an idealistic dreamer who dodged reality, but he did see deeper into reality than those to whom the universe presents a rather unhappy picture.

One can choose the criteria by which he will interpret things. He may insist that the lover is blind who sees the best in his beloved. That is not the attitude of the lover. He believes that the others are blind who cannot see what he does. Will anyone question which brings the most happiness into the world? One may become a cynic. He can find plenty of data for believing that life is a delusion, and love and beauty mere dreams. Recently a member of the graduating class in one of our colleges competed for a prize in oratory. He won with a passionate plea for a high ideal. Afterward in commenting on it he said, "That was all just a lot of 'baloney,' but it is what gets over." That seemed to be his whole philosophy of life. Here was a youth richly endowed with talents, convinced that life is false. Many young people seem to feel that this point of view represents maturity as opposed to the silly notions of idealistic adolescence; that it is a disillusionment from unrealistic dreams into a recognition of life as it really is. The fact is that the man who is pure in heart is happier and more wholesome than one who has lost his faith in others.

There is a second element in this characteristic of being pure in heart. This second element is singleness of purpose.

It has been pointed out that having a purpose in life is one of the surest roads to mental soundness. In every college there are two groups of students: those who know what they expect to do in life, and those who do not. While there are wide individual differences in each group, as groups they are easily distinguished. President Charles W. Eliot pointed out this fact in an address, in which he said:

> In general, professional students in the United States exhibit keen interest in their studies, work hard, advance rapidly, and avail themselves of their opportunities to gain knowledge and skill to the utmost limit of their strength and capacity, no matter whether the profession for which they are preparing be divinity, law, medicine, architecture, engineering, forestry, teaching, business, or corporation service.[4]

The more enthusiastic one is about his purpose, the more valuable its effect on his personality will be. A dominating purpose is one which is constantly in the focus of his attention, is the strongest motive in his behavior, and is the source of his greatest pleasure. Contributions to our knowledge regularly come from men of whom this is characteristic. This is true in the realm of the spiritual as well as the secular fields of knowledge.

The value of a dominating purpose for personality is due to the fact that it brings about integration. All of one's energies are directed toward that one goal. In mental life integration must be achieved; it is not inherited. All mental disorders are the result of the failure to integrate one's drives into a single purpose. What mental disease one has depends upon which of these disintegrating emotional conditions becomes the characteristic response of the individual to his conflicts. Thus, one mental disorder is essentially a condition of constant fatigue. Another is sometimes called the anxiety neurosis. One of the most common of the hospital psychoses is a constant expression of sorrow. The epileptic is devoting his life to anger. Fear is an important character-

[4] Hart, J. K., *Creative Moments in Education*, 395 f., Henry Holt and Company, 1931.

istic in most serious mental conditions. The energy of every one of the urges must be utilized in the healthy personality, but these urges must not conflict with one another. If a life purpose is chosen which leaves any of the natural urges unsatisfied, disintegrating conditions will arise. Purity of heart does not consist in throwing out of one's personality those urges which are not easily integrated, but in finding a purpose about which they can all be integrated.

The pure in heart, then, are always looking for the best in men. Their faith is such that they never despair of finding it. Furthermore they have singleness of purpose. The man who is pure in heart has a vision in life, and he never loses sight of it. It motivates his every act and determines his every attitude. No better example of the pure in heart could be found than the good father or mother. The true parent will find all other phases of his life subordinated to the welfare of his child. It requires no proving, that his faith in his child is unshakable. When men take this attitude toward all their fellows they have learned the Christian virtue of being pure in heart in all of its breadth. When men are pure in heart they will be searching for principles by which they can help men to realize the best that is in them. Whether this searching be so small a task as finding the cause of a child's temper tantrum, or discovering the laws of human nature by which nations can learn to live together peaceably, it is the result of being pure in heart.

It should now be clear why happiness comes to the pure in heart. Jesus described their reward thus, "They shall see God." Many people have believed that they saw God. Even in our hospitals for the insane can be found a number of them. On the other hand, the prophets and saints have had visions of the Divine. How can we distinguish between those who have and those who only think they have seen God? Jesus answered that it is the pure in heart who see God. Urging people to seek mystical experiences by a process of semi-hypnosis is not at all healthy. It encourages people to resort to fantasy as a retreat from their troubles.

We need to recognize in our own religious experiences whether we are indulging in such fantasies or seeing God. Does this seem to be a bit of unreal mysticism? It sounds like an apocalyptic experience.

There is a contrast in the New Testament between the apocalyptic idea of the coming of the kingdom in a sudden burst of glory, and the notion of a gradually growing kingdom in the hearts of righteous men. Are these concepts contradictory? If seeing God or the coming of the kingdom consists in gaining an insight into the spiritual laws, we can use scientific insight as an analogous situation.

Insight into a problem frequently comes in a flash. In describing the psychology of invention or discovery, this flash of insight represents an important stage. Everyone can cite famous instances of it. When Archimedes found a method of determining by specific gravity the purity of the gold in Hiero's crown, the insight was so sudden that he was overjoyed, and in his enthusiasm rushed down the street shouting, "Eureka, I have found it!" It was a steaming teakettle that is said to have given Watt his famous insight into the power of steam. A falling apple brought the insight of gravitation to Newton. Instances might be multiplied. Every experimenter spends hours studying the complex data of his experiments in an effort to discover what they mean. Suddenly an explanation is seen. It is almost as if it had come from without. Most insights into the spiritual realm have been of the same sort.

Observe carefully the causes of these insights. It was not an accident that the millions of others who had observed falling objects failed to discover gravity. Only Newton had the background for such a discovery. Scientific insights have come to those who have learned all of the known facts in their fields of discovery, and have spent hours studying them. Then out of what seems to be chaos come these flashes of insight. Only those who have made it the purpose of their lives to search for such insights, have them. Many have believed that they saw God. Jesus said that only the pure in heart really see Him. We see now what this means. Seeing God is gaining an insight into the spiritual law. Who is likely to do this except he who has made it his dominating purpose in life? As one observes the brilliant insights of Jesus into the spiritual problems of his day, he sees the very incarnation of this Beatitude. Examine the great insights made by the prophets. Jeremiah, Hosea, Amos, Isaiah, and the others were faced with baffling problems. Some of the foundation beliefs of their people were being shattered by circumstances. The temple was destroyed, when they were sure it could not be destroyed. They were made slaves, when they expected to rule the world. But these spiritual scientists, with intense purity of heart, wrestled with these problems until insight came to them. Examine their visions. Compare them with the flashes of insight which come to the scientist. They are strikingly similar. Great discoveries remain to be made both in science and in the spiritual realm. Only the pure in heart will make them.

Finally, let us see how children can be educated to be pure in heart. It should be obvious, in the first place, that these various attitudes are mutually helpful. Forming one of them makes it easier to form the others. In fact, no one of them can be formed except along with all of the others. Being pure in heart is only one trait of this broader attitude which has been called experimental faith. However, a few principles can be suggested for the development of this particular trait.

The most important task is giving the child a faith in others. Indeed, it is not so much giving him such a faith, as keeping him from losing it. Every child is instinctively trusting. Again we find that we can build on an inherited characteristic. There are two ways in which a child often does lose this faith. In the first place, the parents, in an effort to protect him from imposition, teach him to be suspicious of others. They do this in all sincerity, but in so doing they destroy an important part of his personality. On the contrary, they should find every opportunity of giving him more faith in others. The second reason why children sometimes lose their faith in men is because they are taken advantage of. This is a more difficult situation to meet. There are three methods of doing so. First, try to make the child understand that the people who have deceived him are to be pitied, not hated. Explain to him that they do this because of ignorance, that they do not know any better. Secondly, teach him the Beatitudes of fatherly love, and the lessons about anger which are described in the chapter on that subject. Thirdly, utilize his natural tendency to hero-worship. Tell him of heroes who have been pure in heart. Pasteur and Darwin are good examples of scientists who have been pure in heart with respect to the natural law. Many of the Bible heroes and later church heroes provide good examples of the same trait in the religious world. Hosea, Jeremiah, Paul, Jesus, Wesley, and Francis of Assisi are among the best.

Another important task in making the child pure in heart is helping him to find the right life work. Remember that the primary essential is singleness of purpose. The child will have singleness of purpose only if he finds a task about which he can integrate all of his abilities. Two things are necessary for this. In the first place, it must be a purpose which tends to integration. It has been shown and will be shown even more fully that the only motivation about which perfect integration is possible is fatherly love. Hence, give the child this sort of love for others. In the second place, it is important that he find a task especially adapted to his own particular abilities. This means that the parents must know as accurately as possible what his abilities are. That is not always easy to learn. But at least parents who try to learn them will do better than those who do not. Then try to find opportunities for him to use these abilities and to use them in some place where he can serve men.

Here, then, is the last of the four characteristics of an experimental faith, purity of heart, which is to have singleness of purpose and to look for the best in men, with the faith that fundamentally men are potentially good.

AN EXPERIMENTAL FAITH

An experimental faith: what are its values for society, and for you and me? "Now faith is the substance of things hoped for, the evidence of things not seen.... These (heroes) all died in faith, not having received the promises, but having seen them afar off, and were persuaded of them and embraced them.... They desire a better country, that is, a heavenly."[5] No better definition of experimental faith could be found than this portion of the Epistle to the Hebrews. The thrill of discovery, which has driven men to such great efforts throughout the ages, is the motivation that gives zest to research in any field today. A Christian faith that there are spiritual forces waiting to be discovered should be equally challenging to every youth in the Christian church. To challenge the youth of the church to become research workers in the realm of spiritual law may seem quite impractical for a majority of them. There are wide individual differences in inherited capacities and in opportunities. Most of them must fill the more common occupations by which the civilized world functions.

Everyone can in some way discover something about God. A mother who searches for ways of giving her children the character training which will release all of their available power, is contributing quite as much to the advancement of the kingdom of heaven as he who discovers some new way to heal mental disorders. The merchant, whose spirit of service motivates him to seek better ways of making business the servant instead of the master of men, is contributing as much as he who conceives some new plan for the solution of our international difficulties. The only fundamental advance that comes to civilization comes through the development of character. To train a child in these four traits of Christian faith is a worthwhile goal for any man. There is no one, in however humble a position in life, who cannot practice these four habits; and whose personality and usefulness will not be increased by them.

Parents can teach these emotional attitudes of faith to

[5] Hebrews 11:1, 13, 16.

their children with confidence that in so doing they are contributing, not only to the usefulness, but to the happiness and wholesomeness of the child. Whether these attitudes are philosophically, theologically, or ethically valid are questions which might profitably be discussed. However, the purpose of this book is to show that they are psychologically valid. That these four characteristics of experimental faith lead to mental health rather than mental disease and wholesome rather than frustrated personality has been shown to be substantiated by the principles of modern psychology.

Here, then, is the sort of faith Jesus taught. Observe that it is specifically defined. Faith is a tremendous force, but like other great forces it can lead to disaster if ignorantly used. Great things have been done by it, but greater things than these shall be done when men learn the type of faith taught in these four Beatitudes. Men had faith in their magical ceremonies to prevent and cure disease. Men had all sorts of superstitious beliefs in the various fields of nature. It was only when they adopted the experimental faith of modern science that they began to do greater things. The scientist has an unshakable faith that the universe is lawful; that its laws are worth discovering; that whatever happens is in line with them; and that he can devote his whole life to their discovery with confidence. This faith has produced many miracles. That, no one will deny. Jesus urged that exactly this same faith be applied to the spiritual realm. He believed that there are spiritual laws which are the will of God; that those laws are worth finding; that whatever happens is the result of their working; and that if a man devotes his life to their discovery he will find the Divine, inherit the earth, learn of the true nature of the kingdom of God, and experience the happiness which comes to him who lives in the kingdom of heaven. The scientific attitude has been found to be a valuable factor in mental health. Therefore, one who has this faith which Jesus taught will be mentally healthy and achieve great things.

Chapter III

THE DYNAMIC OF FATHERLY LOVE

Man is not saved by faith alone. The Christian personality must be devoted to the service of humanity. "Be ye therefore perfect as your Father." The remaining four Beatitudes describe the characteristics of fatherliness. It will not be sufficient to talk of fatherly love in a vague, meaningless way. These four Beatitudes describe it accurately. They can be made the dominating characteristics of our lives. Let us see exactly what this perfection of fatherliness is, how it may be attained, and what the result will be in terms of wholesome personality.

In spite of the vague way in which brotherly love has been interpreted, it has unquestionably wielded great influence in society. The world is richer for having seen in it an ideal for social relationships. If the concept of fatherly love is to replace it in Christian thinking, it will have to prove itself to be a higher ideal. The findings of the psychology of personality indicate that fatherly love is the best possible motivation about which to integrate one's personality. Furthermore, fatherly love is a type of motivation which can be sustained. It is not subject to the fluctuations which most motivations undergo. It is based on a strong instinctive drive in human nature, and therefore can be easily taught to the child.

The term *fatherly love* may be interpreted quite as vaguely and with as little meaning as the term *brotherly love* has been. Just what is meant by being fatherly to all men? The idea may seem absurd or even objectionable to some. This is because we associate with the word *father* only the more superficial characteristics of parenthood, and not the nature of his love which is the noblest thing on earth. 'Maintaining discipline, pretending to be omniscient, and dictating conduct are not the major characteristics of parenthood. To what kind of a father did Jesus refer? The answer is found in this verse from the Sermon on the Mount. "Be ye therefore perfect, even as your FATHER in heaven is perfect." Jesus taught that we must take the same attitude toward others that God takes toward us. He made this practical by showing how the fatherliness of God works out in everyday life. For example, observe the attitude of the father of the Prodigal Son. Best of all he exemplified it in his own life. "He that hath seen me hath seen the Father." He admonished the disciples, "Love one another as I have loved you." His attitude toward the Twelve was always more like that of a father than of a brother.

Perhaps the most difficult problem in the psychology of motivation is that of sustained effort. It is a fairly simple task to challenge people to momentary enthusiasm. Religious fervor rises high during evangelistic campaigns. Unfortunately, such campaigns have to be repeated at frequent intervals if they are to constitute any important motivation in the lives of those who are stimulated by them. In the fever of war madness patriotism is at its peak. In peace times, it is impossible to stimulate such patriotic fervor even with the aid of numerous flag days, memorial days, and independence days. While still suffering from the painful memories of recent failures or near failures in examinations, students are filled with good resolutions about diligence in the future. The long period of the next semester, however, finds most of them lagging behind again. The tendency for fervor to diminish seems characteristic of most motivations. The whole history of religion is a story of periods of emotional fervor followed by periods of legalism and insincere ritual. Is there a form of love which remains naturally at a high peak? Obviously, that of the parent for a child is the one form that human nature affords. If fatherly love can be taught a child, it will last throughout life. Through it alone can we get sustained motivation.

Let us turn now to the first characteristic which Jesus ascribed to fatherliness. It is not surprising that the first trait he gave is an inner attitude. Many a father has furnished his children with all of the material necessities of life and believed that he had done his full duty. It is all too common to find boys in college whose only close contact with their fathers is through their financial relations. Such fathers insist that they have done their "duty" by their sons. It is true of them as it was of the Pharisees, that they "Tithe mint and anise and cummin, and have left undone the weightier matters of the law, justice, and mercy, and faith." In his description of fatherliness Jesus had nothing to say about financial advantages. The first characteristic he did give seems a strange one at first glance.

Happy are they that mourn: for they shall be comforted.—Matthew 5:4.

Common sense would never have suggested to men that happiness could come from mourning. Yet when its meaning is grasped, this Beatitude describes a trait of character that psychology must recognize as a desirable one. Only the Master with his profound understanding of the spiritual law could have recognized the value of mourning. It is not surprising that many think Jesus was an impractical idealist. This certainly does not sound practical. Yet, as scientific methods replace the "common sense" method of studying the nature of mental life, this "impractical" principle which Jesus taught is standing the test of research.

What, then, is this mourning which is the source of happiness? The word used by Matthew does not refer to outward mourning. There was another word translated *mourning*, which was used to describe outward expression of grief, particularly the activities of the professional mourner. Jesus referred to a much deeper feeling. Very occasionally this term had to do with bereavement, but of the nine times it occurs in Matthew, it refers to bereavement only once. On all of the other occasions it implies a "mourning for the sins of Israel." The Jews mourned for many things but chiefly for their sins, which they believed were retarding the coming of the Messiah and of the kingdom of heaven. They did not always know in just what way they had sinned, but their faith made them sure that any suffering they experienced must be due to their sins. When calamities befell them they did not lose their faith in Jehovah, they tried to discover what they were doing that displeased Him. It was this unshaken faith which produced the religions of Judaism and Christianity. It is the experimental faith which was described in the last chapter. In this meaning of mourning we find our clue to understanding why happiness comes to those who mourn.

> He that lacks time to mourn, lacks time to mend.
> Eternity mourns that. 'Tis an ill cure
> For life's worst ills, to have no time to feel them.
> Where sorrow's held intrusive and turn'd out
> There wisdom will not enter, nor true power,
> Nor aught that dignifies humanity.[1]

We are not dealing, then, with the childish whining which sometimes characterizes even adults in their moments of selfishness. Jonah was hardly to be admired when he mourned the loss of his gourd-vine shade, whereas he had felt no sorrow for the probable destruction of Ninevah's 120,000 people. Many of us are like that. We complain bitterly and loudly because we do not receive all the material benefits we desire. We are only mildly interested in the sufferings of the thousands about us. Since this is the first characteristic of fatherly love, let us turn to parenthood to find its full meaning. Long before a child is born he becomes a source of worry to his parents. That worry is likely to continue as long as the child and the parents both live. They are anxious to bring him up to be a fine, happy, worthwhile man. They mourn when any obstacle gets in the way of that

[1] Gore, Charles, *The Sermon on the Mount*, 31, Charles Scribner's Sons, 1925.

goal. Perhaps this is the fundamental trait of good parents. It is a part of fatherly love. Any father or mother whose son has become a man of whom they are proud, understands why Jesus said that those who mourn are happy.

Here, then, is one characteristic of fatherly love. If a man is sensitive to the sorrows and failures not only of his own children but of all men, he has this personality trait with which we are dealing. Here is a group of young children in our neighborhood. With life before them, we can already see trouble ahead. Many of them will live lives filled with unhappiness, frustration, disappointment, and failure. No man who has fatherly love as a part of his personality will fail to mourn for them. No thoughtful person can see a nation forget its God and lose itself in riotous living, with graft and corruption the mark of its government, and greed and extravagance the characteristics of its people; and not understand the deep emotion of Jesus when he mourned over Jerusalem. Who can watch a group of college students casting their pearls of opportunity before the swine who call themselves jolly good fellows, and not mourn, knowing that sooner or later they must learn the bitterness of disillusionment? Mourning is the inevitable reaction of any man who has a genuine affection for his fellow men. Catholics call their priests, father. It is certainly true that no minister is a real servant of Christ who does not have many of the attributes of a father. As Dean Brown describes it:

> The man who can stand before a waiting congregation of expectant people and not feel in a measure almost overpowering the tug and pull of their need upon his own moral reserves, summoning him into the highest action of which he is capable, is altogether too wooden to be in the ministry for a single hour. Such a man might usefully serve his day and generation by becoming one of those patient figures representing a rapidly vanishing race standing out in front of a cigar store to invite custom.[2]

Jesus' own relationship with those whom he met is replete with examples of fatherly love. When he is described as

[2] Brown, Charles R., *The Art of Preaching*, 11, The Macmillan Company, 1922.

loving the rich young ruler, it was like a father who saw the possibilities in the young man which he had not the character to use.

It is not any longer common for us to let men starve. The religion of Jesus has thoroughly engrained that idea into society. It is, however, very common to commit worse crimes. Consider the young men in any community who become criminals or worthless parasites on society. In almost every case one of the causal factors is a lack of sympathetic and understanding friendship among his elders. Most boys are idealists at heart. If there were older men who were always sensitive to their problems and interested in their welfare, few of them would fail to achieve a manhood of credit to themselves and their country. Unfortunately a boy often finds his most sympathetic friends among the least desirable of his elders.

Consider the sacrifices made by most parents for their children that they may have the best possible advantages; then picture a society where fatherly love is the dominant personality trait of Christian men and women toward all mankind. Here is the so-called "bad element" of the town. Leaders in religion often scorn them, actually expressing fear of contamination with them. What a different result there might be if they took a parental attitude toward them.

How shall such nobility of character be produced in men and women? If it is to become a universal trait, it must be built on some natural drive in human behavior. Psychology has far to go before it can speak very definitely about man's inherited social nature, but it is perfectly certain that man is by nature a social animal. Furthermore, he is by nature sympathetic. Why, then, are there so many unsympathetic people in any social group? The answer is, repression. The church has often been accused, and justly, of teaching the repression of some of man's natural appetites. Here is an innate drive which society itself represses. Curiously enough, it preaches this repression to make men strong, and its result is to make men small.

THE DYNAMIC OF FATHERLY LOVE

There is a common tradition, especially among men, which is vicious to its very core. It has no official name, but it seems to be characteristically American, and perhaps can best be called the "he-man" philosophy. As soon as he can understand words, every boy hears the manly assertion, "Boys don't cry!" During the early years of his life every boy strives with might and main to gain what appears to be the essence of manliness, the capacity to withhold tears. During that time there are hundreds of occasions on which tears fight for exit. He does not see them in his comrades, therefore he develops serious feelings of inferiority, because he thinks that he is the only boy so unmanly as to want to cry. He does not know that his comrades, too, are holding back tears. In his efforts to free himself from such unpleasant feelings he is forced to use many severe methods. In the first place, he avoids all stimulation to tears. When he is grown, habit makes him dodge situations which might arouse his deep sympathy. He is afraid to see suffering. In the second place, he endeavors to harden his heart and make callous his sensitivities, so that he is no longer stimulated to grief even in the presence of suffering and unhappiness. In later life, he is out of tune with the hearts of others and indifferent to their troubles. It is not surprising that women are commonly more sensitive to the finer things of life than men. In his efforts to become a real "he-man," a boy who does not cry, he is forced to become crude, thoughtless, callous, and in fact almost emotionally impotent, having repressed some of his finest qualities. The motivation behind this "boys don't cry" philosophy is perhaps praiseworthy enough. We are, of course, anxious for our sons to be courageous and able to endure hardship, not cowardly and weak, but we have used the wrong methods. We have defeated our very purpose by producing bad inferiority complexes and repressing the sensibilities which make a man noble. If we look through the Bible and list the characters who mourned, we find such names as these: Moses, Abraham, Samuel, David, Elijah, Jeremiah, Isaiah, Amos, Hosea, Jesus, Peter, and Paul. Among those who would answer our description of the real "he-man" would be Samson and Goliath. If we look in our own country for examples of men who have mourned, the names of Washington, Lincoln, Lee, and Grant come to mind. Americans in whom we find the "he-man" ideal exemplified include the most of our gangsters. It is little wonder we have so much heartlessness when this attitude is so completely established in children.

Perhaps it will be asked what one can do with children who cry about every little thing that happens to them. The reason we teach them not to cry is not only that they may learn endurance and courage, but also because they will meet a great deal of ridicule from their fellows if they do cry. This is a good illustration of the danger of confusing outward behavior with true character. Obviously, the purpose of such training is that children may learn to endure pain and have courage to face their own battles bravely. The method used for bringing this about is by teaching them that children do not cry. The result is, that while they may learn to endure pain without crying, they also learn to withhold sympathy for the sufferings of others as well. Children can be taught courage without the dangers of repression or the loss of their capacity for sympathy. The method of accomplishing this will be described fully in the discussion of the last Beatitude.

"They shall be comforted." Some people have tried to win sympathy by their tales of woe. Actually, everyone dreads to be near them. Their doleful complainings are far from pleasant. In the long run they are not comforted. This comfort of which Jesus speaks is found in strength of personality. One who is sympathetic with other men gains a perspective which makes him able to see his own troubles in their true light. Just as parents are usually so concerned about the sufferings of their children that they are almost unaware of their own troubles, so these men who mourn the unhappiness of all men will find their own difficulties so small by comparison that they seem negligible. Their strength of character and depth of sympathy will constitute their own best reward.

One who is not sensitive to the needs of others would be astonished at the amount of suffering that is going on all about him, often in his closest friends. One of the most broadening experiences in life comes to us in moments of deepest sorrow. Because of the habit people have of suppressing the outward signs of grief, we may suppose that the whole world is happy. Then something occurs which is so heart-rending that we cannot withhold our tears. When such an occasion arises, one of the things that impresses us most is the great number of other heavy hearts that open themselves to us in sympathy and comfort. Often they are the hearts of friends whom we have known for a long time, with wounds which we never even suspected. Many a man with a soul full of conflicts, sorrows, and fears, which he has never dared admit to anyone, goes about life handicapped by those unsolved difficulties. Many of them find their way into the study of every true minister and teacher, and to all who have sympathetic ears.

Quite apart from any sense of duty or ethical standards, this attitude of being sensitive to the needs of others is essential to mental health. Most mental disease is fundamentally self-centeredness. The man whose interest is in others is not very susceptible to mental disease. If parents teach their children this Beatitude they will assure them of a high measure of happiness. How, then, shall we go about making them sensitive to the needs of others? Much of what has already been said will suggest the methods. It cannot be emphasized too much that the best single principle of child training consists in taking advantage of his natural behavior. The normal child will naturally show sympathy. Encourage it when it occurs. Stimulate it by giving him opportunities to become aware of its need. This is the positive side. On the negative side, there are certain very common forms of character training which must be carefully avoided. For example, do not tell him that "boys don't cry." Do not make him too much interested in "standing up for his own rights." This only makes him self-centered and mentally unwholesome. Do not teach him class hatred, race prejudice, or national suspicion.

The adage that "the road to hell is paved with good intentions" may be somewhat exaggerated, but it is true that it is the road to a great deal of suffering on earth. There are some people who are sensitive to suffering but do nothing about it. Having learned the lesson of sympathy, let us turn to the active side of fatherly love. Jesus described it in three Beatitudes. The first of these is,

Happy are the merciful: for they shall obtain mercy.—Matthew 5:7.

The word which Jesus translated *mercy* is one rich in meaning throughout the Old Testament. Someone has described it as "the perfection of that mystical relation of one personality to another which is the highest of all possible grades of friendship." Therefore, when Jesus translated it *mercy* he gave to it a meaning far greater than it had ever had, certainly greater than we commonly give to it today. The same Hebrew word is sometimes interpreted as *righteousness*, which is another evidence that righteousness in the Christian era is more of the quality of loving-kindness than of cold justice or negative morality.

Mercy is not a passive process, but one that expresses itself in action. Its simplest definition would be the prevention of suffering in others, whether physical or spiritual. Parents try to predict the hard knocks their children may meet, save them from as many as possible, and give them the strength to meet the others. The fatherliness of God, exemplified in this Beatitude, is not characteristic of the Old Testament teachings. The dominant idea of God in the Old Testament is that of righteousness and justice in the sternest sense. Only Hosea caught a vision of Jesus' type of righteousness, which is characterized by love and forgiveness. The notion that righteousness and love cannot go together has some foundation in experience. Many parents do find it difficult to love their children and be perfectly just with them simultaneously. This is, however, shortsightedness on the part of the parents. To be merciful does not involve a compromise with righteousness, although it does involve forgiveness. Jesus, in all his dealing with sinners, practiced forgiveness, but a forgiveness that made them able "to take up their beds and walk."

Some have thought of mercy as a purely negative virtue by which one refrains from inflicting punishment on another, even though it is a richly deserved punishment. That this is not the meaning of the Beatitude is clearly indicated in the word translated *merciful*. The *merciful* of the Beatitude carries the idea of kindness and beneficence. Forgive and forget is not the stature of Christian mercy.

The best illustrations of Jesus' concept are found in his own life. For example, he was merciful to the woman taken in adultery when the others would have condemned her and stoned her to death. He showed the quality of his mercy in his attitude, "Neither do I condemn thee." Furthermore, he did not stop with lack of punishment, but went on, saying, "Go thy way and sin no more." This involved a forgiveness which extends into regeneration. When he healed the man sick of the palsy, he not only healed his physical illness, but also forgave him his sins.

When we think of this type of mercy we can understand how loving one's enemies is possible. Consider how frequently we are deeply offended at some injustice done to us. We usually find it difficult to forgive even when amends are made. A parent, however, would have no difficulty forgiving a child any number of such offences. For the merciful, then, forgiveness, even of enemies, is a natural part of their personalities. You will recall the incident in Jesus' life when Peter came to him all inflated with a sense of his own magnanimity and asked him, "How often shall we forgive a brother, seven times?" This is one of the occasions on which

Peter probably was not seeking information, but wishing to bask in the sunshine of the Master's approval. It must have been a chastened and amazed Peter who heard Jesus say, "Not seven times, but seventy times seven times." As we contemplate our own capacity for forgiveness, which, if not entirely stunted, rarely approaches even Peter's seven times, we may wonder whether we can ever hope to attain that character which Jesus called merciful. But does not every parent forgive seventy times seven times?

It is not always easy to know how to be merciful. Parents spend many sleepless nights searching for wisdom to keep their children from rushing into sorrow and unhappiness. Mercy does not always express itself by withholding punishment. Often, punishing a child may be more merciful than spoiling him. Flunking a college student may be the most merciful thing one can do for him, although he is not likely to think so at the time. To "spare the rod and spoil the child" is not a universal principle. For one child punishment may be necessary, in another it may produce a sullen, spiritless, and anti-social personality. Permitting a youth to work his way through college may develop a sense of responsibility and idealism in one student, produce an over-materialistic, money-grabbing, philosophy of life in another, and an inferiority complex in a third. Demonstrative affection may be valuable to some children, but produce serious maladjustments in others. An over-strict sex education may result in moral purity, and at the same time be responsible for unhappiness in married life. We are merciful only if we bring it about that righteous behavior is the natural expression of personalities. It will be seen that one needs all the spiritual insight that comes from an experimental faith to know how to be merciful. It is obvious that mercy can prevail only where fatherly love is the dominating motive of one's social behavior. Otherwise he will not always be concerned with the happiness of others.

The same methods used to instill the attitude of mourning apply in teaching the child to be merciful. These attitudes are interrelated and interdependent. When one has learned to mourn, that is, to be sympathetic to the needs of others, it will be a natural impulse to do something about it. He will probably cease to be sympathetic if he does not act on his sympathy.

Since mercy is saving others from suffering, obviously the best way to learn it is to begin with such simple situations as the young child can understand, and gradually bring before him more and more complex ones as he matures in intelligence.

The impulse to help those who are suffering is instinctive. It simply needs to be intelligently developed. The almost universal tendency to favor the under-dog is an expression of this impulse.

Let the young child have opportunities to express this impulse toward animals and younger children. A child at a very early age will respond to the opportunity of protecting weaker children. No finer training in this trait can be found than in the case of those children who are made to feel that they are having a share in bringing up their younger brothers and sisters.

As the child grows older, not only can he do harder tasks of this sort, but he should be given a wider concept of suffering. Here is a high school boy who makes it his job at social gatherings to pay attention to those who are not having a good time. Only those who have been lonely at a social gathering appreciate how much suffering this saves. Here is a college student who takes it upon himself to befriend those of his fellow students whose peculiarities make them the butt of much ridicule. This is mercy of divine proportions. He may quite possibly save someone from a life in an insane hospital. This, then, is a brief picture of growth in this second trait of fatherly love, mercy.

Man is instinctively a social animal. He cannot live alone and remain a healthy personality. He does not, however, inherit, ready-made, the social structure by which he can live with others without friction. Thus, men often seem to be unable to live either with one another or without one another. The man who can resolve these conflicts and make men able to coöperate with one another to form a society of genuine good will, must be of almost superhuman qualities. It was of him that Jesus spoke when he said,

> Happy are the peacemakers: for they shall be called the sons of God.—Matthew 5:9.

In this Beatitude Jesus was preaching unpopular doctrine. The Jews were under the heel of the Roman Empire. They were not anxious for peace until they could first obtain freedom. It is probable that a goodly portion of his audience lost their hope in him when he said, "Happy are the peacemakers." They were looking for military leaders, not peacemakers. Those of us who can still remember our indignation at any pacifistic statements in 1917-18, can appreciate fully the courage required to preach peace at such a time.

Like some of the other qualities which Jesus mentioned, peace has often been defined negatively. In the minds of most of us peace is simply lack of struggle. The epitaph "Rest in peace," implies cessation of effort and work. As the old hymn expresses it, "Work, for the night is coming, when man works no more." However, if we search the teachings of Jesus to determine what he meant by peace, we can hardly attach this negative connotation to his words. Just before he went to Gethsemane and Calvary, facing the certainty of his own death and the probable discouraging behavior of his disciples, he said, "Peace I leave with you, my peace I give unto you." He was not deluded about the future when he said this. He knew perfectly well that these persecutions were upon him, and had prophesied repeatedly the trials and tribulations which would come to his disciples. It would have been sheer hypocrisy to have promised them such a negative peace. The peace of which he spoke was a steadfastness and tranquillity of heart, which would make them able to face the future undismayed. In his words, "Let

THE DYNAMIC OF FATHERLY LOVE 77

not your heart be troubled, neither let it be afraid," he said nothing of external things, but of inner attitudes. The peace of which he spoke involved not so much change outside the man as inside the man, not so much a reduction of struggle as an increase in courage with which to meet that struggle.

There are three kinds of conflict which challenge the peacemaker. The first is the struggle between the various forces within the individual. The second is the conflict which arises between the individual and his society. The third consists of those forms of economic and political warfare which constitute the most serious of our social problems. All three of them are essentially one, however— inner conflict. The most important factors in economic crises are not material resources, but fear and greed. Certainly the only factor which makes it possible for nations to make war any more is the attitude of national conceit and international suspicion, which is so powerfully engrained in the personalities of most of the people under the name of patriotism.

Only within the individual can we find the behavior mechanisms and the consciousness which are fundamental in the interactions between individuals.[3]

Let us examine each of these three kinds of struggle. As it has been pointed out before, a man is born with powerful appetites which motivate his every action. Each of them can be satisfied in many different ways. Sometimes, however, these satisfactions conflict with each other. Sometimes they conflict with the satisfactions of other individuals. If a child is given no direction, and simply adopts the most primitive forms of satisfaction for these wants, numerous conflicts occur. On the other hand, it is possible to find a group of satisfactions which harmonize with one another, and with the interests of others. To build an integrated society of integrated personalities is the fundamental task of the peacemaker. More wars are waged within men than with-

[3] Allport, F. H., *Social Psychology*, vi, Houghton Mifflin Company, 1924.

out. More unhappiness results from inner battles than from external struggles.

These inner conflicts can be classified in three groups: lusts, fears, and angers. These will be recognized as the powerful disintegrating conditions which arise out of conflict. Everyone knows them as the great sources of unhappiness. Only the psychopathic personality, otherwise known as the moral imbecile, can permit his animal appetites to gain control over his whole personality, without a feeling of revulsion and loss of self-respect. A man, who has lain awake nights in terror of possible calamities in the future, does not have to be told the mental torture of fear. When one is constantly losing his temper in violent anger he is indeed unhappy. The man, who can help us gain control of our appetites, gives us courage to meet our dangers, and teaches us magnanimity with which to replace our angers, is a real peacemaker.

Then there are the conflicts between man and his social environment. Fundamentally they are the same conflicts which man has within himself. Lust expresses itself either in out-and-out greed or in the disguise which men call "individual initiative." Social forms of fear are numerous. The many types of panics are only expressions of fear. It is the motivation which produces miserly hoarding, and often is the real drive which men rationalize with the adage, "Charity begins at home." Anger expresses itself in "standing up for one's own rights," and in protesting vigorously about insignificant matters because of "the principle of the thing." How small the things really are that we pursue and worry about and fight for! Most of men's conflicts with one another are concerning matters which do not amount to much objectively. The disastrous results which come from them, however, in broken personalities and unhappy social groups are immeasurable.

Finally, there are the conflicts between larger social groups: economic strife, race hatred, class bitterness, and political antagonism between nations. A close examination

THE DYNAMIC OF FATHERLY LOVE

shows that the same three disintegrating conditions are found in these groups too. Such terms as *national prosperity* and *high standards of living*, which may be admirable ideals, are often only the dignified names of lusts for the satisfaction of primitive appetites. Likewise, fears may be disguised under the names, *national security, self-preservation,* and *race purity;* and *patriotism* is often nothing more than a form of anger. Wars are a result of these same three personality conflicts. War would be impossible between nations composed dominantly of Christian personalities. It is the presence of these three elements which makes propaganda effective.

Propaganda is high-pressure salesmanship, simply the stimulation of certain emotional attitudes. War propaganda appeals to conceit, pride, hate, and suspicion, all unhealthy attitudes. Strong personalities would be impervious to propaganda. Only emotionally unstable people are moved by it. Our educational program of patriotism often consists in developing personalities who respond to a certain group of stimuli with uncritical, disintegrative emotionality. Peacemakers must begin with the emotional education of the child. Fear, anger, and greed must not be dominating forces in men's lives. We are trying to bring about peace by emotional propaganda. Even if it is temporarily successful, it can never be permanently so, as long as our children are taught these other attitudes. During peace times it is fairly easy to persuade thousands to sign pledges of pacifism. However, when another war arises, its propaganda will make it seem more righteous than previous wars, and most of those who have signed these pledges will be certain that here is a situation which warrants their active participation. Why? Because they have been so thoroughly engrained with national conceit and international suspicion that propaganda is effective on them. Here, then, are these three types of conflict, which are all essentially the result of the same cause, maladjusted individuals.

Not everyone who preaches peace is a peacemaker. Often,

methods are employed which produce more conflicts than they solve. Also, some people interfere in the conflicts of others when the motivation for their behavior is not so much a desire for peace as a desire to gain a sense of importance to compensate for their fear of inferiority. This is true of some reformers in every field of activity. Such people are certainly not called "sons of God." This does not mean, however, that the only alternative is "attending to one's own business." One can have a genuine interest in the troubles of other men, just as a father is actively concerned about the interests of his child.

Observe Jesus' method of dealing with inter-group hatreds. Whereas most reformers attempt to win justice by force, Jesus tried to make men capable of rising above injustice without rebellion or strife. This does not mean that Jesus condoned social injustices, but that he used other methods of curing them.

Examples of the superiority of Jesus' method are not hard to find. Here is a young man who was being treated unjustly by an instructor. He was about to leave college because of it. It was pointed out to him that this quick resentment to injustice was a weakness in his personality, so he determined to use this instructor as a means of curing himself of this defect. He did this very successfully. It was a much better solution for him than trying to change the attitude of the instructor by engaging in some bitter quarrel with him. Curiously enough, within a short time the instructor not only ceased his unfair treatment of the boy, but apologized for his former behavior. This is the only good method of fighting injustice.

Rev. Leyton Richards has shown the power of the Christian method in his article on *A Christian Substitute for Armaments*. He tells of the following incident in India:

Another centre of trouble at the present time is the North-West Frontier of India, and we read of air raids and other military measures for holding turbulent tribes in check. Yet another and a better way of ensuring the peace of the Frontier was put into practice by an English Missionary Doctor named Theodore Pennell thirty years ago. With his medicine chest he travelled alone and unarmed among the warlike tribes, ministering to the enemies of his country often at the risk of his life, until he won their confidence and affection. Indeed, so successful was he in this that he was acclaimed by a high military authority as "worth a couple of British regiments" to the peace of North-West India. Again, therefore, it is obvious that the Christian way is more effective—even on the world's level—than the military way.[4]

Many men believe that conflict is inevitable in society, and feel that force is justifiable. No one, however, would deny that we can hardly describe our social order as the kingdom of heaven as long as such conflicts occur. Certainly, there would be unanimous agreement that men who are able to resolve these conflicts are worthy of Jesus' promise for them. "They shall be called the sons of God."

In their anxiety for the happiness of their child, parents often shield him so completely from the world that he fails to become adjusted to his society and suffers greater unhappiness in later life. They sometimes make him so incapable of adjusting to his fellows that he withdraws from society completely, thus gravely endangering his mental health. This is a long way from teaching a child to be a peacemaker.

Since peacemaking consists in dispelling fear, anger, and greed from the world, two factors are necessary in the development of this trait in a child: his own personality must be free from these elements, and he must be capable of influencing others to get rid of them.

In respect to ridding his own personality of them, the best plan is prevention rather than cure. Never permit the child to form them in the first place. A child can learn to be characteristically courageous, magnanimous, and unselfish as easily as to show fear, anger, and greed. The development of experimental faith, which is the foundation of healthy courage, has already been described. The attitudes

[4] Richards, Leyton, "A Christian Substitute for Armaments," *Carrs Lane Journal*, February, 1932.

of mourning and being merciful are wholesome forms of magnanimity and unselfishness.

The best sort of training for preventing the conflicts between a child and his social environment is the development of sportsmanship. To bring about true sportsmanship one must take advantage of all the innate tendencies in the child. Furthermore, the various aspects of sportsmanship can be taught the child only as the necessary inherited capacities for them mature. Team play and being a good loser are utterly impossible for children of seven or eight years of age to learn. It is difficult at that age even to teach them to take turns. It is when the child's affection for other children of his own sex matures that the larger factors in sportsmanship can be developed. This training, which ranges from learning to take turns and obey the rules of the game, to admiring excellence in an opponent and playing cleanly even against a less scrupulous opponent, produces a quality of sportsmanship, which commands admiration and inspires others to emulate it. These aspects of sportsmanship should be applied to all phases of his life as well as to sport.

As for conflicts in the larger social groups such as class, race, and nation, the important efforts are found in training children to hold attitudes of confidence, respect, and generosity toward other groups instead of conceit, fear, and suspicion. There is no reason why a child in studying the history of our country should learn to be suspicious of any other country. There is no inherited reason for the intolerance shown between races. The suspicion between Catholics and Protestants is the result of training and has no fundamental basis in human nature. The child can be as easily taught to hold friendly attitudes as unfriendly attitudes toward other nations, races, classes, and creeds. Furthermore, he can be taught to grasp every opportunity to further these friendly attitudes.

Having developed a personality from which fear, anger, and lust are excluded, the second factor in the development of the peacemaker is making him capable of influencing

THE DYNAMIC OF FATHERLY LOVE 83

others to get rid of them. As a matter of fact, having a personality free of these elements is in itself the strongest force in bringing about the same kind of personality in others. Emotions tend to beget themselves in others. One man who becomes terror-stricken is often enough to throw a whole crowd into a panic. On the other hand, one man who is calm in a time of crisis inspires confidence in those about him. The same thing is true of anger and greed, magnanimity and love. Nations made up of such personalities would never resort to war. The only other principle is to teach him love of peace, so that he actively throws all of his influence on the side of social understanding and sympathy, as opposed to that of suspicion and greed.

"For whosoever will save his life shall lose it: but whosoever will lose his life for my sake shall find it." When all of the tests of historical scholarship have been applied to the Gospels, this verse is the one most certain to have come from the lips of Jesus. There has been a strong tendency in recent years to neglect the cross in Christianity. It remains true, however, that sacrifice plays the central rôle in the teachings of Jesus. It is this phase of strong character which receives the emphasis in the last of these great Beatitudes.

Happy are they which are persecuted for righteousness' sake: for theirs is the kingdom of heaven. Happy are ye, when men shall revile you, and persecute you, and shall say all manner of evil against you falsely, for my sake. Rejoice, and be exceeding glad: for great is your reward in heaven: for so persecuted they the prophets which were before you.—Matthew 5:10-12.

It is significant that Jesus follows peace with persecution. After the Last Supper, where he had given his peace to his disciples, his persecution began and so did theirs. That they were persecuted, no one can deny. Not only the twelve disciples, but all those who have chosen to follow Jesus have suffered persecution. When an old man, we find Paul lying in a Roman prison awaiting execution, and deserted by his friends, but far from being unhappy. In a letter written to his youthful successor, who was becoming somewhat discouraged, Paul, who might have complained bitterly about his own lot, writes in a spirit of extreme joy, "For God hath not given us the spirit of fear; but of power, and of love, and of a sound mind." Centuries later, when two Englishmen were about to be burned at the stake for righteousness' sake, one of them, Latimer, spoke to the other in these words, "Be of good cheer, Master Ridley, we shall this day light such a candle, by God's grace, in England, as I trust never shall be put out." The prophets of the world, of whatever time or creed, have regularly met persecution and just as universally been happy in spite of it. We are no longer thrown to the lions or burned at the stake, but when any man defends an ideal higher than that of the people at large he meets persecution.

We may be sure that Jesus was not preaching asceticism. He does not say a man who is persecuted for righteousness will be happy, because by that token he will know that he is righteous. Jesus himself did many righteous things for which he was not persecuted.

It is obvious, that if this Beatitude is to be descriptive of wholesome personalities, we must find a natural basis for it in normal people. We do not have to look far to find numerous illustrations of those who rejoice even in suffering. The boy, who risks his life for his beloved, gets joy from that very risk. Indeed, every young man, wooing the heart of some young lady, longs for the opportunity to take such a risk and bemoans the disgustingly safe world in which such opportunities are rare. The football player, filled not only with a love of the game but with a loyalty for his college, rejoices in the injuries received while playing for the honor of his school. But highest of all, a mother, whose love for her child more closely approaches divinity than anything else on earth, will gladly sacrifice her life for that of her son. It is not that these people go out seeking injury for injury's sake, but they are happy to serve those whom they love, even if suffering is necessary. "Greater love hath no man than this, that a man lay down his life for his friends." Yet a father is quite willing to lay down his life for his son. It should be clear, then, that being happy even when persecuted has much basis in normal human behavior, especially in parental love.

It requires no great insight to realize why the prophets have been persecuted. Progressive achievement usually brings persecution. History offers abundant evidence that progress is rarely made except through the suffering of some individual or nation, usually of both. It is clear that real courage is always necessary if one is to espouse an unpopular but just cause. The crowd generally opposes progress. As Jesus stated it, "So persecuted they the prophets." This relationship between progress and persecution would probably be admitted by most thinking men. What is not so evident is that the persecuted are happy. It is commonly supposed that strong personalities have the courage to endure persecution for the progress of civilization because they are strong personalities. It has not been as clearly recognized that the persecution is an important factor in producing the strong personality.

Psychologically, why should happiness follow persecution? This Beatitude describes an emotional attitude. In terms of habitual behavior, it means that the individual responds with the emotion of joy to the situation: persecution for doing right. This can be learned, as will be shown a little later. The formation of such an attitude has two results. In the first place, when the individual responds to persecution with joy he obviously avoids responding to it with the unpleasant emotions of fear and anger. This in itself is a source of happiness, for, if by learning to respond to persecution with joy instead of with fear and anger, one rids himself of these disintegrating emotions, he saves himself the inevitable unhappiness which accompanies them. In the second place, one of the innate sources of pleasure, which has been mentioned repeatedly, is achievement. It is easy to teach the child that the greatest achievements cost sacrifice. It is quite normal to get more pleasure from an achievement which has been gained only through many hardships than one which is secured too easily. War seems glorious to some men, because they actually thrill at the idea of giving their lives to their country, a vicarious sacrifice.

Can this attitude of vicarious sacrifice be taught to our children? In all probability it is one of the easiest of all of the Beatitudes to teach them. It can be built on some of the strongest natural drives in human nature. The same natural impulses which have led to courage on the battlefield can be utilized in developing this attitude. Human nature responds to the challenge of courage. It is probable that one reason why so inane a social institution as war can continue, is because of its challenge to this innate love of bravery. Whatever facts research may discover in the future about the social nature of man, it is probable that the desire to appear to himself and to others as a man of courage will be found to be an important element in his natural endowment. Such common forms of expression as vanity, rivalry, self-assertion, fighting, and exhibitionism are learned reactions to this instinctive drive. No one of them is necessary. Other more admirable reactions can be learned just as easily in place of them. The joy which comes from persecution for righteousness' sake is one of these other possible reactions. It is a more adequate satisfaction for this urge than any of the others, and is much more conducive to an integrated personality and mental health.

There are many ways in which this trait can be instilled into the child. However, if this attitude toward vicarious sacrifice is to be learned, it must be done through love coupled with this innate sense of courage. The child's first love, as it has been pointed out, is for his parents, usually his mother. Many opportunities will arise and can be created in which he can sacrifice his own wishes to provide pleasure for his mother. Occasions should be provided in which he sacrifices for the pleasure given his mother, without praise

THE DYNAMIC OF FATHERLY LOVE

from her and often without her knowledge that the sacrifice is being made. As the circle of the child's affections grows, occasions for sacrifice will multiply and should be encouraged, for which his only reward is the joy of making the object of his affection happy. An example of similar unselfish acts on the part of his parents will go far toward instilling this principle in him. Much of his concept of what is manly and courageous will be determined by his estimation of the personality of his father and mother.

Courage, which has held so popular a place in the list of virtues, is not a trait in itself, but always the resultant behavior of some driving emotion. There are many kinds of courage. There is the courage of the gangster, driven by greed and lust for adventure. There is the courage of fear, shown by the animal fighting at bay. There is the courage of anger, demonstrated by one whose rage has so warped his judgment that he rushes into danger in blind fury. There is the courage of the man who is afraid to be afraid, which is a compensation for an inferiority complex. It is found in those individuals who have been trained to the social philosophy, "boys don't cry." Finally, there is the courage of love, exemplified by the parent trying to save a child. This is the highest type of courage, the one which is the surest and most dependable, the one which is mentally healthiest, and from which men derive the greatest satisfaction. One of the most common errors which parents make is the method by which they teach their children courage. They often develop one of these less healthy forms, especially the courage of fear or the courage of anger. Being anxious lest the child be imposed upon, they urge him to "stand up for his rights." The result is all too frequently one of those pitifully small individuals, who goes through life with a "chip on his shoulder," disliked and unhappy. This is a far worse fate than being imposed upon. Courage is highly desirable, but only when it is mentally wholesome.

Let the motivation for courage in the child be love, then, not fear or anger or selfishness. Here is a boy of ten who is afraid of water, and refuses to learn to swim. He is, however, very fond of his mother. When it was suggested to him that his ability to swim might some day save his mother's life, he gritted his teeth, overcame his fear of water, and soon learned to swim. This is courage stimulated by love.

As the child grows older, he may be taught the more difficult sorts of courage. He may learn to face the taunts of other children in serving someone he loves. Then he may learn to return some good service to someone who has mistreated him, if he can be given the same sort of unselfish interest in the other, that characterizes parental love. This is especially easy to teach, if the child is encouraged to take a parental interest in a younger brother or friend. It is quite probable that the object of this interest will very often fail to appreciate it.

When this stage has been reached, we have the groundwork for the personality which is dedicated to serving mankind, even when mankind responds with persecution. Let it be emphasized that such an individual is not unhappy. His persecution does not make him morbid. If he has learned this attitude, which Jesus taught, his personality will be a wholesome and a happy one.

This, then, is the type of love which Jesus taught. He believed that the fatherliness, characteristic of God, is a spiritual law of the whole universe. He believed that if men make this fatherly love the dynamic of their personalities, they will achieve happiness, and the world will consist of a society which will be a veritable heaven on earth. The nature of fatherliness is carefully defined in these last four Beatitudes as the traits which are characteristic of the best in parental love. These traits make one sensitive to the needs of those about him. They make him always anxious to give every man his highest chance for happiness and achievement, by overcoming the forces which would destroy it. They make him eager to solve the conflicts which arise

THE DYNAMIC OF FATHERLY LOVE

within men and between men. And they make him willing to suffer whatever is necessary to accomplish these purposes.

In this brief exposition of the Beatitudes we have listed eight traits which constitute the Christian personality. Four of them seem to be attributes of a type of faith, which has been described as an experimental faith. The other four are descriptive of the sort of love which Jesus urged his followers to have for one another. When the nature of its characteristics is examined, they seem typical of parental love.

The most significant mistake that men have made in interpreting these verses of Jesus is the failure to note the first word in each of them, *happy*. Many people think of these Beatitudes as ethical duties to be performed. In fact, very often they think of them as directly opposed to the more pleasant things of life. Actually, they are very far from being ethical codes of conduct.

Everyone recognizes that moral behavior is necessary. Even those who think of immorality as more attractive, despite that fact, favor a moral code of conduct for society. Such codes of conduct are usually legalistic statements of external behavior classified as right or wrong, and are not thought of as sources of happiness. Such codes are always fraught with difficulties. Codes which fit one group of people in one age are usually unfit for other groups and other times. Even within the group, different individuals fit only imperfectly into the code. All sorts of exceptions to the items of the code have to be made, and many elaborations designed to define it accurately. It is forced upon all members of the group even if it destroys some personalities. Such a code is constructed in view of a certain social theory, with little consideration of whether or not human nature can adjust to it.

Contrast these artificial legalistic codes with the attitudes which Jesus taught. He described traits of personality which can be developed in any normal human being. They utilize human nature instead of neglecting it. They are flexible enough for all individual differences. If men should be inculcated with them, social codes would be unnecessary. Men would behave in a much more normal fashion than under the unnatural artificial systems.

The whole problem of personality, then, is to discover some way by which integration can be secured. However, to discover some form of behavior which satisfies harmoniously all of the instinctive drives is not so simple. The most important contributions to this problem have come from the clinic. Here, psychologists and psychiatrists are constantly facing broken and deformed personalities. By a careful study of the histories of these cases they have gradually discovered the sources of both mental disease and mental health.

When the wrong methods of satisfaction are used, the result is disintegration. Clinical experience has shown that the most certain source of disintegration is the presence of fear and anger. It is possible to analyze each of the functional mental diseases into its characteristic emotional attitudes. (A functional mental disease is one which is not caused by some actual destruction of nervous tissue.) These can be traced back to their origin, which is almost always in early childhood. Mental disease may have its precipitating cause in adult life, but its essential causes have been developing since childhood. It is possible, therefore, to list all of the unhealthy attitudes. For example, the essential attitude of the most common functional mental disease is seclusive behavior, which involves either conscious or unconscious fear of society. The basic attitude of every one of these diseases is some variation of fear or anger.

It is also possible to name a group of attitudes which are the very opposite of these unhealthy ones. If these attitudes are formed it will be impossible for the child to develop a functional mental disease. Thus, if a child is taught to make social contacts, he will not develop this most common mental disease. However, there is the problem of finding healthy

THE DYNAMIC OF FATHERLY LOVE

attitudes which do not conflict with one another. This limits the range of possibilities. Only one such group seems possible. Its characteristics have already been named. It may now be reduced to a single general formula: Find a life purpose, which uses all of your capacities, in some form of social service, in the value of which you have an enthusiastic faith, for which you have faith in your ability to perform, and in the performance of which you get your greatest pleasure. These principles were not worked out by individuals who were anxious to satisfy the requirements of religion, but by scientists who would have described accurately the conditions of mental health even if they were directly contradictory to the teachings of religion. They were interested only in mental health and strong personality, not in religion. This description of the essential factors in mental health is an effort to summarize the results of their studies. Therefore, if one makes the Beatitudes his philosophy of life, he fulfills every requirement of this formula for mental health.

Chapter IV

THE SALT OF THE EARTH

VOCATIONAL guidance has always been a vitally important problem in the life of every individual. A large proportion of the students who enter college each fall do not know what their life tasks are to be. It is evident to every teacher that students who have picked their life work are better adjusted. Yet the task of choosing one is difficult and fraught with dangers which most people face with fear and trembling. The number of misfits in the world bears tragic testimony, in terms of unhappiness, to the great price paid for reaching the wrong decision.

The following passages from the Sermon on the Mount provide valuable criteria for the selection of one's life work. They constitute a standard by which one can estimate his usefulness to society.

> Ye are the salt of the earth!
> But if the salt hath lost its savour, wherewithal shall it be salted? It is thenceforth good for nothing, but to be cast out and trodden under foot of men.
> Ye are the light of the world!
> A city set on a hill cannot be hid. Neither do men light a candle, and put it under a bushel, but on a candlestick; and it giveth light unto all that are in the house. Let your light so shine before men, that they may see your good works and glorify your Father which is in heaven.—Matthew 5:13-16.

An examination of these two illustrations reveals much about the ideals of Jesus. The use of metaphorical comparisons is common to most public speakers. Usually they choose very loose and flattering analogies, which are not meant to be thoughtfully considered. Jesus, in these figures of his, was not casting about for some flattering way to compliment his disciples, and make them feel their own importance. His figures were very carefully chosen. No one else would have thought of calling men the salt of the earth.

The story of salt, in the history of mankind, is an interesting one. In the Orient, during Jesus' day, it was a scarce and valuable article. Sometimes soldiers were paid in salt instead of coins. The word salary had its origin in this fact. It was used in those days for many purposes. It was the only known antiseptic. Furthermore, it was about the only available preservative. We still use it some for this purpose. Finally, it was used then, as now, for flavoring. Jesus was paying a high tribute to his disciples when he called them, "the salt of the earth." They were expected to counteract the poisons which destroy society. They must preserve the good qualities in those with whom they came in contact. And they were to add flavor to the Christian life by their efforts.

Religious sects have often secluded themselves from the contamination of society. In his choice of salt as characteristic of the Christian personality, Jesus showed clearly that this is not the Christian method. Salt alone is not very much good. It may be pure and powerful, but it may as well have lost its savour, if it is not used. Salt is valuable only when it is in the midst of things, making them taste better, preventing them from spoiling, or freeing them from corruption. Here is one criterion for the selection of a vocation. Pick one which is in the midst of life, one in which the goal consists in making other lives better and happier. A life work is valuable when it adds flavor to people's lives. "I came that they might have life, and that they might have it more abundantly."

Let us note another thing about salt. It never gains its end by rejoicing in its own saltiness. It finds itself by losing itself. We speak of well-flavored food, not even mentioning the presence of salt. Indeed, if salt is present in such abundance as to call attention to itself, the food is not well-flavored. On the other hand, no one who has tried to eat unsalted potatoes can forget its value to a meal. Some Christians, who think of themselves more highly than they ought to think, might reflect profitably on the thought that a dish of salt alone would hardly be palatable. As a preservative its value lies in the preservation of other things, never of itself. Indeed, if it is pure salt it does not need preserving. Finally, as an antiseptic, its task is that of preventing the corruption of other things, never of itself, for it cannot be destroyed.

"Ye are the light of the world," was the second figure of speech which Jesus used. This sounds a little more promising to those who wish to shine brilliantly in the eyes of their fellow men. The use of light as a spiritual analogy is a very old one. It was used in every possible connotation in the Bible. It had been employed by other religious teachers. Zoroaster, the founder of the great Persian religion, thought so highly of light that he gave it divinity. The Persian god is named Mazda which means *light*.

If Christians do not attract attention by their spiritual comeliness, they will by their spiritual homeliness. There is evidence for the belief that everyone has some influence upon all those with whom he comes in contact. The question is not whether we have influence, but what sort of influence we have. In whatever vocation a man chooses, he will shed some kind of light. If his choice of a vocation is not motivated by the desire to shed a good light, he will shed a bad one.

As it was true of salt, so is it characteristic of light, that it rarely accomplishes its purpose by attracting attention to itself. The light which glares in one's eyes blinds him, and does not light the way before him. To realize this, one needs only to contrast the value to him of his own automobile lights, with those of a car coming toward him. His own lights usually point out the road in front of him clearly so that he may pursue his way in safety. The lights of an approaching car, however, not only do not help, but are so blinding that they counteract the value of his own lights. The more brilliant the other lights are, the more true this is. It is to be noticed, however, that the more they turn their attention to their job of lighting the road, and the less they waste themselves shining in your eyes, the more valuable they are. Many a Christian leader shines so brilliantly in the eyes of those whom he leads that they are blinded to the Christ whom they propose to follow. It is quite as unchristian to hide one's influence. As Jesus stated it: "Neither do men light a candle, and put it under a bushel, but on a candlestick; and it giveth light unto all that are in the house." The criterion by which one can measure the value of his influence is implied in Paul's assertion, "I live; yet not I, but Christ liveth in me." Not that one who becomes a Christian is to discard all his former personality and repress his natural instincts, but that his purpose shall be to show the light of Christ rather than his own light. That this is psychologically possible has been indicated in the discussion of the wholesome personality described in the Beatitudes. The Christian personality, which has been shown to be a perfectly integrated one, uses the same drives, impulses, and capacities as the sick personality. Changes in personality consist in a reorganization of these drives, not a replacement of them.

Lest his hearers should still imagine that he was preaching a self-centered life, Jesus emphasized the necessity of making one's light serviceable, not glaring. He says, "Let your light so shine before men, that they may see your good works and glorify your Father which is in heaven." Sometimes it is hard for us to keep ourselves out of the way so that men can see our good works. To be able to dazzle the eyes of others with our own brilliance seems a very satisfying thing to do. The star athlete is very frequently of more harm than good, because he cannot lose himself for the best interests of the team. With this brief exposition of these verses before us, let us examine their significance in the problem of choosing a life work.

Vocational adjustment is two-fold. In the first place, one needs to pick out the particular job which is ideal for him, if he can. There are many obstacles which may prevent this. There is the fact that our vocational tests are not yet sufficiently advanced to make it possible to determine exactly what a man is best fitted for. A man, who thinks that he has the only job for him, might have felt the same way about a number of different types of work. But to find just the right job is not so simple. Another factor, which often prevents a man from finding his ideal occupation, is his environment. He may never have the opportunity to get the necessary preparation. There may be no opening in that particular field for him; it may be already overcrowded. He may be thrown into some other work by the sheer force of circumstances. The fact remains that one should, if he can, pick out the life work for which he is best suited.

In the second place, vocational adjustment consists in adapting oneself to whatever life work he does undertake. It is not always possible to discover the ideal vocation. It is possible, however, to make any work a great one. Many a man spends his whole life going from one sort of work to another, always looking for a better one, never making a success of any of them. These men are all maladjusted.

It seems to be a common notion that the only reason a man works is to make a living. Consequently, the vocation is best, which makes the best living. It is this common attitude about work, that is at the root of most of our labor troubles. Employers, to whom business consists only in the greatest amount of profit possible, have no interest in labor, except to get the greatest amount of labor for the least cost. Laborers, whose interest in their work is all included in the pay envelope, will think only in terms of the highest possible wage for the shortest possible working hours. To secure harmony, when this condition prevails, is at best a very temporary and unsatisfactory arrangement. This is the "common sense" attitude toward business and industry. Many business men have said that Jesus' principles were hopelessly idealistic. What of this system? It certainly is not idealistic, but it is hopeless enough.

Other criteria usually listed for choosing a vocation are these: find a job for which you have the ability; find one in which there are opportunities for advancement; if possible, choose one which will lead to fame and honor and power, as well as fortune. Vocations which bring social position are coveted, and jobs which carry with them such responsibility as to enhance one's sense of importance are much sought after.

It is obvious, that if men seek the highest incomes, they must find an occupation for which they have some ability. This brings it about that they often do find a job which uses at least some of their capacities. This in turn brings a certain amount of achievement, which is a source of some measure of happiness. Finally, it provides a dominant purpose in life, and that is healthy. When this has been said, one has completed the list of the good qualities in this method of choosing a vocation.

What are the bad qualities of these criteria? They are much more numerous. In the first place, a comparatively small number of men achieve their purpose, when they use this method of choosing a vocation. A very small percentage of men are sufficiently successful financially to be satisfied with their income. Most of them are continually thinking of how happy they would be if they had just a little more. Or they are looking for get-rich-quick schemes by which they can be certain to acquire a fortune the next year. While the struggle for wealth gives man a purpose in life, it regularly makes him unhappy, usually because he does not attain that purpose. Also, observe the inevitable emotional tones of such a life purpose: suspicion, greed, selfishness, fear and uncertainty, anger and strife. Every one of these brings about unhappiness, both in oneself and in society.

The key to Jesus' method is found in a passage which occurs later in the Sermon on the Mount. "Lay not up for yourselves treasures upon earth: but lay up for yourselves treasures in heaven." Paraphrased, it might read, do not pick out a life work in terms of individual profit, but in terms of righteous achievement. One will, of course, pick out a vocation in terms of his capacities, and in view of the opportunities for such work. But all of the other factors, such as salary, advancement, fame, honor, power, social position, and prestige must be secondary. "Seek ye first the kingdom of God, and all these things shall be added"; or at least all that these things at their best are supposed to give: namely, happiness in life.

Very often such an individual goes into an unprofitable vocation, simply for the sheer delight of achieving things. He stands a better chance of being happy than the profit seeker. If, in addition to this, he strives to make that achievement contribute to social welfare, he will reach the best decision as to what to do with his life. The term *service* has been used so much that it has become hackneyed. It is, however, necessary to happiness.

Granted that a man must choose his life work for social interest, there is still the question of what constitutes serving mankind. Many men set out on life tasks with perfectly good intentions of serving their fellow men, only to discover that they have done them more harm than good. When Jesus gave these two metaphors of salt and light to describe the task of the disciples in the world, he showed what it means to serve men. According to them, there are at least four ways in which we may serve our fellow men. We may add flavor to men's lives. We may preserve men's lives and happiness. We may kill the poisons which corrupt men and society. And we may give men a vision of the divine. These are the tasks of being the salt of the earth and the light of the world. Any vocation can be turned into such channels. Thus, a man can transform the dullest of occupations into a source of genuine pleasure and satisfaction.

Let every young man, then, who is trying to decide what he will do with his life, ask himself these questions. In what field do I have the capacity to help alleviate the unhappiness in the world? Let him also ask himself what he can do to help conserve the best in the world. There are ideals which need to be preserved in human personality, as well as in the arts and social institutions. Men are needed in every phase of life who have not lost their own ideals, and who, through their outstanding moral integrity, are powerful in preserving these ideals in youth. When one sees how widespread the belief is that idealism is baseless, and cynicism the evidence of maturity, one sees how much men and women are needed whose aim in life is the preservation of life and all that matters in it. Furthermore, he should find out what the social poisons are which destroy the happiness of men, and ask himself how he can help to counteract them. Wherever fear, anger, hate, suspicion, greed, and the like are being eliminated from life, there, the poisons of society are being cured. Finally, where are there men who have no vision of high things, to whom he can give a picture of the divine? This is especially the task of the minister and educator. But anyone, who lets his own good works so shine before men that they glorify God, is quite as much at the same task.

Even those to whom life seems unkind, can make their lives a real contribution to the happiness of mankind. The invalid, who inspires men to renewed faith by his own transcending faith and cheerfulness, has a vocation which is of inestimable value. Elderly people, who so often think that they are worn out and useless, if they gain this vision of service may achieve their greatest work in their later years. Young people need courage and steadfastness. Who can give it to them so well as those who have grown old in the service of men, and still believe in them?

Let one choose what vocation he will, from the most responsible to the humblest, from the most adventurous to the most humdrum; in every one of them these tests can be applied. The humdrum, monotonous tasks, which so often make life a drudgery, can be transformed into thrilling achievements. In any walk of life, one will find challenges to his best abilities if he has this vision of becoming the salt of the earth and the light of the world.

Another important side of personality is implied in these two metaphors. It is quite probable that Jesus' hearers, especially the disciples, thought that he was simply paying a compliment to their leadership capacities. They may have squared their shoulders and felt a pride in the possession of such striking personalities that Jesus picked them out as leaders in his cause. However immodest this may seem, the fact remains that a pleasing, attractive personality is important to any sort of leadership and vital to human happiness.

There are two common errors which characterize the thinking of many people about attractiveness: one with respect to its importance, and the other concerning its sources. Some think that attractiveness is only a superficial feature of personality, unworthy of the thoughtful consideration of men and women facing the perplexing problems of life. This attitude, however, overlooks the fact that progress is made only through strong leadership, and that leadership implies an attractive personality. Furthermore, people who insist upon the superficial nature of attractiveness usually think that it consists entirely in outward appearance. An attractive personality, however, is one which possesses the qualities to which people respond positively. Thus, while physical attractiveness is not to be neglected, and has unquestioned value, it is far from being the whole story, or even the most important factor in the attractive personality.

What, then, are the factors of attractiveness as seen by the psychologist? It must be confessed that most of these factors are so complex that it is difficult to get an objective measure of them. By various methods, however, some insight into these characteristics has been gained, which is much more reliable than mere subjective opinion. Using large groups of college students as subjects, I have tried to discover what the significant factors of attractiveness really are, and the relative importance of each. Each student was asked to list his ten best friends, and then to state what characteristic he admired most in each of them. An analysis of these results indicates that four factors are the most important ones in attractiveness. They are: physical attractiveness, intelligence, temperament, and character. By counting the number of times each of these factors was mentioned by the students as the most admired characteristic in a friend's personality, a result was obtained which is some indication of their relative importance. You will notice, of course, that this experiment dealt with attractiveness as found, not in a casual acquaintance, but in a close friend, therefore of a more permanent quality. Almost anyone, on short acquaintance, can make an attractive first impression by the clever use of cosmetics and stylish clothes. It is a very different task to be attractive over a long period of intimate association. The results are quite interesting. Physical attractiveness was mentioned least frequently of all. For each mention of physical attractiveness, intelligence occurred twice, temperament five times, and character eight times. In most popular thinking the emphasis has been placed on physical attractiveness. Here, however, is evidence that it is relatively unimportant.

In view of the fact that many Christians have believed that it is almost unethical to look as attractive as possible, it is worthwhile to see whether a study of Jesus' teachings indicates his attitude toward the question of physical attractiveness. In one verse of the Sermon on the Mount, in which he demonstrated his keen sense of humor, he did offer some advice, which those who are careless about their outward appearance would do well to heed. A habit was prevalent in Judea on the part of ultra pious men, of making a show of their piety. For example, when they fasted, which they very regularly did, they took pains to call their piety to the attention of others. Christians who have tried to impress their self-sacrificing religiosity on others, by their long-faced attitudes and non-attractive appearance, should read Jesus' comment on these persons.

> Moreover when ye fast, be not, as the hypocrites, of a sad countenance: for they disfigure their faces, that they may appear unto men to fast. Verily I say unto you, they have their reward. But thou, when thou fastest, anoint thine head, and wash thy face; that thou appear not unto men to fast, but unto thy Father which is in secret: and thy Father which seeth in secret shall reward thee openly.—Matthew 6:16-18.

No one can read this verse without realizing that Jesus believed in an attractive personality.

What, then, shall we say of physical attractiveness? In a society as cruel as ours, probably no more unhappy person exists than the unattractive girl. No one else can know the bitter heartache which she experiences. If she finally rationalizes herself into the conviction that she does not care about popularity or having men associates, she is only repressing her natural drives and is more maladjusted than ever. She becomes the object of much cruel ridicule on the part of self-styled humorists both on and off the stage. The so-called "old-maid" adjustment is one of the most difficult to make satisfactorily. No religion can meet her needs adequately which does not face it. Fortunately, the important factors of attractiveness are not inherited, and anyone, with however meager a native endowment, can be attractive. It should be noted that the attractiveness of physical beauty is by no means always lasting. It is not at all uncommon to find a remarkably handsome individual who seems downright unattractive, if the handsomeness is not backed up by a deeper form of attractiveness. On the other hand, all of us have known individuals who, by the objective measures of esthetics, were decidedly unattractive. Yet, by the beauty of their personality, they literally change in our eyes, until they seem the very essence of attractiveness. Not every person can be physically beautiful, but everyone can be so attractive that the lack of physical beauty is no great handicap.

The second factor in attractiveness is intelligence. Our

experiment indicates that it is twice as important as physical attractiveness. However, when we examine the objective fact of intelligence as the psychologist views it, which like physical beauty is largely inherited, we find that it has little value for attractiveness. Sometimes intelligence is actually unattractive. Especially when an individual is highly endowed with brains, and seems quite willing to admit that he is "the light of the world," we find him anything but attractive.

Some of the most attractive personalities in history have not been conspicuously intelligent. Jeremiah quite openly admitted his slowness of mind. It seems probable that most of the disciples were of only average intelligence. This may have been an actual advantage for Christianity. If they had all been as brilliant as Paul, we might never have known Jesus directly. Reading Paul, we are forced to see Christ through a Pauline lens.

Jesus certainly did not underrate intelligence. On the contrary, in his figure of "the light of the world," he recognized its desirability. It would be foolish to deny the value of a high intelligence. However, far too much importance has been attached to it. Some psychologists have made almost a religion out of the I. Q. (Intelligence Quotient). Intelligence is not a necessary accompaniment of fine character and strong personality. Both geniuses and morons have done much to make this world liveable.

We have now dealt with the two factors of attractiveness most dependent upon heredity. Unfortunately, we have little control over our hereditary characteristics. But fortunately, they are not the most important factors in the attractive personality.

The third factor in attractiveness is temperament. Temperament is the characteristic emotional tone of an individual's personality. That is, he forms emotional attitudes about most of the phases of his physical and social environment. If most of his attitudes are fear attitudes, he has a timid temperament. If he attaches affection to most of his environment, he has an affectionate temperament. If a large number of anger habits are formed, we describe him as having a bad temper.

It is a very common belief that temperament is inherited. This belief has grown out of the fact that a child's characteristic temperament appears very early in his life, and is often much like that of one or both of his parents. It seems probable, however, that this assumption is incorrect. Temperamental habits are learned reactions formed in the early years. The remarkable temperamental similarities between children and their parents occur, not because of inheritance, but because during these early years, the parents are their only teachers. Much of the fundamental nature of temperament has been determined by the end of the first three years. For example, it seems true that every normal child has a natural tendency to explore strange objects. There is little evidence to show that fear is a natural reaction to any of them. However, if his exploration brings him pain, he may learn to respond to strange objects with fear. If, however, the parents see to it that his early exploratory adventures are happy ones, he may develop the temperament which reacts to new objects with confidence and curiosity. This important distinction may be learned as early as the end of the first year. Other temperamental traits may be formed likewise.

Temperamental types have been described for many centuries. Greek philosophy recognized four such types, which may serve as practical classifications. The sanguine, or happy disposition, is conceded to be the most attractive. The phlegmatic, or apathetic temperament, which appears to be indifferent to emotional stimuli, is often admired but hardly to be described as attractive. The choleric, or anger-dominated personality, while often encouraged by the "he-man" philosophy, nevertheless is not very attractive. Finally, the melancholic, or depressed temperament, is least attractive of all. It is impossible to classify people accurately according to any group of temperamental types. There are so many border-line cases that the number of types may be increased

THE SALT OF THE EARTH

indefinitely. Furthermore, we find that any one individual may have some sanguine habits, some choleric habits, some melancholic habits, and some phlegmatic habits. The pure type is extremely rare.

In the preceding chapter, happiness was shown to be the reward of those who achieve the outlook on life described in the Beatitudes. Now we find the happy disposition to be the most attractive type. It is not by accident that men have universally desired happiness. Nor is it strange that happiness should be a necessary attribute of him who would be attractive. Each of these, in turn, is part of the wholesome, healthy personality. That these principles are mutually helpful is a further indication that Jesus used the spiritual laws of the universe in his philosophy of living. This point will be further illustrated as we continue the study of Jesus' teachings about personality.

We have yet to discuss that factor in attractiveness which was judged by our investigation to be the most important; namely, character. It is, however, so important that the next chapter will be devoted to it.

"Ye are the salt of the earth and the light of the world." What powerful figures these are! In them, Jesus described the effectiveness of the Christian personaity. One choosing a vocation or searching for ways to make his life more useful finds in them the purposes in life which are really worth pursuing. One whose personality is accurately described by them has that quality of attractiveness, which makes his influence among men stronger and his achievements correspondingly greater. Certainly in this day of social and moral chaos, men and women are badly needed whose vital and attractive personalities qualify them to assume that spiritual leadership of which the world is so much in need.

Chapter V

THE INTEGRATION OF CHARACTER

The test of a man's personality is his character. It is well enough to describe methods of developing strong personality. It is quite another thing to face the trying problems of life with courage and nobility. While we are talking of fatherly love and the sources of happiness, there is on every hand murder, adultery, divorce, class and race hatreds, injustice, and dishonesty. It may have seemed to some of Jesus' hearers as they listened to the first part of the Sermon, that he was blissfully unaware of these grim facts of life. If so, Jesus immediately dispelled this delusion by facing each of these very problems squarely with a remarkable description of the only thing that ever has contributed substantially to their solution, character.

"Train up a child in the way he should go, and even when he is old he will not depart from it." There are hundreds of parents who are in grave doubt about the complete truthfulness of this assertion. At least, as they look at the finished product, they often have difficulty recognizing any relationship between it and what they thought they were "training up." Most parents would like their children to become men and women of noble character. Even those parents whose own characters are far from exemplary, wish for their children more admirable ones.

As soon as we face the problem of character, we are confronted with the apparent paradox that some men of most unethical character often appear more attractive than others who are ethically flawless. It is quite common for men of energy and strong native endowment to commit many transgressions against the ten commandments, and despite that fact have much more attractive and admirable personalities than others who obey all the commandments. This has given rise to the popular belief that one must take a fling at some of the immoralities if he is to be a real man, and not a "sissy."

Why this attitude toward morality? Is it necessary to be immoral to be virile? Must one choose between being unattractive and being indecent? This is the honest conviction of hundreds of young men and women entering our colleges and even our high schools every year. Recently a young man commented thus: "I never drank before I came to college. I was quite a boy scout then." He said this in derision of his previous "innocence." The movies have consistently pictured this philosophy of life. For a considerable period the gangster was actually made the hero. Regularly the man of complete moral integrity is made to look foolish and weak, one at whom the real "he-man" sneers with disdain.

Yet, in spite of this widespread philosophy, morality still persists. Laws still frown upon immorality. Society in general recognizes that its very existence depends upon the moral stamina of its constituents. It is obvious, then, that despite this attitude toward ethical morality, we intuitively feel that the stability of our social institutions depends upon moral integrity.

Here, then, is the dilemma: we want our children to be men and women of moral integrity, but we do not want them to be prudish. How shall we solve it? A very common method is the ludicrous one of trying to make them just a little bit bad, just enough so that they will be "human." Is there not some method of securing this double end without resorting to the absurd? Jesus' picture of character offers such a solution.

There are two important reasons why the notion has arisen that the man of strictly moral character is lacking in vitality. The first one involves a confusion between the terms *weakness* and *effeminacy*. This is because there is a prevailing ignorance of the true nature of effeminacy. Effeminacy is an inherited characteristic, and is not influenced much by either environment or behavior. The man who inherits effeminate characteristics may try to compensate for them by endeavoring to be rough and vulgar, but his behavior will fall far short of convincing others of his "cure" from effeminacy. Due to the unfortunate philosophy of life prevalent in our western civilization, which has been mentioned under the name of the "he-man" philosophy, the effeminate man is often ashamed of his nature. As a result he may try to seem masculine. He may enter athletics, use excessive profanity, drink, or live immorally. Or he may resort to religion as an excuse for his behavior, thus assuring the world that he would be quite masculine if it were not for his moral scruples. Neither of these adjustments is a healthy or successful one. As a matter of fact, effeminacy is by no means an undesirable trait. Much of the advancement of civilization has been made by effeminate individuals. In America we make them ashamed of themselves, abnormal, and often perverted. It is probable that we are destroying a great deal of potential achievement by our cruel and ignorant treatment of effeminacy. We must distinguish, then, between the namby-pamby weakling and the so-called effeminate man whose native endowments often combine in him the fine sensitiveness of the woman with the aggressiveness of the man. Such individuals have in themselves resources of strength. No amount of immoral behavior will serve to increase their masculinity. On the other hand, it is also true that rigid adherence to ethical standards will in no way make effeminate the man who inherits a more masculine nature.

There is another reason for the common notion that men who are immoral are for that reason strong. This is the fact that people notice the exceptions to the rule rather than the rank and file of cases. It requires no proving that a majority of the immoral are far from being admirable. Yet there are hundreds who imagine that immorality will make them manly, because of a few such men who have been so highly endowed that they appear strong, despite their immorality.

On the other hand, there are hundreds of splendid, strong personalities who are strictly moral. Yet it is a common conviction that if one is strictly moral he is therefore effeminate, simply because a few men are moral because they are afraid to be anything else, or because they inherit no strong characteristics. Actually it is true that a majority of strong characters are moral, and a majority of immoral characters are weak. Nor can anyone doubt that the dynamic force of a strong character, who has complete moral integrity, is much more admirable than the man who runs roughshod over the customs which generations of men have found necessary to a stable society, simply because he is richly endowed with strong capacities and can "get away with it."

Probably, a majority of people faced with that question would describe a man of good character as one who commits none of the common sins. Such individuals, whose only claim to character is that they see no evil, hear no evil, and speak no evil, hardly typify what the psychologist understands by the term *character*.

If we search for the motivation underlying the fear of being too good, which we have described, we find that it is a desire to be strong. The fear of being weak, especially weak willed, seems to be almost instinctive. At least, it is very close to the inherited drives. If, then, we are to discuss a type of character which men and women covet, it will be strong character rather than merely good character in the ethical sense.

Strong character is not necessarily the function of any type of external behavior, good or bad. Rather it consists of the power with which one behaves. If he can bring to bear upon his purpose all of the strength of which his personality is capable, he has strong character. To whatever extent he loses the power of any of his natural drives, or is so constituted that conflict between them make him less aggressive, to that extent he is a man of weaker character, whether his conduct be good or bad. It is the force of his conduct, then, and not the external nature of it which measures the strength of his character.

There is a second feature of the highest type of character. No one thinks of a completely self-centered man as having character, however dynamic his behavior may be. But the man who can sacrifice his own interests for those of his friends, and do it gladly, has character. It is clear, then, that there is no character apart from love.

It should be obvious that character is not inherited. It must be achieved. If we look for the instinctive basis upon which strength of character can be built, we find it in the tendency to self-realization. This is the same instinctive tendency which is expressed in the commonly less desirable motivations of competition, self-assertion, and aggressiveness. This tendency seems to be an inborn part of all animal nature. Any explanation of animal behavior which assumes that an animal seeks only such things as it needs for its own comforts, is not in accordance with the facts, even among the lower animals. The bee, for example, lays up far more honey than is necessary for its own existence. If this were not true our honey industry would never have thrived. It is improbable that the bee gathers honey with any conscious purpose of laying up food. In all probability it gathers all the honey it is capable of gathering simply because it inherits that capacity and tends to use it. In human life numerous examples of this motivation are easily found. For instance, the man with business ability usually does not cease his business activities as soon as he has saved enough money to satisfy all his wants. His zest for money making is just as keen even after his income is already so great that he cannot spend it. It is probable that to most people in the full vigor of life, the worst possible punishment would be a world in which there was nothing to accomplish. This principle of self-realization, then, is a fundamental one among our inborn characteristics and can obviously be used as the basis for strong character.

THE INTEGRATION OF CHARACTER

Now let us turn to the second feature of character development, unselfishness. To begin with, the child lives only by instinctual impulses. They are unmoral and totally self-centered. The child is motivated by what Freud has termed the pleasure principle. He seeks pleasure and avoids pain. As he grows older, however, and becomes aware of the individuals about him, especially when he begins to love them, he finds that these instinctual impulses not only run into various forms of social taboo, but frequently involve pain for those whom he loves. It is at this point that character begins.

Let us emphasize the significance of this point. It is obvious that a person will receive social punishments if he gives unbridled expression to all of his natural impulses. These punishments are frequently more painful than the pleasure is worth. If he has any intelligence, he quickly learns to inhibit at least those of his instinctive urges which result in more pain than pleasure. This is not character, but caution. There is a philosophy of child training which holds that character is built upon this sort of inhibition. This is the so-called behavioristic approach. It consists in attaching pain or fear to undesirable behavior, and pleasure to desirable behavior. Such training would be excellent to teach children to respond with ethical behavior, but is totally insufficient in developing character. Many parents imagine that they have produced fine characters in their children by some such philosophy as "spare the rod and spoil the child." They would be surprised if they knew how little the rod had to do with the resultant character.

What is the difference between this good behavior motivated by fear of the consequences, and strong character? The difference is found in the word *love*. When we trace the history of psychopathic personalities we find that very often they heartily dislike their parents. Quite commonly the parents have either badly mistreated them or have shown undue favoritism for the other children. (And it should be emphasized that it matters little whether parents actually do show favoritism, as measured by some objective standard. If the child believes that they are discriminating against him, as far as its effect on his personality is concerned, they are.) It should be obvious, then, that strong character can be built only on the fundamental drive of love. Unless parents can inspire such a genuine affection for themselves in a child that he gets pain from hurting them, they cannot develop character in that child. Even the physical punishment which parents give their children finds its greatest effectiveness in this motive. When a boy's mother is whipping him, he is faced with the fact that, for the time being at least, she does not love him. This is the worst part of the punishment. If a boy hates his parents, he will not develop character from any amount of punishment by them. It follows that physical punishment should never be inflicted upon a child except by someone he loves. Punishment from someone whom the child dislikes or even hates will only make him sullen and obstinate. In this modern day, physical punishment is in disrepute. Parents are being urged to accomplish "with love" what formerly they tried to accomplish "with anger." It is well to observe, however, that in physical punishment they were often stimulating more consciousness of love in their children than can be done by most of our modern methods.

Here, then, is the nature of character. It consists, not in forms of external behavior or negative ethics, but in strength and unselfishness of action. It is not inherited, but must be developed. Its motivation is not fear of punishment, but the desire for self-realization and love.

In this section of the Sermon on the Mount, Jesus points out the elements of character. It is interesting to observe that, of the six illustrations by which he describes the Christian character, three have to do with the control of one's anger life. Inasmuch as a later chapter will be devoted entirely to the discussion of anger in personality, these three illustrations from Jesus' discussion will be omitted for the present. The other three will indicate clearly Jesus' methods of character formation.

THE INTEGRATION OF CHARACTER 113

Think not that I am come to destroy the law, or the prophets: I am not come to destroy, but to fulfill.—Matthew 5:17.

It is characteristic of the founders of religious movements to throw over all that has gone before them. Jesus founded his religion in just the opposite way. He did not throw over all the past. Jesus, of course, presented new ideas. This can be done, however, in different ways. One leader may be dominated by the revolutionary spirit, and try to relegate the old order into oblivion. Another may go about changing things by evolution rather than revolution. Jesus was of the latter type. As he expressed it, "I came not to destroy, but to fulfill."

A new concept has come into psychology within recent years which is called the psychogenic principle. It holds that all of our adult behavior patterns represent developments from seeds planted in early childhood. It furthermore teaches that these adult behavior patterns can be changed only when their psychogenic history is taken into consideration. Pseudo-psychologists promise us quick character transformations. It is equally characteristic of evangelists, parents, educators, and even the individuals themselves, to expect revolutionary changes in personalities, regardless of their previous history. Evangelists assure us that our past can be blotted out, and that we can start over as if it had never happened. Every sincere student of psychology knows that such a thing is impossible. It is inevitable that seeds planted in childhood will bear their fruit in adult life. "For whatsoever a man soweth, that shall he also reap." Careful studies of the phenomena of conversion show clearly that there is always a psychogenic basis upon which the experience of conversion is built. In the typical testimony of the converted drunkard, for example, is found some such statement as this: "As I passed by the mission, I heard them singing the song my mother used to sing." Unless some such past experience has developed psychogenic attitudes in the individual, the apparently instantaneous conversion does not occur; or if it does occur it is not lasting. Jesus embraces this genetic principle in his statement, "I am not come to destroy, but to fulfill."

It may be urged by some that Jesus was not thinking of the development of the human personality when he made these statements about the law, but of the development of social laws over many generations. This is probably true. But it should be observed that the same principles which govern social development are applicable to personality development. Furthermore, if we may judge by the principles he set forth, they are all concerned with the individual, not with social institutions as such.

Of course, rules of conduct and etiquette can be learned by adults and put into practice superficially. When a crisis arises, however, the emotional attitudes begun in early childhood are the ones which dominate the behavior of the individual. This is the reason why our various efforts at peace propaganda fail under stress of war. We have been trained from early childhood to respond "patriotically" to warlike stimuli. This is not a rational process. We forget all our peace notions as these warlike stimuli appear. Only when our psychogenic attitudes are of a peace-producing sort can we hope to gain lasting peace. Thus, even apart from the value to personalities, the value to society of this type of emotional education is large. In using the method of fulfillment instead of the method of destruction, Jesus was adopting the only possible plan for permanent change or progress.

In personality the psychogenic principle has three practical implications. In the first place, we must not judge external behavior on the basis of immediate causes, but search the personality of the individual for the more significant ones, which probably date far back into his childhood. In the second place, we cannot hope to influence adult behavior by the use of external motivations only. We must know the psychogenic history of the individual, and deal with him in terms of and through his psychogenic attitudes. Finally, in the education of children, we should not be concerned with the immediate behavior of the child, but with the type of adult personality which it is likely to produce.

THE INTEGRATION OF CHARACTER

The following case history will demonstrate the large number of such psychogenic factors which can enter into what seems to be a simple case of stealing.

Here is a boy of ten, referred for stealing. He was of the hypopituitary type of obesity, which not only made him fat and conspicuous, but also gave him an exaggerated craving for sweets. His particular physiology demanded that the sugar and starches of his food be largely stored as fat in his tissues instead of being burned up to produce the energy required in muscular activity. Because of his weight and awkwardness, and because of fatigue produced by inadequate sugar mobilization and oxidation, when he tried to keep up with the other kids' games, he soon became the butt of their ridicule. Absorption of poison from a pair of chronically infected tonsils further added to his fatigability. So here there were two physical conditions which indirectly produced an intolerable social situation and violated his fundamental wishes for approval and recognition. But, further, he came from a squalid and poverty-stricken home where food was not always sufficient and where the sweets he craved were not to be had. His home offered absolutely no satisfactions to offset the defeats encountered in his contacts with his peers. He was one of five children, two of whom, he felt, had ingratiated themselves into the parents' affections; thus were his fundamental wishes for security and intimate response violated. In this crowded, squalid home he had had no chance to develop a strong sense of property. He had no place to keep inviolate the few possessions he had and they were bestowed upon and used indiscriminately by others. An allowance, which he could budget and use as he liked, was unheard of. In his classroom, when the list of school-savings depositors was posted, his name was conspicuous by its absence; in fact, he was the only one who had no deposits to make. Small wonder, then, that this boy would appropriate whatever nickels, dimes, and quarters he could occasionally find in his mother's purse. With this ill-gotten gain he would (1) buy candy to satisfy his own physically induced craving, (2) buy candy to bestow upon others in exchange for their approval, and (3) retain his self-respect by becoming a school-bank depositor.[1]

If so many factors can enter into the behavior of a ten-year-old child, it is easy to imagine how many factors will be influencing the behavior of an adult. It is obvious, then, that

[1] Timme, A. R., "The Rôle of Physical Conditions in Behavior Problems"; *Mental Hygiene*, XV, 1931, 471.

we must not judge behavior on the basis of its objective appearance. Two men may perform the same act. It may mean entirely different things in the two cases. Only when we have studied the case psychogenically can we hope to diagnose it correctly.

The attempt at influencing adult behavior without taking into consideration its psychogenic factors is very common. Almost every individual has some undesirable habits. The most common methods, employed for trying to break them, are: appeal to reason, physical punishment, social ridicule, and shame. None of these is regularly effective, and some of them are actually harmful. The best methods are reconditioning and reëducation, both of which trace the behavior to its true cause and try to get rid of that cause.

The theory of child training which concerns itself with the future development of the child rather than the immediate behavior is most important. An interesting investigation has been made recently, which points out the difference between the two methods.[2] Two large groups were selected, and given a questionnaire. One group consisted of parents, the other of mental hygienists. They were asked to rate the seriousness of a large number of behavior items which appear in young children. The differences between the groups bring out this principle clearly. Items which seemed serious to the parents, but not to the mental hygienists, included swearing, disrespect for elders, smoking, masturbation, playing with fire, impertinence, contradicting elders, criticizing parents, disobedience, interrupting adult conversation, arguing when corrected, obscene talk, ungratefulness, rudeness, and unresponsiveness to parental love. It is interesting to observe how large a percentage of these consist in recognition of the superiority of the parents. One might almost suppose that a modest, well-behaved child is one who stands in awe of the greatness of his parents. The items mentioned as serious by the mental hygienists, but not emphasized by

[2] Stogdill, Ralph M., "Parental Attitudes and Mental Hygiene Standards"; *Mental Hygiene*, XV, 1931, 813-828.

THE INTEGRATION OF CHARACTER

the parents were: excessive modesty, suspiciousness, bashfulness, withdrawing, desire to play alone, constant whining, fears, depression, daydreaming, shyness, uninterestedness, over-activity, demands for attention, sensitiveness, and sulkiness.

The child is constantly forming emotional attitudes which will determine his future happiness. The most important thing in the early years of his life is not his external behavior, but which emotions are developed. He is incapable of learning abstract ethical principles, and therefore they are of no significance in his early training. Temperament, however, is largely formed during these early years. Thus, if a child is severely punished for stealing, he will not learn that it is wrong to steal. He is too young to learn such an abstract principle. But he may be instilled with a fear which will contribute considerably toward his becoming a timid weakling as an adult. If he is forced to share his possessions with someone he does not like, he will not learn generosity, but he may learn to resent discipline. If he is told that "the policeman will get him" if he does not behave, he may learn little about how to behave, but acquire a deep-set fear of policemen. If he is protected from all of the knocks which he normally gets from his social contacts, he may be in danger of developing the shut-in, unhealthy personality. If parents regularly take the part of their own child in every argument he has with other children, they are taking one of the surest means of causing him heartache and unpopularity when he is grown. If he is taught always to "stand up for his own rights," he is likely to grow up into one of those small, bitter, narrow personalities, so much despised by his associates. If his parents give in to him every time he has a temper tantrum, he may quiet down for the time being, but may thereby be doomed always to react on this infantile level.

From what has already been said, it should be clear that even if one tries to overthrow the past, he will not succeed.

One cannot bring about progress except when he starts with the past and builds on it as a foundation. This is certainly the method employed by Jesus as is further shown in the next verse.

> For verily I say unto you, Till heaven and earth pass, one jot or one tittle shall in no wise pass from the law, till all be fulfilled.—Matthew 5:18.

It is probable that when Jesus spoke of law, he used the term in somewhat the same way as the scientist does. He thought of moral laws as being in the very nature of things, just as the scientist thinks of natural laws. The scientist does not believe that one can break natural laws, or that one jot or tittle shall in any wise pass from them. He does realize, however, that our formulations of the natural laws may be very much in error, and so he is constantly restating them. Likewise, Jesus did not obey all of the Jewish laws. He broke some of them quite openly. This verse would have little meaning unless he believed that, while Moses and the prophets, and for that matter the whole gamut of religious thinkers, had learned much of the will of Jehovah, they had also made many errors.

In an effort to understand the will of God, with respect to both the natural law and the spiritual law, of course many errors have been made. Wrong hypotheses and mistakes in calculation have caused untold tragedy. We have not advanced in science, however, by simply throwing over the past hypotheses because they were not perfect. Progress has been made only when we have improved upon them, not by disregarding them. The same thing holds true for the spiritual law. Spiritual errors cost dearly in broken and unhappy personalities. Sincere and earnest parents totally destroy the happiness of their children through ignorance. Thus, if we may interpret this verse in view of Jesus' general attitude toward the law, he is pointing out both the good and bad in the past, and showing how the old order can be developed to greater perfection.

THE INTEGRATION OF CHARACTER 119

This principle also holds true in personality development. It is a common belief that a youth can do about as he pleases and when he is a man "put away childish things." Actually, as has been shown already, every "jot and tittle" of his infancy, childhood, and youth is forming more and more firmly the nature of his character and personality. And they certainly will not pass away until they have been fulfilled and borne their fruit in adult personality.

Christian leaders have been justly proud of the fact that Jesus taught inner principles rather than outer habits of conduct. They have pointed out that this makes his teachings equally applicable to every time and people, or stating it psychologically, applicable to individual differences. All this is true, but it has its dangers if left at that point. Children do not learn great inner principles. They learn single habits. For example, if one wishes to teach a child to be honest, he will not accomplish this purpose by lecturing to him on the subject. He will bring about this personality trait only by teaching him, one at a time, a great many honest habits. Hartshorne and May [3] found that there was a strong tendency for a child, honest in one situation, always to be honest in that situation. This tendency did not always hold, however, for other parts of his activity. He might be honest in the classroom and not on the playground. Another child might do just the opposite. This makes it possible for us to see the full significance and value of the next verse in Jesus' teaching on character.

Whosoever therefore shall break one of these least commandments, and shall teach men so, he shall be called the least in the kingdom of heaven: but whosoever shall do and teach them, the same shall be called great in the kingdom of heaven.—Matthew 5:19.

The tendency to overlook little things, as of no significance, finds many expressions in human life. In the history

[3] Hartshorne, H. and May, M. A., *Studies in Deceit*, The Macmillan Company, 1928.

of the sciences the first hypotheses were based upon the observation of large natural phenomena. It inevitably happens, however, that as the sciences grow in accuracy, they do so by the study of the smallest particles rather than large wholes. This can be illustrated by popular conceptions in the field of the psychology of personality. Every psychologist is being constantly approached with such statements as this: "I have a bad temper. How can I get rid of it?" There is no such entity as a bad temper. The term simply signifies that the individual has a large number of anger habits. If temper is to be controlled, the method of control has to be applied to each of these individual habits, not to a general trait. The man who resolves to control his temper by thrusting his hands in his pockets, gritting his teeth, and just refusing to loose his temper, is doomed to failure. It is only when he takes each situation which makes him angry, and attaches some other emotion to it, that he makes a real advance with his problem.

Here is a very typical case history. A mother asked a psychologist how to deal with her son who was subject to temper tantrums. When asked what situations brought out anger, she did not know. When she had observed each instance of temper for a short while, she discovered one or two irritating conditions which accounted for most of the difficulty. Remedying these conditions solved the problem. Preaching to him about or punishing him for a bad temper would never have succeeded, and might have done a great deal of harm.

The practical value of this principle lies in the fact that human nature is not changed by dealing with its general features, but in veritable jots and tittles. The more abstract general commandments are only the results of having mastered many specific ones. One cannot teach honesty. He can only teach many honest habits. How many of them will have to be taught before the child is honest depends upon the intelligence of the child. For example, here is a girl in a school for the feeble-minded who has grown to love her

THE INTEGRATION OF CHARACTER   121

matron. She stole a pair of stockings from a girl in her ward to give to the matron. On being reprimanded for this, she took a pair from another girl. After many such experiences, she finally learned that it was wrong to steal stockings. Then she started on handkerchiefs. She did not learn, "Thou shalt not steal," until almost the whole gamut of possibilities had been exhausted. Of course, a very intelligent child would grasp the abstract principle much more quickly, but by exactly the same process. Permitting any exceptions to occur is fatal. One can imagine how difficult it would be to teach the feeble-minded girl honesty, without being strictly consistent.

One of the old-time theological disputes centered around a misunderstanding of this verse. Some believed Jesus meant that it is just as sinful to break a minor moral law as a major one. In a sense, the small sin is worse than a major one. It is a more accurate indicator of personality, and builder of character. The parents, who smile upon the minor but undesirable behavior patterns of the child as being of no consequence, are committing unpardonable sins. A shy child who hides her face in her father's coat may seem cute, but excessive shyness is an enemy to strong personality. It is more malignant than profanity. The child who does not enter into games with other children may be quiet and demure, but this is a serious symptom for the child's future happiness. We cannot deal with such entities as honesty, courage, and philanthropy. They may be very different things in different individuals. We must know the smaller and more fundamental motives from which they come as natural expressions. This distinction becomes clearer when we read the next verse.

For I say unto you, That except your righteousness shall exceed the righteousness of the scribes and Pharisees, ye shall in no case enter into the kingdom of heaven.—Matthew 5:20.

To one not acquainted with the other teachings of Jesus, this sentence might seem to indicate that Jesus was accusing the scribes and Pharisees of leaving some of the least commandments undone, and urging his followers to exceed Pharisaical righteousness by obeying every jot and tittle of the law. Nothing could be further from the facts in the case. If righteousness had consisted in minute legal details, the Pharisees would have been even higher than the angels. They not only obeyed the law, but they kept increasing the "jots and tittles" of the law to absurd lengths. They had made it almost impossible for anyone except a lawyer to understand, much less to obey it.

In order to see what Jesus did mean, we need only to turn to another passage in which he described his attitude toward the righteousness which characterized the religion of the Pharisees.

> Ye tithe mint and anise and cummin, and have left undone the weightier matters of the law, justice, and mercy, and faith: but these ye ought to have done, and not to have left the other undone.—Matthew 23:23.

The practice of tithing was a very old and traditional custom for the Jews. Through the centuries, the law of tithing had been more and more elaborated, until it included such small and unimportant herbs as mint and anise and cummin, as well as corn, wine, and oil.

Jesus certainly did not mean by this verse that his disciples should go further in this regard than the Pharisees. That would have been almost impossible. His whole teaching on the subject shows that he recognized the impossibility of legislating people into having strong character.

Jesus' real meaning is found in the latter part of this last quotation. He accuses the Pharisees of leaving undone the weightier matters of the law, justice and mercy and faith. It is to be noted that these are all emotional attitudes. Jesus is assuming that if these important emotional attitudes are present, ethical outward behavior will come as a matter of course. The Pharisees made the opposite assumption. They contended that if all of the details of moral behavior could be listed, one would become good by performing them. Thus, while Jesus emphasized the least commandments, he did not confine himself to outward behavior, but to the emotional tone underneath the behavior.

The method of the Pharisees has been frequently used in our educational programs. The legalistic teachings of the Christian church are numerous. How many times has the question been asked whether or not it is right to play cards, or dance, or play Sunday baseball? Whence all our blue laws and negative ethics? One will seek in vain in the teachings of Jesus for answers to any such questions. Various parts of the Christian world have disagreed on the form of such ethical prescriptions. Jesus never offered outward rules of behavior. His moral teaching is always in terms of inner principles.

In its attitude toward reform the church has taken an essentially legalistic position. For example, church leaders have enthusiastically backed the various prohibitions which would safeguard our children from temptation. It is not implied that this is wrong, but that Jesus would classify such things as the minor parts of the law. If the church imagines that it can replace strong character with a world in which strong character is not needed, it has certainly misunderstood one of the most important things Jesus taught.

We find the same idea prevalent in the principles on which our formal education is built. It is sometimes thought that an educated man is one who has a large amount of acquired information. Advertisements of various informational books assure us that acquiring the information contained in them will result in our transformation into learned and cultivated men and women. Likewise, culture is supposed to be the reward of a college education. Yet, to those who watch this rote memory sort of education, it is apparent that such a hope is not realized. The only way to change a man is to change his fundamental emotional attitudes. No amount of information can do that effectively.

Finally, in the education for character, parents have commonly believed that the formation of certain external habits, by whatever means, will result in the development of a fine character. Thus, children have been forced against their will to go to church, to give to charity, to be courteous, to refrain from profanity, fighting, gambling, and the like. The common case of children, who have been brought up on these admonitions and yet developed weak characters, is evidence of the futility of the legalistic method, when the nature of the accompanying emotional attitudes is neglected. "Thou shalt not" has been applied with little success for many generations. It is certainly not in accordance with the principles of the Sermon on the Mount.

Character, then, is the power and the unselfishness with which one behaves. The man who carries through his purposes with the greatest force and with the fewest deviations from his purpose is the man of strongest character. It must not be defined in terms of external behavior. If we develop strong character, our behavior will be ethical; but it does not follow that if our behavior is ethical, we have strong character. Far too many Christians are good, not because they are thoroughly inspired by justice and mercy and faith, but because they are afraid to be bad. Such characters are good, but not strong nor even admirable.

Three special problems of character; namely, sex, divorce, and perjury, will now be discussed. The fundamental principles of character development will be clearer when applied to these problems.

Whether we wish it or not, sex is the most difficult social problem we face. It has occupied so prominent a place in the problem of character, that in the minds of many people, *moral character* and *sexual purity* are synonymous terms. Biologically, sex is the second strongest appetite. Second only to hunger, it is the most powerful drive in human behavior. Since hunger does not meet with so many social inhibitions, its problems are largely confined to questions of physical hygiene, diets, calories, and vitamines. Sex also can

THE INTEGRATION OF CHARACTER 125

be partially dealt with by physical hygiene. There is a great need for information along this line. But more than that, there is need of mental and spiritual hygiene; not of repression and inhibition, but of healthy adjustment and wholesome realization.

Sex has always been a problem to civilized man. Mere expressionism is not and cannot be the solution to this problem. On the other hand, various religious teachers have striven to blot it out of human life entirely. The result in weak and distorted personalities is potent evidence of the futility of such a practice. It has often been assumed that marriage is the solution. However, a considerable group of people never marry, and many of those who do, find that marriage is no certain guarantee of a healthy adjustment. Finally, there are the many sex perversions, which bring upon those unfortunate enough to be addicted to them social scorn which destroys their happiness and influence in society. In these unsuccessful attempts at solution, the power which is inherent in the sex drive is lost to the personality, and society is the poorer because of another weak personality in it.

It is characteristic of Jesus that he should have attacked this problem early in his teaching on character.

Ye have heard that it was said by them of old time, Thou shalt not commit adultery: But I say unto you, That whosoever looketh on a woman to lust after her hath committed adultery with her already in his heart.—Matthew 5:27-28.

It is not at all uncommon for the terms *love* and *lust* to be confused. So general is this confusion in our present society, that it is unfortunate that we do not have another term than *love* for the Christian attitude. It should be pointed out emphatically, however, that this does not imply that sex is wrong or should be eliminated by religion. This is not true. No life is complete which does not utilize all of its sources of strength. No religion could be mentally healthy which attempted to throw out this powerful human drive. An illustration of this principle is found in Jesus' treatment of the sinful woman, described in Luke 7:36-50. In discussing her case, Jesus said, "I tell you, many as are her sins, they are forgiven, for she has loved much." This was one of the most daring statements Jesus made in his entire ministry. It is evident in this case, that he considered the source of her sin as also the potential source of her spiritual power.

Jesus' teaching on the subject of the sex drive in the Sermon on the Mount, when read with understanding and judged in the light of his whole teaching, is clear. It is probable that Jesus did not confine this teaching only to sexual impurity. In the first place, the word translated *lust* may be used to refer to any sort of unbridled, selfish desire. Whenever any urge becomes strong enough to dominate one's entire personality, even temporarily, it may be described as lust. On the other hand, it was like Jesus to strike directly at the chief source of trouble. He did not treat the sex drive as something not to be mentioned, as some prudish educators have done. He recognized its presence in human nature and discussed it as frankly and firmly as any other issue.

It has frequently been assumed that Jesus was teaching that sex is always wrong, not only in its overt form, but even in the very implicit thought of such a thing. Hence, children have often been brought up to believe that sex is the very essence of evil, and that they are to feel ashamed of themselves, if they even experience sexual desire. If Jesus had taught such a principle, he would have been responsible for much of the mental illness in the world. For from such teaching there have developed thousands of cases of insanity, millions of unhappy marriages, and countless other maladjustments.

Man often has desires upon which society frowns. When he faces this situation, there are four alternatives open to him. In the first place, he may ignore the edicts of society and give unbridled expression to his desires. This is expressionism. It results, in the long run, in more conflicts and far worse maladjustments. The second possibility is sup-

THE INTEGRATION OF CHARACTER 127

pression. That is, he experiences a desire, recognizes its social sinfulness, and frankly inhibits it. He neither expresses it nor represses it. Psychologically, this is a more healthy attitude to take. Such suppressions are usually necessary, both for social adjustment and for the development of strong character. Suppression is not the healthiest possible reaction, but it is far superior to expressionism as a personality principle.

The third option is the method of repression. The repressionist not only does not express his desire, but he does not even admit that he has it. It is a form of deceiving oneself. It is the most unhealthy of all the methods of dealing with these socially unacceptable urges. The repressionist is trying to throw this urge out of his personality. But one cannot put desires out of the mind. He only pushes them into the mind, and out of consciousness. A large portion of our behavior is unconscious. This is especially true of our motivations. We have many emotional reactions for which we cannot find the reason. Many of these unknown attitudes are due to repression. During this process of repression, then, these desires become a part of the unconscious behavior of the individual. They do not express themselves in the normal way, and usually are not even recognizable as being related to these desires. A repressed sex desire, for example, may show itself in extreme prudishness, frigidity in women, impotence in men, paralyses in hystericals, various forms of sickness, morbid fears, and violent obsessions and compulsions. Whatever form it takes, a repressed desire is not destroyed but only disguised. It is lost from consciousness, and what is more important, from the possibility of being integrated into the total personality.

The fourth way in which desires may be dealt with is called by the psychologist, sublimation. Many have used the term *sublimation* with a very inadequate notion of what it really is. Sublimation consists in taking the power of the drives which lead into socially unacceptable channels and throwing them into socially acceptable channels. Sublimation is not easy. Like most of the other traits of personality it has to be achieved.

Genuine sublimation does not involve repression, although many descriptions of it cannot be distinguished from repression. A person employing the method of sublimation recognizes frankly the presence and nature of the original urge, and then consciously applies the drive to some other type of activity. For example, two elderly ladies, both unmarried, work in the same institution. One of them says that she "never wanted to marry and never saw the man she would have." The nature of her general behavior, however, belies her words. She behaves in a silly manner, and she is especially attentive to any man who comes near her. She is an object of amusement to all who know her, and her influence is limited. This is repression. She will not face the facts. The other feels that marriage is the natural state for a woman. She says frankly that she is sorry she has never married. But since she has not, she throws her whole energy into her work. She is healthy in mind, and powerful in influence, greatly admired by all who know her. This is genuine sublimation. It might be defined as suppression carried into positive action. A third individual in this same situation might admit her socially unacceptable desires, and though not giving open expression to them, build a fantasy world which provides the desired experiences. This is pure suppression. It is the usual form of behavior taken by the child when he first faces urges for which society denies expression. But this behavior should develop into sublimation as one grows to adulthood. Psychogenically, then, we find the child first using unrestrained expression. When social punishments make this unprofitable, he next resorts to suppression and finds satisfaction in his daydreams. Finally, depending on the type of sex education he gets, he learns either to repress, with its resultant evils, or to sublimate, and thus integrate all his energy into acceptable channels.

Some have believed that Jesus was preaching repression. He said, however, that if lust exists in one's heart, adultery is the effect. Any psychologist knows that the heart, that is, one's affective life, includes subconscious and unconscious drives as well as those that are conscious. Hence, a repressed emotion is quite as lustful as a conscious emotion. Some may wonder if Jesus was aware of unconscious behavior. I think there can be no doubt that he was. How else could he have known, better than Peter himself, the nature of that disciple, so that he could predict the denial. Peter did not expect it. It grew out of subconscious drives. Jesus was constantly seeing motives in men, of which they themselves were not aware. He was too well acquainted with human nature not to sense the presence of those drives which are deepest in a man. His teachings would have been futile indeed, had he not recognized them, for they constitute an important part of personality.

If the central desire of a man's personality lies in social welfare, there will be no room for lust. This does not mean that there will be no desire. Jesus does not use the word *desire;* he says *lust*. Here is a man so covetous for money that he sells his self-respect, his honesty, his friends, and his loved ones to secure it. This is lust. Here is a man so ambitious for high rank and social prestige that he sacrifices his friends, his sense of fairness, and his professional integrity for it. This is also lust. Sexual lust, then, is only one kind of lust. To a strong character, no selfish desire becomes so strong that it predominates over his whole personality inhibiting all other drives. Lust is selfishness, regardless of what we lust for. Selfishness is the antithesis both of Jesus' teaching and of mental health. Sex is a natural and powerful force in every person's life. If it is not, this is an indication of abnormality. But it should be a subordinate drive which gives power to one's total personality, and not a master which gains unbridled control of it.

Just how can the sex drive be integrated into personality? How does it become possible to prevent lust in one's heart? To many, this will seem an idealistic impossibility in the teachings of Jesus and a theoretical and unworkable principle in psychology. Fortunately, nature herself provides the means. Observe the nature of the normal, healthy boy's first love. His adoration for his beloved is complete. He is certain that it would be conservative to classify her as "little lower than the angels." Recall that this idealistic love is motivated almost entirely by the sex drive. Yet also notice that the boy is hardly aware of its presence. This is sex integrated into wholesome personality. The effect is apparent in other phases of his life. He is intensely earnest in his religion. He is passionately idealistic in his attitude toward social problems. When this adoration results in marriage, the sex life is simply a beautiful expression of a wholesome affection, and not lust for sex as an end in itself. Such idealistic sex life, then, does not have to be created artificially by much sermonizing. It has a natural basis in man's being and will develop that way unless some environmental force prevents its operation, or perverts it into less noble channels.

A very common behavior problem is involved in the question, is it right to "pet"? "Petting parties" are very common in our present-day younger society. What is the result of this tendency? To the normal individual, "petting" is pleasant. To many it seems harmless. Its danger lies in its stimulation of the sex instinct, when it is not an expression of genuine affection, but an end in itself. When sex becomes an end in itself, it is lust. "Petting parties," then, are likely to break down the natural idealism of adolescent love and replace it with sexual lust. The individual may commit no socially immoral act, nevertheless, he will be committing adultery. This is not to be confused with prudishness. To object to "petting parties" is not to say that sex is wrong. The principle consists, not in the negative ethics of not "petting," but in the positive preservation of adolescent idealism.

Students of psychology are coming to realize that here also lies the danger of the motion picture show. It is not so much in the overt behavior of the actors as in the stimulation of sex as an end in itself, which helps to break down

THE INTEGRATION OF CHARACTER

this adolescent idealism and make sex a lustful appetite. The fact is that motion pictures often stimulate people to lust after money, luxuries, beauty, adventure, and danger, quite as much as after sex. Whatever the thing one lusts for, disintegration and weakened character are the results. It is shortsighted to object only to the sexual features of the theater, when all these other lusts are equally destructive of personality. It is all very well to object to censorship and talk much of realistic art, but the fact remains that even art was made for man and not man for art.

Here, then, is a new definition of adultery and lust. Adultery takes on none of the legalistic character ordinarily ascribed to it. It is an inner attitude and not an outward form. The whole principle of temperance, if it is to have any psychological value, must be built upon this foundation. True temperance does not consist of inhibited activity, but of integrated activity, which may involve moderation in certain phases of the personality. Temperance, for temperance' sake, has no value. Merely acting with less dynamic force has no virtue. The common notion that there is something undignified or wrong about whole-hearted behavior is ridiculous. It is disintegrated behavior that is deserving of this condemnation. Integration should be more dynamic, not less so.

However, most of us do lust from time to time. We find some of our desires getting the best of us, and often causing us to do impulsive things of which later we are very much ashamed. Recognizing quite frankly that this is not the ideal condition, it nevertheless exists. What are we to do about it? For those who believe that Jesus was so idealistic that he could not face problems as they actually exist in most people's lives, one needs only to recommend the thoughtful reading of the next portion of the teaching on adultery. It has been stated already that suppression is frequently necessary in everyday life. Suppression is not harmful to the personality. Indeed, it is strengthening if done whole-heartedly and courageously. Let us examine this next passage closely.

> And if thy right eye offend thee, pluck it out, and cast it from thee: for it is profitable for thee that one of thy members should perish, and not that thy whole body should be cast into hell. And if thy right hand offend thee, cut it off, and cast it from thee: for it is profitable for thee that one of thy members should perish, and not that thy whole body should be cast into hell.—Matthew 5:29-30.

In this verse Jesus admits frankly the power of the sex drive and the difficulty of completely mastering it. It would be ideal to sublimate it all into socially acceptable and socially useful channels. This ideal, however, is rarely attained. It could be, if we were given Christian attitudes in childhood. But most of us are continually finding some of our impulses rebellious and running counter to the rest of our personalities. They make us desire things which we know are beneath a man of strong character. It is then that suppression should become our order of conduct. "If thy right eye offend thee, pluck it out." If the literature we read, or the art we see, or the music we hear, or the theaters we patronize, or the games we play, or the friends with whom we associate, or the jobs we hold cause us to stumble, Jesus urges that we cut them off and cast them from us. Is this a retreat from reality? Jesus taught in the Beatitudes that we should be able to maintain our moral integrity without dodging our social responsibilities. True enough, we should; but it is better "that one member should perish, than that the whole body should be cast into hell." It often happens that a man finds some habit, for which he despises himself, so strongly attached to him that it seems almost impossible to break. In getting rid of it he may have to "pluck out an eye and cast it from him." This figure of speech may be carried into action in several ways. The most effective way is that of finding another habit with which to replace the undesirable one. This actually gets rid of the temptation for the old behavior. Familiar illustrations come to mind. A man

THE INTEGRATION OF CHARACTER 133

who is endeavoring to stop drinking not only stays away from people and places that tempt him to drink, but forms other associates and activities that make this easier.

One of the most difficult moral problems that society faces finds its answer in this teaching. This is the problem of sex for those who do not marry, but who find themselves powerfully driven by their sex appetites. It would be ideal if everyone could go naturally through the experiences of courtship, marriage, and parenthood. Unfortunately, this is not possible in society as it is. There are many thousands who do not succeed in making this normal adjustment to one of life's hardest problems. On the other hand, the history of society has demonstrated that a free love solution works to the disintegration of society as a whole, and commonly to the degradation of the individual. Therefore, this cannot be the solution. Another solution, which has been described as repression, is socially acceptable, but leaves a rather pitiful and frustrated personality.

What, then, is the solution? Jesus suggested it in this verse. "If thy right eye offend thee, pluck it out and cast it from thee: for it is profitable for thee that one of thy members should perish, and not that thy whole body should be cast into hell." There is no suggestion that this is the best possible solution. But it is better than a destruction of the whole personality. To one whose personality has been built around sex, so that he or she is the personification of lust, this is bitter medicine. Indeed, many do not have the courage to take it, and adultery is the result. But to those who have an integrated personality in which sex plays its natural rôle but no more than that, it is perfectly possible, deliberately and consciously, to turn one's back on it and throw all of its energy into the performance of some great purpose in serving mankind. This is not easy, nor accomplished without a vast amount of rigid self-discipline, but is often necessary for individual and social integrity. Society has demonstrated that monogamy and chastity are essential to its health. Psychology has discovered that honest suppression is far healthier than unbridled expressionism. There is a widespread belief that complete sex suppression is detrimental to mental or physical health. This has no foundation in fact. One can, and many do live lives of vigor and usefulness and happiness under this condition.

Here is the basis of dealing with sex as implied in the teachings of Jesus in the Sermon on the Mount. Sex is a very powerful source of energy and should be utilized in the development of the personality. It can never be the center of it, but if it is lost the resultant personality and character are materially weakened.

With this concept of the nature of lust before us, we are prepared to discuss more fully another important phase of character integration. All of us inherit potential sources of strength. Whether we develop strong character or not depends on whether these individual drives are permitted to operate separately as disintegrated lusts, or whether they are each made to contribute its strength into the whole integrated character. Let us consider our affections. Love is not one drive. It is at least five. Whether and to what extent they are genetically related is still an unsolved problem, but no one will deny that they all exist.

The development of the Christian attribute of fatherly love is an integrative process which passes through several stages, from each of which can be derived sources of strength. In the beginning the child may be said to be in love with himself. His whole interest is in his own wants and wishes. Jesus urged his followers to love their neighbors as themselves. This implied, however, that they were to love themselves. Thus, there is a drive in this self-love of the child which can be educated to be useful. If self-love becomes only a seeking after satisfactions of one's elemental urges, then it will result in what we have called the psychopathic personality; weak because of its internal conflicts, and undesirable because of its anti-social tendencies. On the other hand, if the love of self is a genuine interest in becoming the

THE INTEGRATION OF CHARACTER 135

strongest possible character, this drive becomes a very important one in the final Christian personality. It is clear that no one would want his child to grow to manhood with no nobler purpose than this. It is equally true that here is a source of power which should not be lost to strong character. Ambition is built primarily upon this urge. However unselfish one's personality may become, he is not likely to achieve much for society if he has no ambition.

At an early age, love of parents begins to show itself. It is the first unselfish urge to appear in the life of the child. It is the beginning of character as we know it. But this love for parents has become the source of some of the most diseased and unhappy personalities of which we know. Like love of self, it may be educated to do great harm or to be one of the important elements in strong character. As has been shown, it is this love of parents upon which most of the finest virtues of the child are built. Giving to his mother, sacrificing for his mother, suffering for his mother, denying himself for his mother's happiness; these are the beginnings of character. It is an unwise home in which parents do so much for their children that the children never have an opportunity to exercise this tendency. This is what is meant by spoiling a child. The child must learn to give, sacrifice, suffer, and deny himself. He cannot be made to do these things. He will do them only for those whom he loves. If no such opportunities are provided he will grow into a selfish, spoiled individual. Many sincere mothers make slaves of themselves for their children, and unwittingly deny the child his best gift, character.

At a still later time in the life of the child, he is interested only in members of his own sex. Boys run in gangs and are convinced that girls are an abomination. Girls are no more charitable in their opinion of the opposite sex. This stage, if wrongly developed, leads into one of the worst of the sex perversions. These perverts, the homosexuals, become one of our important social problems. On the other hand, if rightly educated, that is, integrated into the total personality, this urge is the basis for the development of true sportsmanship and friendships which are among the most valuable of our social assets. Again, this appears to be an instinctive reaction which matures at about ten to fourteen years of age. Before it appears, what is commonly called brotherly love is not present. Sportsmanship cannot be developed. Even the rudiments of fair play can be produced only by fear motivations. In the development of the mentally healthy personality, it is inadvisable to use fear, when such a strong positive motivation as this one is available. It is much better to wait until this instinct matures, and use it in the development of that splendid characteristic of the strong character, true sportsmanship. This is the period in which such organizations as the Boy Scouts can do their best work. Team play, the art of losing gracefully, and admiring one's opponent can best be built upon this instinct. It is the basis for the friendship which has been so poetically defined in literature. To stimulate this instinct beyond its desirability, however, is another source of maladjustment. Contrary to the sincere praises heaped upon it, friendship, fine as it is, is not the finest thing in the world. But no strong character would fail to have the capacity for deep and sincere friendship. One of the most pathetic notions one finds in dealing with young men is the notion so common among them that all other men are utterly selfish, and that the only practical philosophy of life is "every man for himself." College students are frequently cynics of this sort. Each insists that "he is going out to get his," which means whatever and as much as he can get. During the period of affection for members of his own sex, it is possible to direct his interests into channels of mutual coöperation and faith in his fellow men.

Then comes sexual maturity and the first love affair, if the individual has had a normal sex education. Few things are so idealistic and beautiful as the adolescent love affair. It is the sex drive which causes it, but that fact is usually not very conscious in the minds of the young lovers. A healthy-minded lad in love for the first time is inspired to dreams

THE INTEGRATION OF CHARACTER 137

of great achievement. It is a foolish parent who does not recognize the value of this period in the life of the child. This drive, the second most powerful in human nature, can be woven at this time into the perfectly integrated character. The age of chivalry may be gone, but the need for the spirit that gave it life is not gone. During this period, which is characterized by what is so often called, "puppy love," can be built the idealism which will remain always a guiding power in the life of the individual. The power of this drive constitutes so large a portion of the individual's total resources of strength, that it may safely be said that strong character is impossible without utilizing it. This instinct has such great strength that some individuals, because of their forcefulness in this drive alone, seem more admirable than others who repress it, even though the latter are ethically far more virtuous. When the natural idealism of adolescent love can be made the basis for its integration into character, there will develop the personality with genuine self-control. This will not be the weak inhibited self-control of fear, but the powerful self-control of purpose and vision. It is during this period of idealism at its best that youth should choose his vocation.

There is one further stage in the development of the affections of the individual. This is the parental stage. When a baby arrives in a home, it instantly becomes the most important thing in the minds of the parents. This parental urge is the noblest of the instinctive tendencies, and is the only one about which the total personality can be perfectly integrated. All of the power of the other stages can now be organized and unified about this one. The others need not be lost, nor must they necessarily be suppressed; but it is this one that forms the core of the Christian personality.

In one of Jesus' most striking parables, he points out very clearly the contrast between the possibilities of brotherly love and those of fatherly love as the guiding motivation of one's life. This is the parable of the Prodigal Son. The Prodigal Son is a relatively insignificant part of the story.

He does exemplify the inevitable results of a life based on self-love. But especial attention is called to the contrast between the reception of the Prodigal by his father and by his elder brother. The father, being interested only in the son, is happy in his return. The unworthiness of the Prodigal only intensifies his forgiveness. He is a typical father. The elder brother, however, is not pleased. He objects to the splendid reception of his brother, because of "the principle of the thing." He bases his argument on the cold justice of just reward for external behavior and conformity. The elder brother should not be too bitterly criticized, for this is the natural reaction of brotherly love. Brotherly love believes in fair play. It is willing to conform to fair play, but it is not forgiving in the way fatherly love is forgiving. The disciples must have had a brotherly love for one another, and yet we find them at the Last Supper jealously bickering about the chief places in the kingdom. Jesus rebuked them with the admonition that they love one another in the way he had loved them. An examination of his relationship to them will convince anyone that his attitude toward them was like that of a father toward his sons. Only parental love will persist when not reciprocated.

Intimately related to the problem of adultery is that of divorce. It is an old one, having been prominent from the earliest beginnings of the rise of woman in society. There have been many hypotheses for its solution, one of which is set forth in this teaching of Jesus.

It hath been said, Whosoever shall put away his wife, let him give her a writing of divorcement: But I say unto you, That whosoever shall put away his wife, causeth her to commit adultery: and whosoever shall marry her that is divorced committeth adultery.—Matthew 5:31-32.

In one of the manuscripts from which our New Testament is translated there is another phrase in the passage which reads, "saving for the cause of fornication." Almost all

THE INTEGRATION OF CHARACTER 139

Bible scholars are agreed that it is a later addition to the passage. A psychologist finds it easy to accept this decision. If Jesus had made this sort of rule, it would have been psychologically unsound, as well as not being characteristic of his teaching. Furthermore, to have included this phrase would have forced us to the conclusion that Jesus took a much narrower view of the problem than was characteristic of him. He certainly must have been aware of the complexity of factors which enter into healthy and happy marriage. In this case he would hardly have confined his teaching to only one of them, important though it might be.

When Jesus came, the divorce problem was centered around the question of what the causes were for which divorce might be granted. The Shammaites insisted that adultery was the only justifiable reason for obtaining it. The Hillelites had apparently accepted the principle of incompatability, for they permitted divorce even if a wife should burn her husband's dinner. Divorce with them was as easy as it is in some localities today; It was becoming more and more common. Indeed, it is said to have been so common in Rome that women reckoned time by their husbands. Here, then, was the condition of things as Jesus found them.

A more elaborate statement of Jesus' teaching on divorce is found in Mark. The Pharisees had demanded that he state his position on the subject. Jesus answered with a question.

> What did Moses command you? And they said, Moses suffered to write a bill of divorcement, and to put her away. And Jesus answered and said unto them, For the hardness of your heart he wrote you this precept. But from the beginning of the creation God made them male and female. For this cause shall a man leave his father and mother, and cleave to his wife; And they twain shall be one flesh: so then they are no more twain, but one flesh. What therefore God hath joined together, let no man put asunder.—Mark 10:3-9.

His teaching involved four definite points. In Mark, Jesus clearly points out that divorce is due to "the hardness of your heart." He states that the basis for marriage is in the inherited nature of man. He says that for this reason there rightly ought to be no divorce. Then in the Sermon on the Mount he says that divorce involves adultery, however and whenever it takes place. In other words, when marriage fails it is due to the faulty character of one or both parties. Divorce would never occur between genuine Christian personalities, because marriage is in the very nature of the case right, and when it fails adultery is somewhere in the picture. As a matter of fact, a recent study of divorce has shown that in actual practice, divorce between men and women who are active church members is astonishingly rare. Remember, however, that adultery is an inner attitude that may be quite as common in wedlock as out of it. It is not merely a legal code.

A study of the psychological causes of marriage difficulties will help us in understanding this teaching. Countless causes might be mentioned, for every case has its own peculiar circumstances which mark it off from every other. But when they are all examined they are fundamentally the same thing; namely, the conflict of emotional attitudes. It is inevitable that to some things any two people will attach different emotional tones. Here is a simple example. A husband may enjoy repeating his stories many times, while his wife may find them unbearable. These emotional conflicts may vary in two ways. In the first place, they may vary in the intensity of the emotional responses. It may be, for example, that a husband enjoys playing the radio incessantly whereas his wife is annoyed by it. On the other hand, it may be that a wife is so passionately fond of a gay social life that she cannot live without it, and her husband so utterly detests it that he cannot endure it. When conflicts of this latter sort arise, danger is ahead. In the second place, these conflicts may differ in the inherent seriousness of the thing over which the conflict occurs. For example, if the disagreement is over so simple a matter as back-seat driving, usually it is adjusted fairly easily. But one of the most serious and probably the most common difficulty arises over sex. It will be recalled

THE INTEGRATION OF CHARACTER 141

that despite the fact that the sex appetite is inherited and very powerful, there can be attached to it many different forms of expression and many different emotional tones. It is possible to attach such intense disgust to all of its expressions, that the individual will not admit even the presence of the appetite in himself. It is possible to attach violent emotions to different forms of its expression. Furthermore, perfect physical adjustment is fairly rare. It is not completely clear as yet as to how much of this lack of physical adjustment is actually due to physical conditions and how much of it to psychological factors. Probably most of it is due to the latter. However, almost every element in the causes of marriage failure is due to some unintegrated emotion: fear, anger, jealousy, disgust, hate, or some other form of lust.

Now, what can be done about it? Marriages will fail less frequently if each party is aware of the conflicts between their temperaments, and recognizes the ones that are most likely to cause trouble. Some of these can be changed. Some can be avoided. Some of them are impossible of solution and will result in unhappiness, if not failure in marriage. Many of the questions which are asked by young people will be recalled at this point. Should a Catholic and a Protestant marry? Should a woman marry a man younger than herself? Is a lack of sex adjustment fatal to happy marriage? If anyone answers any of these questions with a dogmatic "yes" or "no," he is failing to consider a fundamental principle in mental life. This is that it is not the objective situation which counts, but the emotional attitude attached to the situation. Catholics and Protestants marry each other frequently. Many of these marriages are perfectly happy and successful. Much depends upon the emotional attitude which each takes toward the other's religion. If that tone is one of violent dislike, then danger lies ahead. If admiration and respect is the attitude, there is no reason why the marriage should not succeed. Many older women have married younger men and have been perfectly adjusted and happy. Again, it depends upon the attitude of each to this fact.

It has been shown that these emotional attitudes are the result of psychogenic development. Most of them were acquired either in whole or in part in the early years of childhood. Those parents who have been so concerned with moral purity that they have attached disgust and shame to the whole sex instinct in the minds of their daughters, and sometimes of their sons, have doomed them to a vast amount of unhappiness, if not divorce. It is all too common to see a young woman who is the victim of this repressive education. She is prudish, narrow, usually very much self-centered, often given to gossip, and of course unattractive. She simply lacks the wholesome, generous, warm-hearted temperament of the normal girl. It is on the basis of learned emotional attitudes that men and women are attractive to each other. Not every boy is attracted to the same girl, fortunately. This is not because of some "divine ordinance" that "fitted them for each other for all eternity." It is because each has attached the emotional tone of attractiveness to certain attributes which he finds in the other. The permanence of their love depends upon the wearing qualities of these attractions. Just when the "honeymoon will be over" depends upon what has attracted them to each other. Some attractions can be satisfied in a week; others require a lifetime.

But it may be asked, how can conflicts help but occur? It is inevitable that two individuals born in different homes, often in different sections of the country or world, or in different strata of society will have acquired many tastes, likes and dislikes, which will not harmonize. This certainly is true. Marriage would be dull and not very mutually helpful if this were not so. It is not because of the presence of conflicts, but because of the intensity of conflicts, that trouble arises. The concept of lust and adultery presented in the last section immediately comes to mind. Lust is an intense emotional attachment of any sort which is not integrated with the total personality. Adultery is its expression. Jesus said that divorces were due to "the hardness of your heart." Is this not exactly that same thing? A girl may lust for money. If she does, marriage to a man without it is almost certain to fail. She may lust for social position or beauty. If she does, a marriage which does not produce them cannot be a happy one. A man may lust for sexual satisfaction. If marriage does not bring it, the marriage will fail. It is the disintegrated personality, then, that fails in marriage. This is what is meant by "hardness of heart." Note that Jesus did not say that there should be no divorce. He did say that there would be no divorce except for "hardness of heart," and that every divorce is the result of some lust and adultery. There is no doubt that some marriages are unbearable for one or both parties. They are much better dissolved. Such dissolution, however, must be admitted as a failure and not the natural or desirable thing.

Now let us consider the marriage of two perfectly integrated personalities. It has been shown that it is only a fatherly type of love about which perfect integration can be made. Consider the probable frequency of divorce if men and women had this type of love for each other. One does not often hear of a good mother resigning her motherhood because of mental incompatability with her child. Hosea in his experience illustrates how this type of love can be applied to marriage. Even though his wife was unfaithful to him, he took her back into his home and tried to reform her, with the promise of forgiveness. This is love of such stature that it requires the tremendous magnanimity of a father to encompass it.

But what of sexual love? Does this concept of integration about a parental type of love imply dropping sex out of marriage? Not at all. But it should be integrated into the total personality and not be the dominating factor. A goodly majority of marriages, of course, have centered around sex. This is the biological reason for marriage. Therefore, when fatherly love comes into marriage, it should not do so to the exclusion of sex but as the integration of it. The biological function of the home is the bearing and rearing of children. Society cannot go on without it. Quite apart from the propagation of the race, society and human personality would be infinitely poorer without the sex drive and without the presence of children. But when two personalities marry, both of whom are integrated about a fatherly type of love, the dominant desire of each will be the success and happiness of the other. They will be much more concerned with giving than getting, just as a parent is toward a child. Perfect sex adjustment is not necessary, though very desirable. Two persons can live happily together without having made it. It is only when sex has been made a dominant emotion, and has become a lust, that it may become a destroyer of happiness and mental health. Furthermore, when sex attraction is the only drive in marriage, then marriage is very likely to cool off in its ardor. This is the way with appetites. Parental love, about which the whole personality is integrated, does not diminish in intensity. It is permanent. So will marriage be between two integrated personalities.

The third teaching of Jesus on character has to do with oaths. In it Jesus emphasizes especially clearly the contrast between outer conduct and inner motivation. It is also a splendid example of the development of ethical codes. It represents a mid-point between the day when no man was expected to tell the truth about anything unless it was to his advantage to do so, and the day when the highest compliment that could be paid a man was to say that "his word was as good as his bond."

Again, ye have heard that it hath been said by them of old time, Thou shalt not foreswear thyself, but shalt perform unto the Lord thine oaths: But I say unto you, Swear not at all; neither by heaven; for it is God's throne: Nor by the earth; for it is his footstool: neither by Jerusalem; for it is the city of the great King. Neither shalt thou swear by thy head, because thou canst not make one hair white or black. But let your communi-

THE INTEGRATION OF CHARACTER 145

cation be, Yea, yea; Nay, nay: for whatsoever is more than these cometh of evil.—Matthew 5:33-37.

From very early Christian days some men have believed that Jesus was legislating against oaths, as such. There are still many who will not take an oath in court because they believe that this teaching forbids it. A careful study of the passage shows that Jesus had no such idea in mind in this teaching. The Jews were accustomed to a gradation of oaths. It was customary to require a man to take an oath to bolster up the credibility of his statements. It was due only to their sincerity in their religion that this was effective. The Jews believed very intensely in their God. They had, furthermore, a deep reverence for His name. The very word *Jehovah* is a substitute for the name of God, which was thought to be too sacred to mention. Hence, they did not dare to tell a lie when they swore by God. Heaven was a little less dangerous, since it was at least not God Himself. Then, as one progressed further away from God, lies were more and more permissible. It was not so much that they felt that telling a lie under any conditions was wrong, but rather that it was more likely to receive Divine punishment the more sacred the thing sworn by. This was somewhat like our childish practice of saying, "Cross your heart and hope to die."

In this passage, Jesus pointed out the inherent falsity of such reasoning. He pointed out that all things are sacred, even a man's word backed up by no oath at all. In other words, he challenged men to make "their words as good as their bonds." He did not mean to imply that oaths in themselves are evil, but that the type of personality which makes oaths necessary is evil.

This tendency to differentiate between the sacredness of things is not confined to oaths. Many Christians feel that it is far more evil to do certain things on Sunday than on other days of the week; that certain behavior is wrong in the church auditorium, which is all right in the church basement; and that a less strict ethics is applicable to one's business than to his religion, and toward strangers than toward friends. This is just as great a violation of this teaching as the example given about oaths.

In psychology, a mental phenomenon is recognized, which is called *logic-tight compartments*. By logic-tight compartments, we refer to the contradictory attitudes which the same individual applies to different situations. For example, he may hold one code of ethics for members of his own family, another for his friends, another for strangers, and another for enemies. Conduct is thought to be permissible in politics, which would be quite wrong in religion. The assertion that "business is business" is another example. A very good illustration is the case of a certain deacon who was one of the pillars in a prominent church. He was quite religious on Sunday. On week days, however, his chief source of income was from a "bootlegging" business. When asked how he reconciled these two activities, he replied that he did not see the necessity of reconciling them. One was his business and had to be run on a business basis. The other was religion and in no way concerned with his business. He insisted that his sincerity in religion was demonstrated by the fact that he never sold liquor on Sunday. The name *logic-tight* indicates that the individual thinks that his behavior is perfectly rational. He sees no inconsistency in it. It is obvious that logic-tight compartments are indications of a lack of integration in personality. Conflicts between these contradictory attitudes, therefore, are certain to arise, and consequent weakness of character is the result.

The church has been responsible for many of these logic-tight compartments, and parents for many others. The education in reverence, as it is taught in many churches, is a common example. It is very common for Protestant churches to confine such education to insisting upon silence in the church auditorium, as if this external conduct constituted reverence. The child is taught a ritual of conduct for the church service, and this, he is told, is reverence. No effort is made to discover what the motivation is behind this silence or this ritual in the mind of the child. Yet, as a matter of

THE INTEGRATION OF CHARACTER 147

fact, this motivation is the only thing that is important in learning reverence. If the church auditorium is so inspirational that the child naturally responds to it with silence, as one does before some awe-inspiring view in nature, that is one thing; but to assume that silence is a sufficient reverence in itself is another thing entirely. Furthermore, no single mode of outward conduct can characterize the behavior of every person who feels true reverence. One may feel a quiet serenity, another a profound awe, but another may experience an enthusiasm that makes him want to shout, "Hallelujah." To reduce these inner inspirations to carefully defined codes of behavior is to destroy the meaning of reverence. The effect of this outward behavior sort of teaching has resulted in a change in the connotation of certain words. *Piety* actually has an unfavorable sound. Few people would like to be called pious today, although originally it was the description of a man with depth of character. *Sacredness* pretty generally is thought of as referring to superstitious taboo. *Reverence* is often regarded as indicating the habit of walking on tiptoe, with bowed head, and speaking in low tones in King James' English.

This method of teaching reverence by outward behavior only is based upon a former theory of education, which believed that if one were taught the right outward habits, he would continue these habits. It is now clear that this is not true. For example, let us consider the church attendance of children. In two different homes the children are required to attend church regularly. In one case, as soon as the children grow up and leave home, they cease all association with the church. In the other case, they become regular church supporters. Outwardly, the habits learned were the same. The difference lies in the motivation, the early emotional attitude formed. In the one home, church attendance may have been regarded as a duty and a boring one. The requirement may have been a tedious one which even the parents themselves failed to perform. The attitude which would be learned in such a case is not favorable toward the church, but rather that church is for children, and that one of the privileges of adulthood is to put away this childish thing. In the other case, the parents may show that they consider religion vitally important. They take an active part in religious work, and stimulate their children to do likewise. In this case, the emotional attitude toward religion is more likely to be one of respect and admiration.

But suppose two boys are brought up in the same home. One of them becomes a fine Christian man, the other a scoundrel. Because of the commonness of this tragic occurrence, many believe in the inheritance of something like original sin, which just makes one depraved, despite the fine influences of his home. This is not true. Actually, no two children are brought up in the same home, psychologically. That is, the home will not seem the same to both of them. The older child may be forced always to give in to the younger child. If he resents this, the home may become a very different thing to him than it is to the younger child. He may even come to hate his parents, and far from endeavoring to emulate them, he may dislike everything they try to teach him.

Let us apply this principle to education in reverence. If the child is taught to respect and admire God with a deep feeling of awe and wonder and love, and if he finds that his elders have that same feeling, and express it in their attitude of quiet worshipfulness in the church, the child will come naturally to express his heartfelt reverence in just the same way. This is true reverence. But if the child is simply made to go through certain modes of behavior in the church auditorium, he is likely to develop logic-tight compartments: practicing an external form of reverence in the church, but without feeling the need for it in any other place. If he learns nothing except a superstitious habit, it is certain that he will not carry it to the other phases of his behavior. Unfortunate is the man who cannot go into a quiet chapel and feel that here he can have a quiet communion with God, away from a busy, noisy, and sometimes very trying world. He will be a better man, a more stable man for these quiet moments. But such worshipful attitudes are not learned by forced behavior patterns in childhood.

The emotional tones of learned habits must be consistent and integrated. If one learns to hold one attitude toward God in church and others elsewhere, logic-tight compartments are inevitable. We hold only those things sacred that we have learned to hold sacred. Probably even the most hardened of our criminals have a superstitious reverence for some places or things. Again we are faced with logic-tight compartments, because they have not been taught reverence for all things sacred. Jesus is saying in this teaching that all things are sacred, both in and out of church. Only he who holds this attitude has the reverence that gives power to character. Isolated reverence habits, however sincere, are of little use. Probably ninety-nine per cent of the people today think of religion and life as being separate and distinct things; one for church and Sunday, the other for all other places and days. Nowadays, even vacation Sundays are being exempted from religion. It is difficult to see just how religion can hope greatly to influence character and personality, as long as it is confined to a logic-tight compartment with no contacts with the rest of life.

Logic-tight compartments are numerous in other phases of life. It is very common to have different standards of truthfulness for different peoples and different occasions. There are many shades of white lies before one gets to pure black. Furthermore, even if there are white lies, which a man of spotless integrity can tell, they must not be taught children too young to recognize their color. Truthfulness on a sliding scale cannot be learned by a child. Etiquette may approve of social lies. The mother and the visitor may understand just what is meant when the report is given that mother "is not in" when actually she is in, but the child will not learn truthfulness by this method. It is only by practicing a general reverence for the truth, and observing such a reverence in the parents, that it is learned by the child. An admired father, who never breaks his word, is worth more in the education of truthfulness than much mouth-washing with soap and many other physical punishments.

Obviously, the integrated personality will be characterized by integrity in every field of action. A healthy personality cannot be built on the dissociated foundation of logic-tight compartments. Observe that in this teaching of Jesus, the logic-tight compartments described are in the inner motivation of the man, not in the external behavior. This is not a teaching on honesty, as much as a teaching on integrity. It seems quite probable that in society there are occasions when the bald truth would be both brutal and fundamentally dishonest. There are, however, no occasions when utter sincerity is undesirable. If one wishes to develop the Christian personality in a child, he will not do so by a system of logic-tight compartments. He cannot teach the child to be poor in spirit with respect to some things and not to others. He cannot expect him to be merciful to members of his own social group and not toward other social classes. When the Beatitudes were discussed, it was pointed out how interdependent they are. When they are thought of as the traits of the Christian personality, it is easy to see how well integrated such a personality would be. When logic-tight compartments are formed, conflicts between attitudes are inevitable. Each conflict subtracts that much from the possible strength of the character of the individual.

Here, then, are the principles which underlie strong character. There are unquestionably some very weak characters inside the Christian church who obey the entire Decalogue. On the outside, there are some strong and even splendid characters. The fact remains that the teachings of Jesus lend themselves to the development of the maximum character of which an individual is capable. Christians can imbue their children with his principles with the confidence that in so doing they will give to their children their best opportunities. It is at least questionable as to whether that opportunity is afforded in any other way. The development of such characters ought to be an inspiring challenge to the program of the church of the future.

Chapter VI

SOURCES OF POWER

Thoughtful young people are asking questions like these. What happens when we pray? Does it make any difference whether we pray or not? Is worship actually communion with a personal deity, or is it sonorous ritual, which at best is nothing more than autosuggestion? How can one get a sense of the presence of God? When he gets this sense of the presence of God, how does he know whether it is real or the sort of hallucinatory experience characteristic of so many mental diseases? When these are all summarized they ask, is there any value in prayer? These are the questions not only of people who are too thoughtless to pray; they are the honest perplexities of hundreds of serious-minded people, who sincerely question the value of any form of mysticism. Psychology does not concern itself with metaphysics. These questions, however, are also of considerable psychological interest. Only in this respect will they be dealt with here.

The psychological problem concerns the differences which appear in mental life as a result of prayer. The objective reality of God is a vital philosophical question. But whether a personal God exists or not, it makes a tremendous difference to a man's mental health as to whether or not he has faith in a personal God. To have the deepest confidence that there is a God, who does hear and answer one's prayer, forms a basis for a courage which makes a man able to meet many of life's severest trials with mental poise. On the other hand, to hold the belief that this is a purely mechanical universe, which has no heart and is utterly unfriendly, has led many a man to a suicide of hopelessness. Just by way of philosophical reflection, would it not be paradoxical if a lawful universe were so ordered that to believe in its true nature would be mentally unhealthy, and to hold a delusion as to its constitution should be the road to mental health?

The history of mysticism has not always been characterized by mental health. Our mental hospitals regularly have among their patients a considerable portion of the world's sincerest mystics. William James, in his monumental work, *The Varieties of Religious Experience,* pointed out many forms of distorted mentality which express themselves in mystical experiences of one sort or another. By the mechanisms of suggestion, auto-suggestion, and hypnotism, it is quite possible to conjure up in our minds almost any sort of vision we desire. Indeed, if one were to assume that having a convincing sense of God's presence is clear evidence of that presence, he would be put to it to explain these abnormal, hallucinatory phenomena. On the other hand, to fail to distinguish between these mental aberrations and those visions which have represented some of the most significant advances in the history of civilization, would be sheer folly. Therefore, it becomes an important problem for psychology to distinguish between the mental characteristics of the two. In either case, they are mental phenomena, and it is the task of the psychologist to ascertain the principles governing their relative merits.

When we turn to an examination of the various forms of worship, we find that they include a variety of behavior, differing widely both in form and in sincerity. When Jesus pointed out that not everyone who says, "Lord, Lord," is to enter the kingdom of heaven, he implied a criticism of a large part of religious expression. Only the most bigoted religious partisan would fail to recognize that a vast amount that goes under the name of worship is very far from being worship. Church services by the hundreds are conducted every Sunday, in a great proportion of which there is no real sense of God or of true worship, but a mere repetition of form. The critics of religion are quick to point out this fact.

But at the same time, as we look back through history at

those men who have contributed most to the advancement of civilization, we are distinctly conscious that they seem to have been "in tune with the infinite." Their prayers seem to have tapped sources of power. They convey to us a depth of understanding and sympathy which warms our hearts and inspires us to greater service. There are such men in every age. They are the greatest power for good in the world. They seem to leaven the world with a peace and calm which gives balance and stability to the many conflicts which try men's souls. Communion with these great characters, whose personalities seem an ever present spiritual inspiration, reveals valuable insight into the nature of divine love. They renew our faith in prayer and inspire us to find their sources of power. Worship will appeal to men generally, only if it does something for them. If one is able to tap reservoirs of power in worship which are closed to him through other means, then he will worship. Jesus would have agreed with this requirement. "By their fruits ye shall know them," was given as a test of the value of religious exercises as well as to detect the false prophets.

What is the place of psychology in this study of worship? A majority of the studies of psychologists on worship have been analytical rather than dynamic. These scholars have observed the experiences of religious devotees through their mental microscopes and tried to describe what they saw. The contributions of these studies have been of considerable theoretical value. They have been of almost no direct help, however, in making the personality of the worshipper more wholesome. They have not pointed out the dynamic functions of the personality, which are active in worship. But the principles set forth here could never have been advanced except for the painstaking work of these analytical studies.

There are three psychological principles which must underlie any adequate understanding of worship; namely, mental incubation, individual differences, and the reciprocal relationship between behavior and personality attitudes.

In the first place, the value of quiet meditation in mental

adjustments can hardly be denied, especially for minds of any considerable intelligence. While many of the features of what we call mental incubation are far from clear to us, its phenomena are unquestioned. A simple experiment will demonstrate this to any sceptic. Choose any problem;—let us say your reaction to this chapter. Write out this reaction as quickly as you can. Then lay aside your paper, and rewrite it again a week later. It is very improbable that anyone will be satisfied with his first reaction. Something has taken place in the meantime, even if no conscious thought has been given to the matter. This is known as mental incubation. The thought which has thus lain fallow for a week is likely to be of considerably greater maturity and depth than the first reaction. This incubation takes place only in the mind of a man who has given deep thought to his problem first. It is most common to him who practices frequent periods of meditation. It is impossible not to sense the shallowness of editorials, sermons, and books which are written in a hurry and without the aid of this meditation. Just what this mental incubation is, is a debated problem about which we can say almost nothing with certainty at the present time. One psychologist has suggested that it is contact with an inherited source of racial knowledge. Others call it communion with God. Whatever it is, it is valuable to mental health. If worship accomplished nothing more than the stimulation of this habit, it would be worthwhile.

The second psychological principle explains why there are so many forms of worship, and why some forms are unhealthy and others are sources of power. This principle is that, since worship is a learned reaction, many individual differences will appear. For many years men believed that there was a religious instinct. There is fairly common agreement among psychologists today that this is not true. Religious experiences form a satisfaction for several powerful instinctive drives in man, but religion is not in itself instinctive. Indeed, *religion* is a term which covers many phenomena which, psychologically at least, are not closely related.

There are some forms of religion which are nothing more than satisfactions for fear reactions. In other cases religion is an expression of one or more of the forms of love. In other instances it is an esthetic experience, and in still others it is the response to the desire for quiet and peace. It is inevitable that religion shall serve each man according to his need. This accounts for its wide diversity.

One of the fundamental concepts of modern psychology is the concept of individual differences. People differ in every important respect. One can choose any function of the mind and find all gradations of its appearance in people. Hence, it is not strange that different people worship in different ways. To one, the majestic mass in a Catholic cathedral stirs his heart as does some vast panorama from a mountain peak. To such a person the very homely and ultra-simple services of some churches would be far from satisfying, often even offensive. To another the simple service is impressive because of its very simplicity. To him it seems much more sincere and real, and to him it is the true setting for worship. But to a great majority, sincere worship is impossible wherever they are. In this case, they either discontinue worship entirely, or drop into the habit of going through the motions at regular intervals.

Whether or not a man finds satisfaction in worship depends upon his education in worship. In advice to those who would reconstruct their own personalities, Dr. James Gordon Gilkey has said that "as they struggle to make their finer traits dominant they will find it immensely helpful to expose themselves regularly to the spiritual influences they find inspiring." Then he goes on to say, "Obviously these influences vary with different people. One man derives his greatest spiritual stimulus from music, another from friendship, another from contact with the beauty and the silence of Nature."[1] This is indeed true. These differences occur partly because of the difference in the inherited nature of

[1] Gilkey, J. G., *Solving Life's Everyday Problems*, 97. The Macmillan Company, 1931.

the individual, but mostly because of the stimuli to which he has been taught to respond with spiritual inspiration. It is possible to attach a spiritual emotional tone to almost anything. However, if one's education for worship is of the legalistic, outward behavior variety, it is not likely that he will find any sources of power in it.

The third psychological principle in the value and nature of worship is, that it is a function of the personality of the worshipper. It is the disintegrated personality who finds little value in it. It will be seen that there is a reciprocal relationship between the strength of personality and the power of worship.

In the discussion of the Beatitudes, the fundamental spiritual emotional attitudes were described and shown to be mentally healthy. There were eight of those characteristics of the Christian personality. Any true worship experience will need to be built upon them. The unhealthy and morbid forms of mysticism are not likely to occur when these attitudes have become an integral part of the individual. And in turn, a genuine worship experience will deeply strengthen these traits. An individual with a well-grounded experimental faith, for example, will not accept some utterly irrational idea about God, or perform some fantastic and abnormal type of worship. If he has the experimental attitude, he will test the validity of his concepts. If he has faith in the goodness of God and the universe, he will not become discouraged in the face of what seems to be unanswered prayers. On the other hand, spiritual meditation is a form of research into the spiritual nature of the universe. Also, he whose life is integrated about a fatherly type of love will not confine his prayer to, "Dear Lord, I thank you for what you have done for me. Now, please get busy and do some more." Nor will he find the fervency of his prayers cooling into meaningless ritual. Furthermore, meditation on the needs of humanity will broaden his sympathy with it. The pure in heart with his high vision of purpose, which stimulates his ambition and inspires his every act, will find prayer a natural expression of his dominant desire, and reciprocally an intensifying of it. Those to whom the law of vicarious sacrifice is the very spirit of their endeavor, and in whom vicarious sacrifice arouses the happiness of genuine achievement, will know, as no one else can, the power that lies in prayer.

In this next section of the Sermon on the Mount Jesus deals directly with the expressions of religion. He points out clearly some of the unhealthy forms of worship, and the type of worship from which one may gain a sense of power. As one reads these verses, he will see that the central point which Jesus makes about worship has to do with its motivation. The very first verse, which contains the underlying principle of the whole section, is a warning against worship which does not have the right motivation. If the psychologist seeks for ways to make worship contribute to the health and power of the personality, he can do no better than to use these same words:

Take heed that ye do not your righteousness before men, to be seen of them: else ye have no reward of your Father which is in heaven.—Matthew 6:1.

The motives which cause people to worship are many. In the first place, a great proportion of people who worship do so as a sort of superstitious rite. They simply drone through their liturgy in much the same way as men in some religions turn their prayer wheels, with the idea that it will exert some magic influence of protection over them. It is done with much the same reasoning used in nailing a horseshoe over the door to procure luck.

Another motivation is indicated in the verse just quoted. Some people worship in order "to be seen of men." The clause "to be seen of men" is a translation of the Greek word *theathanai* from which our word *theatrical* is derived. Jesus, then, objects to the theatrical in worship. The number of things we do "to be seen of men" is large. Many individuals go to church, build or rent a house, choose a car, read certain books, listen to lectures, attend classical musicals, and scores of other things "to be seen of men." Bernard Shaw has said that some people will go to heaven because they owe it to their social position. This motivation is such a powerful one in human nature, that it is important to know its value in personality, and especially its effect on worship.

A third motive for worship is found in a sense of duty. Many church members go to church because they feel they ought to. This sense of duty is behind their religious exercises. Many young people sign pledges promising such things as to spend at least fifteen minutes each day in religious meditation and direct communion with God. Most of them feel very religious because of having taken this pledge, but many of them are soon watching the clock to be sure that they do not fall below the prescribed fifteen minutes. This is worship from a sense of duty.

Let us observe the rewards which come from these sorts of worship. Since a large percentage of worship is either entirely or partly motivated by the desire "to be seen of men," it should be considered first. Often this sort of worship has been described as hypocrisy, and totally undesirable. Actually, it is of considerable value. It will carry with it a reward. Indeed, Jesus stated this fact in his teachings. It may or may not be consciously hypocritical. The desire for social approval is a worthy motive and a strong one. In this sort of worship many men have found strength for resisting temptations that they would never have been able to meet otherwise. But the element of fear is too prominent in it to make it the healthiest possible motive. It is the fear of social disapproval that constitutes its strongest drive. Those who have contributed to the progress of civilization have very regularly faced this same disapproval. But these men have not worshipped "to be seen of men." This is not the only false motivation for worship which gains its reward. A fairly common type of behavior on the part of some people seems to be the very opposite of this seeking social approval. They pretend to scorn social approval, and to seek social disapproval. They try to be different. They can be accurately described as simply negativistic. They are quite as much worshipping "to be seen of men" as those who seek social approval. They too gain a reward, though a much smaller one than even the first group. When a person seeks social disapproval, he is usually compensating for an unconscious fear that he cannot get social approval. His reward, then, is in saving his pride from the pain of failure.

It is clear, then, that the rewards of worship depend upon the motivations which prompt it. This will become increasingly obvious when we deal with the three phases of worship behavior. But it should be pointed out immediately that the motivation of one's worship may not always be known, even to the worshipper. Worship, the motivation of which is unknown to the worshipper, constitutes a large part of it, and is the most significant factor in the failure of most people to derive power from it.

In psychology we recognize a mechanism which is called *rationalization*. It might be loosely described as doing what one wants to do and then subconsciously finding a good excuse for having done it. It is exceptional for us to be aware of what the real reasons for our behavior are. Rationalizations are the rule rather than the exception. Many people enlarge with enthusiasm upon the pleasure they get in reading the Bible or in hearing some lecture or musical recital, when the truth is that they do these things because they believe they are the things to do. They fool themselves into believing that they enjoy them. They are not consciously lying. They believe their rationalizations. In this lies the danger of this mental habit.

A brief examination of this mechanism of rationalization and its psychogenic development will be necessary for understanding some of the problems in the psychology of worship. It is sometimes thought that a clear-cut contrast can be made between sincere worshippers and out-and-out hypocrites. This is not true. The number of individuals who are consciously hypocritical is probably very small. On the other hand, the number of those great souls to whom worship is a source of real power is equally small. In between the two and in all gradations between the two comes the great host of honest and sincere worshippers, who believe that they are really praying.

Rationalization is a very common form of behavior. All of us use it on occasion. A student goes to a show instead of studying. He offers as his excuse, "All work and no play make Jack a dull boy." He sows his wild oats, and prattles seriously about mid-Victorian ethics and breadth of experience. We neglect our church attendance, and emphasize the need for a day of rest. Indeed, most of our excuses are rationalizations, in whole or in part. This habit begins in early childhood, when we are searching for a convincing excuse to offer for having engaged in some forbidden conduct, and thus avoid the wrath that is to come.

People, then, who worship "to be seen of men" can offer all sorts of reasons why they must be sensitive to the demands of social convention; and they believe their own rationalizations. We like to imagine that we are rational beings. Actually, we are governed by our desires and urges. Our intelligence serves for the most part only in finding satisfactions for these desires, and good reasons for our behavior. Unbiased behavior is impossible. The important thing is to have the right biases, although it is possible to become aware of one's prejudices and make some adjustment for them, in the same way an aviator compensates for a cross-wind. But continuing the analogy, having the right motivation is much more efficient than compensating for the wrong one. Probably the most important reason why the publican rather than the Pharisee went to his home justified after his prayer in the temple was because he was painfully but actually aware of his true motivation. The Pharisee was really not interested in praying at all. He was anxious to tell other men how good he was. He used the prayer as a rationalization for doing this. Jesus evidently was well aware that even his own disciples were in danger of this type of worship. He warned them that they must "take heed" that they do not worship for social approval.

How is one to avoid these rationalizations? How can he know whether his reasons are real or only excuses? This is no simple question. To be sure that one is acting on a given motive it is necessary, in the first place, to take heed that there are no other motives present. Children are naturally quite honest, often embarrassingly so in the eyes of their parents. They have to be taught this sort of dishonesty. The only motives which are hidden from consciousness are those that we repress. The only motives that we repress are those to which we attach shame or guilt. Rationalization would never occur if we did not teach the child to be ashamed of some of his native drives. If an individual is ashamed to admit that he does things for social approval, he will repress his true motive, and find some rationalization for the social nature of his worship. In an earlier chapter the formation of logic-tight compartments was discussed. Rationalizations usually grow out of them. Both are caused by repression. The use of shame or guilt as a motivation for right conduct is a very dangerous practice. Every time it is used it pushes out of consciousness some motivation in the mental equipment of the individual, and he becomes less sincere and is less aware of his true nature. One who is acquainted with the mechanism of rationalization hears them every day and can recognize them easily (except perhaps his own), but only the most rigorous self-examination and mental discipline can enable the individual to become aware of them in himself.

Perhaps a few illustrations of reasoning in connection with religion, which are generally rationalizations, will make this principle clearer. Here is a minister who attends corrupt "movies" because he insists he must know what to preach against. Here is a mother who neglects her children because of her self-admitted importance in the Lord's work of the Ladies' Aid. Here is a man who fails to take a courageous stand on moral issues because he says that one should not parade his righteousness. Here is a man who stays home and listens to a radio sermon because it is so much better than the one his pastor preaches. Here is a pastor who does not preach his honest convictions because he does not want to offend the sincere beliefs of his people.

Here are hundreds who worship, believing that they do it sincerely. They do not receive the "reward of the Father." They wonder why. Many a person comes to the worship services of the church expecting that the ritual will open up for him this power. Religion is not the only field in which this confusion of form and reality exists. Many a student enters college every year with the firm conviction that if he passes his courses he is an educated man. He elects "snap" courses; he pleads for "cuts" and "bolts"; he uses bluff and dishonest methods; in other words, resists every effort to educate him; and then is amazed at the end to find that a college education "does not mean anything." He eventually comes to recognize that his diploma is a counterfeit, but remains blissfully ignorant of the reason for this fact. Such a student believes that a diploma guarantees an education, whether it is the result of well-mastered work, or an evidence of having stayed in college four years without being dismissed. Many worshippers feel that going through the form gains the reward. Jesus is saying that the reward in worship is in the spiritual power gained by communion with God, and in no other way than in communion with God will this power be gained.

Let us turn to the three main types of worship: almsgiving, fasting, and prayer. A study of each of these will reveal the motivations which prompt them, the rewards which come from them, and the reward which Jesus described as being "of the Father."

Money is said to be the source of all evil. The corruption through which man will drag himself for it is disheartening. Despite this fact, it is perhaps more generally believed that money is the source of all good. We may talk of "filthy lucre," but the temples that have been made a place for selling merchandise were not confined to Jesus' day. "It is more blessed to give than to receive," but most of us find receiving a very satisfying experience.

There has never been a religion in which almsgiving was not an important function. That this system of financial operation should be contaminated by much that is not godly is to be expected. There are undoubtedly some churches that spend money unwisely, even extravagantly. There have been and are ministers who consciously and unconsciously place far more importance on money than the tenets of religion would seem to warrant. There are many who give their money ostentatiously, consciously or subconsciously "to be seen of men." Perfectly sincere religious leaders assure their hearers that money given to religious work is laying up treasure in heaven, as if one's religious reward could be bought. The people who are not in sympathy with religion can see these superficialities in the church. They listen with considerable disgust to the unworthy appeals made for money by the church. But giving is an indispensable form of worship. The proper education in almsgiving should be a source of power in the development of personality. Jesus met this problem squarely and effectively.

When therefore thou doest alms, sound not a trumpet before thee, as the hypocrites do in the synagogues and in the streets, that they may have glory of men. Verily I say unto you, They have received their reward. But when thou doest alms, let not thy left hand know what thy right hand doeth: that thine alms may be in secret: and thy Father who seeth in secret shall recompense thee openly.—Matthew 6:2-4.

There were three main forms of worship in the religion of Israel: almsgiving, fasting, and prayer. It was natural that almsgiving should come to be the most important of these. Prayer often becomes more and more superficial, and fasting is increasingly neglected. Then almsgiving is resorted to, to quiet a rebellious conscience. Many a man imagines that he can buy salvation by more or less substantial contributions to the church coffers and charity organizations. Even these soon reach a minimum unless the pastor publicly recognizes the largest gifts from the pulpit, or unless the names of the givers are reported in the newspaper in proportion to the size of their gifts.

Almsgiving had always been an important part of the Jewish religion. Tithing was one of the first religious rules. It was supposed to act as a form of protection or, as suggested before, a sort of luck token. It was expected to pay for immortal life and freedom from death. This notion of worship is far from dead. One hears many appeals made for money in churches in which it is guaranteed that the giver will never starve, but that his "bread cast upon the waters" will return to him. The Psalmist tried to renew the faith of doubting Jews in the verse, "I have been young and now am old, yet have I not seen the righteous forsaken, nor his seed begging for bread." It is probable, however, that the book of Job had already been written, and many could have shown him righteous men who were forsaken and whose children were begging for bread. Thousands of religious people have cited, as examples of divine intervention, times when unexpected resources of wealth came to them at critical hours. Unfortunately there are many thousands who give alms just as sincerely, to whom no such divine intervention is forthcoming.

"Sound not a trumpet before thee." It was customary for a Jew who wanted an unusual portion of God's blessing or forgiveness for some sin, to do penance in the form of almsgiving. One of the customary ways was to buy a skin of water and give it to the poor. Water was scarce in Palestine, and usually obtainable only from a water-carrier. Then the carrier would stand in the street with the giver beside him and sound a trumpet and shout, "O thirsty, come for drink offering." The poor who accepted this charity paid for it by good wishes to the giver, such as, "God forgive thy sins, O giver of drink." In this way the giver obtained considerable free advertising, and supposedly some forgiveness. This sounds strangely like some of our modern givers who love "to be seen of men" to give, and who bask in the sunshine of public approval.

"They have received their reward." It would be foolish to say that one does not gain a reward from insincere giving. One finds genuine pleasure in thanks and flattery from whatever source. If he gains the plaudits of the crowd for his charity, this is pleasure of a sort. But that is as far as the reward goes. It can soon be described in the past tense.

It is to be noted that Jesus is not decrying fame and glory, but is objecting to it as the motive for worship. "That thine alms may be in secret" is not meant as an objective description. The admonition of the right and left hand indicates that Jesus wanted the fact of almsgiving to be secret, not only from other men but even from the giver himself. Many Christians have interpreted this verse as meaning that they must not make a public show in giving their alms, but rather a private show. Such men feel that there is more reward in giving privately, and so are proud of their superior righteousness. To Jesus, this would be quite as far from the spirit of worship as the other. Genuine worship is that in which almsgiving springs from the unselfish motivation of a loving heart.

Jesus is more concerned with the growth in the spiritual power of the worshipper, than in the recipient of the alms or in the external reward of the giver. Let us examine almsgiving, then, in the light of the psychology of personality. Since the spirit of love is one of the essential prerequisites for strong personality, it is obvious that almsgiving is only valuable when it is attached to the emotional tone of love. Adult forms of almsgiving are of many varieties when classified according to the motivations of the givers. During the Great War we were urged to "give until it hurts." To many Christians, this is the acme of real charity. This attitude has caused much poverty in the power of our churches. Official boards discuss proposed projects on the basis of whether they can be afforded or not. Rather, the Christian point of view should be, "Give until the need is met."

"But when thou doest alms, let not thy left hand know what thy right hand doeth." Here again, Jesus indulges in a bit of humor. This verse has been read, often attributing an anthropomorphic explanation to the two hands, which of course do not have the capacity of knowing anything. Let us use two illustrations to bring out Jesus' message. Here is a man who is asked to give to charity. He believes that he must give according to his abundance, but no more. In other words, he gives only what he can "afford." So he pulls his money from his purse with his right hand and counts it carefully. This requires the coöperation of the left hand. Here then, the left hand does know what the right hand doeth. Consider the second illustration. Here are some parents whose son needs educating. What is likely to be the motivation behind their giving? Obviously, the need of the boy for the education. Many a boy goes to college on money furnished by a father whose left hand never knew what the right hand paid for his education, for the father simply reached in his pocket for all there was there. His difficulty was not to divide it according to his ability to give. If he used his left hand, it was to discover if there was any more in the other pocket. This is like fatherly love.

The important thing in giving, as a part of worship, is the emotional tone attached to it. "Though I bestow all my goods to feed the poor, but have not love, it profiteth me nothing." In this verse Paul recognized Jesus' principle. To make the child want to give aid to the extent of his capacity, to those whom he loves, is effective education in almsgiving. Many parents, believing that external habits, in themselves, are character building, have compelled their children to give regularly to worthy causes. They have done this often when the children were not only indifferent to the worthy cause, but were keenly disappointed in the resultant inability to buy something else which they wanted. But habits are only valuable in terms of their emotional tone. In fact, they are different habits when they have different emotional tones. Placing a dollar on the church plate each week may be one sort of habit in one person, and an entirely different one in another. A child should never be made to give, except to those whom he loves.

There are two ways in particular in which stronger personality is the reward of him who gives alms. A great deal has been said about the proper emotional tone being attached to behavior. There is the other side to it, however. There are some people who have nothing except emotional tone. They are sympathetic but they do not act upon their good impulses. Obviously, a personality is not very strong which does not act. This conversion of impulses into action is what the psychologist describes as will power, or volition. Almsgiving is of especial value in this connection because it provides the opportunity for putting one's affections into active helpfulness. The whole development of will power is based upon this principle. Thus will be seen more clearly the principle of the reciprocal value to each other of behavior and inner attitudes of healthy personality.

The other great reward which comes from genuine almsgiving is implied in the word, "secret." It carries the connotation of "casting down one's eyes" and so "to acknowledge one's inferiority." To worship God "in secret" is equivalent to being "poor in spirit." In almsgiving, then, we find one of the best sources of learning to be poor in spirit.

Here, then, are the great rewards of worship in almsgiving: strengthened personality, will power, and poverty of spirit. It will be seen that the reason why the Father does not give these rewards to those who give alms "to be seen of men," is not an arbitrary requirement. It is just in the very nature of things. Only "secret" almsgiving has as its effect on personality these sources of power.

When our Western mind looks about for "those influences which it finds spiritually stimulating," fasting is conspicuous by its absence. To be sure, many Christian churches insist upon certain regular restrictions of diet or even total abstinence from food during religious holidays. But probably the most devout Catholic would not deny that there is much Friday fish-eating which is, to say the least, not deeply worshipful. As for days without food, many are they who find them anything but spiritually stimulating. It is safe to say that to a great majority of people, if they practice fasting at all, such religious observance is entirely ritualistic, done from a sense of duty and not in a spirit of worship. It is doubtful if personalities are any stronger or one's religion any more profound as a result of such fasting. Yet here is Jesus describing fasting as the second form of worship from which one may derive power.

Moreover when ye fast, be not, as the hypocrites, of a sad countenance: for they disfigure their faces, that they may be seen of men to fast. Verily I say unto you, They have received their reward. But thou, when thou fastest, anoint thine head and wash thy face; That thou be not seen of men to fast, but of thy Father which is in secret: and thy Father which seeth in secret shall reward thee openly.—Matthew 6:16-18.

Fasting is found in all Oriental religions. It usually consists in a voluntary deprivation from food for a period of time: sometimes short, sometimes long. In our Western forms of religion we have pretty largely cast it aside with the belief that it does not constitute an essential part of Christianity. Just how we have reached this conclusion is a little difficult to see. Jesus certainly taught fasting. And although he did not always obey the Jewish laws with respect to it, he fasted himself and commanded his disciples to fast. It may be that our Western Christianity has lost much of its potential power by having discarded fasting. It is at least significant that all of the great religions, whether they had contact with other religions or not, have practiced fasting. Such universal customs are usually symptomatic of something in the very nature of things.

In the Orient fasting was practiced for two reasons. On the one hand, people fasted as a rite, somewhat on the order of our ordinance of baptism. It was a demonstration of one's faithfulness to the cause of the deity. This ritual was also performed sometimes as a matter of form, to indicate mourning. It was usually practiced "to be seen of men." There was nothing "secret" about it. Even if the motive was "to be seen of God," it was on the assumption that God, seeing their religiosity, would give them unusually large rewards, here and hereafter. In other words, it was very closely related to superstition. It was this sort of fasting to which Jesus objected in this passage. "Verily they have received their reward." Jesus did not deny that to their fellow men they would seem to be more religious than other folk, if they fasted and took pains that everyone saw their fasting. There is a reward in that. The over-worked minister, who constantly impresses upon his people that he is being worked to death and tries to look as tired as possible, is one of our Western examples of this sort of fasting. Jesus urged his disciples "to wash their faces and anoint their heads so that they be not seen of men to fast." He was not thereby urging them to take pride in the head anointment and face washing, thus imagining that they were any the better for it. He did want them to fast from such a motive that his sort of external behavior would be characteristic of their fasting. It is clear, then, that Jesus was not referring to ritualistic fasting in his teaching on the subject. Indeed, he and his disciples constantly broke the fasting rituals of the Jewish church. His Jewish enemies criticized him because of this. It was not characteristic of his teaching to emphasize so superficial a thing as fasting ritual, especially merely to replace one form of liturgy with another. Some of the early Christians made rules for fasting, the purpose of which was that Christians might be distinguished from the "hypocrites." One of the Jewish customs was to fast on Monday, the day Moses went to Sinai; and on Thursday, the day on which he returned. An early Christian writer said: "Be not as the hypocrites, who fast on Monday and Thursday, but do thou, when thou fastest, fast on Wednesday and Friday." It

SOURCES OF POWER

should be obvious to any student of Jesus that he would never have made a rule like that.

The second motivation for fasting in the Orient was to permit a long period of deep meditation. When a religious leader wished to get in close contact with the divine, he retreated from society and fasted for many days, while he concentrated on his problem. Jesus did this at the beginning of his ministry. When he realized, at the time of his baptism, that he was called to be a leader, he went into the wilderness for forty days to meditate upon the tasks which confronted him. Paul, Elijah, Amos, Jeremiah, Buddha, and Mohammed are other famous examples which come to mind.

But why fast at all? We are much more accustomed to think on a full stomach. The effectiveness of meditation depends partly upon the intensity of concentration attained. Concentration depends in turn upon the absence of distracting stimuli. It is difficult to concentrate with the radio sending forth the "sounding brass and tinkling cymbal" from our jazz bands, and the wildly "scientific" promises of advertisers. We usually find hunger, thirst, noise, discomfort, and many other such things distracting. There are three ways to prevent the disturbance of our thoughts by these distractions. The first is our Western method, which is to eliminate the distraction. If we are well fed we will not be distracted by hunger and thirst. We turn off the radio and sit in a comfortable morris chair under the most favorable light. This is getting rid of distractions by avoiding as many of them as possible.

The Oriental way is by ignoring the stimuli or adapting to them. Fasting was often for this purpose. It is known, for example, that if fasting is carried beyond three days the sensations of hunger disappear, and hunger is no longer a distraction. Furthermore, the one who fasts usually chooses uncomfortable conditions for his fast. Indeed, we may include under the term *fasting* any other sort of bodily discomforts as well as hunger. One soon becomes adapted to them and they cease to be distractive. This is the condition which we describe as a trance. There is nothing abnormal about it except that it is rather uncommon.

Now what is the essential difference between these two extremes? It is easy to see that it is in the motivation. This brings us to the third method of getting rid of distracting stimuli; namely, to have such a motivation that the stimuli cease to be distracting. For example, if one becomes deeply interested in a novel, he becomes oblivious to many stimuli to which he would normally respond.

We shall not have measured up to Jesus' concept of fasting until fasting is the natural expression of our inner attitudes. We do not need to guess long to discover what that motivation must be. It must be the natural outcome of devotion to a dominating purpose. And when this absorbing task is dominated by a love for one's fellow man, fasting will reach its highest peak. Here is the real spirit of the law of vicarious sacrifice, which Jesus has shown to be the central law of the spiritual universe. When one is dominated by fatherly love, it is obvious that he will find no price too great to pay for serving his fellows. To be sure, such a purpose may result in problems so perplexing that the one who fasts is driven to "the wilderness" to search for their solution. On the other hand, ministering to the needs of others may so deplete his resources that he will find himself fasting on most of the days of the week; but it is love that motivates Christian fasting.

While formal fasting is not characteristic of our Western civilization, there are many other varieties of fasting practiced, which are not in the formal ritual of any religious organization. Furthermore, they are frequently practiced "to be seen of men." The Oriental fakir, who disfigures himself as much as possible in the hope of getting a greater abundance of alms, has his counterpart on the streets of all of our own cities. Beggars, who sometimes have a considerable bank account, disfigure themselves in the hope of getting their reward. They usually do. Such fasting pays, after a fashion. Many a housewife assumes a harassed countenance, and spends much of her energy impressing upon the rest of the household how oppressive her duties are and how much she needs rest and sympathy. She receives a reward, of a sort. It is quite probable that she would think twice about this reward, if she realized its price in terms of the respect and affection of her family. Then there are those poor souls who think that they suffer from every conceivable infirmity. An hour's conversation with one of them is little short of a medical education. They fast, but with what disfigured faces. They receive their reward. Even college undergraduates disfigure their faces for some time before examination periods, that they may be seen of their instructors to fast. They receive their rewards—sometimes. All about us in every walk of life are hundreds of people who rush about madly, appearing to be working feverishly, and professing that they are having none of the pleasures of life. In many instances they are figuratively, at least, disfiguring their faces that they may be seen of others to fast: sometimes for sympathy, sometimes for admiration, sometimes for money or raises in rank, and sometimes to hide from themselves the smallness of their own personalities. Very commonly they receive their reward, such as it is.

Then on the other hand, here is an old man, a preacher, never a very successful one, retired by infirmity, living in sheer poverty, not blessed with a sympathetic family, unable to leave an invalid's chair, yet happy. He fasts by the force of circumstances, a fast that is almost continuous. Yet from some source he draws a power which makes him able to "wash his face and anoint his head, that he appear not unto men to fast." We cannot help feeling that with all his outward poverty, he is infinitely rich.

"That thou be not seen of men to fast, but of thy Father which is in secret: and thy Father which seeth in secret shall reward thee openly." When we look about for the best illustration of this principle working itself out in everyday life, we immediately turn to the parent. Probably no transformation of personality is so complete as that often made by the coming of a baby into a home. It cannot be denied that a baby is a constant source of all kinds of fasting: deprivation, worry, sleepless nights, and fatigue, from the moment of his birth on. Yet that great and divine element which we call parental love, simply transforms those who thus fast until they are hardly aware of their fasting. No one observing them can fail to recognize that in strength and nobility of character they have been rewarded many fold by a God who seeth in secret. To be sure, their former selfish attitudes show themselves over and over again. Also there are some parents who do "disfigure their faces," that their children may grow up with a full recognition of how much sacrificing they have caused their "fasting" parents. Such parents commonly receive their reward. But they are likely to find that this reward is accompanied by children who do not respect them, neighbors who deride them, and minds that believe their own tales of woe. The reward is certainly not worth the unhappiness accompanying it.

In early childhood, fasting must be of a material nature. If the child can be placed in situations in which he wants something badly and has no resources with which to obtain it, this is the beginning of fasting. If this can be brought about when the thing he wants is the means with which to do something for someone whom he loves, this is the beginning of worshipful fasting.

Many children are forced to fast because their parents believe in it, and think the child should form the habit as soon as possible. Here is a man, a leader and an outstanding personality. Yet his attitude toward religion is one of cynicism and doubt. He is the son of a minister. His father believed that Jesus taught an ascetic type of religion. The result was that the family many times went hungry and without sufficient clothing because the father had given away all of their money. The boy, therefore, was forced to fast. Let us observe the effect of this sort of fasting education on children. The boy lost, perhaps forever, the power of religion. He resented this hardship, and believing it to be a part of Christianity he rejected religion. Despite his unusually attractive personality and his splendid endowments and education, he failed at his biggest job. But some of those who know him intimately wonder if an abiding faith in a personal God might not have given him the necessary strength to succeed.

We can see the true rewards of fasting by examining Jesus' own experience. Let us follow Jesus into the wilderness when he fasted for forty days and forty nights, during which he planned his life work. When we consider how prominent a place food plays in the choice of a vocation in the lives of most of us, and how important bread is in our minds, we can appreciate the significance of the first temptation. Jesus was considering the nature of God and the spiritual laws. Therefore, when he was tempted to eat, bread seemed pitifully unimportant. He who has gained a vision of the whole spiritual universe finds a new sense of values in which material bread plays a very subordinate position. Every man who has achieved something of permanent value will find it easy to understand why Jesus chose spiritual insight in preference to bread. Here is a man who is graduating from college, having majored in chemistry. Two possible positions are before him. One pays a good salary but is not in his chosen field of interest; the other does not pay well but is in his major field of chemistry. Many a boy would have chosen the salary. After considerable temptation this boy chose the job in which he was interested. Today he is a prominent chemist. The tendency of the present age to worship money is causing many hundreds of young people to choose the "bread" of salary in preference to the task for which their abilities and opportunities for service so preeminently fit them. This does not mean that a boy must not choose business as a career. This is manifestly not so. But it does mean that the mere acquiring of wealth must not be the dominant purpose even in this life work. Such a man is able to think much less selfishly and is much less guided by secondary values. The medical student who is motivated only by the desire to make money, is much less likely to contribute to the relief of the suffering of mankind than the one who dedicates his life to that end because of a desire to serve mankind. Even when we translate this temptation of Jesus into what was more probably its meaning; namely, the temptation to use men as servants for his own pleasure rather than as foundation stones on which to build a church, we recognize how small such a selfish purpose must have seemed to him as compared to the greater vision of serving and inspiring men to great achievement. Not every man "comes to minister." Most of us enjoy to the fullest "being ministered unto." Only those who have learned this principle of fasting can know how much greater happiness comes from serving. Here then is the first reward of this form of worship. Through it one gains such a perspective that he more wisely guides the course of his life.

In the second temptation Jesus is urged to seek the reward of fame. Many a man sells his soul for the front lines of the newspaper. Fame is undoubtedly sweet, but rather weak in its achievement value. To Jesus, this too seemed pitifully small in comparison with learning of God. He would not tempt God; that is, bring upon his cause the inevitable wages of breaking the spiritual law. He realized that fame is not the road to progress. He was anxious to learn the will of God. Whether or not this brought fame, seemed insignificant. Can you imagine that the great scientists have been concerned with how much fame they might receive? The joy of achievement that comes from finding something new in the universe is by far their greatest joy. By comparison, fame seems a dilute and almost worthless form of pleasure. Here is a great research scientist who has won wide recognition for his work. Yet he is less famous by far than many a gangster. Indeed, he would probably scorn such fame. He is constantly discovering new things in his field. This is his reward. He knows how to fast; that is, to spend long years in preparation, and long hours in experimenting. He would not give one iota of his scientific integrity for any amount of fame. His is the abundant life. Such an attitude is possible only to him who has found love of achievement forcing him to fast. It is to men like this that God speaks, as He has spoken to such scientists during the last century. It is only when love of service dominates a man that he can learn of the spiritual laws in which love is the center. Few temptations are so great as the desire for fame. From its simplest forms in a youth who does things to gain the appreciative applause of his fellows, to the genius who is tempted to sell his soul for fame, this temptation destroys integrity, sincerity, and courage. If the worship of Christian fasting can overcome this temptation, it will have been indeed a source of power.

Even when a world empire was the promise of his tempter, Jesus turned his back upon it with ease and looked to spiritual empires. Jesus was willing even to die in obscurity and misunderstanding, as a criminal and a failure, because he was building for permanent power, not for a short-lived earthly kingdom. If fasting can make a man oblivious of hunger, fame, and power, it is obvious that he will be able to see more deeply into the nature of things. We see, then, why fasting is so important a part of worship, if through worship one is to come "into tune with the infinite." It gives one a sense of orientation, which places things according to their importance in the universe, not to the individual. Usually hunger, pain, fear, and anger seem vitally important to a person at the moment. He overestimates their significance, and is biased in his judgments by them. It is much easier to talk of keeping one's ideals in the face of suffering, when he is not losing his job and actually facing privation. A mother, however, can entirely forget her own comforts when considering those of her child. The man who has such an affection for humanity can look with calmness and self-forgetfulness upon the problems of the world. It is he who can fast with such complete devotion that he truly learns of God and His spiritual law.

When a man is as interested in mankind as a father is in his son, he will give alms. He will pour out both his material and his spiritual resources to help others. When his resources are exhausted and he finds himself fasting, he will become keenly aware of how much he needs a power greater than his own to help him in his efforts to serve men. When he has reached the point where his problems so deeply perplex him that he does not know where to turn next, then he will pray.

And when ye pray, ye shall not be as the hypocrites: for they love to stand and pray in the synagogues and in the corners of the streets, that they may be seen of men. Verily I say unto you, They have received their reward. But thou, when thou prayest, enter into thine inner chamber, and having shut thy door, pray to thy Father who is in secret, and thy Father who seeth in secret shall recompense thee. And in praying use not vain repetitions, as the Gentiles do: for they think that they shall be heard for their much speaking. Be not therefore like unto them: for your Father knoweth what things ye have need of, before ye ask Him.
—Matthew 6:5-8.

How to pray is a problem that is probably as old as the human mind. Some of us are brought up in religious homes, and are taught all of the customary prayers, from "Now I lay me down to sleep," to "Our Father which art in heaven." We listen with decorous respect to the best offerings of our various ministers on numerous occasions. Then we are suddenly faced with a critical need in the life of someone we love, and become painfully aware of our lack of resources to satisfy that need and our inability to pray. Then we too are willing to stand with the disciples and say, "Lord, teach us to pray."

The prayers of the Orient are much more numerous and common than they are with us. Whole populations have prayer periods daily. The audience that faced Jesus was not ignorant of the ordinary methods of prayer. Yet, it is probable that they listened to no section of the Sermon on the Mount with any more intense eagerness than this section on prayer. If any group of high school or college young people is given a choice of topics for discussion, no topic will exceed the problem of prayer in popularity. Even the most sceptical will be deeply interested. Whether one believes in prayer or not, deep in his heart he hopes that it is real.

One needs only to compare common types of prayer with some of those found in the Bible to realize that there is a wide range in the quality of praying. The petition to have an automobile, to pass an examination, to save one's life from disease, to bless the dime given for foreign missions that it may do a dollar's worth of good, to help our church and save China, are so different in quality from some of the prayers of the Bible, that the same name should not be applied to both of them. "Lord, be merciful to me a sinner," earnestly prayed the publican in the temple; "I will not let thee go, until thou bless me," said Jacob wrestling with the angel; "Thy will be done," prayed Jesus at Gethsemane. These make the former group shrivel into insignificance.

The motivations that lead men to pray are as numerous as the types of prayer. The child looks at God as a sort of super-Santa Claus, who will give him whatever he asks for. Some people never outgrow this childish attitude. Most adults pray from a sense of duty, with an element of superstitious faith that the very act of praying will protect them against some unforeseen harm. Others pray in order to seem to the world to be religious. Some have simply formed the habit of praying and go on automatically. Still others pray only when they are in trouble. Some use prayer as a form of auto-suggestion. The athlete says with gritted teeth, "God help me make this touchdown," when he is really not praying at all but making himself a morale lecture. Some pray when facing a task which overwhelms them with its magnitude and, feeling the great need of assistance, pray for it. Finally, some great souls seem to be intimately in contact with the infinite, and by their prayer reach into the resources of divinity for a strength which the rest of us do not understand.

The hypocrites are described as loving to stand in public places for their prayer. Jesus refers here to a practice of some religious men, who were anxious that the world should see their piety. There were certain prayer hours, as in most Oriental religions. These men took care that they should be on a busy corner or in a crowded synagogue when this hour arrived. Such individuals certainly are praying "to be seen of men." As has been said of almsgiving and fasting, they have a reward, such as it is. But it is of a very fickle and dubious sort.

"Enter into thine inner chamber." The inner chamber was the storeroom where the treasure was kept. "Where thy treasure is, there will thy heart be also." Public prayer may sometimes be as much in the inner chamber of the minister's heart, as if he were in the darkest cellar.

"Pray to thy Father who is in secret." Much has been said of the immanent presence of God. Oratory has been used to emphasize how completely God is everywhere and in everything. However, when we appeal to the experience of men and women, a very small percentage of them have ever actually felt His presence. To most of mankind, He is very much "in secret." Even to hundreds who have sought Him with all their hearts, He has not been found. Just as our sense organs are capable of receiving only a small percentage of the physical energy about us, so that we are blind to most of the light, deaf to most of the sound waves, and insensitive to most of the stimuli in all the sense fields; so human hearts are rare which are sensitive to the spiritual values in the universe.

"Use not vain repetitions." The word which is translated "vain repetitions" is the one from which we derive our word *stammering*. The stammerer uses vain repetitions. Notice that Jesus does not object to repetition, but to vain repetition. Effective prayer consists in wrestling with some problem of a spiritual nature. We may need to repeat it many hundreds of times before we are able to find a solution. Everyone who has tackled such problems in any field of knowledge is well aware of the necessity for perseverance. Nature does not reveal her laws easily. Jesus clearly pointed out the value of perseverance in prayer in several parables.

Profound prayer requires both persistence and an unwavering faith in the friendliness of the universe. The contrast between such prayer and vain repetition is like that between a student who studies long and hard to grasp a difficult principle in physics and a child who keeps on begging for some selfish request to be granted. Trying to gain an audience with God by simply saying, "Lord, Lord," does not insure an entrance into the kingdom of heaven. A passage in Ecclesiastes illustrates this principle. "A dream cometh with a multitude of business, and a fool's voice with a multitude of words."

Probably the child's earliest concept of God and prayer is the divine Santa Claus idea. The child asks for God's protection from harm and for such gifts as his heart desires. A little later he comes to have affections, first for his parents, and then for others. As these mature, his prayers broaden into petitions for his loved ones. This must be encouraged. Then he should be given the idea of actively assisting in the answer to his prayers. The next step is the beginning of an experimental faith. Doubt, of a type, is almost certain to arise in the intelligent child. One of the great mistakes that Christian parents often make in training children is in teaching them memorized prayers, and thus depriving them of the great rewards that should come from prayer. The Lord's Prayer may be memorized quickly by the young child. But it must be made to grow through the years, if the child is to grasp its full significance. Some individuals never rise above childhood levels, and utter meaningless liturgy or selfish petitions as their only form of prayer life.

The various sorts of prayer are accompanied by different rewards. A consideration of a few of these types will help us to distinguish between true and false prayer. There are, of course, some real hypocrites in religion. Men who, like the ones described by Jesus, pray in public with great pomp, and who do so for no reason except "to be seen of men." They are aware of this fact and are consciously trying to make an impression, and they get their reward. If they are clever, they may even produce a spirit of worship in the churches. They may win the confidence and admiration of men. This is a reward.

But by no manner of means are all prayers either hypocritical or true prayer. There are many earnest people who pray "to be seen of men," but who are totally unaware that they are doing so. They may, for example, have a type of inferiority complex, which makes them choose this method of bolstering up their influence, while they believe that they are really praying to God. This may be so satisfactory that they cease to be aware of their inferiority. Their reward is of the same sort that ether brings to a person in pain. They no longer suffer the pain, although they have done nothing to cure the inferiority feelings.

Then, there is a group of prayers which grow out of fear. When men are faced with a sudden danger, terror may strike their hearts, and some of them pray in a form of minor hysteria for protection from that danger. It is said that Dwight L. Moody used an experience of his own to illustrate answer to prayer. During a sea voyage, the ship on which he was sailing caught fire. While he was praying for God's help, the steam pipes burst and put out the fire. Such stories are common. It seems quite probable, however, that the effect of prayer on physical forces is unimportant. If men are saved from danger or recover from disease, they may ascribe it to answered prayer; there seems to be no evidence, however, that prayer has any effect upon the working of the natural laws. On the other hand, it is not at all uncommon for men to gain through such prayer a sense of security and faith which makes them able to face the danger with equanimity and dignity. This is a reward, and one that is not to be underestimated.

There are prayers of determination which are akin to these. Men faced with a test of skill, a game to be won, a battle to be fought, or some other testing time, may pray to God to help them win. Most nations believe that all their wars are righteous wars and that God will protect them. The victors are likely to consider their military success an evidence of God's favor. There is no evidence, however, that prayer in any objective way enhances their chance to win. It may give them the courage and confidence that they need in their struggle. This is their reward.

Next there are prayers of perplexity. When the publican said, "Be merciful to me," what he meant was, "Can you find a way of forgiveness for me?" Some men, praying for mercy, simply want a withholding of punishment; others, like this publican, want regeneration. When one faces a baffling problem, and has considered all of the available evidence, and still cannot determine between two courses of solution, he often prays for guidance. The vast number of wrong solutions which have followed sincere prayers indicates that this is no sure way of solving problems quickly. There is no evidence that God will in any supernatural way give the answer after the fashion of an oracle or a ouija board. On the other hand, such prayers impress upon us the poverty of our own ability at solution, and we are much more open to further evidence. In many cases of this sort there is a real danger. Many a man has prayed thus for the will of God, reached a conclusion, and been perfectly certain that it was an answer to prayer, only to discover later that it was a tragically wrong answer. The preacher who prays on Saturday night for the Holy Spirit to guide his preparation of a sermon for Sunday morning, will do well to be sceptical that the resultant manuscript is of divine quality. The solution of problems, however, is one of the legitimate causes for which prayer should be employed in great abundance. Such prayers, however, have to be of great length, often lasting over a long period of years. A young preacher just finishing his seminary work went into one of the graduate departments of science to work for a doctor's degree. The head of the science department said something to him which carries more significance than appears on the surface. "Young man, you had better stick to preaching. You can prove more in one sermon than you can prove in this laboratory in a hundred years." Such prayers may not be answered for many generations. The writer of the book of Job prayed for a solution to the problem of evil, but got no further than, "Though He slay me, yet will I trust in Him." This is also implied in a statement Jesus once made to his disciples. "Blessed are your eyes, for they see; and your ears, for they hear. For verily I say unto you, That many prophets and righteous men have desired to see the things which you see, and saw them not; and to hear the things which you hear, and heard them not." In the prayer for spiritual knowledge, as well as for knowledge of the physical laws, many years and generations have been required for the insights which have come to us by slow and painful degrees. Yet no one has gained one of these insights without the feeling of a source of power greater than himself.

This does not exhaust or even liberally sample the possible types of prayer. It does, however, give some notion of the rewards which one may expect from these various sorts of prayer. There are many who believe that since there is no intervention in the realm of physical law, there is no real value to prayer. Many a person has lost his religion because some prayer which represented his soul's deepest desire was apparently unanswered. He becomes cynical and hardened for the rest of his life.

There are a number of rewards of prayer which are much more worthwhile than supernatural interventions could possibly be. The man who lacks the power which can be found in genuine worship is poor indeed. There is a beautiful little memorial chapel on the shore of Lake Keuka in northern New York. A more inspiring spot could hardly be found. Yet, the crypt of this chapel has been closed to the public because some people had gone there to eat their picnic lunches. One cannot be angry with such people. He can only pity them.

When a man has a profound faith in a personal God, when he feels the tremendous need of spiritual values on earth, when he recognizes his own inadequacy in understanding those values, when he has dedicated his life to spiritual progress, he will come into a place of worship driven by the problems of life, and gain a sense of power and insight that literally fills his soul.

Prayer is a source of mental peace. Not the negative peace which dodges from one's troubles, but the peace which comes to him who can transcend the trials of his life, and meet them with courage and equanimity. This is not self-hypnosis. It is perfectly wholesome mental procedure. If one prays to the Father sincerely, it is because he has faith in Him. When psychologists set out to understand fear, they found that one of the most important factors in its control is a sense of dependence. This is natural. When the frightened child can place his hand in the hand of his mother or father, fear disappears. When a man driven by fear can come to the altar with a perfect faith in God, he can, through that sense of dependence, gain a courage which sends him back to his danger with that calmness of mind so necessary to efficient action. The mental mechanisms by which this takes place should be perfectly clear. Anger, the other great enemy of strong personality, which has such devastating effects in shriveling up our personalities, will also disappear at the altar, if we go there in a spirit of fatherly love. "If thy brother hath aught against thee; first be reconciled to thy brother, and then come" to the altar. This teaching of Jesus is neither a dutiful command nor an over-idealistic dream. Even Christian men and women sometimes lose their tempers. An examination of the causes of these losses of temper will usually reveal a narrow view of the situation. Like the child to whom the loss of an ice-cream cone seems for the moment to be a major tragedy, so we become angry at things almost as small. Someone hurts our feelings, or fails to recognize our importance, and we are angry. Such an anger occurs only because we are looking too closely at this isolated incident. However, if we have been trained in true worship, we can hardly approach the altar without becoming conscious of a much wider horizon. When we find ourselves in this larger world, our own small anger-filled situations shrivel into insignificance, and we are calm again. This is true even if the causes of our anger are of vital importance to us. Consider the mastery of fear which Jesus achieved at Gethsemane when he shifted his horizon from his own will to the will of God. There is nothing supernatural about this. Our own troubles always seem larger to us until we compare them to the troubles of the whole world. It is perfectly natural, then, that fears and angers and lusts shall cease to be effective when their stimuli dwindle into insignificance.

It is in this phase of worship that a man gains the courage to "pluck out an eye" or "cut off a hand" that "offends" him. Here is a man whose personality and training have led him to a position of moral leadership in his community. Other men look up to him for spiritual strength. Then he finds ignoble impulses in himself. He is attracted strongly to another man's wife. This is a battle which has torn many a man, including even the great Augustine. Let such a man go to whatever altar brings him closest to God, and try to think with God. Let him consider the responsibilities and opportunities for service which his position and personality have trusted to his care. Let him contemplate the price that will have to be paid in self-respect, happiness, and the faith that others have in him, if he gives in to his impulses. Then he will reorient his lust into its actual importance. Every man and every woman will find some such ignoble impulse in his or her life. There is no easy painless process for getting rid of it. It requires courage and self-discipline. But one who has learned the art of true worship will find in his Garden of Gethsemane a ministering angel in the form of strength to meet the test. True worship, then, gives us a sense of peace from the strife within us. We go out unafraid and forgiving. Such people have power.

This suggests the second reward that comes in true worship. Having overcome fear and anger, one grows in faith and love. Just as the fundamental attitudes described in the

Beatitudes are prerequisite to true prayer, so prayer in turn makes them deeper and more secure. They have been shown to be the foundations of personality. It requires no mysterious violation of spiritual laws for prayer to build personality. Religion has always taught that one can go to God in prayer for strength. Here are the very spiritual laws of God, which psychologically are seen to be also the laws of human personality by which that can be done. This is the second reward of the Father.

The third reward is perspective. As was implied in connection with anger, so is it true of the rest of our vision. We become so engrossed in our particular problems that we magnify them out of all proportion. They seem much more important than they really are. A college professor is tempted to think that his field and his course is the most important one in college, because he studies it so much more than everything else that he inevitably disorients it. For that matter, most individuals refer to their small jobs and their problems as if they were of universal importance. Then one comes to prayer. He has learned of God and His interest in all mankind and all times. One cannot meditate on such things without a reorientation of his own problems and a much wider perspective upon things as they are. If he has a great faith in God, this will permeate his thinking on his own problems. If he has a fatherly love, his whole attitude toward his own life will be altered in terms of it. It is small wonder that such men make the great steps in human progress. It is less wonder that they seem totally unconcerned with their own difficulties. They have been looking at mountains, and molehills seem insignificant.

Perhaps the noblest motive that calls men to prayer is the desire to learn more of God. In science, men accumulate great quantities of data carefully described. Then they try to make it tell them something of the nature of the world. They wrestle with it in a meditation that is like, and indeed almost is, a form of prayer. Their reward comes if they gain the insight which they so much desire. The man who comes to prayer desiring to know more about the spiritual laws, if he is wise, comes with as much data as he can gather together on spiritual problems, and then, like Jacob, wrestles with them until they bless him. It may well be asked, why does one need to pray to God? Why should he not simply meditate about them as the scientist does? If the scientist starts looking for the answer to his problem with the wrong mental set, he usually comes to the wrong answer unless he is very open-minded. (By mental set we refer to the fundamental principles by which one interprets his data.) Here is a scientist who, in an effort to demonstrate the validity of a certain scientific theory, made a large number of measurements of a certain phenomenon in nature. In commenting on the results he said that they were worthless, that they did not mean anything. What really was the case was that they did not fit the theory he was determined to prove. Another scientist without this bias could have seen a great deal of meaning in his data. In the spiritual realm, men have often approached the throne of God with the wrong mental sets and have come away with the wrong answers. Thus, men have believed in the righteousness of wars, on both sides. Many doctrines have been taught which have since proved to be wrong. One will always have some mental set. It is important that he have the right one. A young scientist is trained in scientific reasoning. Scientific reasoning consists in the mental sets which have been found necessary to good scientific theory. The most important one that the scientist has is that the universe is lawful. One of the important mental sets that one must have if he is to gain insight into the spiritual law is that the universe is friendly, fatherly. Furthermore, God must have the attributes which Jesus ascribed to Him. It is no accident that the advance of psychology has everywhere shown the validity of Jesus' teachings. Hypotheses which have been opposed to Jesus' teachings have regularly been discarded when further evidence was obtained. It is because Jesus gave the right hypotheses or mental sets upon which the spiritual law must be built. Just as no greater happiness comes to the scientist than to gain a new insight into the laws of nature, so no greater joy can come to the spiritual scientist than to learn more of God.

Here then, are the great rewards of prayer: peacefulness of soul that raises men above fear and anger, growth in strength and wholesomeness of personality, perspective in the solution of life's problems, insight into the spiritual nature of the universe. This may not be an exhaustive list, but beside it the rewards of other sorts of prayer dwindle into insignificance. The church is no true steward of its sources of power if it forces its youth into an insincere quiet, while it mumbles a few liturgical phrases and calls it worship. It will become a tremendous influence in the life of its youth if it teaches them to pray. As Dr. Fosdick puts it:

> To you, therefore, who are going out to preach, I say, Make men believe in miracle. But do it by leading them into the experience of God's power in their own lives now. Teach them so to find conversion, direction, commission in their fellowship with God, so to explore the possibilities of prayer, so to believe in God's providence for a willing nation and an obedient world, that they will find their minds at home when in other terms than theirs the Bible presents them with the same experiences. Never let the mechanistic philosophy imprison your mind. Keep the doors of hope and expectancy open. Above all, believe in the living God until you see him, in ways surprising in your eyes, working out his will for you and for the world.[2]

The most interesting thing of all is that it can be done. It is perfectly practical. Any child can be taught the attitudes of the Beatitudes. Any child can be taught to worship so that he will gain these rewards. He may not climb the entire ladder of them because his native endowments of intelligence may not permit that, but he can gain some of them.

Here then, is Jesus' teaching on worship as a psychologist

[2] Fosdick, H. E., *Modern Use of the Bible*, 167. The Macmillan Company, 1924.

sees it. No theological implications have been considered. Even without them the rewards of worship of this sort are tremendous. If his faith is of the experimental kind, one will make every fact of his experience, sufferings as well as joys, contribute to his understanding of God. He will have complete faith that whatever happens is the will of a fatherly God, which awaits the spiritual scientist to discover it. This prayer will carry with it the reward of peace of soul, courage and magnanimity, strength of character and personality, perspective of vision, and insight into the very nature of God. With such a prospect before them it is little wonder that the disciples asked Jesus to teach them to pray.

Chapter VII

CREATIVE THINKING

No one can converse very successfully with another person who does not understand his language. One will find it hard to master the intricacies of a science who does not know how to study it. It is difficult to accomplish any important purpose without a good plan of action. Listen to the average discussions of a social group spending an evening together. The trend of the conversation will go from one thing to another for the whole evening. Most of the immediate problems of the universe and of one's own home town will come up for learned pronouncement. When an end has come, determined by the clock and not the conversation, a good time may have been had by all, but probably nothing new will have been added to the present store of knowledge. If college classes were run on this principle, very little would be accomplished toward the education of the class. Much prayer is like that: miscellaneous, pious, platitudinal, thoughtless, or selfish; and people wonder why they get nothing of value from it.

Consider what the true worshipper is asking, and then it will be clear why it is so hard to pray. If he has advanced beyond the Santa Claus stage of prayer he will be asking for the secrets of transforming personality, for insight into the nature of the kingdom of heaven, and for knowledge of how this kingdom can be brought about on earth. These are far-reaching requests. By their very nature they require time and patient striving after answers, and sometimes long suffering over many generations. Just as the scientist must know how to interpret his data, so the spiritual scientist must know how to pray. The Lord's Prayer is far more than a liturgical poem. It is a road to spiritual power which every Christian must learn to travel.

When one goes about changing his personality, it is not so simple as just a decision to be a different man in the future. Here is a boy on the road to mental disease. He promises his father repeatedly that he will turn over a new leaf in certain respects. Each time he tries but fails. Paul must have become aware of the same baffling weakness when he said: "The good which I would I do not: but the evil which I would not, that I practice. Wretched man that I am! who shall deliver me out of the body of this death? I thank God through Jesus Christ our Lord." Most men have experienced times when they were utterly disgusted with themselves, because they had no strength to do the things they knew to be right or to resist the evil of fear and anger, hate and suspicion. Some men have even committed suicide because they found no source of strength great enough to deliver them out of the "body of this death."

Paul said that Jesus was his deliverer. To many of us, that explanation may seem somewhat mystical. We want to know just what this means in everyday life. If the average minister is consulted, his answer is likely to be that the source of power is found in prayer. Indeed it is, but how? Not everyone who pours out his soul in fervent petition is helped. If prayer is to be a source of power, we must know how to pray. The Lord's Prayer is Jesus' answer to that.

In order that we may better understand the significance of this great prayer, let us recall the psychological mechanisms which are available for changing personality, and then see if these mechanisms are implied in the Lord's Prayer.

It has been pointed out that personality is changed very little, if at all, by logical reasoning. Paul's statement quoted above would never have been written if reasoning were sufficient. One of the older notions of education was based upon the assumption that all sin is ignorance. An educated population, therefore, would be entirely good. That this is fallacious is evident to anyone who has struggled without success to even approach being the best he knows how. One can reason with a group of men until every member of the group is convinced that his behavior is undesirable; but this does not guarantee that he will change his behavior, or even be able to do so if he wants to. Reason is, of course, a valuable criterion in our choice of ethical standards. It is very little help in living up to them.

The futility of a disintegrating emotional appeal has also been emphasized. Who has not found himself, led on by the emotional fervor of some experience, making a pledge which he regretted the next day and broke soon after? Under strong emotional strain almost anything can be wrung from the average person. Every religious organization is familiar with the man who pledges himself during a revival period to great Christian effort, only to slump into indifference shortly after the work begins. Many a drunkard, impressed by the sight of his suffering family, has sworn off liquor, only to find himself drunk again in the near future. Such emotional appeals fail because the emotion disappears. When other emotions become dominant, the first one is lost sight of. The appeal to shame or ridicule is a very effective motivation. Its effect, however, is repression and a less healthy personality. It can never be used to bring about desirable changes in the personality.

Two methods, however, are effective in bringing about a permanent and healthy change in our personalities. The first one is what the psychologist describes as *reconditioning*. The other one is called *identification*. When the whole emotional set of a situation can be changed, so that a stimulus which once brought out an undesirable response is attached to another response, then a real change has been wrought. This is reconditioning. Can we, by praying the Lord's Prayer, bring about such changes in ourselves? Identification, which is really a form of reconditioning, is effective whenever the influence of another personality which we have come to admire has its results in our lives. We are very likely to adopt, not only the mannerisms and habits, but also some of the philosophy and ideals of someone whom we greatly admire. Can the Lord's Prayer bring about this sort of change in us?

It should be obvious, then, that to pray the Lord's Prayer cannot be confined to the mere repetition of its words, as if they were some magic formula which, by the very force of the words themselves, does something. If one is to use it as a form of worship which will effect a change in him, he must be conscious of its meaning, throw himself into its spirit, and think himself into its problems.

It has been pointed out that true worship consists in discovering and applying the spiritual laws to the problems about which we are praying. Furthermore, prayer must be in the spirit of the Christian attitudes. One will not gain an insight into the spiritual law who is not "poor in spirit." One can hardly hope to gain a message from a fatherly God, who does not live the meaning of, "Happy are they that mourn." On the other hand, the ideal prayer should be able to help one become more "poor in spirit" and make one more sensitive to the needs of his fellow men. It must have that source of strength if it is to be the true prayer.

After this manner therefore pray ye.—Matthew 6:9.

This prayer, which is the most famous one in history, consists of sixty-four words, forty-nine of which are of one syllable. It can be said in thirty seconds. It is simple enough to have meaning for a seven-year-old child. Its complete interpretation will challenge the intelligence of the profoundest minds. It can be prayed by Hindhu, Mohammedan, or Buddhist, as well as Christians and Jews. It indicates the attitudes one must have in prayer and the things for which one should pray. When one reads it thoughtfully, he wonders how Christians fit many of their ordinary prayers into this pattern. It sounds very little like our prayers of profuse thanks and selfish petitions.

It requires depth of character and a highly integrated personality to pray it with sincerity. Almost any flaw in one's character makes some part of it impossible to pray. If we are angry we find it difficult to say, "Forgive as we forgive." When our greed is dominant in our thoughts we are dubious about the simple petition, "Give us this day our daily bread." When we let our pride induce in us race prejudice, class distinctions, or national conceit, we cannot say, "Our Father" with much enthusiasm. If the world seems to be against us and things are not going our way we find it difficult to pray, "Thy will be done." As our religion cools from its first enthusiasm there is little meaning in our petition, "Hallowed be Thy name." This may seem discouraging, but if we are to solve spiritual problems we must satisfy all the necessary conditions. If we cannot, our prayer has little value for that purpose. Less perfect prayer may have some value. Jesus admitted that it did. It is only to be pointed out that if we expect our prayer to tap the greatest possible resources of power, it is necessary to be able to pray this prayer with sincerity, understanding, and conviction.

The prayer has been divided in various ways. For the purposes of this psychological study it will be considered in six sections. In the first section of the prayer man approaches the Divine. He does so by recognizing the nature of God, and the significant power of that nature. This immediately gives the worshipper a point of view from which to solve his problems. Any other hypothesis than fatherliness in the spiritual realm would fail of success, because the spiritual universe has as its most powerful attribute, fatherliness. Following this, comes the overwhelming determination to make this power available to the world, as it is in heaven. The third section portrays the spirit of meekness in all of the strength of that attitude. Then follows the description of divine forgiveness, the full significance of which is one of the most tremendous concepts in the teachings of Jesus. The fifth section is an intelligent dedication of oneself to God's work, recognizing one's own shortcomings and the power of evil. The last section is a statement of faith.

Where is God? What is His nature? These have been problems in the minds of men for many generations. Jesus teaches that if one is to gain God's help in prayer he must start with a knowledge of His nature. Jesus' hypothesis is the simplest and yet the most profound that has yet been suggested.

Our Father who art in heaven, Hallowed be Thy name.—Matthew 6:9.

Jesus called Him Father. Any follower of Moses would have been horrified at the prospect of having Jehovah for a father. But Jesus based his whole religion on the assumption that the universe is fatherly. The Christian must act on this assumption. To whatever extent he loses his faith in the fatherliness of things, to that extent he ceases to be a Christian.

We are not concerned with the philosophical problem of the nature of God, but with the results of this concept in personality. In other words, if we live under the assumption that God is a father, what will be the result in mental health and social adjustment? When the Jews were taught to believe in a national God who would lead them to victory over all other nations, hate for other nations was the inevitable result in behavior. Hate in the minds of men is psychologically unhealthy. This is sufficient to disprove this concept, psychologically. Following Jesus' teaching of "Our Father" we should find ourselves brothers and sisters of all mankind. In this, the motivation is love, which is productive of mental health. This is pragmatic proof of its validity.

Then there are the atheistic concepts of God, which conceive of the universe as utterly impersonal. As Harry Emerson Fosdick puts it:

Haeckel says that there is no God—only "mobile, cosmic ether." Imagine a congregation of people, under Haeckel's leadership, rising to pray, "O Mobile Cosmic Ether, blessed be thy name!" It is absurd. Unless God is personal, the deepest meanings of gratitude in human hearts for life and its benedictions have no proper place in the universe.[1]

Furthermore, such a concept of God will inevitably lead to fear and pessimism. One of the most famous lawyers of our day, an atheist, looking back on life advises youth to "chuck it all as soon as possible." This is not mentally healthy. No concept of God so contributes to the development of strong personality as that of Jesus.

Note that Jesus said "our" Father not "my" Father. It requires little knowledge of Jesus to know who would be included in "our." His beautiful parable of the Good Samaritan, his treatment of the woman of the Samaritans whom the Jews were taught to hate, the great command for loving enemies, convince us that he would include every living person in "our." When we read the other teachings of Jesus on fatherhood we realize how much is involved in this statement.

We have talked much of the brotherhood of man. To most of us it has been a beautiful thought carrying very little serious conviction with it. The same man can talk of brotherhood on Sunday and hate his enemy and despise his inferior on Monday. Such a man cannot, with sincerity, pray even the first two words of the Lord's Prayer. Yet, if we examine the growth of society, the formation of communities, the development of nations, the extension of commerce, the gradual progress toward international peace, we shall see that a workable attitude of genuine interest in others is one of the spiritual laws of the universe and a necessary essential to any advance in civilization. If human brotherhood is to be anything more than a set of words, which men say with their lips but forget in their hearts, they will have to develop the attitude implied in the words "Our Father." This means that one is not prepared to pray until he has a fatherlike spirit in his heart for all nations and all classes of men.

[1] Fosdick, H. E., *The Meaning of Faith*, 54. Association Press, 1921.

Not many men have contributed to our knowledge of the spiritual law. It requires a growth of soul which only a few men have attained. Yet here is a source of power which, if utilized, may become the possession of any man. By what process can this kind of a brotherhood be developed? Many brothers are too jealous of each other to sacrifice themselves for each other. Yet when we do find men willing to sacrifice themselves for others, how powerful it is. Who has not at some time in his life been righteously indignant at the behavior of some man who has cheated and lied and stolen and wrought physical injury. It is probable that our attitude toward him is far from resembling any sort of love. If we meet his mother, however, she tells us of her love for him. She pleads for our help in making him a better man. That simple experience transforms our whole attitude toward him. We now see him, not as an enemy, but as the son of his mother. We immediately seek to discover ways of helping him. Our own anger and even our own interests dwindle into insignificance. Observe what has happened. We have learned a fatherly type of love for the man, and it is fatherly love that "suffereth long, and is kind."

Now we see the value of the mental attitude implied in the first two words of the Lord's Prayer. We approach our problems with the assumption that the power which governs the universe is fatherly. If one makes this assumption with all his heart, it will strongly influence his attitudes both toward himself and toward others. If he has faith that the universe is fatherly, it will follow that he is being treated as a good father would treat his son. Things that seemed fearful and hateful are viewed in a new light. He will examine them more closely for their potential values, which his faith assures him are there. Then, if the universe is fatherly, all men are of great value, as children are to their parents. Sin, crime, and injustice will then arouse pity and sorrow for those who commit them, not fear and anger. Our desire will be to reform the sinner, not to avenge the sin. Is this attitude rational? At least it is mentally and socially healthy.

"Who art in heaven." The word translated "heaven" is actually plural, "in the heavens." It certainly does not refer to some place beyond the sky. Dr. Harry Lathrop Reed has suggested that heaven is "the realm of the highest." In our worship, then, we are contemplating the fact that heaven, the noblest characteristic of which is fatherliness, is the highest possible condition of the spiritual universe.

In everyday speech we use the term *heaven* in two ways. One refers to the theological concept of some mysterious place, as usually described, rather dull and monotonous, certainly not very thrilling. Also we use the term as the description of any place or condition in which we are supremely happy. It is this last use of the word that Jesus taught, rather than the former. Imagine a world in which fatherliness is the prevailing spirit being anything except the very picture of happiness; not the rather empty happiness which is only the lack of suffering, sorrow, or hardship, but the more dynamic happiness of achievement.

"Hallowed be Thy name" is also involved in this relationship between the worshipper and God. The word "hallowed" has lost its meaning to most of us. A majority of us are about as intelligent as to what it signifies as the little boy who said that it refers to the fact that God is hollow like a spirit. "Sacred be Thy name" would be a better translation, or "Revered be Thy name."

The Jews placed much more emphasis upon a name than we do. They gave names that had special meaning. If the character of the individual did not accord with that name, they changed it. The cases of changing Simon to Peter and of Saul to Paul are instances of this custom. Therefore, when such a wish as "Hallowed be Thy name" was uttered in prayer, it was full of significance. To them the name of God was tremendously important. Furthermore, a son could disgrace his father's name. A father was held responsible for his son. The best way in which the son could hallow the name of his father was to become a fine character himself. To the Jew then, this petition would not connote merely a sort of good wish for the Father, but a consecration of his own life as well, in order that he might honor the Father's name.

Here then, is the first of the six teachings involved in the Lord's Prayer. With whatever problems one comes to the place of worship, his first task is to think in terms of the true nature of God. When one considers himself the son of God and God the Father of all mankind, when he has confidence that fatherliness is the spiritual principle which must govern all our social adjustments, when he has faith that the Father loves all men and desires their happiness, then and only then will these problems assume their proper perspective. With this feeling before him he will approach their solution without fear and with love in his heart. This is the first mental set which must characterize the problem solving of the spiritual scientist; namely, that the universe is fatherly.

It is not always easy to accept the will of God, even when it is known. Each of us faces times when the spiritual values are perfectly clear, but other values tempt us powerfully. All of our desires and all of our happiness seem to lie in the opposite direction. It is hard not to let our own wishes govern our thinking. It is necessary to gain the right mental set with which to compensate for our biases. This mental set is involved in the next petition.

Thy kingdom come. Thy will be done on earth, as it is in heaven.—Matthew 6:10.

"Thy will" is the religious equivalent of "spiritual law." "Heaven" is where it is practiced. If this world is to be a part of the kingdom of heaven, it must practice the spiritual law. This petition, then, is that men shall learn and practice the spiritual law here.

The accusation that because God made man in His own image, man has been returning the compliment ever since, is true for the man who cannot pray this petition. One's values, joys, hopes, and ambitions are his heaven. Many a scientist has missed discovering some important things in the natural world, because he was biased ahead of time as to what he wanted to find. He was not willing to discover the world as it actually is. We think with our biases. We need to consider carefully whether or not we are able to pray earnestly this section of the prayer. Not my will be done, not my notion of the kingdom, but Thy will and Thy kingdom come. This is the attitude of meekness.

Obviously, it is not possible to do the will of anyone until it has been discovered what that will is. How great a number of Christians pray with deep piety for God's will to be done, and then refuse to spend any time at all finding out what it is. The doctor spends many years learning the principles of medicine. The lawyer spends as long a period mastering his profession. Even the contract bridge devotee spends hours in study and practice perfecting his avocation. But the church member spends a pitifully short time trying to understand what Jesus taught.

It is all very well to bemoan this fact, and urge a renewal of interest on the part of church people. Unfortunately, this does not solve the problem. Merely to persuade men that they ought to do something has at most only a temporary effect. There is some reason why this state of affairs exists, and this must be remedied before conditions can be changed. The young medical student looks ahead to his reward. He sees it and finds it worth working and sacrificing for. The same may be said of the lawyer. Even the contract bridge devotee sees social approval and popularity, the joy of victory and the thrill of competition. But what is there in the program of the church to challenge the youth to study? Give the child a vision of a real kingdom. Let him see something of the great needs which face this world, that the spirit of Christ can best solve. The spirit of Christ can be used instead of war in international relations. The spirit of Christ can bring light instead of ignorance, healing to the sick, and happiness where there is sorrow, strength of character where there is wasted life, and strength and wholesomeness of personality where there is weakness and morbidness. Suppose the youth of the church were being constantly faced with these problems, and challenged to find their solution; then the prayer "Thy kingdom come" would become the dominant desire of their lives. Then men would study to know the will of God.

When one meets a triumphant soul with a brilliant vision of a better world and the power of the sacrificial love of Christianity, one can see how challenging and absorbing a vision of the kingdom can be. Men need vision to make this part of their prayer one of reality, challenging them to thought and achievement. When such visions are taught to children, they will never tire of praying, "Thy kingdom come."

Here, then, is the second guiding principle for the correct solution of spiritual problems; namely, using the will of God as the conscious criterion of value. This may seem like nothing more than common sense. Actually, it is very significant. In the first place, one must be aware as far as possible of his own biases, or his prayer is likely to become a mere petition for selfish desires, and a dangerous rationalization to deceive himself into believing that all of his own behavior is right. In the next place, he must be "poor in spirit." If he "thanks God that he is not as other men," he will be much less likely to overcome his own prejudices. Thirdly, he must think about his spiritual problems always with the objective attitude, "What is the will of God?" No one can pray this petition who does not study the spiritual teachings of Jesus thoroughly. Finally, one must be prepared to make many self-sacrifices. Even Jesus at Gethsemane found his own will opposed to what he knew to be the will of God. Perhaps it will be clearer now how impossible it is just to meditate on spiritual problems without praying at all. Many brilliant men have written whole philosophies of life which were manifestly projections of their own desires. They do not contribute much to our knowledge of spiritual problems.

CREATIVE THINKING 203

With the spirit in mind in which spiritual problems are to be solved, and the goal to be obtained before us, we can proceed with some assurance of gaining insight into our problems. Here is a man whose heart is filled with fear; fear that seems hopelessly justified in reality, and for which there seems no escape. He wants to pray to God for delivery from this unhappiness in which he lives. Here is another who finds himself burning with anger at some great injustice done him or his loved ones. The spirit of revenge rankles in his heart, and shrivels his soul. How shall he solve his problem in prayer? Another finds himself unable to live up to the best he knows. His feeling of an utter lack of manhood makes him desperate in his prayer. There seems no escape from these things in life. Let us see whether God can answer prayer which is motivated by desire for security, revenge, and power.

Give us this day our daily bread.—Matthew 6:11.

When we consider our multitudinous desires for luxuries, pleasures, and wealth, which we usually include in our requests to a God who is said to be distributing blessings in great abundance, we may well look with some misgivings upon this petition. When we are laying away "something for a rainy day," and also a few sunshiny days by way of good measure, it seems nothing less than shortsightedness to ask only for enough to eat for one day. What of tomorrow? Of course we might pray again, but experience has made us a bit dubious of material answers to prayer. Only the most superficial study of this petition would ever result in such a narrow interpretation. Let us examine it more closely.

In the first place, notice that the second word is "us," not "me." Nor must it be imagined that this is a case of editorial "us." Nor is it a sort of liturgical "us" such as ministers might use when representing a sleeping congregation before the Lord. If one prays this petition sincerely, it is because others have an important place in his innermost heart. Then he can pray meaningfully, "Give us." If he has the mental set of a fatherly universe, involved in the first two words of the prayer, "us" will include all mankind. If he has been able to pray, "Thy will be done," he will not be dogmatic as to just what constitutes "bread." It is not possible to solve spiritual problems with a selfish wish, with the rest of mankind left out, even if it be so small a wish as for just enough bread for the day. Many of the people who complain most bitterly about political graft, official corruption, and governmental inefficiency vote for a congressman only on the basis of the narrow desires of their own community. Fundamentally, such evils as well as most international misunderstandings are a result of the attitude that says, "Give *me my* daily bread." There is nothing surprising about the presence of these evils. They are inevitable. We are certainly not likely to solve our social, political, and spiritual problems until we can sincerely pray, "Give *us* this day *our* daily bread." The universe spiritually is made up that way. We can no more solve spiritual problems on any other basis, than in physics we can repeal the laws of gravitation. When we consider these facts, interpretations of this verse which suggest that Jesus wants us to be irresponsible and take no intelligent forethought for the morrow, are obviously small and beneath the level of Jesus' teaching.

Furthermore, as we come to know Jesus better, we begin to doubt whether the term "bread" is confined to the ordinary material food that goes by that name. He is frequently talking of bread of which most individuals know nothing. "Every word that proceedeth from the mouth of God" is spoken of as if it too were spiritual bread. Spiritual bread, then, is as much a part of our needs as material bread. "Give us this day our daily bread" must be a request for knowledge of the spiritual law as well as for actual food. This is a petition that we be given a part in the great task of making "His kingdom come and His will be done on earth." Many of us, not appreciating the breadth of this vision, may not be very "poor in spirit," or see the responsibility involved. A Sunday school teacher with a half-dozen boys under his charge has a weight of responsibility on his heart, which would tax the spiritual wealth of a prophet. Only one who is thoughtless and spiritually anemic dares to assume this responsibility without fear and trembling, lest he become a stumbling-block in their paths. Experience makes us increasingly humble about our tasks. It is easy for a youth to visualize a better world. For example, who has not contemplated what would happen if all people and nations practiced the Golden Rule? It is easy enough to set forth panaceas by which the whole world can be transformed quickly. Experience, however, and a more profound knowledge of the problems involved make us much more humble, and we look for some less ambitious problem which will contribute, however slightly, to human happiness. Apparently, then, this need of bread refers to the poor, whether in spirit or in body. Most of us do not need to pray for material bread. We have plenty and too much. Not many of us, however, are overburdened with spiritual bread.

Another thought is involved in this petition. A little later in the sermon, Jesus urges that we shall "Take no thought for the morrow, about what we shall eat or wear." This is a challenge to our faith. Many people have believed that the request for daily bread is a simple petition to be fed. Actually, what is behind it is the assumption that the one who prays is devoting his whole life to the service of the will of God with the confidence that His will is just. Suppose one does not get bread; suppose he starves in God's service. Shall he then believe that God has not heard and answered his prayer? This petition implies that he believes that whatever happens is the will of God, and is his just portion of bread for the day. "Though He slay me, yet will I trust in Him." Many a man suffers trouble, the value of which seems doubtful to him at the moment, only to discover later that he is much richer for it. Many a man dies for his cause and leaves the world enriched by his life. Consider the prophets who have suffered and died for righteousness' sake.

Did they not get their daily bread? "Give us this day our daily bread," whether in the form of nourishment for our bodies, food for our souls, or spiritual opportunities to make the world more like heaven, can hardly be so naïve a petition as some would make it.

The world often seems cruel. Most of us are born with obvious lacks in our native equipment. We may have bodies that are not beautiful, homes that are not comfortable, social inheritance that makes our manners crude and our habits little short of vulgar. We may be trained in a temperament that is unattractive. We may be men with effeminate inheritance, or women whose native characteristics are strikingly masculine. We may lack all of the special aptitudes with which to compensate. We may not be naturally athletic, nor good at painting or music, nor given to wit and humor. We may seem to have nothing to commend us. The unattractive girl is permitted to remain a wall flower, while her beautiful sister is very popular. The effeminate boy is hazed and tormented by his big "he-man" fellows, until his life is sheer torture. The world is not kind. It ridicules us, bullies us, taunts us, persecutes us, or worst of all totally neglects us. It is little wonder that we grow up with timid souls, with inferiority complexes that weaken us, fears that fill our lives with terror, bitter angers and hatreds that shrivel our souls, or unattainable lusts for the things we crave so much. To satisfy all these rebellious urges and appetites Jesus suggests that we pray, "Give us this day our daily bread." At first glance it seems utterly inadequate. But let us search for the spiritual strength which underlies it.

Who prays for bread? Obviously, the poor. The wealthy have all the bread they want. They feel no need to pray for it. Then, who will pray for spiritual bread? Again the answer is, the poor in spirit. It is only the poor in spirit who gain the kingdom of heaven. It may be that the very handicaps which we bemoan so much are sources of strength, if they make us poor in spirit. It is probable that the least endowed men contribute more to the spiritual law than men with great native endowment. This is the reason why suffering is so essential to the development of strong character; because only those who suffer become aware of their poverty of spirit, and truly pray. Perhaps the greatest handicap the church has to meet is the lack of poverty of spirit.

This petition implies a faith in divine providence. Divine providence does not signify that God purposely plans every experience that befalls us. But it is true that, since the spiritual law is always working, we can use every one of these experiences, however painful, to learn something new about the spiritual law. Necessity is the mother of invention in this realm as well as in any other. Unfortunate is the man whose life flows along so undisturbed that he feels no need of help. He has no chance to get daily spiritual bread. When we pray, "Give us this day our daily bread," we may even be praying for starvation or suffering or even death; for in such experiences does the world advance spiritually.

Will this form of prayer, then, get rid of our fears and angers? Can we be happy even if the world remains just as cruel and we just as handicapped? The answer now seems obvious. We approach the altar feeling that these handicaps are sources of fear and anger, but there we learn to see them as sources of spiritual power. When we can regard persecution as a source of strength, we are not likely to greatly fear it any longer. This is reconditioning. It is getting rid of the destructive forces of personality, and replacing them with strength. No one can doubt that the man who not only is unafraid of persecution, but actually turns it into a source of great blessing, has strength of character which will force other men to admire him.

When one is bemoaning his own suffering, let him recall the example of Jesus, and see him as he met his cross with the response, "Father, forgive them, for they know not what they do." This is indeed an inspiration. He will find himself filled with pride at the great personality of his leader. This is identification, the other method of changing personality.

Thus we see why the inspiring example of Jesus has contributed so much to the spiritual progress of men and institutions.

The training in the attitudes which underlie this petition is not easy. For sharing our bread with others there is ample opportunity, but seldom the correct training. Too many parents try to teach their children the habit of sharing by forcing them actually to give part of whatever they have to others, without regard to what emotional tone is attached to this behavior. The only effective training for sharing is to bring about situations in which the child will naturally take the attitude of, "Give us this day our daily bread."

When we have thus turned any defeat into a victory, we have received abundant answer to our prayer for daily bread. It is not always easy. Here are two parents who have lost their only son in a tragedy. They have given their whole lives to him for twenty years. With him gone, life seems empty to them. Happy are they if they can pray, "Give us this day our daily bread." The more baffling and difficult the problem, the greater and more significant the answer. These parents may come from this prayer understanding a little better the nature of God, and the breaking of His law which caused the loss of their son. They may make the spirit of their son live on in some other boy. They may, by their own lives of increased depth and understanding, bring the world a little bit closer to the kingdom, so that other such tragedies shall be impossible. When they have won such a victory, these parents will know that God has not "given them a stone when they asked for bread."

If one has gained a vision of his task in the spiritual progress of mankind, he is prepared to do creative thinking; that is, to learn a little bit more about the spiritual law. If we observe the contributions which have been made to natural science, we find that one important element in scientific discovery is intelligence. Not everyone could have made the brilliant discoveries of Galileo, Newton, and Darwin. There is no reason to believe that great spiritual insights require any less intelligence than the natural law. This does not mean that those less highly endowed can do nothing of creative value. It is true, however, that the extent of one's insight is limited by his intelligence. If we turn to psychology we find that while inheritance sets the top limit to one's intelligence, there are many ways of lowering that limit, or more technically speaking, of contracting the field of consciousness. The most common agent in the destruction of intelligence is the emergency emotion. When a man is struck with terror or seized with rage, he cannot think clearly. He says that he has "lost his head." That is literally true, he cannot do creative thinking during a temper tantrum. Many a brilliant mind has been blind to great visions because of his emotions. When we consider this fact, we begin to understand why the forgiving spirit is so necessary to spiritual progress.

And forgive us our debts, as we forgive our debtors. For if ye forgive men their trespasses, your heavenly Father will also forgive you: But if ye forgive not men their trespasses, neither will your Father forgive your trespasses.—Matthew 6:12, 14-15.

Each new vision of the kingdom of heaven makes us more aware of our own poverty of spirit, and we naturally pray, "Forgive us our debts." Probably every man who has wasted his opportunities in school has come later to the realization of how foolish this has been. No experience is so revealing of one's own shortcomings as a careful study of the teachings of Jesus. One may be pretty well satisfied with himself, but a close study of the Gospels will soon make him able to pray with deep sincerity, "Forgive us our debts." Then there are those lusts over which we seem to have so little control. All of us face temptations when something seems immensely attractive to us, which we know to be destructive of our own happiness and often of that of many others about us. As we view this weakness and the social responsibility that is ours, we become painfully conscious of how far short of our spiritual capacity we have fallen. We feel the need of forgiveness.

"Forgive us" comes to be the most earnest petition of the whole prayer when we have compared ourselves to God. God has endowed us with talents; some of us with many, some of us with few. Most of us have used them for selfish purposes. We have buried them in the earth of lust, where they cannot grow. We have brains, strength, physical attractiveness, talents in art and literature, powerful emotional urges—all sources of dynamic power. We use them to bring us pleasures, comforts, power, fame, popularity. If all of these talents were integrated into one all-consuming purpose centered around love of our fellow man, we could do great things toward mastering the spiritual law. Letting any one of the emotional urges act apart from the whole produces spiritual loss and is fatal to strong personality. We have talents but we sell them for a "mess of pottage." We let them one by one rule us in selfish desires. Thus we lust after gold, security, revenge, sexual satisfaction, and many other desires, and thus dissociate some of our greatest talents from our total personality and reduce them to the level of lust. These are only a few of the "debts" for which we need forgiveness.

It will be recalled that in discussing the Beatitude of mercy, forgiveness was described as regeneration. Asking God to forgive us is to petition not for a mere cancelling of our sins, but for regeneration to spiritual power. When the church sold indulgences, which one might buy to cancel out his sin without any effort on his part to become better, the process of penance became a bargain counter, where for a stipulated price one bought the privilege of sinning as much as he pleased. Forgiveness for which we pray here, is of a very different sort. It means, "Give us the capacity for insight into our spiritual and social problems. Help us to use all our capacities, to harness all our native urges, and to solve our problems in the Christian way."

How are we to obtain this sort of forgiveness? We must not answer this question by quoting some theological doctrine such as "God's mercy endureth forever." We must find spiritual and psychological laws by which this transformation is accomplished. When Jesus described the method of obtaining Divine forgiveness he said, "As we forgive our debtors." That is, we must take this same spirit of regenerative love toward others. Our own forgiveness is brought about in forgiving others. This calls up three questions in our minds. Who are indebted to us? How do we go about forgiving them? And why does this help in our own forgiveness? It is very easy for us to recognize our own debts to God. It requires little spiritual insight for us to discover how much we fail of achieving all the things for which our talents make us responsible. But who owes us any such debts? We may recall a few people who have done us minor injuries or even more serious ones, but certainly not in any such magnitude as the debts we owe to God.

To answer this let us turn again to psychology. Everyone knows that emotions have a strong tendency to beget themselves in other individuals. If a man hates another, it is pretty hard for the other not to return the feeling. When others are angry with us, we are very likely to repay anger with anger. When others persecute us, we want to fight back. It is a rare soul who can take persecution, ridicule, reviling, and gossip, without feeling his blood boil and a great desire to get revenge. If someone becomes terrified in a fire, a whole crowd may go into a panic. This is true for all of the emergency emotions. Such emotions are disintegrating factors in personality. When a man by his behavior forces me to become angry, or afraid, or lustful in any other way, he tears down my personality and weakens my character. He is my debtor.

But how shall I go about forgiving him? Love also begets love and faith begets faith. It is difficult to remain angry with one who loves you. A soft answer does turn away wrath. If my neighbor makes me angry by being angry himself, he is "missing the mark" and weakening his own personality, for anger is a disintegrating factor. How shall I forgive him, that is, regenerate him? Obviously, if he is to grow in personality, his anger must be changed to love. What part can I play in that? I can return love for anger; for love begets love, and his anger will be softened and thereby his personality strengthened. This is forgiveness which is regeneration. Quite apart from anything beyond the bounds of our normal mental processes, we can see this principle working without any outside influence. Let us summarize this point. Anger is a disintegrating factor. Love is the only emotion about which strong personality can be built. An emotion begets itself in another. If anger is responded to with anger, both parties grow weaker in character and personality. If either returns love for anger he strengthens himself, and if his love begets love in the other he also strengthens the personality of the other. This is forgiving our debtors; that is, returning to those who would make us weaker, a response that makes both us and them stronger. It was said of Henry Ward Beecher that the easiest way to get affection from him was to do him an injury, for he never rested then until he could do something good in retaliation. In this way he changed many men from lives of meanness of soul to lives of power and love.

If this process is so simple, why pray about it? Why not simply set out on a policy of returning good for evil? The answer is, that this is impossible. Anger begets anger, and if one is to return it with love he must get that love from some source. Love is not the sort of thing that can be acquired by just deciding to adopt it. Praying for forgiveness is asking for the love of God. When one contemplates the love of God, he becomes conscious of its greatness, and finds it generating in him a responsive emotion and a desire to be like Him.

Does this idea of getting love from God seem rather mystical and out of touch with our known mental and spiritual laws? Let us recall a former illustration. Here is a man who is unjust to us, who does us great injury, and who hates us. Our natural response is anger. But we meet his mother. She tells us of her love, and hopes, and fears for him. Almost at once he is seen in a new light, not as an enemy but as his mother's son. We actually come to love him. In the future, if he tries our patience severely, we need only to think again of that mother. Now let us apply this to prayer. If our prayer is contemplation of a loving Father, we shall find that in just the same way our anger and fear for other men is being replaced by faith and love. It can be seen that this is exactly what will happen mentally if one learns to pray this petition in this spirit.

What man can come to know Jesus well, sense the warmth of his love, and not return that love? When we think of his twelve disciples at the Last Supper bickering about which would be greatest, we are angry with them. But far from losing his patience with them, Jesus washed their feet. Our hearts thrill before such transcendent love. It was a much humbler group of disciples after this loving ministration to them. And as their selfish pride descended, their spiritual power increased. When we are discouraged or find ourselves impatient and angry at the attitude of those whom we are trying to help, we can contemplate the stature of Jesus. Our strength is renewed, and we are able once more to forgive those who trespass against us. In this very act we strengthen our own character as well. This is the process of identification at work again. The church has made one of its major errors in picturing Jesus as a teacher of negative ethics, and failing to inspire its youth with a picture of his heroic qualities. Hero worship is founded on inherited characteristics of the individual. Failing to use it where there is such abundant possibility is criminal negligence in religious education.

As we look at our own shortcomings, we are aware that they are the results either of ignorance or of weakness. When Jesus surveyed the group of his crucifiers, he was aware that most of them were perfectly sincere in their action. They thought that his death would put an end to his heresies. On the contrary, persecution has regularly brought life not death to any doctrine. The persistence of the doctrine is its own vindication. Hence, Jesus said, "Father, forgive them, for they know not what they do." The stimulus which might justly have been followed by a sense of injustice and anger, is followed by the same attitude which one would take toward children; namely, the desire to help them. The power of such a retaliation is evident. It is said that the centurion at the crucifixion was impressed by the attitude of Jesus. He would not have been impressed with anger. When nations learn and use this method of retaliation, then we shall have really invincible nations.

This insight into the psychology of forgiveness gives us a comprehension of another very important principle; namely, the principle of vicarious sacrifice. Recognizing the power of vicarious sacrifice, we have often wondered why it is that advance in civilization is brought about only through persecution and suffering. The answer is clear. Advancement in civilization can come only through the development of strong personalities and high characters in mankind. This involves returning love for anger and faith for fear.

We owe it to God to use all of our talents in His service. We need forgiveness whenever we do not. However, this is not meant to imply, as has been frequently done, that God is a commercial banker who lends us talents and demands their return to Him with interest for His enrichment. Jesus made this clear when he presented his great Judgment scene. He accuses those on the left hand of not having ministered unto him on various occasions of his need. In perplexity they asked when they had ever seen the Lord in trouble. Jesus' answer was, "Inasmuch as ye did it not to one of the least of these, ye did it not to me." This is no esoteric theological process. It is a living human principle. Our debt to God is paid in service to our fellow men. Disregarding theological implications, we can easily see that this is a spiritual law. When we have returned good for evil in love, we receive the reward in our own growth of character.

The law of vicarious sacrifice is clearly a part of the spiritual law. But it is not instinctive. Our inherited appetites call for many things but not for self-sacrifice. Yet in this law is the secret of the perfectly integrated personality. But always there are the natural appetites which will demand other sorts of rewards than are found in crosses and burdens. However strong a man becomes sometimes he finds himself face to face with temptation, which requires every fiber of his being to resist. However, if he has been trained in the spiritual laws, it takes a stronger and stronger force to become a temptation to him. That which is temptation for the child is no trial at all for the adult. Likewise, that which is temptation for a man who has not learned to control his appetites, will seem unattractive to the Christian. But to every man there will come trials which seem too great for him to bear, and he will be impelled to pray.

And lead us not into temptation, but deliver us from evil.—Matthew 6:13.

Again we face the danger of rationalization. Who has not found himself face to face with a strong desire which at first seemed wrong, only to discover that scores of good excuses for the desired behavior were coming into his mind? Our reason is like that. One of its most exercised habits is finding excuses for doing what we want to do.

The difficulty with temptation is that it comes when one is unprepared for it, and usually comes in disguise. This is almost a definition; for if one is prepared for it, it is not temptation. We are not tempted while under the inspiring influence of some fine worship service. During our mountain-top experiences we are filled with power. The danger comes when, in the bustle and worry of everyday life, we are suddenly faced with some unrighteous desire. Here is where strength is most needed. How can one find in prayer the power that will strengthen him later? That it can be done, is seen in the experience of Jesus in the Garden of Gethsemane. He was looking forward with sorrow to the dangers that were before him. He prayed for strength to meet them. He did not cease praying until he had found that strength. Three times he prayed before he finally found it. But having gained it, there is no indication that his courage failed him in the face of his terrible suffering. In prayer he had found the strength he needed.

In Jesus' teachings two kinds of temptation are mentioned. The first is to use one's abilities for wrong purposes. This is exemplified in the life of Jesus in the three temptations in the wilderness, and by the disciples on the occasion when Jesus washed their feet. A life dominated by this desire is certain to be filled with lust, anger, and suspicion. Such a purpose inevitably defeats its own ends; for these attitudes can lead to neither happiness nor strong personality. The second one is the temptation to become discouraged or frightened, and to give up in one's life work. This is exemplified in Jesus' prayer at Gethsemane, and the admonition to the disciples to watch and pray lest they enter into temptation. People are so sensitive to any effort to change them that they resent the efforts of reformers. Their maddening indifference to the needs of the world and narrow selfishness in their own pleasures are certainly causes for "righteous indignation." But anger neither solves the problems of society nor secures the happiness of the individual. It is a temptation. One, then, is the temptation to take the instinctive desires of our nature, which in their crude form crave pleasure and comforts, and let them rule our lives and prevent us from living by the spiritual laws. This use of one's abilities is evil, even when perfectly good rationalizations can be offered for such behavior, such as those which Satan suggested to Jesus in the wilderness. The second type refers to the disintegrating emotional attitudes, especially fear and anger, which would make us forget our purpose and would themselves gain domination over us. When Jesus was arrested Peter showed these negative traits. At first he became angry and cut off the ear of a high priest's servant. He demonstrated fear when at the trial he denied Jesus with oaths. Peter indeed needed to pray lest he enter into temptation.

Such temptations do try a man. Peter was tried and on this occasion found wanting, but he could have met a lesser temptation with great ease, to which most of us would have fallen. This one was too much for him. His spiritual power was not yet strong enough. Fear and anger still played dominating rôles in his personality. However, behold him some time later when he faced the same court. The Sanhedrin commanded him to discontinue preaching about Jesus, threatening him with dire punishment if he did. Peter's answer contrasts strikingly with his weakness at Jesus' trial. "Whether it be right to harken unto you more than unto God, judge ye. For we cannot but speak the things which we have seen and heard." Peter had finally let the love of Jesus transform his personality until fear and anger were completely dominated by that love.

It is to be noted that the first word in this verse is "lead." The meaning of this petition will be found in this prayer, "Lead us. But recognizing how poor in spirit we are, and how far we are from having perfected the strength of our personalities, do not give us tasks we cannot perform, nor trials we cannot meet." Many a youth is not strong enough to refuse a large salary for faith in what he believes to be the right task for him. Others with a great vision before them, are tempted by positions which bring fame and honor.

How shall we meet these temptations? It is all too common an experience to make all sorts of good resolutions, only to break them in time of temptation. This prayer then is not one of mere self-suggestion. Psychologically, if one is to cease making an undesirable response to any particular situation, he will have to bring it about that the situation brings out some other response. Can we do this for temptation? Obviously, temptation is really a spiritual problem. To gain strength to meet it consists in reorienting the tempting situation. For example, many things seem vitally important until one considers them in the wider perspective of the universe. Many dangers seem terrifying until one thinks of them in a fatherly universe. Praying this petition, then, does not consist in giving oneself a morale lecture, but orienting the environment in terms of God's will.

The second part of this petition is a prayer that we shall continue to grow in spiritual power. We are weak and may have temptations which are far too strong for us. Yet we recognize that if we are to help deliver the world from evil, we will have to meet temptation. As we compare our own weakness with the vision of service that is before us, we need to pray for strength against temptation and strength to do our share in solving the problems that are given us. This petition against temptation and for deliverance from evil might almost be the prayer of Jesus at Gethsemane. "If it be possible, let this cup pass from me." This was like the prayer against temptation. "Nevertheless, not my will, but thine, be done," is the spirit of, "Deliver us from evil."

This petition brings out clearly the need of the right orientation for creative thinking. Many a man with all the capacity and training for solving the world's problems is confined to the narrow realm of his own wishes and troubles. One must remember that whatever his problems, he must avoid the temptation to solve them as a rationalization of his own wishes. If he is to contribute toward delivering the world from evil, he must be led only by the ideals of the Master.

Here then is our confession of weakness, and a prayer for strength, which we can have if we let love become more and more the dominating drive of our lives. If the great temptation is fear, the great evil is anger. "Deliver us from evil," if it is to be through the power of love, must gain its momentum from the overcoming of anger.

The most important source of temptation is the apparent power of evil. When we look about us, military strength and material wealth seem to be "the kingdom and the power." Evil seems so attractive, pleasure the very basis of happiness, all our angers examples of righteous indignation, our suspicions justified and the basis for a prudent preparedness. Security seems to rest in obtaining material resources which are greater than any possible opposing strength. Probably a vast majority, even of those who are professing Christians, are very doubtful as to whether it can be said of the Christian method that here is "the kingdom and the power and the glory."

This final section of the prayer is a renewal of our faith in the Christian method. When we look at the apparent weakness of love, the persecution which follows integrity, and the ingratitude which follows serving, we are likely to become doubtful of the Christian method. Yet it is true that fatherly love is the greatest force in the world. It is the strongest in the production of personality, and the most effective in the solution of social problems.

For Thine is the kingdom and the power, and the glory, forever. Amen.—Matthew 6:13.

Most scholars believe that this is a later addition to the Lord's Prayer. If this is true, whoever added it had learned much about Jesus, for it is representative of his spirit. Most of us are inclined to believe that a kingdom can best be built by conquests, large armies and navies, a considerable gold reserve, and a well-developed nationalistic spirit among its citizens. To say that the only kingdom is found in the practice of these spiritual laws requires a tremendous change in our ordinary modes of thought. Certainly, even the most Christian of nations still prefer to have prosperity in material things, than to advance civilization through vicarious sacrifice.

Power seems to most men to rest in money. "Money talks" and "every man has his price." Many of our wealthy men imagine that they rule our nation, and for that matter the world, because they are wealthy. As long as wealth is the basis for our definition of power, we can hardly call ourselves Christians, who should recognize love as the greatest and only power there is.

Glory is usually looked for by a majority of us in victories and applause. The laurels of a "crown of thorns" are two thousand years in the past for us. To die in poverty and disgrace is hardly our definition of glory. We want fame and honor among men. So much so is this true, that we commonly pick our life work on the basis of such criteria of achievement.

It should be clear that "Thine" really means, "Thy method." This petition is not simply an enthusiastic approval of whatever triumphs one has, whether in the attainment of wealth, fame, or power. It is much more a final test of the correctness of the solution we have obtained to our spiritual problems. We have been trying to determine what the answer to them is. We have reached a decision. Is it correct? Only if it is according to "God's method." There too, the solution may not seem to be filled with kingdoms and power and glory. Certainly, an unbiased observer would hardly have thought so at the crucifixion. It often does require a very deep-lying faith to face such a situation, still certain that, "Thine is the kingdom and the power and the glory forever." But the reason for prayer is to know the will of God. We are not likely to discover that will unless we have faith in it. If our faith is in these other things, our prayers will not unfold the mysteries of the spiritual law. This statement of faith simply implies that in the effort to solve our social problems, we shall not even consider these other sources of power and glory. We start with the assumption that the Christian method is right, and try to discover how that method can be applied to these problems. Only by this method can we hope to do creative thinking.

Chapter VIII

THE CHAOS OF FEAR

More than half a century ago a housekeeper, in the absence of a five-year-old boy's parents, sought to punish him effectually for a childish naughtiness of which she believed him guilty. She shut the little one up in a room at the top of the house, and told him he must live on bread and water until he confessed to having committed the misdemeanor of which she accused him. Unable to pretend a guilt that was not his, the little fellow lived alone in the third floor room for three days, when his parents unexpectedly returned home. In his sixtieth year the boy, now an old man, had a serious illness during which he became delirious. He constantly implored his nurse to go with him up to the attic. Finally while she was out for exercise he persuaded his fifteen-year-old daughter to accompany him to the attic. Here he sat on a chest weeping, signed to the daughter to be perfectly quiet and whispered, "They told me to come. They told me to come." He stayed in the attic, listening for outside sounds, weeping and softly moaning, "They told me to come," until his daughter prevailed on him to return to his bed lest the nurse find out that he had left it. During the rest of that day and on the next day the sick man tried unceasingly to get someone to go with him to the attic. He must go, he said, but he dared not go alone. While watching by his bedside during the night his eldest son heard the father say, "They wouldn't come near me. Nobody came. I listened and listened. Three days and three nights. A little room. All alone. Nobody came." [1]

Who can estimate how much unhappiness and how much loss of power was caused in the entire life of this man by this one cruel act of torture on the part of an ignorant housekeeper? No enemy of mankind has caused so much misery

[1] Groves, E. R., *Personality and Social Adjustment*, 93. Longmans, Green and Co., 1931.

as fear. Even anger with its devastating destruction of personality does not make its victims as unhappy as fear does.

When some instinctive drive is thwarted, usually either fear or anger results. The situation which produced the thwarting may thereafter be a conditioned stimulus for one of these emotions, whether the original instinctive drive is present or not. The average adult has scores of such situations to which he responds with fear. Every one of them diminishes his potential power of character and personality. Each one of them causes him more or less mental anguish every time it occurs.

This thwarting of instinctive urges is one form of mental conflict, which has been described as the chief source of mental disease. Fear, then, is simply an expression of conflict. When conflicts occur, a number of things result. In the first place, these conflicts always weaken personality because mental drives neutralize one another instead of combining their forces toward one end. A convincing demonstration of this is found in many common responses to fear. Everyone has felt his knees give way under him with fear or has been "rooted to the spot." The reason for these forms of behavior is that fear brings about a loss of coördination through the conflict of impulses. Thus, if one suddenly meets a bear in the woods, he may not know what to do.

For, upon the sight of the bear, he tends simultaneously to yell, to climb a tree, to run away, to throw a stone, to grasp a club, and what not. All of these impulses seek motor expression, get jammed in the process, and the result is a state of discoördination.[2]

This illustrates beautifully the effect of this emotion both upon motor behavior and upon the mental mechanisms.

These conflicts with their resultant disintegrative effects upon the personality are even more serious when we are not aware of them. This happens when we thrust them out of consciousness. This process is called by the term *dissocia-*

[2] From Howard, D. T., "A Functional Theory of the Emotions." In *The Wittenberg Symposium on Feelings and Emotions.* Clark University Press, 1928, p. 143.

tion. No emotional desire can be put out of the mental life, but it can be repressed into unconscious behavior where its effects will not be consciously recognized, but will be none the less maladjustive. Such a repressed fear is called a *phobia*. Consider the following case which is typical of phobias.

A young woman of good heredity developed during her childhood a severe phobia of running water. She was unable to give any explanation of her disorder, which persisted without noticeable improvement from approximately her seventh to her twentieth year. Her fear of splashing sounds was especially intense. For instance, it was necessary for her to be in a distant part of the house when the bathtub was being filled for her bath, and during the early years it often required the combined efforts of three members of the family to secure a satisfactory washing. She always struggled violently and screamed. During one school session a drinking-fountain was in the hall outside her classroom. If the children of the school made much noise drinking, she became very frightened, actually fainting on one occasion. When she rode on trains, it was necessary to keep the window curtain down so that she might not see the streams over which the train passed. (Whence this phobia?) The mother, the aunt, and the little girl—she was seven years old at the time—had gone on a picnic. Late in the afternoon, the mother decided to return home but the child insisted on being permitted to stay a while longer with her aunt. This was promptly arranged on the child's promise to be strictly obedient and the two friends went into the woods for a walk. A short time later the little girl, neglecting her agreement, ran off alone. When she was finally found she was lying wedged among the rocks of a small stream with a waterfall pouring down over her head. She was screaming with terror. They proceeded immediately to a farm house where the wet clothes were dried, but, even after this, the child continued to express great alarm lest her mother should learn of her disobedience. However, her aunt reassured her with the promise, "I will never tell." So at last they returned home and to bed. As the older woman left the next morning for a distant city, the girl had no one in whom she could confide. On the contrary she repressed all thought of her accident and presently she was unable to recall the facts even when a serious effort was made to have her do so. (The fear remained in the form of a phobia for running water.)[3]

[3] Bagby, E., *The Psychology of Personality*, 44-46. Henry Holt and Company, 1928.

No one who is unacquainted with the vast multitudes of phobias and obsessions which torment people can imagine the unhappiness which results from these unconscious fears. It is probable that there was a time in the history of the race when fear was necessary for self-preservation. A little fear does make one physically stronger in a crisis. And if there is one definite response to be made, such as running from danger, it will increase the chances of escape. However, in our modern life such occasions are seldom experienced. On all other occasions dissociation occurs, and fear is disruptive of the highest adjustment. Of course, this does not mean that one should never experience any apprehension about his behavior. The nervousness which public speakers feel before they address an audience is actually productive of a better speech. But a genuine fear of an audience only drives what they have to say out of their minds. This is certainly not helpful. The same principle holds for every important undertaking in life. Cautious planning and concentrated effort are invaluable but fear is not.

Fears may be of many varieties. They may be the constant characteristic of our behavior. The timid soul who is afraid of almost everything is a most common and miserable reality. They may occur only in times of crises, such as Peter's fear which made him deny Jesus even after his many brave assertions of a few hours before. Furthermore, fears may be of many degrees of consciousness. We may be afraid of snakes and know that we are. We may have phobias which are conscious, but the causes of them are totally unknown. Then there is behavior which the psychologist recognizes as caused by fear, whereas the patient is not aware that he is afraid at all. Being "yellow" on the athletic field, being sensitive, irritable, or conceited, are examples of such unconscious fears. To understand the extensive nature of fear, we must grasp more carefully the meaning of another important psychological concept.

The last few years of popularized Freudianism has made the term *complex* a household word. Many people talk of complexes, are afraid of them, or are intrigued by them; but very few know what they are. The widespread notion that complexes are like overgrown germs, which live in some damp sub-cellar of the mind ready to spring forth and devour us when we open the cellar door, is far from true.

Increasing evidence convinces psychologists that there is no such thing as unemotional or unbiased thinking. Every mental reaction, however cold and rational it may seem on the surface, will be found to have its roots in some emotional core. Of course, not all of these emotional habits are conscious. For convenience, we may classify them into three groups.

The first group consists of our conscious attitudes, which include our convictions, our loyalties, and our allegiances. We are loyal to our family and to our country. We give allegiance to the flag. We believe in the creed of our own church. All of these are conscious attitudes founded on powerful emotions, but often very far from being rational. Then there are subconscious attitudes of which we are not so much aware, but on the basis of which we make many decisions. These are at the bottom of most of our tastes. We like this thing and not that. But just why we have these preferences is rarely conscious in our minds and can be correctly analyzed only with considerable difficulty. Finally, there are unconscious attitudes, or complexes. By unconscious attitudes we mean those emotional cores which are not acceptable to our conscious minds and which we therefore repress. They govern our thinking and behavior more completely than the conscious attitudes, but in unrecognized forms. Fear attitudes may be of all three types. They are disintegrative in any case, but especially so when unconscious. The case previously cited of fear of running water is an illustration. There was a conscious fear, but the important factor was an unconscious fear of an entirely different thing.

Religion has not always been free from fear. Indeed, some of the worst crimes for which the church is responsible are crimes of filling young lives with fear. When an evangelist draws vivid pictures of a burning hell and brings a group of young children quivering with fear to the altar, he does them irreparable damage from which they may not recover throughout life. Here is the confession of a young woman suffering from a nervous breakdown, which was essentially fear.

> Fear has been a predominant element in my illness. Theoretically I would not have admitted that my God was preëminently a God to be feared and held in terror but all my practices were based upon that idea and I was ever afraid of offending and dishonoring Him; all my ceremonials partook of this fear and my whole life was pervaded by a sense of terror. Most distinct among my early experiences and impressions is this fear in the form of an ever present dread of death, which possessed me powerfully at the age of eight and thereafter, so that I was filled with dread anticipation as day drew to its close and lay awake in secret terror when night had actually come. This fear was with me all the years of my illness with also other manifestations of it, fear of injury in play, terror of rocks falling upon me, of being buried alive, of drowning, of any experience of being smothered, excessive fear of snakes, all these closely connected with the fear of death and the hereafter.[4]

Fear is involved in every complex, because fear is the underlying cause of all repressions. Repression, it will be recalled, is the result of attaching shame or guilt to certain behavior. Shame is simply one form of fear. The "boys don't cry" philosophy is really making the boy afraid to be afraid. This means that the original fear is repressed out of consciousness and replaced by a disguised fear which is much worse. The boy who is always bragging about his physical achievements is an example of this repressed fear. Another example is seen in the fighter who is often referred to as the "bantam rooster type." He is always ready to be offended and to fight for his rights. Usually he is small of stature.

[4] Jelliffe, S. E., and X. Z., "Compulsion Neurosis and Primitive Culture," *Psychoanalytic Review:* 1, Oct. 1914. 384.
Quoted from Groves, E. R., *Personality and Social Adjustment*, 87. Longmans, Green and Co., 1931.

This is one cause of his pugnacity. Actually, he is afraid of being afraid.

Fear complexes express themselves in so many ways that it is impossible to list them all. The panics which occur in crises are indications of the tremendous number of people who are potentially fear personalities. Watch a crowd destroy itself in a theater fire. Watch men disgrace themselves in terror on a sinking ship. Observe the terrified crowd before a bank which is undergoing a run. Consider the presence of fear in such a time as the last economic depression. Is it any wonder that Jesus described fear as one of the major sins of humanity?

Here, then, are these hidden drives which we have pushed out of our conscious thinking. They are lost to our voluntary control, and color all our behavior. The boy on the athletic field whom we call "yellow" finds it impossible to throw himself wholly into the play. He draws back imperceptibly from violent physical contacts. The term "yellow" has come to have a connotation among boys which is indeed unfortunate for him to whom it is applied. But how did he become that way? Is he consciously afraid? Seldom ever. It is a complex. When he was a young child his parents probably filled him with scores of fears. They warned him not to fall down the stairs and hurt himself, not to cut himself with the butcher knife, not to burn himself with the matches, not to fall in the water and get drowned. His fear-filled life moves along fairly satisfactorily until he becomes old enough to dread the accusations of cowardice. Then he realizes he must not be afraid. He determines that he will not be afraid. It is here that he begins to repress his fear. Later he goes out for athletics not aware of any fear at all, but these imperceptible bits of behavior in his athletic activities show that the fears have only been repressed and are still exerting their power over his behavior. These complexes include in their number some of the most powerful motives that rule us, all the more dangerous because they are unrecognized and unrecognizable.

It must not be implied that all of our unconscious behavior is undesirable. It is not. It is only these complexes which are formed around repressed motives that are maladjustive. Many a person represses his sex drive until the power of that urge is lost to achievement, and acts only to make the individual queer, abnormal, and ineffective socially. It is fear in the form of shame or guilt which brings about sex repression. Freud has assigned the source of most maladjustment to sex. When one meets a large number of maladjusted individuals, he does find sex playing an important part in a majority of cases. But it is not so much sex as the thwarting of sex which leads to the maladjustment, and this is fear.

Here is a case which will typify many people. Miss X. age 50. She considers herself a "shut-in." She always feels too exhausted and will not trust herself to leave her home. She is usually depressed, has "brain-fag," and self-occupation whenever she is visited. Active in the church, she has decided that she is not getting a "square deal" there, and has expressed a desire to leave it. She has always been obsessed with a fear of death, and that it may come when no one is around. No one familiar with personality difficulties will fail to see the presence of sex in this. But it will also be observed that the cure is not in sex, which is now beyond its stage of potency, but in fear, which has grown out of it. This is the most common story behind inferiority complexes. Indeed, the "conscience that makes cowards of us all" is fundamentally fear. Much that we recognize as conscience is only an abnormal expression of a morbid complex.

When one considers the extensive use that is made of fear in society, he shudders at the wholesale destruction of happiness and character. Jealousy is fear. Think of the toll of pain it alone causes. Whole nations try to terrify their enemies into submission and their own people into patriotism. Some mothers scare their children into being good, especially by the use of shame. Law tries to bring about order through intimidation. When the fears which come from the frustration of the natural appetites are added to these, the total

THE CHAOS OF FEAR

is staggering. Every whit of it, every jot and tittle takes its toll in human personality. And "not one jot or tittle" is lost to the individual until it has come to its inevitable fruition. Let him who wonders what miracles could possibly be wrought in the mental realm, to compare with those that have come from natural science, consider what the social results would be, if fear could be overcome.

Has Christianity anything with which to combat this enemy of mankind? If it has, the church has at its disposal a greater source of power than it has yet employed. One will examine the words of Jesus in vain to find any teaching approving of the use of fear for making people good. On the contrary, Jesus not only taught that fear is sin, but laid down principles which are psychologically valid for overcoming fear in men. Let us examine those of his teachings that have significance for the problem of fear.

Again recall the case of the girl who was afraid of running water. Actually, she was not afraid of running water, but of what running water represented in her mind. The phobia did not disappear until it was discovered just what this running water did stand for. Sometimes such an unconscious fear will arise which is compensated for, not by a phobia, but by a seemingly satisfactory protection. In this case the individual will attach a type of love to the protecting element. The love of money is an example of this. Actually, money has no value in itself, and certainly is not an adequate stimulus for affection. Any thrill or affection that one experiences for money must be a conditioned response. When this is a real conscious emotion of love for money, it is based on the subconscious fear of insecurity and deprivation. When a nation is economically deficient, this is described as a crisis and a type of war. All this leads to fear. This fear in connection with money carries over into industry. Working men are afraid of losing their jobs, or of not getting their share of the incoming wealth. Capital is afraid of bankruptcy. These two fears are at the basis of most of the trouble between capital and labor. Money being the most commonly worshipped god, it is not surprising that Jesus began his teachings about fear on this point.

> Lay not up for yourselves treasures upon earth, where moth and rust doth corrupt, and where thieves break through and steal: But lay up for yourselves treasures in heaven, where neither moth nor rust doth corrupt, and where thieves do not break through nor steal: For where your treasure is, there will your heart be also.—Matthew 6:19-21.

When Paul said that love of money is the root of all evil he was probably as wrong as Freud is when he insists that sex is the root of all evil. However, no one can deny that love of money has caused much suffering in the world. We need only to consider the fact that almost every war from the earliest times has been caused by the desire for wealth, to realize to what extremes of depravity money leads men and nations. Wealth has served some men, enslaved others, and worried most of us no little bit. Men who have purposes which have loving service as their emotional tone, have found money a source of greater power and increased opportunity for service. Others, however, have fear as the underlying motivation of their lives. To them, money comes to be the most important value in the world. They are desperately afraid to be without it.

If it is suggested that selfishness not fear is the motivation of wealth seeking, it need only be asked what the emotional tone of selfishness is. In most selfishness, fear is a dominant element. It is curious to note how often the acquisition of wealth makes people afraid. Here is a woman who scrubbed floors for a living for many years. During this period she gave liberally to the church. Then she married a wealthy man. After that her gifts were few, small, and difficult to secure. She suddenly had become afraid to lose her money. Fear now dominated her giving.

It is interesting to remember that despite the fact that this sermon was addressed largely to poor men, Jesus dwelt upon the dangers of wealth. Money can be as great a peril to the poor as to the rich. Men have faith in money, then, as the source for dispelling fear. But Jesus points out that it has no lasting qualities. It is always in danger of disappearing. Hence, anyone who bases his whole life on money will also live in constant fear of its loss. Quite apart from any ethical consideration, it is impossible to build a strong personality around faith in money, because by its very nature fear is involved.

"Not on earth but in heaven." What is the distinction between them? Rather carelessly many have believed that any acquiring of money on earth is "laying up treasures on earth." Any charity is "laying up treasures in heaven." Jesus, however, defines the term "earth" as wherever "moth" and "rust" and "thieves" bring about destruction. "Heaven" is defined here as where there are permanent values; implying that heavenly things are infinite. In another passage he tells the rich young ruler who has great possessions "to sell all he has and give to the poor." Then he shall have "treasure in heaven." Why should selling all that he had give the rich young ruler "treasure in heaven"? There are those who believe that giving to the poor, in itself, is building up a sort of celestial bank account. Without considering the theological implications of this assumption, which are outside the realm of this study, let us see what the result would be in his own life. The very answer he made to Jesus indicated that he placed great faith in his wealth. He believed that Jesus had the secret of salvation, but his faith in money was so great and his fear of poverty so deep-seated, that he could not follow Jesus' advice.

Wealth in itself is not evil. In only this one instance did Jesus urge the abolishing of wealth. Jesus said that Zaccheus was saved, when he had given a much smaller proportion of his wealth. Still others became disciples, in connection with whom wealth was not mentioned. Therefore, it is obviously not money, but the emotional value attached to money, that determines its effect on personality. Jesus did not say that it is impossible to acquire great wealth and be a Christian.

In fact, he says very clearly that it is possible. But he does say that it is difficult. "It is easier for a camel to go through the eye of a needle, than for a rich man to enter into the kingdom of God."

There is some evidence that the fear of the loss of money is usually stronger than the fear of serious disease. To lose one's job quite frequently causes actual mental disease because of fear. The same sort of fear is back of the belief in immortality in the minds of many people. Even a superficial survey of their behavior shows that they have no positive desire for life after death, at least not enough to make death attractive. This explanation is probably not true for all belief in immortality, but it certainly is true for the more unhealthy varieties of it. Whatever protects man from fear he treasures, and has faith in.

In the stock market crash of 1929, many men lost all that they possessed. At first they thought that life had been deprived of all its meaning. Some even killed themselves, because they were so desperately afraid to be without money. A number of them, however, discovered a deep sense of relief when the first shock was over. More than one have said that they would never again become such slaves to money.

Observe in passing, another striking thing about Jesus' dealing with the rich young ruler; namely, that he did not appeal to shame and guilt. Rather he pointed out higher levels of achievement. This is characteristic of his dealing with men. He was quick to discourage false pride and conceit when men began to think of themselves too highly, but in no case did he appeal to shame, not even with the adulterers. This is especially significant now that psychology recognizes so well the mental dangers which the use of these motivations incurs.

The fear of poverty, or as it usually appears, love of money, is so common that it is sometimes thought to be instinctive. Actually, it would be utterly impossible to inherit such a fear. There may be some stimuli to which the child does respond instinctively with fear. However, they are very

THE CHAOS OF FEAR

few and simple, and fear of poverty is not one of them. It has to be learned. The child quickly acquires the fears of his parents, for fear begets fear. A case history will demonstrate the mechanism involved.

The mother of a little girl, age eleven months, was in constant fear lest her child be bitten or otherwise molested by dogs, the truth being, that she herself was very much afraid of dogs. For this reason the child had had no experience with dogs until one day, while playing on the lawn, a big collie approached, seemed friendly, and not at all averse to the hesitant pats of the child. Interest, not fear, was engendered by this shaggy-haired stranger. Their little tête-à-tête had not progressed far, however, when the mother appeared on the scene. With a scream she rushed in upon them, gesturing frantically at the dog which was not slow to make his departure. Her screams and violent reactions not only scared off the dog but thoroughly frightened the child. Henceforth, she could not be approached by a dog without an evident show of fear. What is more, she could not even be induced to play with her pet rabbits, whose fur coats apparently served to remind her of the dog.[5]

Exactly the same methods are used, perhaps in less dramatic form, in learning to fear poverty. Fear must not be confused with caution. For example, every child must learn to be cautious in crossing streets, to avoid automobiles. But to teach a child to be afraid of the automobiles is likely to bring about frantic and totally maladjustive behavior, defeating its own purpose. Caution in the matter of wealth is not fear of poverty. It is not the man who uses money, but the man who worships money who has the weak personality.

Two other types of "treasures" are often made the sources of fear. One is health and the other sex. Both are perfectly desirable and wholesome, but not to be made so important that fears are built up around them.

The constant terror of germs in which some parents seem to live, often engenders in a child so irrational a fear of disease that when he is sick his personality goes to pieces, and his whole body reacts with fear. This includes the cessa-

[5] Lund, F. H., *Emotions of Men*, 101. Whittlesey House, 1930.

tion of all digestive processes, the over-stimulation of the heart, and many other physiological effects, which decrease his resistance to the disease and put him in much graver danger than if he had not become afraid. When epidemics occur and whole populations become afraid of the disease, it is very doubtful as to which causes more cases, the germs or the fear. Health is very desirable, but when it is made one of the things without which one simply cannot be happy, it becomes a "treasure on earth."

The most insidious sorts of fear are developed around sex. This is true for both sexes, but especially for girls. Here is a natural appetite, the second strongest one which man possesses. To inhibit it by any means whatever is certain to produce fear. When to this fear shame is added, which produces another fear, we develop those personalities which make up such a large portion of our mental diseases. The fears that are associated with sex are numerous. There is the fear of not getting married, fear of sin, fear of pregnancy, fear of the loss of manhood, fear of disease, fear of marital failure, even fear of death. Life cannot be built around sex any more than around wealth or health, because of consequent fear. Caution and sex hygiene are important parts of any healthy person's education. But fear is the enemy of mankind. Not only does it weaken the personality, but it defeats the very purpose for which it was devised. It may bring about sexual abstinence, but at what a price! Here, then, is "laying up treasures on earth." What to do about it is the problem.

"But lay up for yourselves treasures in heaven, where neither moth nor rust doth corrupt, and where thieves do not break through nor steal." It has been pointed out several times that the most efficient way to change personality is by the process of reconditioning. Is this not exactly what Jesus is doing here? Let us see what this teaching has said. Here is the first condition. Lack of money is followed by fear. On the positive side, money and other perishable values are made the treasure of the individual, because these things have come to have security value. They seem to constitute adequate satisfactions for certain instinctive drives. If we are to change this, we must attach a new emotional value to them. This is done through the fact that these things actually are very perishable. They are subject to all sorts of destructive agencies. This ought not to be difficult to understand, for a world that has just gone through a long economic depression. It is evident, therefore, that money is not the basis of security. It ceases to be followed by confidence. It no longer satisfies the instinctive drive for security. As a result, it is necessary to replace it with some more satisfying value. Jesus does this in his concept of "heavenly treasures." These treasures include the values described under the term *fatherly love*. Compare the attitude toward money described in the section on almsgiving with that so commonly held by people. Both involve money, but one produces power and the other fear. Jesus points out that these values are permanent and indestructible. Anyone examining them can see that they are. Therefore, if one chooses wealth he will be afraid always of losing it. If his treasure consists in this "heavenly" type he will have no fear of ever losing it. Fear disappears. Here is the basic principle on which the problem of fear is to be solved. The next two teachings are applicable to the special problems which arise out of fear, and out of the complexes of fear.

A man, thirty-eight years old, was busy cleaning a machine. A rag full of grease and petroleum caught in a gear and lashed him on the face. The face was only dirtied, and he did not trouble about the accident. He washed himself, but he had much difficulty in clearing his skin and eyelids of these fatty substances. Remark that nothing penetrated into his eyes and that he felt no pain in them. However, after an hour, he seemed to see as it were a mist before him; this mist grew thicker and two hours later he could no longer see at all. From time to time he could see a little, chiefly with his right eye. These fluctuations lasted for a month, then they disappeared absolutely and for four years he remained quite blind.[6]

[6] Janet, P., *The Major Symptoms of Hysteria*, 186. The Macmillan Company, 1920.

This man was not blind in the organic sense. Both his eyes were perfectly all right. However, he was functionally blind. This rather dramatic incident is only an analogous case of what happens to many people of whom Jesus spoke in the next verses.

The light of the body is the eye: if therefore thine eye be single, thy whole body shall be full of light. But if thine eye be evil, thy whole body shall be full of darkness. If therefore the light that is in thee be darkness, how great is that darkness!—Matthew 6:22-23.

The "single eye" and "evil eye" were Jewish idioms which would have been understood perfectly by Jesus' audience. The "single eye" referred to soundness on the physical side and liberality on the spiritual side. The man with the "single eye" is one who has no disease and who is liberal in his giving. He is able to see the need for charity and to give liberally to it. The "evil eye," on the other hand, refers to disease on the physical side and niggardliness on the religious side. The man with the "evil eye" is diseased so that he cannot see the needs of others and therefore gives very niggardly. This figure was used especially to refer to miserliness. It is probable that in that day of little reading, the chief eye disease of which they knew anything was nearsightedness or some other form of visual abnormality which makes distance vision difficult.

The clause, "Thy whole body shall be full of darkness," has interesting significance. Many people think that a blind man lives in blackness. This is not true of genuine blindness. Black is a very definite and positive sensation, which is just as real as vision of light and color. The blind man sees nothing at all. Furthermore, the eyes do not record the external world accurately. Stimuli from the external world fall on the retina and cause certain sensations in the nervous system. What vision we have depends upon the nature of our nervous system and sense organs and upon our emotional education. This is far from being alike for everyone. For example, many individuals are color-blind from birth and never discover it. Some are even totally blind in one eye without discovering it until adult life. Any form of visual abnormality will result in abnormal visual experiences for the individual, which usually he never realizes are different from those of other individuals.

"If therefore the light that is in thee be darkness, how great is that darkness." If one is aware of his blindness, he adjusts for it by getting assistance from someone who can see. However, if one is blind and does not know that he is blind, he thinks that he sees aright. Many an individual who has no appreciation for the best in art, literature, and music scoffs at those who do. He is not only blind, but blind to his blindness, which is a much more serious abnormality.

This figure was happily chosen. The psychologist could easily use it as a literal illustration of the principle which underlies Jesus' statement. Jesus suggests that the niggardly, selfish life is a diseased, nearsighted life. It is possible for mental qualities really to change our field of vision. Most of us imagine that our eyes are like cameras which accurately record the nature of the external world. This is far from being true. Actually, they search out for us in the external world what we are looking for, and interpret what they see in the light of the emotions with which they are seen. As a matter of fact, we do not see things, as such, at all. Rather, we see the meanings of things. These are what we call perceptions. Our perceptions are the meanings attached to external objects by our own emotional impulses. For example, we often add to the external stimuli and see in them whatever else is necessary for a complete perception. To illustrate: a group of non-meaningful lines and curves which are about the size and shape of a word are drawn on a card. This card is shown to a group of people for a fraction of a second. Then each one is asked what he has seen. Most subjects will see words. In a group of subjects each may see a different word. Actually, there is no word there at all. Each sees what he is looking for. If he is hungry, he will probably see the name of some food. If he is looking for pleasure, it will probably be the name of some theater or game, and so forth.[7]

On the other hand, many things are left unobserved unless they serve some purpose in the life of the observer. Every man who has tried to describe to his wife the clothes worn at some social event which he has attended, knows how easy it is to overlook entirely things in which he has no active interest. We may pass places every day for years without ever realizing that they exist. Everyone has had the experience of walking down a familiar street and suddenly becoming aware of a sense of strangeness, as if he had never seen it before. This is literally true. He never really has seen it before. These differences are due to the emotions.

If the eye is diseased, this inability to perceive is still greater. Any of us may overlook color, but if our attention is called to it we can perceive it. However, if we are totally color-blind, we are incapable of seeing it at all. In this case, color simply does not play a part in our behavior. An emotion which has been repressed into the unconscious is like a diseased eye. It cannot be recalled. It colors our perceptions and makes us blind to many things.

A fear-filled mind is able to conjure up many visual phenomena of which it is afraid. For example, here is a boy who was taught fear rather than caution in the crossing of streets. As a result his imagination ran wild. He told of scores of drunken drivers careening about the streets which he had to traverse on his way to school, and driving at terrific speeds. A young person who is afraid that other young people do not like him will find all sorts of substantiating evidence in their behavior.

Consider the effects of fear complexes on our attitude toward society. If one becomes afraid that a friend is trying to do him some harm, his fear makes him see in the friend despicable characteristics which were not observed before, as well as a great deal of suspicious behavior. A man afraid of losing his job will interpret every act of his employer as

[7] Hollingworth, H. L., *Psychology*, 6 f. D. Appleton and Company, 1928.

THE CHAOS OF FEAR

further evidence to support the reasonableness of this fear. The basis of conflict between different classes of society is usually not an actual provocation, but a fear of what the other might do.

Many a young couple has married in the full expectation of life-long happiness, only for each to discover that the other has no "common sense." This source of conflict is in fear. The dominant fear in the mind of the young man may be financial failure. It may be repressed within him, but it dominates his whole life and his system of values. He does not realize that he is afraid. He calls it "common sense," and really believes himself. On the other hand, the young lady may believe that beauty is the most important thing in life. She fears more than any other one thing not to be well dressed or not to have a beautiful home. To her, this is "common sense." It is obvious that these two brands of "common sense" clash. Actually of course, each is simply a rationalization for a repressed fear. The proof that they are unaware of the existence of these fears is in the fact that each appeals to "common sense," which is, of course, a purely mythical entity in which many have confidence, but which actually does not exist.

No man can serve two masters: for either he will hate the one, and love the other; or else he will hold to the one, and despise the other. Ye cannot serve God and mammon.—Matthew 6:24.

No man can do his best work with conflicting loyalties. The word translated "serve" does not mean simply to "work for." It implies serving as a slave, the dedication of all of one's energies. Jesus is saying that it is impossible to dedicate one's whole life to two masters. Many of us try to do just that.

"Either he will hate the one, and love the other." When one tries to serve two opposing masters, it can be only because he fears one of them. When one serves a master whom he fears, he will inevitably hate him. Many a man has come to love God, and very truly hate the selfishness which draws him away from God, and yet the repressed fear in his heart keeps him serving the hated master. He despises himself for it, he does his job very poorly and half-heartedly, but he does not have the courage to stop serving this hated master.

"Mammon" is untranslated. However, it seems to connote the personification of wealth. The meaning of the sentence, then, is not, "Ye cannot serve God and have riches," but, "Ye cannot be faithful to God and make an idol of riches." Note that Jesus is not condemning wealth, as such. The reason given for not "laying up treasures on earth" is not so much in having them, as in the fact that they involve a divided allegiance, a split personality, a division of interest.

Parents who are religious commonly try to teach their children a "common sense" balance between practical economy and religion. They feel that it is possible and desirable to teach the child to serve two masters. But just as it is impossible to be a good father and think of one's own economic welfare when it comes into conflict with the best interests of the child, so it is impossible to pay too much attention to one's economic status and be a good Christian. One must choose which one he will serve.

Parents can teach their children what they will. They may teach him that money is the source of security. But when they do they assure the child of a life of fear and weakness of character, whether he gets the money or not. He will be afraid if he is rich, and panic-stricken if he is poor.

However, parents can teach the child that loving service is the most important value. They can teach him the use of money as one of the best ways of making greater service possible. If he grows up to believe that service is the greatest good, he is certain to have courage. In this respect he can be wealthy, for there will always be ample opportunities to serve. With respect to material wealth he will not be afraid, whether he has much or little, for his values are in other things.

One thing is certain, if one's early training is centered

around wealth, he will not change his personality quickly, or perhaps ever completely. In the case of mammon we not only rationalize our money making, but we become blind to the needs about us so that our consciences do not bother us too much. The principle, "Charity begins at home," covers a multitude of sins and much fear.

It should be clear now that fear is the most disintegrating of all the enemies of personality. Worry, anxiety, terror, inferiority complexes, pessimism, greed, and the like are all varieties of this one great evil. We lie awake nights dreading the possible calamities of the morrow. We do and say cowardly things prompted by it. We are selfish and thoughtless of others in times of danger. Our minds become confused and frantic when it masters us. It undermines our personalities, makes us afraid to stand up for what we believe to be right, and afraid to dedicate our lives to the purpose which challenges our best selves. In disease it is one of the most destructive factors. Quoting Burnham:

> Among physicians it is largely recognized today that the symptoms of heart disease usually complained of do not come from cardiac disturbances. In regard to all forms of disease it is well to recall the lesson taught by the Dervish, in extravagant Oriental manner to be sure, but largely true. He met the Cholera to whom he said, "Where are you going?" The Cholera replied, "I'm going to Bagdad, to kill twenty thousand." Some time afterward the same Dervish met the Cholera returning, and said, "You vagabond! You killed ninety thousand." "No! No!" said the Cholera, "I killed twenty thousand; fear killed the rest." [8]

Children are born with very few fears. But in the early years parents teach them hundreds of them. There is some evidence now that fear, as such, is not inherited at all. Watson's famous experiments, showing that the new-born child exhibits fear to some stimuli and anger to a few others, are not meeting the test of further research. It seems possible, therefore, that the child does not necessarily have to acquire any fears at all, since all fear patterns are learned.

[8] Burnham, W. H., *The Wholesome Personality*, 300. D. Appleton and Company, 1932. By permission of D. Appleton-Century Company.

242 PSYCHOLOGY OF CHRISTIAN PERSONALITY

We have now seen the far-reaching effects of fear. Three general psychological principles have been set forth by which the problem of fear is to be solved. We now turn to the specific methods by which we shall go about eliminating our fears.

Consider the pitifully inadequate methods which are often employed to overcome fear. Some try to get rid of its external causes, others run away from it, dodge it, or devise some superstitious ritual against it. Everyone is ashamed of it. This leads to destructive inferiority complexes and pushes the whole problem out of conscious control. Let us read carefully this passage.

> Therefore I say unto you, Be not anxious for your life, what ye shall eat, or what ye shall drink; nor yet for your body, what ye shall put on. Is not the life more than the food, and the body than the raiment? Behold the birds of the heaven, that they sew not, neither do they reap, nor gather into barns; and your heavenly Father feedeth them. Are not ye of much more value than they? And which of you by being anxious can add one cubit unto the measure of his life? And why are ye anxious concerning raiment? Consider the lilies of the field, how they grow; they toil not, neither do they spin: yet I say unto you, that even Solomon in all his glory was not arrayed like one of these. But if God doth so clothe the grass of the field, which today is, and tomorrow is cast into the oven, shall he not much more clothe you, O ye of little faith? Be not therefore anxious, saying, What shall we eat? or, What shall we drink? or, Wherewithal shall we be clothed? For after all these things do the Gentiles seek; for your heavenly Father knoweth that ye have need of all these things. But seek ye first His kingdom, and His righteousness; and all these things shall be added unto you. Be not therefore anxious for the morrow: for the morrow will be anxious for itself. Sufficient unto the day is the evil thereof.—Matthew 6:25-34.

Few passages have been more misunderstood than this one. It sounds on first reading as if it were a plea for irresponsibility and shortsightedness. It impresses one as being a mystical, dreamy, utterly impractical bit of beautiful poetry, which can easily be read in the church liturgy, but should be completely forgotten in the cold facts of everyday life. The King James version reads, "Take no thought." This accounts for much of the misunderstanding. Actually, it should read, "Be not anxious." This is the key word of the passage. "Be not afraid" about the morrow and food and clothes. The passage is not a plea for irresponsibility, but for faith.

It is not universally agreed that fear is totally undesirable. We all admire courage and wish it both for ourselves and for our children. Yet we are quite likely to teach our children some fears, which we feel are necessary for survival in our everyday life. Jesus comments on this practice in the passage just quoted. "And which of you by being anxious can add one cubit unto the measure of his life?" Jesus uses here a bit of humor to make his point, when he asks of what value fear is in securing height or length of life. The word translated "measure of his life" might also be rendered, "his stature." Many of us imagine that we do add to the length of life by being afraid. In other words, we show the curious paradox of having faith in fear. If a man caught in a critical place becomes afraid, his fear quickly drives out his intelligence and he frantically tries to do several things at once, and often ends by doing the wrong thing or nothing at all. This is more likely to subtract cubits from his stature, and for that matter from the measure of his life as well.

In discussing fear in connection with life and stature, let us describe briefly the physiological reaction of fear. When a fear stimulus presents itself to an individual, his whole body reacts in such a manner as to make him able to run as rapidly as possible. It decreases his ability to do anything else. Even when one is so badly frightened that he is "rooted to the spot," actually what is happening is that he is trying to move his legs faster than they can be moved, with the result that he trembles violently without getting anywhere. Certain neural mechanisms bring it about that all of the unnecessary bodily activities cease and throw their energies into the skeletal musculature of the body to get him prepared for flight. Digestion ceases. Blood from the stomach and head rush to the arms and legs. The heart beats faster to provide more fuel for strenuous activity. Blood sugar is secreted in greater quantities into the blood stream, with the result that the muscles are actually stronger than normally. The pupils of the eyes are dilated to make better vision possible, and muscle tension is increased. This would be invaluable in a life in which fleeing from danger is important. In our own civilization, however, the usual effect is to give us indigestion because of the digestive processes ceasing to function, eye strain due to the increased brightness of light on the eyes, and decreased resistance to disease because the unused fuel thrown into the muscles has to be carried off or is left there to stagnate. The fighting forces of our blood which give us resistance to germs, have to waste their energy in scavenger service, and leave us less protected from disease. Fear certainly does not add much to our length of life or stature.

Every doctor tries to instill confidence in his patients as soon as he starts treating their illness, because he knows that fear is almost as important an element in the disease as the germs are. It is against this sort of fear that Jesus' teaching is so potent. In what way will "being anxious" increase the strength or length of your life? Here is another excellent example of reconditioning. Parents have used fear because they believed that it is helpful to the safety of their children. Jesus points out that it is not. If one of us is afraid of something, the nature of which he does not understand, and then discovers that it has no fearful qualities, his fear disappears. If parents realize the power of Jesus' words, that fear is of no value in fighting the enemies of human life, they will cease to use it in training their children.

Many people imagine that they can overcome their fears and angers by some process of will power. A man says to himself, "I am not going to let myself be afraid again." But when the next fear stimulus comes along, he finds his resolution difficult to keep. If we are going to increase our courage and decrease our fears, we must take each of the fear-toned stimuli and attach it to some other emotion. In the example to which Jesus refers, men have attached faith to food and clothes as the source of security. Jesus shows that they do not warrant such faith and inevitably lead to fear. There is no better way to help the fear-filled life than to replace the cause of fear with faith. The psychologist cannot treat fear as an entity. He must deal with each separate fear habit. Note that Jesus does not discuss the generality called fear, but deals with special fear habits; namely, those which arise from too much faith in money, food, and clothes. In these, he names the ones which play the largest part in our everyday life. If we place our faith in some other power than these things, we shall have gone a long way toward overcoming our fears. It is certainly interesting that Jesus should have approached the problem in the way which mental hygiene has found necessary. Most philosophers in the past have generalized, and dealt with fear as if it were an entity, instead of treating specific fear habits.

Psychology has shown the effectiveness of a number of methods of dealing with fear. A list of the more important of them will give a basis for evaluating Jesus' methods.

Among the preventatives and remedies for fear are coördinated activity, knowledge, direct action, love and a sense of dependence upon some adequate protection.[9]

The first attack made upon fear is that of knowledge. In the clinic we find people afraid of a number of things, because they have not thought of the irrationality of such fears. Many a student fears examinations, who can find no grounds for his fear at all. He does not know why he should be afraid of failing, or what there is to be afraid of even if he does fail. Often a recognition of this is sufficient to dispel the fear entirely. It is not at all uncommon to find a man afraid of something simply because he always has been afraid of it,

[9] Burnham, W. H., *The Wholesome Personality*, 328. D. Appleton and Company, 1932. By permission of D. Appleton-Century Company.

without ever questioning the rationality of his fear. That is, the thing is attached to the emotional tone of fear only because of his unfamiliarity with it. A rational analysis of it shows that it should be attached to some other emotion. If he can make this analysis and change its emotional tone, the fear will disappear.

This does not mean that mere logic is likely to change personality. One may convince an individual logically that his fear is foolish and wrong without making the slightest impression on the fear. It is only when reconditioning can be accomplished through the process of reasoning that reasoning changes fears. That is, when a situation brings out fear, not because of its fearful characteristics, but because it has been associated with something else of which the individual is afraid, then the fear will disappear if this association is dissolved. How easily this can be done depends upon the intelligence and age of the individual and the nature of the fear. A case history will demonstrate the way in which knowledge enters into the formation and the cure of fear.

A little boy, not quite three, was very fond of being taken to a nearby lake to bathe. He showed not the slightest fear of the water and delighted in being taken far out from the shore by his father, who was an expert swimmer. One day he was taken fishing in the same lake and this too he appeared to enjoy greatly. He sat in the boat, "fished" with a light rod, and shrieked with glee when he succeeded in catching a small fish. A few days later he was again taken swimming. To the amazement of everyone he refused, with every sign of fear, to go near the water. His father finally undressed him by force and attempted to carry him in, but no sooner had his feet touched the water than he began screaming in such extreme terror that it was thought best not to force or urge him further. He could give no explanation of his fear at the time, but a few days later he confided to his mother, "Mummy, do you know why I couldn't go in ze water one day? I was apraid ze pish would bite my peet." . . . It was explained to him that fish do not bite little boys but only fishworms and that when little boys come into the water all the fishes swim away fast. In this case the fear disappeared within a few days and never returned.[10]

[10] Goodenough, F. L., *Developmental Psychology*, 279, 291. D. Appleton-Century Company, 1934.

THE CHAOS OF FEAR

It is easy to see the child's reasoning. The men in the boat were talking of the fish "biting." This had only one meaning for the child. If knowledge is to be effective then it must be of this sort. People are not often changed by Paul's deep polemics, because he argued in abstract logic. People are often changed by Jesus' reasoning, because it obeys the principle of simplicity. Observe the type of reasoning which Jesus uses, especially in this analogy he draws between God's care of man and His care of the birds of the air and the lilies of the field.

As it has been pointed out, most of us are brought up to pay especial attention to what we shall eat and drink and wear. These things are so impressed upon us that we are very much afraid of being without them. Boys and girls go to college because they think a college education will increase their salary. If it does not it seems worthless. So much are these things emphasized, that the idealist to whom achievement is more important than these things, is usually thought to be somewhat abnormal. Yet Jesus said, "Is not life more than food?" We are afraid for what we shall eat, drink, or wear because we believe that they are life. With this simple statement Jesus shows that this is not true. This requires no extended argument. It is obvious immediately that life really is more than food. Thus, an undesirable emotional habit of fear is overcome with a stronger and more important emotional habit.

In the year 800 B.C. Joel said, "Your old men shall dream dreams, your young men shall see visions." Every young man with talents sees visions of achievement in line with his talents. Often he is offered a higher salary in another field and sells his soul for what is really a very low price. However, some seek first the type of work they want and let the salary be a very secondary matter. Many a boy graduating from college, even in times when jobs are scarce, is working for little or nothing in order to do what he wants to do. Still others are going into fields in which the pay is certain always to be small, because their interest is in those fields. These men have discovered that "Life is more than food." Jesus does not say that food, drink, and raiment are not important. He says that the Father knows that we have need of these things. He insists only that other things are of more significance. Note that the force of the argument depends not upon a deep philosophical polemic, but upon a rearrangement of fundamental attitudes. It should be obvious that this whole fear is the result of early education. If parents had given their children a faith in achievement rather than a faith in food and raiment, the fear would never have occurred.

This, then, is the first of the specific methods suggested by Jesus for eliminating fears, especially those fundamental fears that make our whole lives unhappy. We are to examine the situations in which they occur and see whether they actually contain sources of fear. In psychology this method of dealing with emotions is called the *objective attitude*. This was discussed briefly in connection with the Beatitudes. In its highest form it is the scientific attitude. Many people are afraid of things which have no significance, and which would lose their fear value if they were scientifically evaluated. For example, men have been afraid that they would become insane or lose their manhood, because they masturbated in early life, and were told that insanity and impotency would result. The worry in this case is a more common source of insanity than the habit, which is now known never to be a cause of mental disease. The fear of it is much more malignant. Many a person is afraid that he or she is low in intelligence, and is afraid to take an intelligence test or to try important tasks, because of this feared inferiority. Many an individual gets some disease and is afraid to have it treated by a doctor, because of the fear that it may prove to be fatal. Men find queer things happening to their hearts and fail to consult a physician, because they are afraid they have some serious heart disease. This fear to face the facts is a most important source of unhappiness. Jesus urged, just as mental hygiene is now urging, that we face the facts, weigh them carefully, and reason out their significance. It may happen that in some of these situations there is something to be afraid of, but in most cases there is not, and we shall face the situation more intelligently if we know all the facts in the case. This objective attitude, then, is a habit which we must form like any other habit. It runs through all of Jesus' teachings on both fear and anger.

Here is the second method for overcoming fear. It is the development of a sense of dependence. The child may be afraid, but if he can place his hand in that of his father or mother, his fear disappears. He has faith. He is dependent upon them, and believes in their ability to protect him. Men who believe in God can accomplish more than those who do not. Here is at least a partial explanation of that fact. He trusts God to care for him. This releases all his power for the achievement of his vision. He throws all his heart into his work without the hampering fear that it may not pay him a living.

This sense of dependence, when it is unquestioning, has the power to cast out fear even when the dependence is upon some magic charm.

A boy had just seen his companion devoured by a crocodile, but insisted on swimming back across the river; and although Mr. Akeley denounced the boy's foolhardiness and shook him violently the boy showed no resentment, stood smiling before him, pointed proudly to his fetishes, tiny antelope horns, packed by the witch doctor, and calmly assured him that he was safe from the crocodiles when he wore this medicine.[11]

Youth may balk at being taught a faith which is nothing more than superstition. It will rise with enthusiasm to a faith which is adventurous. The faith of the scientist took courage at first. To dedicate one's life to an unproved hypothesis seemed nothing short of foolhardiness. The faith which Jesus taught, laying down the fundamental hypothesis

---

[11] Akeley, D. J., "Crocodiles," *Saturday Evening Post,* Vol. 201, July 28, 1928, pp. 34-40.
Quoted from Burnham, W. H., *The Wholesome Personality,* 316. D. Appleton and Company, 1932. By permission of D. Appleton-Century Company.

of the fatherliness of the spiritual universe, challenges the youth to dedicate his life to discovering more about the nature of the kingdom of heaven, and bringing to people the happiness which they have so long sought, but which their fearful methods could never secure for them. When one considers strikes and other labor troubles, and thinks of the vast amount of fear and hatred which is the inevitable by-product, he mourns the consequent destruction of personality. This, then, is the second method for getting rid of fears; namely, a sense of dependence on God.

The third cure for fear is one with which we are already very familiar, a dominating purpose in life. Every one of us has worried about some little thing and had it disappear with the conception of a purpose. Jesus states this clearly in his admonition, "Seek ye first His kingdom, and His righteousness; and all these things shall be added unto you." Jesus is telling us to get a vision. Fear not the consequences in lack of wealth or comfort. The happiness which comes from achievement is permanent. Horace Mann, classed by some as the greatest educator the Western Hemisphere has produced, is a splendid example of a man who followed his ideals far beyond the thoughts of "food and raiment." In 1837 he resigned as president of the Massachusetts State Senate to accept the newly created position of secretary of the State Board of Education, at a fraction of his former salary. To his friends, it seemed that he had resigned a brilliant political career for an unimportant job. They were astonished at his action.

To some who said that the position was not one of sufficient dignity, he replied:

"If the title is not sufficiently honorable now, then it is clearly left to me to elevate it; and I had rather be creditor than debtor to the title." Others, more practical, urged that it was sheer madness for one of the best lawyers in Massachusetts to give his whole time in exchange for a beggarly $1500 a year. "Well, one thing is certain," said Mann. "If I live, and have health, I will be

THE CHAOS OF FEAR 251

avenged on them; I will do them more than $1500 worth of good." [12]

He had a dominating purpose, which he carried out with signal efficiency. Our whole educational system in America is indebted to his remarkable work.

"Be not therefore anxious for the morrow: for the morrow will be anxious for itself. Sufficient unto the day is the evil thereof." This verse gives us another method for overcoming fear. Psychologists insist that one of the best remedies is action. Do something about it. A soldier will admit that fear is strongest before he goes into action. Athletes are not afraid after they get into the game. Speakers lose their stage fright when they are well embarked upon their speeches. Action uses some of the excess energy being supplied by the fear, and takes one's mind off of it. This is not a plea for irresponsibility, but for the banishing of fear for the future. One is not urged to make no plans for the future, but to "be not anxious" for the future. The fear of the future is a very common one. It may concern not only the next day, but even the next hour. A simple example might be found in a tennis match, especially when it is of considerable importance. If the player lets his mind try to grasp the whole match, and considers the great number of points still to be played before he is the victor, he is likely to become afraid, which is fatal to good tennis. However, if he realizes that each play is the only one he has to play for the time being, and plays it as if it were the only one, this fear will disappear. When a large amount of work is before us, we are likely to wonder whether or not it will ever be finished. This worry makes us fatigued and restless, even before we start. But if we estimate the time that remains before it must be finished, and budget the work to cover that time, then each day consider only what has to be done for that day, this worry disappears. When we look at the vast resources of

[12] From "The American Spirit in Education," Volume 33, *The Chronicles of America.* Copyright Yale University Press.

evil about us, we become discouraged about ever overcoming them. When we consider only the task which lies before us for this day, and tackle it, this discouragement is lost. Many a man gives up before he starts because of this fear of the future. "Sufficient unto the day is the evil thereof."

Two other principles are involved in this teaching. One is called the principle of direct action or repeated contact. Some fears will disappear by meeting them directly and frequently. This is not true of all fears, or even of a majority of them, but it is effective for some of them. This is especially true of fears which make us hesitate to tackle some great task. Looking at the forces against us, we become afraid of them. One of the best ways to dispel that fear is to meet the fearful elements of these forces one at a time and vanquish them. Gradually the sense of victory over each part of this formidable foe makes fear disappear. A young man looking ahead at the vast amount of education necessary before he is prepared for a profession may be depressed by fear. But as he tackles each course, and each day of that course, it is easily mastered, and he soon has a sense of victory over the whole.

Here, then, are the specific methods for getting rid of our fears. First, we must approach them with an objective attitude, and intelligently trim out the dead wood of fears which have no basis at all. We must have faith in God so that fear disappears, because of a sense of confident dependence. We must get a great purpose. Our former discussions have shown that this can best be done in service, for fatherly love is the only emotion about which perfect integration is possible. Then, each day do the tasks for that day, with no fear for the future. Tackle directly the elements that seem fearful. Victory over them inspires confidence. Finally, as far as possible, bring up a child in situations which he can meet successfully. No mental hygienist can find a better program than this. It will not only destroy the negative fear, but will restore its wasted energy to the positive side of achievement.

Chapter IX

THE MEASURE OF A MAN

"Whoever is angry, is in danger!" This is the center of Jesus' teaching on anger. For one who wishes to become great, to have the strongest possible personality, to command the greatest respect from his fellow men, to accomplish the greatest achievements, psychology could also say, "Whoever is angry, is in danger."

Enough emphasis has not been put upon anger. It is probable that it is even more destructive of personality than fear. The old saying, "The measure of a man is the size of the thing it takes to get his goat," certainly has a large measure of truth. Jesus placed more emphasis upon these two emotions, than upon any other phases of human behavior. When the Jews paid tribute to Rome, they were slaves of fear and anger. Jesus had ample opportunity to observe the effects of these emotions, since they dominated the lives of most of those about him.

Do you resent being imposed upon? Does it make you angry for people to take advantage of you? If so, this portion of the teachings of Jesus is valuable for you. There may be times when we "do well to be angry." There are said to be times when one should take strychnine as a medicine, but no one has ever adopted strychnine as a steady diet and increased his stature in length of years. Nor has anyone indulged in the poison of anger freely, and failed to shrivel up under its deadly effects. The small personality goes about with a "chip on his shoulder" ready to get angry at the slightest provocation. The great man can go to a cross and pray for the forgiveness of his crucifiers. The rest of us come in between the two, but the number and intensity of our angers is in inverse proportion to our greatness. Most of us are pitifully small in respect to anger. "Standing up for our rights" and insisting on "the principle of the thing" dwindles our statures to pigmy size. The Christian church could easily prevent much of this tremendous loss, if it used to the fullest extent the principles set forth by Jesus.

"Love your enemies," has been described as the impossible commandment. Jesus himself followed it with the admonition to be perfect, as if it were next door to perfection. In our enthusiasm for serving our friends, it is very easy to forget that there are any enemies. It would seem a good excuse to say that we are kept completely busy serving our loved ones. Why bother about enemies?

Yet Jesus obviously did not describe this simply as a desirable trait to be practiced if one could find time for it after serving his friends. He taught in unmistakable terms that anger and hate have no place in civilization, and that we are even more obligated to love enemies than friends. "Bless them that curse you, do good to them that hate you." These words do not sound like personality frills which can be added to the character after all the more fundamental things have been acquired. It is clear that Jesus believed that the Christian personality involves the complete elimination of anger and hate.

Learn to control your temper. Most of us have heard this advice since we were little children. Our parents have been diligent in their admonitions to this effect. It is a difficult lesson to learn, however, and in adult life the characters of most of us still leave much to be desired in this respect. Some of us, indeed, are fixated at infantile stages of development and show the same anger picture as the young child. Temper tantrums are of this infantile character. No adult should have them. Outbursts of anger are most frequent in children between one and two years of age. They should decrease from then on to adult life.[1] Yet at the same

[1] Goodenough, F. L., *Anger in Young Children*, 72. University of Minnesota Press, 1931.

time that parents urge their children to control their tempers, they are also usually training their children in the art of being angry. For example, here is a mother trying to bring up her child to be even-tempered, but who also teaches him that he is considerably better than other children. What chance has he of not angering others and being angered hundreds of times when he begins to associate with his fellows? Here is a father who insists that his young son shall sit still while guests are present. No child can do this and remain healthy. The result is inevitably an irritable disposition. He may learn to control his outward conduct, but he will boil beneath the surface, for he will become angry. If every time a child becomes angry at others he receives the sympathy of his parents, he is likely to become an almost unbearable person. Parents commonly insist that their children shall have their just due. But they are so biased about what that just due is, that they often inflict upon the child many sources of anger. Strong personality cannot be built upon this principle, even if the just due is gained.

An angry person is never a very pretty sight at best. Most of us admit the desirability of self-control, especially on the part of the other fellow. We almost always despise a show of temper in any one else. This does not seem so applicable to our own behavior, however, for each experience of anger in ourselves always seems to be a case of "righteous indignation," never a mere loss of temper. There is probably no field of human action in which we see others and ourselves in such different lights as in our anger life. The notion of "turning the other cheek" is pretty far from the actual working ethics of most of us. Of course, as we look back at the very frequent occasions on which we have practiced this virtue of "standing up for our rights," we often have some misgivings as to the virtue, to say nothing of the dignity, of some of our behavior on those occasions. Of our right to be angry, however, we are seldom in doubt. It is to be noted that whenever men have been anxious to find weaknesses to criticize in the character of Jesus, they have invariably pointed out those occasions on which he seems to have been angry. And paradoxically enough for those who insist upon the necessity of "standing up for one's rights," when we look for the most admirable deeds of Jesus, we usually point to those events in which he most obviously did not stand for his rights. Jesus struck the keynote for this emotion when he asked, "If ye love them which love you, what do ye more than others?" No one can doubt that this is a test of strong character. As Booker T. Washington once said, "I am determined to permit no man to narrow or degrade my soul by making me hate him."

Occasionally, it is said of a young lady that she is much prettier when angry. One desiring to be attractive, however, will do well not to consider this method too seriously. When one is roused to anger, he may feel that he is being cowardly if he does not give expression to his anger. Yet when he sees exactly the same behavior in another, it looks disgustingly small.

Usually Annette was as amiable as a June morning. She was celebrated, however, for occasional outbursts of rage which were reminiscent of a stormy December night. One curious thing about them was the insignificance of their provocation. One of her sorority sisters had agreed to accompany her, one evening, to a movie, with two men friends. As the hour approached, her sister found herself disabled with a severe headache and suggested that she and her caller might remain at home while Annette and her man went to the movie alone. The suggestion was not out of the girl's mouth a second before anyone who knew Annette knew what was to follow. Her face turned white, then very red; she clenched her fists, she pounded her heels into the floor, she fairly foamed with fury. "That's the way you do, is it?" she hurled at the astonished sister; "you try to ditch me, do you? You frame up something and then crawl out of it, do you? I might have known it. Someone said you were yellow. You're pretending to have a headache and you're just a damned quitter, that's what you are . . ." And so on, for half an hour, at the end of which time her hair and clothes were in disarray, her face was stained with sweat and tears, her eyes bloodshot.[2]

[2] Menninger, K. A., *The Human Mind*, 198 f. Alfred A. Knopf, 1930.

Such a case history seems abnormal. But any one of us can be aroused to just these absurd lengths, if we are subject to anger at all. No wonder Jesus said that the law against murder should be directed against its cause, anger. When we observe individuals driving their cars and shouting at almost everyone they meet, about the right of way, lights, cutting in, and stop signs, they look pretty small. On the other hand, when we meet those occasional souls who always seem even-tempered and unruffled, who are able to return a soft answer for wrath, we envy them. They seem somehow powerful.

An important characteristic of anger is its power to beget itself in others. When others become angry at us, it is very difficult for us not to return that anger in kind, even with interest. When someone hates us, we are likely to return the compliment with usury. One who has listened to two small boys calling each other names and has heard their voices rise higher and higher with their anger, or has watched the growth of a riot at a football game, or has studied the development of propaganda during a war, knows that anger is the most contagious of emotions. Its results in unattractiveness, disintegrated personalities, and social tragedies make it as great or greater than fear as an enemy of personality. Murder, war, mobs, race prejudice, narrow nationalism; all these would be far less dangerous to civilization without the poison of anger.

The conscious stimuli are not always the real causes of anger. Often, psychogenic causes from early childhood or repressed urges of which the individual is unaware are the real causes, while the causes which he assigns to his anger are only rationalizations.

An illustration of this mechanism of rationalization of anger is described by Bernard Hart. It is especially significant for this book, because of its religious nature.

One of my patients, a former Sunday school teacher, had become a convinced atheist. He insisted that he had reached this standpoint after a long and careful study of the literature of the subject, and, as a matter of fact, he really had acquired a remarkably wide knowledge of religious apologetics. He discoursed at length upon the evidence of Genesis, marshalling his arguments with considerable skill, and producing a coherent and well-reasoned case. Subsequent psychological analysis, however, revealed the real complex responsible for his atheism; the girl to whom he had been engaged had eloped with the most enthusiastic of his fellow Sunday school teachers. We see that in this patient the causal complex, resentment against his successful rival, had expressed itself by a repudiation of the beliefs which had formerly constituted the principal bond between them. The arguments, the study, and the quotations were merely an elaborate rationalization.[3]

Let us now examine Jesus' teaching on anger: its nature and effects on human character, the various causes which give rise to it, and what is to be done about it.

Ye have heard that it was said by them of old time, Thou shalt not kill; and whosoever shall kill shall be in danger of the judgment: But I say unto you, That whosoever is angry with his brother shall be in danger of the judgment: and whosoever shall say to his brother, Raca, shall be in danger of the council: but whosoever shall say, Thou fool, shall be in danger of hell fire.—Matthew 5:21-22.

Laws against killing have existed for many centuries. Yet killing has continued. It remained for Jesus to show that the way to stop killing is not in pointing out and presenting its evils, but to place the emphasis upon the emotions which produce it. Killing is the result of anger and hate. If we are to prevent it, we must prevent them. Perhaps Jesus would paraphrase a statement here and say, "He who looks upon his brother in anger and desires to kill him has committed murder already in his heart."

Here is a fine genetic picture of the development of murder. All of us have observed anger rise. We have seen a person first get a bit angry, then say something, then curse, and finally strike or murder. These are the steps indicated in Jesus' description of this ugly behavior. First, one is angry

[3] Hart, Bernard, *The Psychology of Insanity*, 71 f. Cambridge University Press, 1922.

with his brother, then he utters, "Raca," probably a statement of contempt, and finally, "Thou fool," which carried a much worse connotation to them than to us. It was as insulting a term as one could use. All these are steps on the road to murder. Jesus suggests that all these stages are in need of punishment, and that if we are effectively to avoid murder, we must go to the root of it.

In all this discussion of murder, unlike the legalism of Moses, Jesus is concerned with the man who is angry. It is his personality that needs more consideration than the one at whom he is angry. It will be recalled that the King James translation says, "Angry *without cause*." This qualification, however, would seem unnecessary, and psychologically incorrect, if Jesus was concerned only with the angry personality. There is very strong evidence that this phrase is a later addition and not part of the original Sermon. Jesus was not concerned with the justice or injustice of anger. It was not like him to be. He is concerned with angry behavior in its bad effects upon the individual who indulges in it. Its effects are just as bad when there is a just cause for it as when there is not.

What happens to an individual when he gets angry? As in fear, there are widespread physiological effects. There are two nervous systems in the human body. One of them, called the autonomic nervous system, takes care of all the automatic duties in the body, such as keeping the heart beating, the lungs breathing, the digestive organs functioning, and so on. If one wants to think, it sends as much blood as possible to his brain, and after meals to his stomach to facilitate digestion. One part of this autonomic nervous system is active only when one is experiencing fear or anger. Thus, when one gets angry it begins to function. It prepares him for engaging in physical struggle, and gets him as ready for this occasion as possible. It immediately calls a halt on any unnecessary bodily processes. One of these is digestion. All the blood is rushed to the great muscles of the arms and legs. The heart starts working faster to increase the blood supply. Sugar is thrown into the blood stream, giving additional fuel to be burned in energy. The individual is now physically stronger by far than without the emotion. He is better prepared to fight, as far as strength is concerned. But usually in our modern world, he does not fight. He only grips the steering wheel a little tighter, grinds his teeth a couple of times, and drives on, thinking only of what he would like to do to the other driver. As a result, not only is his food undigested, but this excess sugar, unused, stagnates in the system, or has to be carried off as waste matter. He has then taken the first step toward becoming a dyspeptic and a chronic grouch.[4] It is not a figure of speech to say that anger is poisonous.

We differ widely in the things that make us angry. At birth we apparently start out alike, being made angry only by restraint of some of our movements. Thus, if the baby's head is held still or his arms pinned to his side when he wants to move them, he often shows general emotionality. This seems to be the only thing which resembles anger in the new-born baby. When the baby has reached the age of twenty, however, the variety of things which will arouse his ire are remarkable for their number. One hundred college women reported 274 different stimuli for anger. Thirty-five college men have listed 251 different causes. A vast majority of the causes cited were mentioned only once each. What is the significance of this fact? From the point of view of learning to control our anger, this diversity of anger stimuli is hopeful. It certainly shows that anger stimuli are not inherited.

Let us observe two points. In the first place, although animals become angry frequently and easily, there are few types of stimuli which will produce the emotion in them. It is only the adult human who is irritated by many things. Functionally, we may divide the brain into two sections.[5]

[4] Cannon, W. B., *Bodily Changes in Fear, Anger, Hunger and Rage* (2nd rev. ed.). D. Appleton and Company, 1929.
[5] Cannon, W. B., "Neural Organization for Emotional Expression," *The Wittenberg Symposium on the Feelings and Emotions.* Clark University Press, 1928.

The old brain, so-called because of its presence in earlier stages of evolutionary development, is the seat of instinctive activity, and has a minimum of conscious or voluntary control. The new brain, or cerebral cortex, is the other division. This is the seat of the conscious mind. Through it we exert whatever voluntary control we have over our behavior. Since man's mind is different from that of the animal by virtue of his greater new brain, it follows that the causes for anger are probably located in the new or thinking brain. Thus, while anger itself is located in the old brain, it is directed by the new brain. This is very significant. If it were not true, changing one's anger life would be almost impossible. In the second place, the animal carries his every impulse into action, while the human adult may repress and keep more or less under control most of his grosser impulses. This shows that the control of anger also is located in the new thinking brain.

It follows that we have two alternatives. On the one hand, we can show anger to a great many different stimuli and then repress and subdue our savage impulses. In this case, the mind is a house divided against itself. The new and old brains constantly fight each other and hence we accomplish little. Furthermore, there is always the danger that the old brain in an unguarded moment may gain control and cause us to perform violence or even murder. On the other hand, one can study the situations which produce anger in him, change and limit them, until few if any will arouse his wrath. Then he can utilize all the courage, added strength, and driving force which formerly was wasted in anger to achieve results otherwise impossible, results of which he can be justly proud. The new and old brains, then, work together, doing great things and exhibiting that strength of character which is a criterion of strong personality.

The dynamic personality does not repress his anger. Anger is the result of a thwarted urge. To place the emphasis upon the emotion itself is at best a makeshift. One must find some other way to satisfy the urge. This consists in a change in one's attitude toward the objective situation. Just how this is to be accomplished in specific situations will be illustrated many times throughout the chapter. To repress or suppress the anger without doing this simply loses the strength of the urge from the personality power of the individual.

It is obvious that the seriousness of anger as an enemy of personality is in proportion to the intensity and frequency of the anger. When one becomes angry in his heart, it may be only one of those temporary explosions which quickly passes. Nevertheless, it is dangerous for strong personality. If one becomes angry enough to let it express itself in personal incriminations, it is still more serious for the personality. If it causes one to say those harsh things which leave incurable wounds, and so often produce permanent ruptures between friends, it is still worse. When the disease of anger has progressed to the point of murder, it is far too late for efficient treatment to be rendered. It does no good to hang a man after he has committed murder. It were better that he had appeared before the "judgment," when he first became angry. Something might have been done then. Jesus was saying exactly what modern medicine and modern mental hygiene are now emphasizing. Prevention is better than cure. The place to stop murder is in the growth of the anger life of the child. If this phase of his personality is permitted to develop along pathological lines and become morbid and diseased, we need not be surprised when killing is the natural outcome. To try to cure it then, is about as effective as cutting out all the spots to cure measles. The history of the punishment of murder has shown, that implicitly we have seen its malignant nature, and prescribed the death penalty, which after all is hardly an effective method of curing personality.

The fallacy of trying to build character by controlling external acts has been emphasized again and again. Here, once more Jesus urges the futility of this sort of legislation. Murder is only a symptom of a certain type of personality reaction. It is the personality which needs curing. Children have been told that they must learn to control their tempers. When this is more specifically stated, it is resolved into certain forms of external behavior which must not be exhibited. The outgrowth of this sort of training, if it is successful, is the suave, smooth individual who can smile to one's face and hate him at the same time. It may be socially acceptable, but it can hardly be called strong personality.

How is the emotion of anger to be dealt with? The various possibilities in its growth can be pointed out. Every child will become angry when his desires are thwarted. Instinctively, then, his anger is selfish or at least self-centered. The response which his instinct urges him to make is socially undesirable. The instinctive response to anger is one of the most definite and universal inherited response patterns in human behavior. But it is obvious that he cannot go on all his life losing his temper every time some wish of his is refused. What can be done about it? Again we meet the same four forms of emotional release: expression, suppression, repression, and sublimation. In relation to anger, how does each of them operate?

The old method of child training is that of suppression and repression. In the case of anger, repression has not been used as much as suppression. In the case of fear and sex, repression has been used more. Children have been urged to suppress their temper. The futility of this program has become apparent, at least to students of human nature, and a new doctrine has gained considerable following. This is expressionism. Parents are urged to permit the child to express himself. From this has grown the term, the uninhibited child, which all too often is synonymous with unruly and undisciplined. How any serious student of personality could have imagined that unbridled expression would solve the problem is difficult to see.

Sublimation consists in finding some other way to satisfy the instinctive drive than through the channel in which it is being thwarted and which results in anger. This is not always easy to do. Here is a college student who was extremely angry with one of his instructors, who, he said, had insulted him. This student had been subject to temper tantrums all his life. In this particular instance, the facts did seem to warrant his resentment. It was pointed out to him, however, that there was this weakness in his personality, and that if he could learn to endure the taunts of this instructor without anger, he would have gone far toward curing this weakness in himself. This simple suggestion proved adequate in his case, because his original anger was really wounded vanity at not being treated with sufficient respect by his instructor. In other words, the instinctive drive was the desire to excel. When another source of greatness was pointed out to him the anger disappeared, because the original drive was no longer being thwarted.

The fact has been pointed out already that the only road to progress is, in the last analysis, the replacing of anger and fear with love and faith. The law of vicarious sacrifice means essentially that one faces the angers, hates, and fears of others and responds to them with love and faith. The world advances only when this is done. In this next passage Jesus strikes directly at the heart of the doctrine of righteous indignation, and urges us to overcome anger with love.

> Therefore if thou bring thy gift to the altar, and there rememberest that thy brother hath aught against thee; Leave there thy gift before the altar, and go thy way; first be reconciled to thy brother, and then come and offer thy gift.—Matthew 5:23-24.

"If thou rememberest that thy brother hath aught against thee." One will remember it all right if he comes to the altar with sincerity. It is all very well to excuse ourselves and defend our rights when we are comparing our case with that of our brother. It becomes quite another matter when we approach the altar with a widened sense of right and wrong. If we are conscious of the fatherliness of God and of our own shortcomings, we are very likely to remember this anger with our brother, and feel rather small about it.

There may be occasions for anger, but the way to distinguish such occasions is by the criterion, not of one's own rights, but of those of the person at whom one is angry. If there are occasions in which our anger brings about growth of the personality of the other individual, if through it all we have a genuine interest in him, it seems possible that such anger is desirable. Certainly such occasions are few and far between. Probably, there are times when parents contribute to the growth of the character and personality of their children by displaying a form of anger, rather than by outward expression of love; but if there are, the very anger must be of a fatherly variety. These parental angers are in kind far above our petty explosions of wounded vanity.

"If thy brother hath aught against thee." There is no question of whether it is justly or unjustly. It does not even read, "If thou hast aught against thy brother," but rather, "If thy brother has anything of anger in his heart against thee." The little man is likely to return the anger of his brother with anger. But Jesus preaches a righteousness which "exceeds the righteousness of the scribes and Pharisees."

Notice also that it does not read: "When two brothers find themselves at odds let them get together and be reconciled." That would be more according to ordinary brotherly love. What usually happens is that each waits for the other, and as a result neither does anything about it at all. A young minister called one day on one of the families of his parish. When he was leaving he asked some question about another family in his church, who lived next door. Quite calmly but coolly they replied that they could give no information, not having spoken to the other family for twenty years. Here they were, both members of the same church, living next door to each other without greeting each other for twenty years. Surely they must never have read this verse. Otherwise, how could they ever have come to the altar to pray? Only diseased minds could hold anger in their hearts for so long a time.

There is something beautiful in a brotherly love that would make a man obey Jesus' command before he came to the altar. Actually, it is brotherly love permeated with fatherly elements. Dr. Reed tells the story of a young boy, who, when told that a man's automobile had been given him by his brother, said, "When I grow up, I am going to be a brother like that." Most boys would have said, "I wish I had a brother like that." This particular boy was older than his brother, and had probably been taught to take a fatherly interest in him. It will require this sort of love to make men able to master this teaching whole-heartedly.

"If thou bring thy gift to the altar." There is a symbolic significance to this ceremony. Many of us come frequently to the Lord's Supper without the slightest preparation of this sort. Jesus gave his life for those who hated him and were angry at him. Jesus might say today, that no Christian should come to the Communion table until he has prepared himself by offering love to someone who hates him. Many people outside the church insist that they are quite as good as those in the church. Sometimes it is difficult to see in what way our righteousness does "exceed the righteousness of the scribes and Pharisees." But if every Christian, before each Lord's Supper, became reconciled with one brother who held hate against him, what a power the Communion would be in the world and how influential the church would become. This is exactly what Jesus commanded.

But is there no time when righteous indignation is the right attitude to take? This term *righteous indignation* has been a cover for many multitudes of sins. The smug, self-satisfied way in which most of us judge our own behavior as compared to that of our neighbor is nothing short of astonishing when we look at it objectively. So few of us ever criticize our own behavior negatively, that if we become angry whenever we think we have just cause, we shall find no diminution in our own anger, but will see many desirable changes that others should make. As a bishop once expressed it: "There are times when I do well to be angry, but I have mistaken the times." There can be no denying, however, that there are many injustices in the world, both in ourselves and others. Furthermore, there must be such a thing, then, as righteous indignation. Let us see if Jesus taught how this should be expressed. If we are to determine accurately the times and methods of its use, we must use an objective attitude of some sort. Jesus did use righteous indignation at times. He furthermore demonstrated how it should be expressed.

Among the irritating factors in Jesus' life, probably none was so great as the attitude of the disciples themselves. Probably the most beautiful example of his method of showing righteous indignation was at the Last Supper. In Jesus' day, men went barefoot except for their sandals. It was customary, therefore, to provide guests with a basin of water and a towel for washing their feet. Usually a servant did it. In such a large group as the disciples, however, it was customary to take turns in performing this ministry. At the Last Supper the disciples were bickering as to which would be greatest in the kingdom of heaven. Probably, each studiously avoided noticing the bathing materials. It was here that Jesus demonstrated again the right way to show righteous indignation. He himself washed their feet. No group of men were more completely ashamed or rebuked than the disciples were. No angry words could have been nearly so effective. Yet Jesus did it in a spirit of perfect love for them. There was nothing of anger in this act. It completely overcame them. None failed to feel the sting of its rebuke or the healing power of the love which prompted it. If there is a time for righteous indignation, this is the way in which the anger ought to express itself. Otherwise, it may be indignation but it cannot be righteous, for it will not cure, nor will it increase one's own strength of personality.

Probably, there is no more firmly established principle in

modern civilization than the righteousness of justice. From individuals to nations, we insist on securing what is justly our own. We establish courts to settle the inevitable disputes, and talk about the corruption of the courts if the decision is on the other side. Justice has regularly failed as an ideal. It is all right in principle. It is impossible of fulfillment.

The spiritual law is that of "Be ye therefore perfect, like the Father." Let the characteristics of fatherliness prevail. A much more profound justice will be obtained. Anger will disappear from the earth. Personalities will be finer and happier. Surely, as we observe the nobility of the mother instinct and praise the fine character of fathers, we can realize what the world would be like if this same noble spirit characterized the attitude of all men toward one another.

Some may ask what is to be done with the scoundrels who seem so utterly without conscience. Many cases of this sort can be quoted. Some children ingratiate themselves in the eyes of their parents in order to obtain a major portion of the estate. When the estate is settled, they fight over the settlement like a pack of wolves. Unscrupulous real estate dealers defraud innocent people out of their property by technicalities of the law. Dishonest bankers embezzle the trust funds of the poor. Fraudulent stock companies literally steal the hard-earned money of unsuspecting victims. Men cash checks that are not good. Counterfeiters pass imitation money. The suffering and privation which come from these dishonesties make our blood boil. Surely, here are occasions for righteous indignation. Jesus' reply to this problem is certainly astonishing.

> Agree with thine adversary quickly, while thou art in the way with him; lest at any time the adversary deliver thee to the judge, and the judge deliver thee to the officer, and thou be cast into prison. Verily I say unto thee, Thou shalt by no means come out thence, till thou hast paid the uttermost farthing.—Matthew 5:25-26.

In this picture which Jesus draws of a common scene in his day, this sort of experience is described. It was the custom of the courts of that day to cause the defendant and plaintiff to walk into court together. It was hoped that they might settle their differences on the way and save the trouble of a trial. The plan did not work well, however. Most people are far too stiff-necked for that. Usually, both walked into court with an air of complete disdain. One can almost see these two men, each looking something like a bantam rooster, marching in self-satisfied pride, perfectly confident of the righteousness of his own indignation. Vanity kept them from anything but a haughty anger against their adversary. In this rather picturesque way Jesus indicated the true nature of anger. Far from being manly, it is disgusting and childlike.

Psychologically, anger behavior has three basic causes. These three types of cause seem to be so universal that they can be considered native. They are: blocked behavior, being prevented from doing what we want to do; wounded vanity, having others think less highly of us than we think we deserve; and injustices to ourselves or our friends. Jesus deals with all three of them in this section, and all in connection with the hypothesis of justice as the goal of righteousness.

While there are many cases such as the ones described on the preceding pages which really are injustices, there are many more cases when it is simply "the principle of the thing," wounded vanity. When others do not think of us as highly as we think they should, our vanity is hurt and we are angry. The first important reason for losing our tempers is, strangely enough, our desire to be great. All of us covet greatness. Most of us never attain it. We all want to be leaders, but seldom find followers. When one drives an automobile, however, he has his opportunity. If he just drives fast enough he can be a leader, and hence achieve a feeling of greatness. The automobile is the most democratic power-giver in the world. In the cheapest second-hand car we can make the pedestrian jump and occasionally can pass the larger cars. Why does anyone want to drive eighty miles an hour? To get there sooner? Very rarely. He does the same thing on a Sunday afternoon drive. The real reason is that most of us like to pass people. This is also why we try to get ahead of the other car when the light turns. It explains why we will not let another car into the line, or why we pass a whole line of cars at a light without waiting our turn as we would in any other situation in life. Why does one get angry when a car beats him at the turn of the light? It is not because he feels that he has been done an injustice, or that he is in a hurry. It is because he thinks that the other driver considers himself a better driver.

This verse has often been interpreted as a duty which one should try to perform. Jesus shows that there is in human nature a native drive in which it is the natural thing to do. Every preacher knows how futile it is to preach duty to congregations. Years of such preaching produce almost no impression. If we are to have unselfishness, some natural sources of unselfishness must be tapped. Jesus teaches that this natural source is found in parental love.

At the same time, it should be pointed out that many a parent loses the respect and confidence of his son by vanity. Read again the list of things which parents classified as serious misbehavior in their children: interrupting adult conversation, disobeying parents, talking back when spoken to, and so forth. It is not that the parents want the child to realize that they are greater than their children, but simply that they are great. It is no accident that every boy thinks his father can whip any man in the world, or that he is the greatest man in the world. The boy learned that somewhere. The father taught him. Because of this professed infallibility many a boy finds his father a poor source of comfort and understanding in time of difficulty.

Many a minister and church repels young people from its doors by vanity. The minister professes a sense of divinity which he does not possess, and holds up his hands in horror at the sins and troubles of his young people. The church leaders have stilted manners and sanctimonious attitudes which bespeak their own hypocrisy. It is no wonder that young people do not find them sources of strength in time of temptation or of power for great achievement.

Here, then, is another philosophy of child education. Many parents honestly believe that if they can make their children think themselves better than other people, they will be better. Of course, most parents believe their children really are better than other people's children, so this is a temptation at best. Here is a woman who is the daughter of the town's leading family. She is aware of this fact and grows up to be something of a snob. She wins the respect but not the affection of the townspeople. She teaches her son that he is the cream of the town's youth. Is he the better for this? Anyone who has watched this common drama knows the answer. He becomes an insufferable egotist. He is unpopular and unhappy. He finds himself living in a lonely world. He is laid open to the most common and incurable of the mental diseases, schizophrenia.

We all desire to have a high opinion of ourselves. This usually requires a submissive attitude on the part of others, who openly acknowledge our superiority. If we do not get this submission, we resent the fact, and the more we feel we deserve it, the more angry we become at its absence. For some reason, the customer frequently assumes that he is vastly superior to the clerk who waits upon him. He becomes angry indeed if the clerk does not at least outwardly acknowledge this superiority. This would not be at all the case if we were dealing with those recognized as superiors or even equals. The man who objects to the talkative clerk will find himself anxiously listening to every word of his guest that evening. The clerk who irritates us by telling us what to buy would be graciously thanked for his advice, if he were the leader of our social set. The reason why it makes a woman angry to have a sales-girl call her "dearie" is because this wounds her vanity and sense of social prestige. If a social leader should do the same thing she probably would be elated. The clerk becomes so thoroughly imbued with this attitude that he does not expect submission on the part of his customers. There are some stimuli for loss of self-feeling, however, which do rankle. He is deeply incensed when he is utterly ignored by a customer. The condescending customer and the "know it all" customer are trying to his self-control. There is nothing which makes the sales-girl so angry as to have the customer take a haughty, superior attitude toward her.

The outward expression of anger changes with the growth of the individual, but the inward impulses do not. If the stimulation were strong enough, primitive forms of expression would be forthcoming. Outward control of anger is only valuable so long as the temptation is not too strong.

Goodenough has shown that the proportion of anger outbursts which involve display of undirected energy decreases rapidly with age.[6]

Few if any of the primitive emotions are permitted free expression under modern conditions of civilized life. Take anger as an example. You do not as a rule give the waitress a black eye because she puts her thumb in the soup, but you may refrain from giving her a tip. When one of your classmates offends you, you are not likely to attack him with your fists, but you may make a sarcastic retort. The process of substitution begins very early. A little boy not yet two when restrained from investigating the contents of his father's pockets ran screaming to the floor lamp, jerked at the cord and pretended he was going to tip the lamp over. A little girl of about the same age when punished for some small misdemeanor pulled all the cushions off the davenport. Somewhat later the day-dream comes in as a form of substitution for emotions that are denied more active expression. In the daydream you are exalted, while the rival who has made you angry or jealous or afraid is made to suffer all the punishment that you were unable to inflict at the time.[7]

Sometimes, the daydream carries itself into certain types

[6] Goodenough, F. L., *Anger in Young Children*, 51. University of Minnesota Press, 1931.
[7] Goodenough, F. L., *Developmental Psychology*, 283 f. D. Appleton-Century Company, 1934. By permission of D. Appleton-Century Company.

of action. Perhaps the most common of these is the child's deciding to run away from home. Usually, this follows a daydream of how deeply grieved his parents will be at his loss. The child's desire to die is of the same sort. He does not so much want to die as to have his parents suffer for their crimes. Fundamentally, however, the expression of anger is universally similar. These substitutions are little more than veneers which disappear under stress.

Wounded vanity may be a cause for anger. Anger, however, is certainly nothing to be vain about. "Agree with thine adversary quickly." This may seem to involve a loss of dignity and the giving up of some of our "divine" rights. Anger, however, is hardly a better alternative. Despite our enthusiastic claims to the right of righteous indignation, we are most angry when we are in the wrong. We are much more angered by just than by unjust criticism. This is especially true in connection with vanity. Consider the case of conceit. Conceit is most commonly a compensation for an inferiority complex. The conceited individual is calling attention to his good qualities to take attention away from his bad ones. To have the less desirable ones pointed out is always a potent source of anger.

Jesus shows another sympathetic but keen insight into human nature by the use of the word "quickly." It is common knowledge that every minute's delay in admitting a wrong makes the admission increasingly difficult. It is better to agree quickly.

Here, then, is the first great cause of anger, wounded vanity. In adult life it is by far the most common. Most of the cases which individuals ascribe to injustice are actually wounded vanity. Why are people vain? The desire for achievement has been described as one if not the fundamental drive of human life. But a sense of achievement is relative to the standards of the social environment in which one lives. Obviously, a vast majority of individuals in any social organization cannot excel the others. These individuals often seek abnormal ways of getting rid of the resultant inferiority feeling. There are many mechanisms which are used in this respect. Vanity is the most common one. Many pseudo-psychological books have been written on, "You are what you think you are." Much is made of the courage of the man who refuses to admit defeat, of the man who holds his head high when everything is against him. Properly interpreted, these are worthwhile virtues. To the great majority, they lead to a deceiving of oneself, which the rest of the world recognizes as vanity or conceit. There may be in them a modicum of safety from the fear of inferiority, but they lead to worry and especially to anger. They make for a hard, cruel, heartless personality, which is far below its maximum capacity. Like some other philosophies of life, this one does not accomplish its purpose.

Over against this philosophy, Jesus puts fatherly love. "Agree with thine adversary quickly." The word translated "agree" carries a much deeper meaning than is usually connoted by our English word. It means literally, "to be in good mind," or "to be well inclined toward," "to be favorable." In other words, Jesus is not recommending cowardice, but love. To be stiff-necked as most men are in this situation never settles the case. When one remains angry, it matters little whether the case is won or lost, it is lost anyway. No despicable cowardice and cringing attitude needs to be taken. It is the same attitude that a father would take toward his son. The father would be most concerned about being reconciled with his son. He would not be greatly concerned about the merits of the case or the cost to him, if he could win back his son's love and help him become a finer man. Jesus, then, is not condoning evil, he is simply showing a new method of meeting it.

This right method is more explicitly stated in Jesus' next teaching on anger, which has to do especially with cases in which there really is injustice. It includes the famous statement, "Resist not evil." It is this statement which has inspired the non-resistance campaign of Gandhi. Notice, how-

THE MEASURE OF A MAN

ever, that Jesus does not stop with the negative command of, "Resist not evil." He goes on to a positive substitute method of dealing with evil. Let us examine it psychologically. It can best be discussed in two sections. One contains the basic principle, with the famous teaching about "turning the other cheek." In the other, Jesus gives several illustrations of how the Christian goes about "turning the other cheek." This has always been considered as one of the impossibly idealistic teachings of Jesus. Read it with the attitude of a father dealing with his son, and see how naturally it reads.

Ye have heard that it hath been said, An eye for an eye, and a tooth for a tooth: But I say unto you, That ye resist not evil: but whosoever shall smite thee on thy right cheek, turn to him the other also.—Matthew 5:38-39.

The first of the three fundamental causes for anger is wounded vanity. We now turn to the second one. It is real or imagined injustice. Certainly, if there is a place for righteous anger, it is in the case of injustice. Yet, here is Jesus saying, "Resist not evil!"

"An eye for an eye, and a tooth for a tooth" has come to have a sort of undesirable flavor. Yet, most of us live by it, and endeavor to build our foundations of justice upon it. It was a tremendous advance over the ethics of the day in which it was written. "A head for an eye, and a life for a tooth," was much more in keeping with preceding codes of morals. As long as anger is the dominating motive of behavior, such ethics are likely to prevail. Watch two boys retaliate blow for blow, each making his a little harder than the one received. Anger is like that. It wants a "head for an eye." It was, then, a high ideal to try to reach the level of "An eye for an eye, and a tooth for a tooth." The difficulty with it, like that of all negative codes of ethics, is that it cannot be achieved. There is always the question of the relative value of different "eyes," and the comparative importance of "teeth." Those who have tried to make fine distinctions in values are too well aware of this difficulty.

Couples who have seen their marriages torn apart on the rock of "each one going halfway" but ending an infinite distance apart, should recognize how impossible it is.

The chief difficulty in the program of justice, then, is in agreeing as to what is just. The powerful drives or appetites which motivate our behavior, color all our judgments of value and insist on being satisfied. Furthermore, they motivate the building up of rationalizations to defend their satisfaction. It is not difficult for any man to prove, at least to his own satisfaction, that the world owes him a living. It is easy for the student with low marks to believe that the fault lies with the teacher rather than with himself. The man who loses his job commonly has a story of pull and favoritism on the part of his employer toward some one else. It is obvious, then, that no two persons with conflicting desires can hope to agree upon a middle ground. It is the task of our courts to make such decisions objectively. However, the loser in a court decision is usually angry about the result, which seems unjust to him.

The numerous situations which make people angry because of injustice are infinite in their scope. Let us observe a few of the most familiar. Being short-changed or having goods misrepresented to them makes people very angry. The inability to depend upon the word of a merchant is a source of wrath. The laundry comes back minus some article and anger is the result. Despite our suspicion of the clerk, we arouse his anger for injustices done him much more often than he does ours. People who handle or demolish merchandise, those who ask very unfair favors, those who comment upon how much cheaper the article can be bought elsewhere, and those who find fault with everything, arouse a great deal of anger. The things which make us angry in religion along this line are numerous. By far the most frequent source of irritation is insincerity. The hypocrite, who is religious on Sunday and dishonest during the rest of the week is the most frequently mentioned single stimulus. Others in this group are the "holier than thou" church member, those who wear elaborate clothes to church to display them, churches giving shows, refreshments, and the like to bribe people into them, men who are church members for business reasons, insincere prayers, and Easter and Christmas church members, who never go to church any other time in the year, are among the most common varieties. The next greatest source of anger is the sermon. If the minister wishes to avoid making any of his congregation angry, apparently he will have some difficulty; for all of these things are mentioned as causing anger: the moralizing sermon, the abstract sermon, the long sermon, the read sermon, the dogmatic sermon, the erudite sermon, the "modern age" sermon, and the sermons on subjects in which the preacher is not well informed. It is indeed a straight and narrow way that the minister must tread to avoid all of these. All of these are related to this fundamental principle of injustice.

It is not the intention here to discuss the objective possibility of determining justice. The point is, that it is impossible to determine a justice which will not leave one or both parties angry. Since the object of our study is personality, this is the only factor to be considered. The principle, then, of "An eye for an eye, and a tooth for a tooth" can never be the basis for a religion in which strong personality is the end goal. What is Jesus' answer to the problem of injustice? "Resist not evil."

This command of Jesus has received many connotations in the centuries since he gave it. The last individual to give it publicity was Gandhi. In his non-resistance campaign he professed to be following this principle. Gandhi has missed the very essence of Jesus' doctrine. Gandhi's program is not really a non-resistance campaign, but a non-resistance-with-force campaign. Gandhi seems to have made the assumption that if one does not resist with force, he is not resisting. If that were true, the Jewish leaders of Jesus' day, against whom he preached most frequently, were engaged in a non-resistance campaign against Rome. The Jews hated the Romans. However, the Pharisees, at least, were convinced of the futility of resistance, and urged a submission of hate. This is about what Gandhi preaches. This very problem was presented to Jesus in the question of rendering tribute to Cæsar. One party, the resistance party, urged that taxes not be paid. The non-resistance party urged that they be paid. It is to be observed that Jesus did not side with either. He pointed out an entirely different method of meeting evil.

There are, then, three methods for overcoming evil. Each has been tried. We have experimental evidence for each of them. There is the common method of which war is a part, which overcomes evil with evil. Three things stand out against it. First, it does not work. It never has worked in history for any length of time. It cannot hope to do so because its only possible permanence depends upon fear. We may have great naval displays to inspire fear in our potential enemies, but they are not afraid any more than we are at their displays. Secondly, it invariably produces greater evils than it solves. Thirdly, it is based upon anger and destroys personality.

The second method of overcoming evil is the negative method of non-resistance. It cannot work because it engenders hate, suspicion, and anger on both sides of the quarrel.

The third method is the Christian method, which is "overcoming evil with good." It returns love for hate, even though it costs one's life on a cross to do so. It maintains courage where others are afraid. It forgives where others hate, and suffers where others try to gain revenge. Notice, then, that to read the sentence, "Resist not evil," is an incomplete statement of Jesus' teaching. Jesus did not stop with the admonition against resisting evil but went on to say, "But whosoever shall smite thee on thy right cheek, turn to him the other also." This is a very interesting method. It is to be observed that if one were being struck a blow, his assailant would probably use the right hand, and so strike him on the left cheek. But if one were insulting him, he would slap him with the back of his right hand, as was the custom in that day, and so strike him on the right cheek. It is probable that Jesus referred to this sort of insulting blow.

It has been emphasized that the law of vicarious sacrifice implies returning love for hate. It was pointed out, however, that in so doing, one is likely to suffer the abuse of him who hates. Jesus did not say that one will not be struck if he turns the left cheek. In his own case, he was crucified. But he did teach that the only source of civilized advance is the return of love for hate. When this interpretation is given to the passage, we recall some other great words of Jesus: "Forgive us as we forgive," and, "Forgive, not seven times, but seventy times seven."

It is to be carefully observed that Jesus does not urge the returning of fear for hate. Many who have commented upon the doubtful value of not "resisting evil" and "turning the other cheek," have objected that these would be acts of cowardice. Examine again Jesus' behavior at Gethsemane when he was arrested. Hear him on the cross praying for the forgiveness of those who crucified him. These are certainly not examples of cowardice. He does not teach fear. That would be no better than hate and anger.

Here, then, is the basic principle for meeting injustice. In the next verses, Jesus applies the principle in a few characteristic situations.

And if any man will sue thee at the law, and take away thy coat, let him have thy cloak also. And whosoever shall compel thee to go a mile, go with him twain. Give to him that asketh thee, and from him that would borrow of thee turn not thou away.—Matthew 5:40-42.

"Whosoever shall compel thee to go a mile, go with him twain." This passage recalls an incident recorded in the diary of John Wesley. He was riding through the country on horseback one rainy day. Another man came up beside him. In the course of the ensuing conversation the other asked him if he knew John Wesley. Then he began a tirade against

Wesley, denouncing him as a menace to England and to society in general. Upon learning that he was speaking to Wesley, to use Wesley's words (as nearly as I can remember them), "He spurred his horse to leave me. But I, being better mounted than he, overtook him, and never let him go until I had him on his knees in the mud praying for the salvation of his soul." This story about Wesley will go far toward helping us to understand this passage in the way in which Jesus meant it.

At birth, as it has been pointed out, we apparently can be made angry only by restraint of some of our movements. Thus, if the baby's head is held still or his arms pinned to his sides, he usually shows anger behavior. But this seems to be the complete catalogue of the causes which will produce it in the new-born infant. If we observe adult behavior, we find scores of irritating situations which look suspiciously like this earliest form of the philosophy: "I want, what I want, when I want it."

Among causes for anger in automobile driving, the one most frequently mentioned is being forced to follow some slow car, truck, bus, or street-car. There is usually not the slightest reason why these situations should make us angry, except that they restrain some of our movements. Many other similar stimuli for anger will be recognized instantly as coming under this head. The more intent one is upon getting ahead, the more it hurts to be held back. It will be found that we lose our tempers a lot more often at sixty miles per hour than at thirty.

The blocking of some initiated behavior includes many of the customers' complaints. Among these are: not being waited upon in turn, the slow clerk, the clerk who insists upon talking to some one else while waiting upon you, the clerk who with maddening deliberation finishes some task about the store before attending to your wants. These are all illustrations of what we call, in more popular language, being impatient. It is interesting to note that the slow customer is about as irritating to the clerk as the slow clerk is to the customer. If the customer does not know what he wants, or if he looks at everything and buys little or nothing, or if he delays unnecessarily when others are waiting, or if he regularly comes in at closing time and delays the finish of the day's work, he arouses wrath in the salesman.

In religion, the ministers also get angry. For them, the greatest annoyance is the lack of enthusiasm on the part of their congregations, especially in their unwillingness to back large programs. Next in importance is the religious penury of the people, who buy automobiles and go to theaters but give almost nothing to the church. Then comes the tendency of church members to sit in the back seats, being criticized by those who do not know what they are talking about, being told what he can or cannot preach about, and having people quit the church when they do not like him. Even here, the chief cause of anger is in being held back from some projected program of action.

From our early infantile beginnings, then, we have conditioned and reconditioned this restraint source of anger until the number of varieties possible to it are countless. Their expression is seldom so powerful as those in connection with wounded vanity and injustice. Rather, under this cause can be listed most of the little irritating factors in life. No one of them seems important, but the whole list of them constantly keeps us a little cross and grouchy. Having the door slam shut just after one has gotten his key back into his pocket is typical of many of these stimuli. Indeed, many people might consider them just amiable weaknesses, of no great significance either one way or another. It is to be noticed, however, that personality is made up of little habits, not of large traits. These little anger habits can be the disintegrating factors which do us far more harm than the more occasional anger explosions which seem far worse. What is Jesus' method for dealing with them?

Jesus mentioned a number of these irritating stimuli and suggested a remedy for each; that is, a new attitude to take toward it. Jesus always used examples which involve our attitude toward other people. "If any man will sue thee at the law, and take away thy coat, let him have thy cloak also." It is to be observed that this illustration does not refer to some major circumstance in which one's whole property or life is lost. It is a small trial in which only a trifle is taken away. Such circumstances are irritating. The anger will be all the stronger because the coat obviously has been taken only against the opposition of the individual who loses it. The average individual is likely to feel that the court has been unjust. The strong personality, however, will use love in his response to the situation and give the cloak also. The mere outer act is of no significance, of course. The individual must have such an attitude that the giving of the cloak will be a natural expression of his good will toward him who took away his coat.

"Whosoever would compel thee to go a mile, go with him twain." It was quite common for the Roman soldiers to use the beasts of the people for their own purposes, or even to compel the people themselves to do work for them. Such behavior was certainly a source of tremendous irritation on the part of the people so treated. Most of us feel that we do not like to be imposed upon. Jesus urges that if one compels us to do something for him, we should do more than he asks. This seems a strange way to get justice. Yet, there are those great souls who actually seem to get pleasure from being imposed upon. They are an inspiration and look pretty big when we compare them with ourselves, who are constantly ready to become indignant at those who "compel us to go with them a mile." It is not easy to love those who impose upon us in any way. An old preacher once gave this sage philosophy to a young man preparing for the ministry. "You will find in every congregation some man, usually wealthy and a high official in your church, who will throw cold water on all your plans and hold back the church on every occasion. You must not hate that man. You must love and understand him if you are to be a great minister." This is a perfect example of Jesus' method of dealing with such difficulties.

"Give to him that asketh thee." Whenever we have any desirable assets, there are always some who will be continually asking us for them. Our tendency is to become angry and refuse them. As a matter of fact, many times it would be very undesirable to give them the things for which they ask. No parent would give a child everything he asks for. Jesus does not say that they should be given what they ask. He says only that we should give them love and not anger. Give them something, something that will truly help them. Often, when beggars approach us, we give to them rather irritatedly to keep from being bothered further. This is quite as contrary to the spirit of Jesus' teaching as if we had not given at all. "Give to him that asketh thee" of those things which you have that will make him a stronger character.

"From him that would borrow of thee, turn not thou away." I suppose few pests are so distasteful to the average person as the chronic borrower. The tendency is to turn him away and refuse to lend him anything further. Probably, Jesus was not teaching us always to lend him what he asks for. He does not say that. He does say that we must not turn him away in anger. Perhaps Jesus mentioned the borrower because of the very pettiness of the situation. Many a man who could love his enemy might fail at this point. There are plenty of thoroughly bad people in the world who need saving, but most of our trials will be with those individuals who irritate and bore us, and toward whom we need a great deal of affection to be patient. Yet, they are as much in need of service as anyone. If one can learn to be above these petty irritations, and return love instead of anger here, he has made a vast improvement in his strength of personality.

Consider the question of the professional tramp and beggar. Should one always give to them, thus encouraging them in their parasitic life? There is an increasing number of people who are perfectly willing that charity shall furnish them with food and clothing, for which they make no return at all. During the recent economic depression, the government has fed a great many people who could obtain no employment. Among that number were many who never wanted employment. It was quite agreeable to them to do nothing while others fed them. Shall we simply encourage them and "Turn them not away?" The answer is found in a more intimate study of the passage. The verb which is translated "turn away" actually has a stronger meaning. It means, "drive away," "to turn to flight." Let us seek understanding by turning again to fatherly love. When a child comes to his father, does the father turn him away? He certainly does not drive him away, nor does he always give him what he asks. As a father, he is interested in giving the child what is best for the development of the child. This may be exactly what the child asks for, or it may be something else. Many a college professor has had a boy of whom he was really fond come and ask to be given a passing grade in a course which he had flunked. He usually does not grant this request, but if he is a true teacher he may use the occasion to help the boy grow into a better student. Many a boy has been changed from the college house-party type of student into a serious-minded student by one such flunk. The only true course is that of fatherly love. This is not the easy way. It is the right way; better for him that asks, and for him that grants the request.

Here they are then, the three sources of anger: wounded vanity, injustice, and blocked behavior. What can we do about them? Our emotional attitudes are pretty securely fixed and do not disappear just by our willing it. Even when we frequently experience some anger for which we are very much ashamed, we often find it difficult to dislodge. They do not seem at all rational or subject to reason. It has been repeatedly emphasized that if we are to change an emotional habit, the stimulus which arouses it must be made to arouse some other emotion. Now, with respect to anger, we have these scores of anger habits. They seem each to have some reason behind it. But we have discovered that fundamentally they can be resolved into these three groups. This means, then, that every time we change an anger habit, we are changing one of these fundamental attitudes. To do this, in principle, is simple. We must make the situation which wounds our vanity cease to do so, or even if possible increase our self-feeling. We must make the situations which block our desires cease to do this. The situations which seem unjust to us must be changed so that they do not give this interpretation. A consideration of the practical ways in which each of these can be brought about will help us to solve our anger problems.

Obviously, there are theoretically two ways to enhance the self-feeling. We may find superior characteristics in ourselves, or inferior characteristics in others. That is, a situation which seems to give the other person superiority and us inferiority must be found to be the reverse of that. Obviously, what we consider superiority and inferiority is not determined by some objective criterion, but by what we have learned to consider superior and inferior. If "standing up for one's rights," or "the principle of the thing," constitute our notion of greatness, there are many occasions on which we are certain to be angry. On the other hand, if our ideal of greatness is according to the ideal set forth by Jesus in his life and teaching, and for that matter in the lives of all great men, then stimuli which will irritate the small man will have no effect on us. One of the common ways to get a sense of enhanced self-feeling is to emulate great men. When one considers that one of the outstanding characteristics of great men is their ability to meet irritating situations without anger, then he will actually get pleasure from being able to face irritating situations calmly. Furthermore, as he reflects upon the fact that an easy way to detect the small man is to find one who is constantly losing his temper, he becomes even less inclined to meet situations with this emotion. As Jesus expresses it in a later verse, "If ye love them which love you, what do ye more than others?"

To change those stimuli which cause us anger because they

block our behavior is not so simply done as this. The slow clerk will continue to be slow. The slow traffic will not speed up for us. We shall always find many of our desires being denied. Perhaps it may be suggested that at least one method is to cease being in a hurry. This is actually effective to whatever extent it can be used, but it is dodging the problem, not solving it. It is impossible to offer general principles which will fit every situation, but one or two examples will show the general method by which it can be accomplished. Here is an animal experimenter watching his first maze experiment. The animals seemed maddeningly slow and he lost his temper many times. Then he discovered that if he spent the time trying to determine the reason for the animals' behavior, he was fully occupied. The animals no longer seemed to be slow. In other words, he had used the situation for a positive purpose. Many situations can be treated in a similar manner. Then, there are many obstacles which constitute a challenge to achievement. To accept them as such, and find the solution to them, gives pleasure which will soon dispel the original anger.

What about recovering our wounded sense of justice? In the first place, one needs to be sure that there is any injustice. We have a strange tendency in our nature to hate most in other people those things of which we ourselves are guilty. However, if we find that beyond all doubt there is injustice, we can deal with it as Socrates did. When a friend was bemoaning the fact that the great philosopher must die innocent, he replied, "What, would you have me die guilty?" And perhaps the happiest persons are not those who worry a great deal about their injustices, but those who make injustices impossible. I once asked a friend of mine, a Jewish grocer, if I might "bother" him for a certain favor. His reply was: "It is no bother at all, but if there is anything that I can do for you which you would consider a bother, I would consider it a pleasure." And his life certainly backed up his words. Apparently, he did not think of himself often enough to find out whether he was being treated unjustly or not. He was too busy trying to be of service to some one else.

Perhaps now it can be seen why a great man seldom loses his temper; why the man who is always busy "standing up for his rights" seldom has any to stand up for; and why "The measure of a man is the size of the thing it takes to get his goat." "Agree with thine adversary quickly." "Resist not evil." "If a man would compel thee to go a mile, go with him twain." These are three great commands. If we make them a part of our own characters, they constitute the very foundation stones of strong personality.

These teachings must have seemed astonishing to Jesus' hearers. When we take time to consider their meaning, they still seem astonishing. In the final passage on anger, he offers a philosophy of social behavior.

Ye have heard that it hath been said, Thou shalt love thy neighbor, and hate thine enemy. But I say unto you, Love your enemies, bless them that curse you, do good to them that hate you, and pray for them which despitefully use you, and persecute you: That ye may be the children of your Father which is in heaven: for he maketh his sun to rise on the evil and on the good, and sendeth rain on the just and on the unjust. For if ye love them which love you, what reward have ye? do not even the publicans the same? And if ye salute your brethren only, what do ye more than others? do not even the publicans so?— Matthew 5:43-47.

"Love your enemies," the so-called impossible commandment. With the exception of the Golden Rule, this passage is perhaps more often quoted as best representing the spirit of Christianity than any other. "Turning the other cheek" sounds cowardly to some. "Resisting not evil" seems unjust to others. But none can fail to feel the power of this ideal of "loving enemies." Christians can quote it with the pride of ownership. This is the Christian ideal. However, this verse has a convenient characteristic for some people. It can be repeated with great devotion and sincerity and mean absolutely nothing in one's daily life. It is a little difficult to make empty phrases out of "Turn the other cheek" and "Resist not evil." This can be done, however, with "love your enemies." We can broaden the term "love" into a rather vague feeling of well-wishing to the world in general. As for "enemies," who are they? In time of war they are so far away that they never come into personal contact with us. In time of peace they consist in a sort of unseen possibility which has no real existence. How easy it is to say, "Love your enemies," without the slightest inconvenience to our ordinary modes of living. This is partly because our language fails to give us the full meaning of the word translated "enemy," which does not refer to enemies in war or to a mortal enemy. The word used in this passage really means, "hated one." In other words, Jesus says, "Love those whom you hate." This leaves less room for a meaningless interpretation. One must replace his hate with love. Furthermore, it refers especially to someone who formerly has been a friend and is now estranged. It was not Jesus' method to set forth principles which are far removed from our daily lives. If we are to get rid of anger, we must bring it about that the stimuli which formerly brought out anger, now bring out some other emotion. Jesus did not preach an impossible "self-control." He preached what is psychologically far more possible, the replacement of anger with a new emotion. Where formerly you have hated, now love.

In order that the practical value of this teaching may be more apparent, let us turn to psychology and see what methods are ordinarily used for changing anger attachments. We have seen the psychological principles involved in such changes: curing wounded vanity, overcoming obstacles, and changing our feeling of injustice. Now let us see more specifically how any one of these changes is to be made. Then we shall see whether the Christian method satisfies them. Each of the methods to be described has been applied to other emotions. Let us now apply them to anger. Deeply set emotional attachments are hard to change. The task of making our emotions intelligent is a difficult one.

Everyone should make a list of his attitudes, to discover what things make him angry. Then he should examine the reasonableness of these anger habits. He will need to be on his guard here, lest he rationalize; that is, find reasons where none exist. The safest way is to try to prove that each attitude is irrational. Then he is a little more likely to detect the false ones. Now, let him consider the list of irrational anger attitudes and begin to resolve them one by one by three methods.

The first one is called *reëducation*. This is especially valuable when the emotion is relatively weak, and when its whole history can be recalled consciously. If one can recall the original experience of an emotional attitude, and relive in his imagination this unpleasant early experience, realizing how childish and irrational it was, he will often find that the emotion will entirely disappear. In any case, the tracing back of each emotional attitude to its origin is a valuable step in its resolution if it can be made. This method is basically a recognition on the part of the person that his attitude is the result of childhood fixation. If he can see that his emotional reaction is very infantile in its nature, he will be likely to replace it with a more mature emotional habit. To "Bless them that curse you," is easily recognized as a manly attitude. This gives a high motivation for its attainment. To "Hate them that curse you" is very obviously an infantile reaction.

Often, however, the emotion is too deeply set to respond to simple reëducation. It is frequently impossible to trace it to its origin. In this case, the second method becomes more effective. This is called the method of *catharsis*. It consists in a detailed analysis of the situation. Emotional attachments are often so irrational that they fall down under close scrutiny. For example, if you are always angry at some people, analyze this anger carefully. Just what about them makes you irritated? Just how angry are you? This often makes your emotion seem ridiculous and less important, and the anger-arousing stimuli disappear. When we are faced with the command, "Love your enemies," it seems to be a pretty large order. But Jesus immediately points out a number of small habits. We could learn any one of them. When we have finished, we find that we do "Love our enemies." It seems rather difficult to "Resist not evil." That becomes much simpler when each of its elements is described. These commands of Jesus involved important situations, but they consist in replacing childish reactions with more manly ones. If a man "compels me to go with him a mile," unjustly, I shall be "standing up for my own rights" if I hold back. I shall be more "manly" if I go with him two miles. He may be stronger than I and force me to go with him one. But I shall have won the battle by a wide margin if I go with him two. This method of catharsis is valuable when an undesirable emotional attachment is made to a situation in which all of the elements call out other emotions. Therefore, when we analyze the situation, we are detaching the undesirable emotion and attaching a desirable one.

The last method is called *reconditioning*. This means the attachment of a new emotion to the situation, instead of an undesirable one. A child who is afraid of a rabbit will lose that fear if the rabbit is introduced at meal-time each day. The emotion of fear in the presence of the rabbit is replaced by that of pleasure, because the rabbit becomes associated with eating. In human relations, it is difficult to dislike people when we know them well. If one has difficulty controlling his temper toward members of another social group, let him simply cultivate a few close friends among them. In a vast majority of cases, we find our prejudices attached to groups with whom we are not intimate. As soon as intimacy is established, much of the prejudice disappears. "Do good to them that hate you."

Many believe that there is power in anger. Because the man who is angry goes at things so viciously, it might seem that to take anger out of personality would make a man lose some of his vigor. No power is lost, however. Contrast the relative power of an angry man trying to wreak vengeance upon his enemy and a father throwing all his energy into the development of his son. Jesus is giving us a way to use every bit of our energy and ability without even facing the thwarting which results in anger. "One man with the method of Christ is better than two regiments of armed men with the methods of anger and hate."

We shall find that a great majority of our poorly founded anger attitudes disappear under these three forms of treatment. But a certain number will persist and a bias will be left as a residue. And when attitudes persist, we can at least be conscious of them and recognize our bias in order to compensate for it. When Hamilton championed the election of his most bitter political enemy, Jefferson, for the Presidency, he showed a mastery over his prejudices that bespeaks a great man. When Lincoln appointed to his cabinet one of his bitterest critics, we recognize a personality of great proportions. "Love your enemies." This command is no mere ideal which Jesus gave, to be sought after only by the great man. It is an essential part of the Christian character. Psychology indicates that it is an essential part of any strong personality. No great man in history has had so little to recommend him to the world in a material way as Jesus had. He was poor, obscure, and in a small unimportant corner of the world. He preached a very short time, reached a relatively small number of people, and died unpopular, as a common criminal. What has given Jesus his great influence over mankind? We shall probably find it in his ability to love his enemies. Jesus' prayer on the cross, "Father forgive them, for they know not what they do," is the supreme example of his power. The hardened Roman centurion at the crucifixion was so impressed that he is said to have become a Christian. The power of Jesus over the world is found in this ability of his to apply love to every situation. He was no weakling. He was the most powerful personality ever to walk on earth.

We shall fail to appreciate the full value of Jesus' teaching for overcoming anger and fear, if we do not grasp the significance of his concept of a fatherly God. The value of faith has already been emphasized. That this faith shall be in a fatherly God is essential to a religion which can lift men to their highest power.

"That ye may be children of your Father which is in heaven." Let us consider a group of data to which several hypotheses have been ascribed. "He maketh His sun to rise on the evil and on the good, and sendeth rain on the just and on the unjust." On the one hand, we may choose the hypothesis that is expressed in Bertrand Russell's philosophy:

> Brief and powerless is man's life; on him and all his race the slow sure doom falls pitiless and dark. Blind to good and evil, reckless of destruction, omnipotent matter rolls on its relentless way; for Man condemned today to lose his dearest, tomorrow himself to pass through the gates of darkness, it remains only to cherish, ere yet the blow falls, the lofty thoughts that ennoble his little day—proudly defiant of the irresistible forces that tolerate for a moment his knowledge and his condemnation, to sustain alone a weary but unyielding Atlas, the world that his own ideals have fashioned despite the trampling march of unconscious power.[8]

This is a possible explanation of the phenomena that Jesus has honestly described in the above sentence.

Jesus offers another explanation of the same data. It is the explanation of fatherliness. The two are as far apart as they can be. When two such hypotheses are possible in science, we look for further data to offer confirmation to one or the other of them. Let us turn to human personality. After all, humanity is a part of the universe which the scientist and philosopher describe. What would be the effect on human personality of the hypothesis held by Bertrand Russell? All that is noble and best in man would inevitably be destroyed. His courage and love and honor would become the mere delusions of a mechanistic mind. Quite unable to cease to be human, he would be forced to a life of fear and complete pessimism. There would be no force by which man could learn to return love for anger and hate. Anger would

[8] Quoted from Fosdick, H. E., *The Meaning of Faith*, 18 f. Association Press, 1921.

grow more and more dominant, and eventually would destroy mankind. Accept Jesus' hypothesis and see what happens in human personality. Let us consider fatherliness as the most important principle of life, as Jesus did. Integration becomes possible. Fear and anger can be dispelled. Man can rise to his greatest achievement. Here is pragmatic evidence which can be offered to support Jesus' faith in a fatherly God.

>Be ye therefore perfect, even as your Father which is in heaven is perfect.—Matthew 5:48.

It is interesting to note that Jesus followed the command to love one's enemies with the concept of perfection. This concept of perfection has been a popular rationalization for many of our weaknesses. Insisting that we cannot hope to reach perfection, we simply do not try. A student once said that he would not take abnormal psychology because he thought a little abnormality is good for a person. It was suggested to him that after he had gotten rid of all the abnormalities he could, he would still have quite enough left for all practical purposes. Jesus is not satisfied with a personality that is good enough, or as good as those of other people. He insists that one of the qualifications of high character is striving toward perfection. Character is no static condition. It is a process. One who has ceased growing in character has no character at all.

Men have had many concepts of God. It remained for Jesus to call him Father. If it is true that this is the perfection of the Father, then Jesus is urging that we increase the power and breadth of our love until it transcends everything else, and utilizes all the other forces of our personality to its ends. If the size of a man's love, then, is the measure of the man, and if this in turn is determined by his capacity to love where there was once anger and hate, we can measure personality by one's anger.

"If any man will come after me, let him deny himself, and take up his cross, and follow me." Anger, hate, and suspicion are largely responsible for the sorrows and troubles of the world. Not only do they produce themselves in others, but they narrow and degrade the souls of those who hate.

Look to your angry brother for reconciliation in brotherly love. Respond to your legal oppressor by giving him more than he extorts from you. Look upon the beggar with true compassion. Retaliate the persecution of your tormentor with a desire to help him. Return the hate of those who despise you with doing good for them. "Pray for those who despitefully use you." Respond to your enemies with love. When all these emotional attachments have been changed from anger to love, one will have gone far toward becoming perfect "even as the Father is perfect."

Here, then, is the Christian method of destroying the power of anger over human personality. And here is the most significant fact of all. Psychology has long recognized that fear and anger are the two greatest enemies of strong personality, but has not always suggested a workable way out. Psychology has recognized the value of faith and love in human personality, but it has not had the resources from which to provide that faith. It has seen the need for love, not only to overcome anger but to overcome lust. It has not found a way in which to inspire that love. Jesus has given a philosophy of God and man, which requires the sort of faith that psychology finds healthy and which has been the very source of the power of science. It gives a basis for a type of love which overcomes lust, without losing any of its power, and which inspires us to the highest achievement of which man is capable. Let those who think that psychology can cure all of our mental ills without religion reflect upon these facts. Religion is indispensable to human happiness. Finally, when one sees the tremendous waste in human personality: small mean people, selfish people, dishonest people, social parasites, criminals, unhappy people, he finds that the forces of fear and anger are responsible for most of them. Jesus has given the only solution that has thus far been found. "Love your enemies" is not the impossible commandment. It is the commandment which it is impossible to be without.

Chapter X

THE RÔLE OF INFERIORITY IN HUMAN BEHAVIOR

Have you ever wondered why some people are so very sensitive and others so extremely conceited? Curiously enough, both reactions serve exactly the same purpose. Here are a few others which we make for the same reason: vanity, jealousy, envy, anxiety, always having hard luck, bullying, gossip, inability to take criticism, pretending to know it all, refusing to join groups, extreme desire for flattery, grandstand playing, being a poor loser, extreme profanity, pugnacity, suspiciousness, and many others. In fact, most of the things which make people seem small and petty. About ninety per cent of the time the reason, or one of the reasons, is an *inferiority complex*.

At two points, which we have already discussed, Jesus struck at the sources of most of the unhappiness of the world. "Be ye therefore perfect," is the natural desire of every person. Achievement is the greatest source of happiness in the world. It is the only satisfying one. To most of us, however, perfection seems impossible of fulfillment. "Be not anxious," is a command most of us would like to be able to obey, but feel unable to do so. Because we are certain of our incapacity to become perfect, we feel inferior and are decidedly anxious. This is the basis for the inferiority complex. Every one of us has one, and no two of us have the same one. It is far from being a homogeneous condition. Inferiority complexes differ widely in their causes, intensity, expressions, and methods of compensation. In the seventh chapter of

Matthew Jesus deals extensively with types of behavior which we know to be related to inferiority complexes.

To assume that Jesus was consciously dealing with this mechanism and only this mechanism in these portions of the Sermon would of course be false. Especially the Golden Rule has far wider implications. Yet if he had had nothing else in mind, he would have aimed at one of the greatest sources of unhappiness and weak personality to which mankind is subject. It is impossible for one who has not made a thorough study of it to realize how widespread is its devastating destruction of personality.

Many people nowadays talk about the inferiority complex with a very inadequate notion of its true nature. Hollingworth has pointed out that it has four principle features.[1] First there is some constitutional inferiority which serves as the starting point. Secondly, the individual has the "mastery motive," which seeks expression. Thirdly, he compensates for the inferiority. Finally, he develops a "guiding fiction," or ideal toward which he strives, as the essence of mastery.

Each of us is born with the innate desire for self-expression, or as Adler expresses it, to become "a complete man." Any lack of perfection in ourselves of which we become aware can be the cause of much unhappiness and numerous maladjustments. Such imperfections may be physical impairments, such as skin blemishes, deformities, speech defects, or acute illness in childhood. They may be abnormalities that call out ridicule, such as bow-legs, knock-knees, cross-eyes, and the like. Nervous disorders may arise in childhood, such as fears, compulsions, and anxieties. There may be social pressures, such as ridicule on the part of parents and teachers. Unfavorable contrasts are often made, as when parents compare a child with the one next door. Favoritism between children is of the same sort. It should be emphasized at this point that the justice or injustice of this feeling is of no significance. If the child thinks there is favor-

---

[1] Hollingworth, H. L., *Abnormal Psychology*, 333. The Ronald Press Company, 1930.

itism, from the psychological point of view, there is. Bullies are always producers of inferiority feelings, as well as being victims of inferiority complexes. A very important cause is the broken promises of elders. Often a father does not feel that his engagements with his child are sacred. This makes the child feel unimportant and inferior. A kindred habit is that of speaking to the child in baby talk. The growing child likes to think that he is becoming a man, and the obvious assumption that he is still a child results in feelings of inferiority. Finally, we may mention corporeal punishment. It is not to be concluded that corporeal punishment is never valuable. However, it is the habit of many parents to make very frequent, indeed almost constant use of slapping and striking for minor annoyances. Most of the naughty acts of the child are no more than innocent curiosity and over-abundant energy. To treat them all with punishment inevitably leads to feelings of inferiority.

The wide scope of these sources of inferiority makes it easy to see that it is impossible to avoid the production of some inferiority feelings in every child. It goes without saying that the fewer of these there are, the better for the child. The important problem is what he does about them. Adler, the psychologist who first described the inferiority complex, gives the name *compensation* to the reactions that we make to feelings of inferiority. The individual who has some weakness usually tries to compensate for that weakness by being very sensitive about it and by emphasizing its opposite characteristic. For example, the effeminate individual is most likely to be sensitive to being called effeminate, and compensates by trying to behave in a masculine manner. Likewise, the stout woman will be easily insulted by references to this characteristic.

Many sorts of compensation can be made to inferiority feelings. However, they can be subsumed under two groupings. On the one hand, there are the aggressive reactions by which one endeavors to compensate by fighting the inferiority. The others are in the submissive group in which the individual is so much impressed with his inferiority that he surrenders to the situation. Some characteristic reactions common to the first group include conceit, vanity, jealousy, envy, avarice, hate, and imperiousness. Among the submissive attitudes are sensitiveness, anxiety, phobias, seclusiveness, obsessions, compulsions, faint-heartedness, and pessimism.

The mechanism of repression has been dealt with at several points before. Here, it comes in again. It will be recalled that repression is the pushing out of consciousness of undesirable emotional elements. The factor which brings about this dissociation is always shame or guilt. Thus it is, in the case of the inferiority complex. If a sense of shame or guilt is attached to the factors which produce feelings of inferiority, they are repressed, and express themselves in undesirable attributes of character and personality. These are not recognized by the individual for what they really are, expressions of inferiority. Indeed, often the very opposite is true. Bluff, conceit, sarcasm, bullying, bluster, and ridicule are examples of such expressions which are most commonly recognized as the very opposite of inferiority.

It will be clear, then, that the inferiority complex is a behavior reaction which the individual uses as a substitute for the ideal reaction of superiority. The desire to excel seems universal. The ability to excel is of course far from that, especially when the wrong notions of excellence or the wrong methods of developing excellence are learned. If a boy who inherits a small stature is taught that the acme of excellence is found in being a big strong man, he is almost certain to have feelings of inferiority. He may then compensate for it by becoming especially pugnacious. This illustration is chosen because this particular reaction is among the most common there are. It is indeed rare to find a small man who has not felt some inferiority feelings, and has not made some violent reaction to prove his manhood.

The little man swaggers and talks in a loud voice, the woman without brains uses every device to be beautiful and charming, the woman who cannot be beautiful goes to college and takes an interest in "higher" things, the menial compensates by insolence to superiors. The Southerner clings to his belief in his aristocratic descent and the tradition of *noblesse oblige*, seeking to forget the relative inferiority of his section in economic and intellectual development. The New Englander makes a virtue of necessity and cherishes the faults as well as the excellences of the middle class. The Westerner boasts the material greatness of his country because he has not yet taken time to acquire cultural greatness.[2]

Adler has always insisted that this complex is the drive which makes men do things. He says that one's achievement is a compensation for an inferiority complex. No one would deny that a feeling of inferiority does cause compensatory behavior. It should be recognized, however, that it is usually abnormal behavior. Classic examples such as Demosthenes and Beethoven could be cited. It seems more probable that the apparent power behind the inferiority complex is the original drive for excellence. If some adequate means could be found for gaining this excellence, it is possible that no inferiority complex would need to be developed at all, and that such a condition would be far healthier and more normal than the inferiority compensation could ever be.

In the next few passages of the Sermon on the Mount, Jesus discusses some of these abnormal activities that are common forms of inferiority compensations at the unconscious level. In other words, they are forms of the inferiority complex.

Judge not, that ye be not judged. For with what judgment ye judge, ye shall be judged; and with what measure ye mete, it shall be measured to you again.—Matthew 7:1-2.

"Judge not" must not be interpreted to mean, "seek not to estimate." Many individuals have used this verse as a good excuse to be indifferent to the behavior of others completely. The word which is translated "judge" means, "judge ad-

[2] Pruett, L., "Inferiority Complex and Pluralistic Behavior," *Psychoanalytic Review*, 9, 1922. 22.

versely." In other words, Jesus is saying, "Do not always look for the worst in men." Luke, in his more elaborate report of the passage, shows that Jesus goes on to urge the positive attitude. "Forgive and ye shall be forgiven." This passage, then, is no curt suggestion that we "Attend to our own business," as if it involved a let-alone doctrine toward our neighbor, for whom we would take no responsibility. However, he does warn against that type of adverse criticism which looks for the evil in people, and seeing it, tears their characters to pieces.

One of the most insidious and abnormal of all the forms of compensation for an inferiority complex is the habit of gossip. There are two ways in which one may gain a higher opinion of himself than of his neighbor. The first is to increase his estimate of himself. The other is to lower his estimate of his neighbor. This is expressed in an effort to make others think more highly of him than of his neighbor. Thus, if I can call enough attention to the faults of my neighbor, I may lower him beneath myself. This is the aim of gossip. The gossip is rarely maliciously anxious to injure his neighbor. He is interested in helping himself. It will be observed that he seldom gossips about a person in a lower social scale than his own. Usually, gossip is restricted within the same social set.

A very significant investigation has been reported by Spearman on the tendency of individuals to exalt themselves.[3] Doubting that self-exaltation is an entity, he chose six different versions of it, so as to ascertain how far they correlated with each other. The six versions he used may be briefly described as: (1) simply the desire to excel, (2) the desire to impose one's will on other people, (3) excessive belief in his ability, (4) feeling of satisfaction with himself, (5) eagerness for admiration, (6) offensive manifestations of this self-esteem. Assuming that self-exaltation is one entity, these various versions of it ought to correlate with each

[3] Spearman, C. E., "A New Method for Investigating the Springs of Action," *The Wittenberg Symposium on Feelings and Emotions*, 39-48. Clark University Press, 1928.

other perfectly. Actually they do not. This would indicate that there is a common element in each of them, but that they are not identical. It will be observed that the first version is a native drive. All men desire to excel. The other five are commonly compensations for an inferiority complex. All of the other five correlate much more highly with each other than they do with the first. Here, then, are six ways of trying to obtain a positive self-feeling. What effect does each of them have upon character? When these six traits are compared with the six desirable character traits: kindness on impulse, kindness on principle, corporate spirit, trustworthiness, conscientiousness, and interest in religion, the desire to excel always has a positive correlation with these desirable traits. This would seem to show that whereas the natural desire to excel is perfectly wholesome, these forms of compensations for inferiority complexes are always failures in producing the desired results. Like fear and anger they miss the mark toward which they are aimed.

Another very interesting feature of gossip is that it usually represents characteristics of which the gossiper himself is guilty. Paul, in commenting upon this passage, expressed it correctly when he said: "Therefore thou art inexcusable, O man, whosoever thou art that judgest: for wherein thou judgest another, thou condemnest thyself; for thou that judgest doest the same things." In psychology this mechanism is called *projection*. Stated in popular terminology, it means the tendency to judge others by oneself. When one has a fault he does not like to admit it himself. Hence, he represses it from his own consciousness, and attributes it by way of compensation to his neighbor. For example, the dishonest man is invariably suspicious of the honesty of his fellow men. The liar never believes his neighbor's story. The unfaithful wife or husband usually suspects the fidelity of the other. It does not follow that one will attribute his good qualities to others, but it is certain that he will do so with his bad ones. It is correct insight into human nature to judge a man as he judges his neighbor adversely.

A case in illustration is that of a man whose inferiority obsession arose from the fact of an inferior education. Being thrown continually with people of a higher culture and training, he was subjected to humiliating realizations of incompleteness. Habits of behavior in the nature of defense reactions developed. He became offensively contemptuous of all things "high brow." Teachers were all "grafters" and "educated fools." The schools were hopelessly misguided and ineffectual. Nothing in education was right. As Bret Harte would put it, "his language was frequent and painful"; and in his efforts to prove that he ranked with the best in spite of a meagre education, his manner grew loudly controversial and bombastic.[4]

There is another aspect to the danger of adverse judgment, which has been discussed previously. That is, that hate begets hate. The one who is the object of gossip is likely to return in kind that which is said about him, The personalities of both individuals are lowered. There are few forms of anger behavior so difficult to return with love, as slander. When one gossips he makes an enemy, which is bad enough in itself; but also in becoming an enemy the other experiences hate and hence becomes a weaker character.

The notion that people in glass houses should not throw stones has deterred many a man in the carrying out of his obvious duty. Jesus' answer to this is very clear. It is the attitude with which one judges that is emphasized. Adverse criticism is returning evil with evil, anger with anger, and hate with hate. This has nothing to do with an honest estimate of one's fellow men. Luke describes the Christian attitude beautifully in the clause, "Forgive, and ye shall be forgiven." We have examined the word "forgive" at length. In brief, it is the loving regeneration of one's fellow men. It does involve a recognition of the shortcomings of the other. One cannot help his neighbor if he does not know his needs, but he can, by meeting his faults with a different attitude—the attitude of fatherly love. Every one of us has been criticized over and over again by two different individuals. On the one

[4] Valentine, P. F., *The Psychology of Personality*, 287. D. Appleton and Company, 1927. By permission of D. Appleton-Century Company.

hand, the criticism made us angry. The other was so kindly done that we appreciated it. The latter is the sort of criticism which regenerates us and makes us better. This is forgiveness. Jesus, then, is saying that we shall look for the best in men, and see even in their failings the foundations for greater characters and stronger personalities.

"For with what judgment ye judge, ye shall be judged." We have much more need to be afraid of giving adverse criticism than of the original sense of inferiority. It never helps our social standing to gossip. This was clearly shown in Spearman's experiment, previously cited. Our inferiority complex only becomes worse. It is an abnormal adjustment. Gossiping has long been recognized as a great sin. In the early days of our own country it was subject to severe penalty. It was soon evident, however, that these severities had little or no deterring effect upon the guilty parties. They only gossiped more slyly and more insidiously. Psychology recognizes that it is not so much a sin in the ethical sense of the term as it is a disease. It is really a form of paranoia, and is very difficult to cure. If it is to be cured, it has to be done by a fundamental change of attitude and not of external behavior. The fundamental attitude on which it is built is the selfish fear of the inferiority complex. Obviously, its cure is found in Jesus' doctrine of love. If one assumes the attitude of love toward his fellow men and forgets himself in his effort to serve them, like the parent toward the child, he will see in every fault of his fellows an opportunity to change them for the better. If this is his method of approach to all such problems, he is likely to find that love is met with love. Soon his fellows trust him, then love him, and thus give to him the regenerative power of love which makes him stronger. Thus his inferiority complex is soon lost. Men like to be served and they love the servant. He may be imposed upon, but will not even consider it an imposition. Many an individual suffering from the worst sort of inferiority complex, with the narrow, cruel, poisonous character which so often accompanies it, finds some task of real service, and is transformed into a splendid, generous character. There is nothing necessarily mysterious about the transforming power of Jesus' love. Love always begets love and transforms its recipients.

An individual, then, who wishes to excel others, and tries to do so by gossip, uses the most hopeless type of compensation for his inferiority complex, because it implies that he has no hope of building himself up. He only hopes to bring others down to his level. Compare this method of excelling with the effort to excel by fatherly love. It is obvious which is more likely to succeed in the effort to get a sense of achievement.

Here is a man who seems to be a fanatic. He seems to think that the salvation of the world depends upon the elimination of Sunday baseball. Many people oppose that. He preaches against it, spends his money in propaganda against it, is constantly wrought up about it. He has unquestionably exaggerated it out of all proportion to its actual importance. The next teaching of Jesus to be discussed fits this sort of behavior perfectly.

And why beholdest thou the mote that is in thy brother's eye, but considerest not the beam that is in thine own eye? Or how wilt thou say, to thy brother, Let me pull out the mote out of thine eye; and, behold, the beam is in thine own eye? Thou hypocrite, first cast out the beam out of thine own eye; and then shalt thou see clearly to cast out the mote out of thy brother's eye.—Matthew 7:3-5.

Here is another of those humorous but poignant analogies used so frequently by Jesus in his teaching. Employing the substance of an old Jewish proverb, Jesus gave it a freshness and personal touch which accounts for its strength to us. The "mote" was a bit of chaff or particle of wood. The "beam" was about the same as our own word, beam; that is, a large piece of timber. Obviously, having a beam in one's eye is an impossibility. However, a beam could stand in front of us and obstruct our whole vision. Here, then, are individuals with great sins trying to reform those with small ones. One is reminded of a later sermon, when Jesus criticized the scribes and Pharisees as "tithing mint and anise and cummin and omitting the weightier matters of the law, justice and mercy and faith." Jesus' way of putting it brings a smile, but a rather rueful one to the man with a "beam."

In this figure is found the second form of compensation for an inferiority complex. When one's inferiority consists in a lack of moral stamina, he is ashamed of his sinfulness and is anxious that it shall not be seen, and that others shall seem as sinful as he. Therefore, he picks flaws in others. It differs from the gossip reaction just discussed. In gossip, the individual is trying to pull the other person down to his level. In this reaction, he is dealing with the object of his criticism directly, and trying to gain a feeling of supremacy by endeavoring to help the other, thus directing attention from his own "beams" to the other's "motes."

The moral realm is not the only one in which this type of mechanism occurs. Wherever we are lacking, we are likely to compensate in some fashion or other.

This tendency to cast out "motes" from others, especially when they are like one's own "beams," is a very common one. The liar is very likely to be particularly sensitive to being deceived by some one else. The egotist will despise conceit in another. The gossip will most bitterly resent any gossip about him. These people commonly think they see "motes" when really they are looking at their own "beams."

When this tendency is carried to its extreme form, we find a condition which we call reformatory paranoia. The patient usually has some deep-lying sin which he has repressed. To prevent others from discovering it, and to satisfy his own conscience as to his moral stamina, he becomes an ardent reformer. Of course, this is entirely an unconscious process. The patient is consciously quite sincere in his behavior. Usually, the sin chosen for the subject of reformation is a rather minor one. He magnifies it out of all proportion, and soon believes and teaches that it is the root of all evil and its reformation the only source of world salvation.

It must be recalled that an individual is unaware of the presence of "beams" in his own eye. The attitudes so described are quite unconscious. They bias his behavior without his knowing that it is biased. "Common sense" is usually one such unconscious prejudice. If one examines his own brand of "common sense" carefully, he is likely to discover that it is "common" only to himself. Actually, it is likely to be only a compensation for an inferiority complex. He likes to think that his own notions are so well established as to be just good "horse sense." If this mechanism is unconscious and we are sincere in our reforming, how can we discover and cure our "beams"?

"Thou hypocrite, cast out first the beam out of thine own eye; and then shalt thou see clearly to cast out the mote out of thy brother's eye." If a modern psychologist should give this same advice he would say that one must first gain an objective attitude, and then he will be sufficiently able to avoid his own shortcomings to help others. One of the most common things in the world is advice given by people who have no objective foundations for their advice.

Much has been said about this objective attitude. Now it will be discussed more thoroughly. In discussing the Beatitudes, the scientific attitude was described in some detail, especially in the discussion of the "poor in spirit," whom we found to represent the very essence of the scientific or objective attitude. Essentially, it consists in casting the "beam" out of one's eye in order that he may see clearly in his efforts to cast "motes" out of the eyes of others. Jesus does not deny that this latter needs to be done, but he does insist that clear vision is essential to doing it well. We shall not be concerned with the "motes" in this discussion, however, but with the man with the "beam." How shall we cast out the "beam"? In other words, how can the objective attitude be attained and of what value is it?

In the history of mental therapy, numerous methods of

cure have arisen and been tried. The most recent of these involves the use of this objective attitude. A goodly number of the former theories rested, fundamentally, on the power of suggestion or auto-suggestion. A patient suffering from some physical or mental malady was told that if he recited a certain formula frequently enough, such as: "Every day in every way I am getting better and better," he would soon be healed. There is no denying the value of faith in therapy. Very definite physiological healing agencies are thereby facilitated. However, to blind oneself to a real pathological condition can never be efficacious. A woman suffering from a painful heart disease was told by her physician that she must never exert herself. A faith healer told her that if she believed herself well, she would be well. She accepted this, decided that she was well, and went forth for a brisk walk. She dropped dead from heart failure. Such suggestion was blind ignorance. Contrast that case history with this one. A boy announced that he was severely depressed and was about to drop out of college. When the causes of his depression were sought, it was discovered that most of them long antedated the depression itself, and none of them was especially serious, or had ever been depressing before. This is commonly characteristic of the mental disease known as manic-depressive insanity. Of this disease it is also known that if one waits long enough it clears up of its own accord. This was pointed out to the student. He was advised to continue his work, paying as little attention as possible to his depression, and not to worry about it at all. He recognized the truth of this advice, obeyed instructions, and soon found that his depression was gone, with no irreparable damage done. Here was a fine example of the objective attitude. The boy stood off and looked at himself objectively. He found out just what was wrong with himself and what to expect. If he had maintained his subjective attitude, he would have insisted upon the excuses for his depression, worried about it excessively, perhaps dropped out of college, and regretted it all the rest of his life. Here was the "beam" of depression, which this boy was able to "cast out" and solve his problem objectively.

We may not always be able to prevent our feelings, emotions, biases, prejudices, fears, and angers from occurring. We can, however, develop the ability to weigh them objectively, in order that we may estimate their true importance. This does not mean that thereby one is doing unemotional thinking. Attitudes are emotional habits. The objective attitude is such an emotional habit. One simply develops the emotional urge to be objective. Often we see a man in the midst of the most trying circumstances keep calm and self-possessed. In a recent meeting, the whole audience assailed the speaker from every point of view with the most sarcastic and bitter remarks. He sat through the whole discussion quietly making notes. When the time came for his answer, he replied to each criticism in the calmest possible spirit and in the fairest possible way. He completely carried his point because of his objective attitude. Here is a man assailed by fear. If he can meet the situation calmly in the face of that fear, his is the objective attitude. The story is told of one of Napoleon's generals, who, just before a battle, noticed his knees shaking against the saddle. He looked at them a minute and then remarked: "Shake on, O knees, you will shake worse than that before you get out of here." We do many foolish things under emotion. If we can develop a powerful objective attitude, we shall go a long way toward sublimating all our emotions, so that we can use them rather than have them dominate us.

Of all the emotions that disintegrate our effectiveness, perhaps the most devastating is the inferiority complex. The reason such abnormal means are used to compensate for it, such as gossip and fanatical reformation, is that we fear to face the facts. Many a student has refused to study psychology, because he feared lest he find out undoubted evidences of his inferiority, and know what he now only suspects. Actually, each of us has limitations and capacities. An objective estimate of these is essential to the fullest and most efficient administration of them.

It is not uncommon to hear it said that one should not endeavor to make a psychological self-examination, because that leads to morbid introspection, which is undesirable. This is not true. When morbid introspection occurs, it is a symptom of a diseased personality, and not the result of objective analysis. No one need fear an accurate estimate of himself.

If, then, one finds himself tremendously interested in the "motes" in other people's eyes, he can be suspicious of the presence of a "beam" in his own. He will do well to adopt the objective attitude, "cast out the beam," and make his social adjustment more efficient both for his neighbor and for himself.

Delinquent conduct as a compensation for feelings of inferiority is clearly shown in the behavior of a ten-year-old boy who because of glandular imbalance was too obese to hold his own in competitive games on the playground at school. The other boys made fun of him, and he felt that he had to "put himself across" with them in some fashion. He began to invent tales of himself as a daring burglar, but the boys laughed at these. Then he actually began to take money, at first from his parents, and displayed it flourishingly in treating his companions. Next he advanced to stealing from his teachers and others outside the family circle. His misdemeanors soon brought him to Juvenile Court, but this was only an added advantage to his boasting. He succeeded in winning the respectful admiration of his comrades by his antisocial behavior when he had been unable to do so in any other way. Medical treatment and a strenuous course of athletic training which reduced his weight and enabled him to participate successfully in group games solved his problem.[5]

This is a rather extreme though very common case. However, most of us at some time do things which we would not ordinarily do except for the desire to impress others when we feel inferior. Most of us who do such things to win acclaim find that the acclaimers are hardly worth the trouble, and that they are likely to despise us for our efforts. Jesus' next teaching applies to such problems.

[5] Groves, E. R., and Blanchard, P., *Introduction to Mental Hygiene*, 68. Henry Holt and Company, 1930.

> Give not that which is holy unto the dogs, neither cast ye your pearls before swine, lest they trample them under their feet, and turn again and rend you.—Matthew 7:6.

Of course, dogs cannot understand holiness, and are quite as likely to rend the holy as readily as the unholy. Anyone who has seen a lively pup tear up a costly article realizes that he does so with no appreciation or capacity for appreciation of its value. The dog is capable of recognizing certain characteristics in an article. In this case he discovers its tearability. Other differences are negligible. Hence, no one gives a dog expensive things to tear up when old rags are quite as satisfactory to the dog. To carry the analogy to human realms, the man who has no appreciation for things holy will treat them as he does other things. It is foolish, then, to give holy things to him. Likewise, swine judge most things according to their edibility. They investigate everything in an effort to discover whether it can be eaten or not. If it cannot, they trample it under their feet. Pearls would be worthless in the mind of a hog, because they are not something to eat. He would most certainly walk on them. Again, in the human realm, it is foolish to give "pearls" to him for whom the bodily appetites are the only values in life. Culture is the subject of ridicule to him whose life consists in the satisfaction of his physical desires.

In this verse is found the third form of compensation for an inferiority complex. This expresses itself in an excessive seeking after popularity. How tragic it is to see a boy enter college with the highest of ideals, and then be swayed by a group of "jolly good fellows" who inform him that the art of being popular consists in becoming one of them. He takes the best that is in him and throws it to the "dogs," and casts his talents before "swine." Why? Is it because he wants to do these things? On the contrary, it is because he has so little confidence in himself that he seeks to bolster up what he considers his inferiority by buying this popularity. The unfortunate part of it is that it does not work.

Here is a boy who entered college, and was laughed at because he insisted upon hard work and moral integrity. But in his senior year he was elected to positions of leadership, and graduated with the wholesome respect of all his fellows. On the other hand, the "jolly good fellow" is popular, but neither trusted nor given responsibility.

Here is a girl who falls in love with a young man. He tells her that her morals are old-fashioned, and that he will lose interest unless she deserts her ideals. If she feels some inferiority for her power over him, she may compensate by a lowering of her ideals. In so doing, she soon finds her ideals trampled upon, herself discarded, and her opportunity lost to help one man evolve from swinehood to manhood.

On the other hand, here is a young man who was hardly ever sober long enough to go to classes for the first part of his college career. He met a fine girl. She pointed out firmly that the only path to winning her affections was a different sort of behavior. He followed that path, and did great work for the last part of his academic career. This story could be multiplied over and over again.

Possibly there is no sort of inferiority feeling more distressing and more of a weight upon happiness than that which comes to the woman who supposes that she must constantly explain her not marrying. She comes to imagine that her status needs to be defended. Although she may prefer single life, she nevertheless suffers from a notion that she is counted among those lacking in appeal to men. Instead of making the most of the lot that she has either willed or had forced upon her by circumstances, she allows chronic inferiority to rob her of most of its compensations. She becomes extremely sensitive and awkwardly self-conscious in the presence of men, especially when they are unmarried, by her conduct deepening her inferiority and losing opportunities of marriage that might otherwise come to her. The dissatisfaction of the unmarried woman is often a reaction against the feeling of inferiority rather than a conscious sense of the loss of the matrimonial experience or parenthood.[6]

[6] Groves, E. R., *Personality and Social Adjustment*, 242 f. Longmans, Green and Company, 1931.

Here then is the form of a very common type of inferiority complex. Fear of the opinion of others, even when it brings out behavior which is opposed to our principles, is its chief feature. Almost none of us is entirely free from its influence. Most of us do things because we are afraid of what people will think if we do not, instead of doing them because we sincerely wish to. The very word, prude, has come to have a very undesirable connotation, because it implies over-morality. Many people lower their moral level to avoid this terrible condemnation of being a prude. This can never be anything except a compensation for inferiority.

Let us analyze this type of reaction. Again, the fundamental drive is for excelling. In this case, we have learned that excelling brings popularity. Hence, we may assume that to gain popularity is the end justifiable by whatever means. Therefore, we think that we may well invest our "pearls" and that which is "holy" in the effort to gain this popularity. We discover that it is fickle, and likely to change at a moment's warning. However, we shall not lose the complex by pointing out this fact alone. We must find some other way by which the original drive can be satisfied. In the temptations, Jesus discarded three very common notions as to the criteria of excelling: money, popularity, and power. His teaching would have been very ineffective to meet this problem, if he had not offered some better way of satisfying this drive.

To whom shall we "give that which is holy" and before whom "cast our pearls"? Obviously, it is implied, only to those who are prepared to receive them as befits their nature. If we recognize that integration of personality is the psychological correlate of divinity and holiness, it is obvious that disintegration will be its opposite and characteristic of "dogs" and "swine."

It is with a true understanding of some of the great sorrows of human nature, coming from an ignorant but fear-ridden inferiority complex, that Jesus urges us not to "give that which is holy to the dogs" nor to "cast our pearls before swine."

INFERIORITY IN HUMAN BEHAVIOR

Men have always looked for short cuts to fame and fortune. The concept of prayer which makes of God a sort of divine Santa Claus is carried into many phases of life. Men invest in get-rich-quick stocks. They buy patent medicines for the same reason. They go through college with the idea that a college education, in itself, works a magical transformation. They follow panaceas for our social ills. But above all they expect to obtain a powerful personality cheaply and quickly. Orthodox psychology has often been condemned because it does not promise this quick transformation. But no child ever had as much faith in Santa Claus as some men have in the promises of the pseudo-psychologies.

Several summers ago I met a bank clerk in the Rocky Mountains. When he found that I was a psychologist he came to me for advice. He had been working conscientiously for years and planning ways of "getting ahead" to buy a home, but for some reason he seemed to be avoided by Lady Luck. He decided that it might be something beside enthusiastic work day in and day out that brought the vague reward we call "success." One day an advertisement caught his eye. It started: "You, too, may have this amazing secret of success." After reading through the advertisement he sent in the coupon and soon had the books in his possession. Eagerly he drank in every word, feeling that here he had found exactly what he needed. Then he saw another advertisement of an "Inner Power Now Revealed" book. He bought that. And another, and another until he had two shelves filled with books of this sort when I first made his acquaintance. These books I borrowed and read. In not one of them did I find anything that would help one in any other way than by reassuring him of his great potency for success—and assurance will not butter bread or buy a home.[7]

This is another result of the native desire to excel. It is really an inferiority complex when one loses confidence in the possibilities of obtaining this feeling of achievement by his own efforts. He then turns to these miraculous methods for self-improvement. Many hundreds of people are de-

[7] Laird, D. A., *Increasing Human Efficiency*. Harper & Brothers, 1929.
Quoted from Valentine, P. F., *The Psychology of Personality*, 354. D. Appleton and Company, 1927. By permission of D. Appleton-Century Company.

frauded of their money by these pseudo-psychologies every year, because there are no short cuts.

On the other hand, men have certainly not utilized even the major portion of their potential personality power. With the right methods they could be more powerful. They could excel. They could achieve great things, but not by short cuts.

Ask, and it shall be given you; seek, and ye shall find; knock, and it shall be opened unto you: for everyone that asketh receiveth; and he that seeketh findeth; and to him that knocketh it shall be opened.—Matthew 7:7-8.

Anyone who imagines that this is a "Santa Claus" teaching has made no effort either to understand the teaching itself or to interpret it in terms of Jesus' total teaching. It is a plea for faith, but examination will show that it is for an experimental faith.

Fatalism, pessimism, and mechanism are very often nothing more than types of reaction to an inferiority complex. One who has not succeeded feels inferior. But if he believes in fatalism, he can throw the blame for his failure on the nature of the universe. This is much more comforting. Here is a similar reaction. A student is afraid he will flunk a course. He becomes ill and misses the final examination. He is flunked, to be sure, but he can lay the blame on something else than his own inferiority. He can always think that he could have passed if only he had not been ill. Between this utter surrender reaction of the fatalist, and the ignorant and naïve credulity of the dupe there is a principle which is implied in this verse, which does meet the problem of how to achieve things in life. "Ask, seek, knock."

This passage has not received its just due when one interprets it simply as a redundant admonition to the practice of prayer. It is no careless promise on the part of Jesus that every prayer will be answered instantly. Its meaning is much deeper than that. It is a plea for faith. In this passage is implied the fourth way in which an inferiority complex expresses itself. It is obvious that faith is the very antithesis of inferiority. No Christian who believes in the power of God can very well have an inferiority complex. It follows that if one has a strong inferiority complex with respect to his ability to do things he lacks faith. Here is a group of people who think they have prayed and found their prayers unanswered; that they have sought for power and have not received it; that they have knocked at the door of opportunity and have not found it open to them. They now stand before Jesus and seek help. Jesus teaches them the meaning of faith. He urges them to ask, believing.

Many a student has "asked" fervently, has even "sought" for the answer, only to find blocks in the way which seemed impassable. Only to him who "knocks" can the answer be forthcoming. Here is the scientist again. He asks his question of nature, he seeks for an answer. When none is forthcoming, he goes into his laboratory and experiments. This is the truest form of "knocking." Individuals with an inferiority complex seldom get this far in the process. They have long since given up. It is only the individual who has faith in receiving an answer who continues until he has found it.

Finally in exposition, it is to be noted that there is no promise that one will be given that for which he asks, or that he will find exactly what he is seeking, or that the door on which he is knocking is the one which will open. An incident in one of my own researches will illustrate this point. I was testing the learning ability of white rats under different periods of hunger. I anticipated that there would be a regular relationship between the amount of hunger and the degree of learning. A few trials convinced me that one group was learning in a way very much contrary to my expectations. At first, I was angry and disappointed, thinking that my experiment was destroyed. However, it turned out that this was an important discovery. My major professor in commenting upon it said this: "In experimenting, you will seldom find what you expect to find, but what you do find will usually be far more interesting."

Here, then, is a philosophy of experimental faith to replace pessimism or credulity. It is the assumption that the universe is fatherly, and that if we find unsatisfactory things about it, the cause lies in our method of trying to get satisfaction and not in the universe. Perhaps it may be asked whether there is any evidence that such faith is justified. The answer is, that aside from the demonstrated evidence of the validity of Jesus' social principles in society, there is always the fact that such a faith is mentally healthier. This is especially true in connection with this surrender type of inferiority complex. The fact that such a faith does work in human personality is strong evidence of its validity.

Many, indeed, are the reactions made to the surrender type of inferiority complex. Mention has already been made of pessimism, atheism, and fatalism. One of the most common of the minor mental diseases is essentially such a reaction. It is one form of what is commonly called a nervous breakdown; more technically, neurasthenia. Here is a case history.

An unmarried woman, aged 26, complained to the writer of the following symptoms: She suffered extreme fatigue, particularly in the morning, and found it quite impossible to sustain effort in a given direction for any length of time. She complained of being frequently nauseated in the morning, of a poor and very irregular appetite, of indigestion, and constipation. She was troubled by frequent headaches; and eye-strain and blurred vision preventing her reading even the headlines in the newspapers. Severe pains in the back and legs made it impossible for her to sit, lie, or stand in comfort. She had "ringings" and "buzzings" in her ears and in order to drown these distracting and highly unpleasant noises she carried a man's watch which she held to her left ear. She complained of being extremely nervous and distractable and was very irritable, becoming immediately exasperated at the sound of a slamming door, footsteps in the hallway, and even noises on the street. Finally this patient was in a constant state of anxiety particularly concerning her health and physical appearance. And, as is usually the case, she stated that she was unable to sleep on account of her illness. She explained that her aches and pains and akoasms kept her from getting any rest and that the need of rest kept her from regaining her health and left her in a continuous state of fatigue.[8]

This is such a common mental difficulty that a great many people at some time or other suffer more or less from it. A man wakes up in the morning as tired as when he went to sleep. He has periods in which he cannot sleep. He feels a constant tired feeling which makes him irritable and unhealthy. These are usually indications of neurasthenia. They are regularly forms of reaction to an inferiority complex. The minister who is about to fail in his work may have a nervous breakdown, the unconscious motive of which is to hide both from his people and from himself the fact of his failure. He seems to be "working himself to death." How many people have sought medical relief for such difficulties, when actually what they needed was faith! Indeed, many of them have been cured by faith. This is one explanation of many of the faith cures. The disease is essentially a defense mechanism for an inferiority complex. The faith destroys the basis for the feeling of inferiority and the physical symtoms disappear.

This lack of faith is behind most laziness and lack of ambition. The desire to excel is inherited. It will be a potent drive to achievement unless the hope of achievement is lost. When a boy decides that he cannot accomplish anything, he is likely to be lazy and lack ambition. Many a splendid boy has been lost because his parents destroyed his self-confidence. In other cases, they have taught him to look for get-rich-quick schemes as the only source of excelling.

For this sense of inferiority the objective attitude is a sovereign preventative and remedy. If this enables the youth to discover self, it becomes clear that one's limited ability is similar to that of all other individuals, that one's own self, whatever it may be, is one's own unique gift and usually represents, at least potentially, superiority in some small field. This insight helps one to give up trying to do many things imperfectly and enables one to

---

[8] Fisher, V. E., *An Introduction to Abnormal Psychology*, 162 f. The Macmillan Company, 1929.

achieve a superiority in a limited field that would be impossible otherwise.[9]

This passage involves also one of the most effective methods for obtaining the objective attitude. The whole method of science is experiment. In science, one never thinks of reaching a conclusion without experimental data upon which to found that conclusion. In this passage, the same process is urged for gaining faith. Experiment with prayer and faith and get objective data for strengthening your faith. When one is afflicted with an inferiority complex of any sort, there is no better beginning for its cure than this objective method of experiment. None of us is born so completely lacking in talent that he cannot do good work in some field. If there are exceptions to this rule in the feebleminded, there is the accompanying condition that they do not feel inferior, and so do not have inferiority complexes. The very presence of an inferiority complex indicates the presence of some ability. Hence, even if one has started out on some venture for which he does not have the ability, an intelligent analysis of his own personality will reveal places in which he can excel. Far less unhappiness would exist in the world if all men took such objective attitudes.

A student who had flunked a course went to a psychologist and asked whether or not he had the ability to pass the course. He said that if he did not have the ability, he would start in some other field in which he could succeed. On the other hand, if the ability was present, he would try again and seek the cause of his failure, so that it would not occur again. This is a good example of the objective attitude at its best.

A salesman had not been successful for a time. He tried to find out if he was a misfit for his job; whether or not he could succeed if he tried harder.

This is sometimes called the method of direct attack. Some individuals approach their inferiority complexes with complete surrender. They just give up. Direct attack does not

[9] Burnham, W. H., *The Wholesome Personality*, 236. D. Appleton and Company, 1932. By permission of D. Appleton-Century Company.

mean that the subject will butt his head against a stone wall, but that he will tackle the situation courageously to discover what the real reason is for his lack of success, and find out in which field he can do his best work.

However, it must be remembered that this lack of faith will not be recognized by its owner as an expression of an inferiority complex. He will most likely talk at length on the ineffectiveness of prayer, or even become a professing atheist. This is why the cure is so difficult, because the patient does not realize that he is sick. Jesus does not try a method of logical argument. We are all aware of the futility of such procedure. He suggests the pragmatic test of science, experiment.

When Syngo first attracted the attention of a clinical psychologist, he was standing just inside the main entrance of a school building looking out upon the playground. He was timidly watching a game of football and as the boy-players drew near he shrank back into a shadow, emerging again only when the play had passed to a distant part of the yard. Finally, he summoned his courage, dashed down the steps, then through the gate, and was still running when he disappeared from sight two blocks away. Syngo's timidity was not a passing psychological condition. His conduct upon all occasions had the same mark upon it. In classroom, when he was called upon to recite, he stood abashed, stammering and nervously wincing when the other pupils laughed at him and whispered. At recess he remained always in the general assembly room where he might have, and frequently required, the protection of one of the masters. He was abused at every opportunity and was a constant object of ridicule and uncomplimentary invective. An interview with the boy served to bring out the rest of the picture of an inferiority complex in the primary stage of its development. He complained, "I can't fight and I can't play any games." Syngo was frail and was incompetent in athletics. He had an adult manner of speech and conduct. And his scholarship was so nearly perfect that he was held up as a sort of model. All of these qualities were, of course, sources of violent irritation.[10]

Probably Syngo would have insisted that the Lord had

[10] Bagby, E., *The Psychology of Personality*, 181. Henry Holt and Company, 1928.

treated him badly in his physical and social inheritance. Being of considerable intelligence, he might easily have been convinced that the notion of a good God was very much of a delusion. Certainly, he would have felt that all of the "asking, seeking, or knocking" he could do would be futile in the face of such insurmountable difficulties.

Syngo was cured of his inferiority complex. He learned to play football. Due to his mental superiority he was taught the position of quarterback. He studied the theory of the game until he was a master at it. He also learned to forward pass. This gave him the necessary prestige for social adjustment and a sense of achievement which made him regain his self-confidence. The very attributes which had seemed his downfall now became his source of success. Many a man has felt as Syngo did, that his inheritance was lacking, and that he stood no chance of success. To him, Jesus would say:

> Or what man is there of you, whom if his son ask bread, will he give him a stone? Or if he ask a fish, will he give him a serpent? If ye then, being evil, know how to give good gifts unto your children, how much more shall your Father which is in heaven give good things to them that ask Him?—Matthew 7:9-11.

Considerable emphasis has been laid upon the faith of science in the lawfulness of the universe. To many an individual, this very fact has been the source of a depressing form of the inferiority complex. The psalmist expressed it: "When I consider thy heavens, the work of thy fingers, the moon and the stars, which thou hast ordained; what is man, that thou art mindful of him? And the son of man, that thou visitest him?" The natural laws seem so cold and soulless that we are almost afraid of them. How, then, shall we know that even if we obey the spiritual laws, we shall not find ourselves still in sorrow and misfortune? How can we discover whether or not the universe is friendly? It is not easy to persuade the youth to follow Jesus, if that path leads to certain unhappiness. To many, this has been accepted as a natural consequence of being religious. Many an individual who accepts Christianity believes that his conversion consists in giving up a lot of pleasures because they are wrong.

Man is essentially a dependent individual. However courageous he may be or pretend to be, he needs someone upon whom he can depend. In the discussion of the psychology of fear, this sense of dependence was pointed out as one of the greatest sources of overcoming fear. Thus, if one feels himself to be in the midst of a heartless and soulless universe, his sense of dependence upon its friendliness is lost, and he feels insignificant and inferior. He then becomes the true pessimist, and insists that life is all an illusion, that actually one is quite likely to receive a "stone" in answer to his prayer for "bread" and a "serpent" instead of "fish." This is not the result of sound reasoning, but the rationalized expression of an inferiority complex. Let us follow Jesus' reasoning on this question.

Observe the nature of his reasoning. It is not a deep philosophical argument. The reasoning which Jesus used is essentially a reconditioning process. He takes situations which ordinarily we attach to one emotional tone, and attaches them to another. Stimuli which we ordinarily see as "stones" and "serpents," Jesus points out are not. Even your earthly father would not give you "stones" and "serpents." Your heavenly Father is much wiser than he. Hence, there must be some other explanation of these seemingly disagreeable things.

This, again, is our experimental faith. It is what is meant by divine providence. It is the implicit faith that behind everything there is some secret, some law which it is possible for us to learn with which to accomplish miracles.

We are already beginning to see that some of the things which seem to be "serpents" are actually food. The Jews gradually discovered that suffering was like that. The law of vicarious sacrifice is the resultant "food." As one looks at the troubles of those about him and at his own, he may feel that the universe is heartless and cold. Actually, if he has faith in its fatherliness, he may discover, as did the Jews, that out of suffering come some of the finest spiritual gifts.

Jesus, then, insists that God is such a father that He will give only good gifts to His children. If "stones" are given them when they ask for "bread," we should search for their meaning, being sure that it is out of love that they are given. Furthermore, when gifts are taken from us which seem all right to us, we should believe that they are really "serpents" which a good father would not give to his children. How often we have begged for something which seemed very valuable to us at the time. We were refused, and later discovered that it was a "serpent." The spirit of this teaching is beautifully illustrated by a prayer written by an anonymous Confederate soldier. It is entitled *The Creed of a Soldier.*

He asked for strength that he might achieve; he was made weak that he might obey.
He asked for health that he might do greater things; he was given infirmity that he might do better things.
He asked for riches that he might be happy; he was given poverty that he might be wise.
He asked for power that he might have the praise of men; he was given weakness that he might feel the need of God.
He asked for all things that he might enjoy life; he was given life that he might enjoy all things.
He had nothing that he asked for, but everything that he hoped for.
His prayer is answered.
He is most blessed.[11]

Science has been built by men who had faith in the laws which they were discovering. It is common to hear people talk of the heartlessness of natural law. Yet, scientists use it to contribute greatly to our comfort and pleasure. Consider the courage that scientists have exhibited because of their faith in the lawfulness of the universe. Columbus had enough confidence in his scientific knowledge to pit his faith against the opinions of the world. The first fliers constructed planes which were made to utilize certain laws of nature to

[11] This prayer was given to the author by Dr. Harry Lathrop Reed.

making flying possible. It must have taken faith to trust oneself to them at first. Such instances might be multiplied over and over again. The same has been true in the spiritual world. Jesus believed that he could overcome the world better by dying on a cross than by living a long life. His faith has proved to have been well founded. Here, then, is the cure for those inferiority complexes that rest on pure lack of confidence in one's ability to do things. Jesus' answer is, "Learn to have faith in the fatherliness of God."

One of the things which we are most sure is essential to mental health is social contact. When a child refuses to play with other children and prefers to be alone, this is grave cause for concern. Those who do withdraw from society do so because of an inferiority complex. They feel that society does not want them. How can they make contact with others? How should they behave toward others in an effort to overcome this deadly source of inferiority? Jesus' answer is well known.

Therefore all things whatsoever ye would that men should do to you, do ye even so to them: for this is the law and the prophets.—Matthew 7:12.

Certainly, no passage has been so widely used as the core of Jesus' teaching as the Golden Rule. Indeed, the two seem almost synonymous in the mind of the average person. It has been more used and more abused than any other passage of scripture. We shall do well to examine it carefully.

The fact that it is a spiritual law inherent in the very nature of the social world is strongly indicated by its appearance in various forms in a number of widely divergent places. This phenomenon of truths appearing in different places independently of each other and sometimes simultaneously is a very interesting one in history. It certainly offers strong evidence for the inherent truth of such discoveries or revelations. Jesus' statement differs in some important respects from the previous ones. The most important of these differences is that it is positive. The others are all negative, in that they tell us what we must *not do*. It should be observed that it refers to all our social relationships. It says "all things," not "some things." The "would" is important in its full interpretation. The subjunctive indicates a condition. In this case the meaning is clear. "Do unto others what you would that they should do unto you, if you were in their place." This is very significant, and its oversight is the basis for many misinterpretations of Jesus' teaching.

Many people professing to follow the Golden Rule have given it some strange interpretations. To some of them, if we judge by their lives, it must seem to read, "Do unto thy neighbor as he does unto you." If psychology should apply its best established principles to social problems, it would be forced to agree with Jesus that a retaliation form of justice can never bring about social welfare.

Other professed followers of the Golden Rule even carry this retaliation over into the paranoid pattern, and read the Golden Rule thus, "Do unto others as others do unto you, only you do it first." Their lives are made up of one continual expression of self-defense. There are few forms of the inferiority complex so unhappy as this one. Here is a man who feels his inferiority, and is therefore envious of the success of his neighbor. If his neighbor gets a better job or a higher salary or more honor than himself, he is intensely unhappy. The fundamental reason for this is that his neighbor's success seems to be further evidence of his own inferiority. One does not like to admit inferiority, however, and tries to explain it in some other way. The best and most satisfactory method of doing this is to feel that the neighbor obtained his success through the use of unfair methods. This is only a step from believing that his neighbor wishes to harm him and prevent his success. He then reads evil connotations into all of his neighbor's behavior, and then performs acts of retaliation to prevent the harm that he is sure is coming to him from his neighbor. This form of behavior is far more common than we can believe, and is the source of a tremendous amount of unhappiness and mental disease.

Another connotation given to the Golden Rule may be best described as the "let alone" doctrine. I may wish that my neighbor would just let me alone, and so by applying the Golden Rule, I let him alone. Especially those who are well off are apt to take this attitude toward those less fortunate. Often, this is due to a fear that they will be unable to maintain their socially well-off position if they do too much for others. This is another form of the inferiority reaction. It is characteristic of those who have no confidence in their ability to maintain their superiority.

It is obvious that Jesus would not have given any of these interpretations. In the first place, his doctrine would imply doing something, never doing nothing. When he described the judgment scene, the chief difference between the good and the bad was that the good had done something for their neighbors, the bad had not. In the next place, there would be involved doing something which we would like to have done for us. This does not mean that we should do nice things for our neighbor in order that possibly he might return them in kind. It is unselfishly loving one's neighbor as one loves himself. As has been pointed out, it implies "doing unto one's neighbor what you would want done unto you" if you were in his place.

How easy it is to criticize and condemn others when we do not apply the Golden Rule. It is so easy to watch the misbehavior of our neighbor's children and criticize their upbringing, indicating very emphatically what would happen if they were our children for a day. Often the exact procedure is left unmentioned, but the tone of voice indicates that we have in mind some very efficient and effective program of child training to apply to such cases.

For the man with an inferiority complex, the negative form of the Golden Rule is much more comfortable. That imposes only a guarded restraint upon our behavior. In that sort of behavior the inferiority individual is quite adept. He is afraid to do anything else. The timid soul does not infringe upon his neighbor's rights, but neither does he do anything else. The positive form of the Golden Rule involves a tremendous responsibility, forcing us to be constantly considering our neighbor's welfare as well as our own, endeavoring to discover what we would like him to do for us if we were in his place, and then doing it. All too frequently such behavior is very thanklessly received by our neighbor, sometimes even violently resented. Yet, because we are sure that it would be best for us if we were in his place, we are bound to do it even if it brings us punishment. Indeed, this is the only way in which the practice of the Golden Rule can make the world better.

The reason for the form of inferiority complex referred to in this verse is not so much physical fear, though that occasionally enters in. Rather, it is a fear of our own righteousness. We do not dare to judge others and their needs. We are afraid of our lack of strength to do good. How can we overcome this weakness? Summarized to a single point, psychology would tell us to replace bad habits with good ones. The Golden Rule has this very effect. One who keeps busy doing things for others is likely to find his own selfishness in the background and along with it his fears.

This involves seeking out the objective relations in the social world and living by them. There are few ways in which the objective attitude can be so effectively developed. When the child is growing up, if there is pointed out to him every opportunity for social welfare, he will certainly have a healthy objective attitude and a minimum of inferiority complex. A few years ago in a summer camp a boy stole some firecrackers from one of his tentmates. The loser discovered who had done the deed and went to one of the counselors for help to regain them. It happened that the thief had come from a very poor family and had no money to buy such luxuries. The other boy had an abundance of spending money. This fact was pointed out to him, and it was suggested that instead of punishing the boy who stole them, he give him some more firecrackers. He had a difficult time understanding this method of "getting even," but finally adopted it. The offender was much more severely punished than he could possibly have been by any other method. The giver had grown in character. The two remained fast friends from that time on. Such training is very much needed in teaching children how to become good citizens.

Here, then, is another form of the inferiority complex. No one can imagine the immense amount of suffering that goes on in the minds of many people, because they are afraid to associate with their fellows. Often, their fellows have no inkling of this. They frequently compensate by behavior which is interpreted by others as being snobbish. Here is a boy who went through college, one of the most unpopular boys in the institution because of this sort of stand-offish behavior. Actually, he feared the society of others. He felt subconsciously that they did not want him. Hence, he stood off from them. Sometimes, parents give this attitude to their children by urging them to be independent. Sometimes, they learn it by a few unhappy experiences in childhood. Every psychologist who listens to the unhappinesses of people finds that this is a cause in a vast number of cases.

How is the individual himself to overcome this form of inferiority? The answer is, practice the Golden Rule. The most timid of parents is likely to have the courage of a lion when his child is in danger. The same will become true for anyone who has fatherly love as the characteristic of his nature. If his interest in men is in what to do to help them, and if he does what he would like them to do for him if he were in their place, his attention will soon be on them instead of himself.

Another form of the fear of society is found in the fear to go against the will of the crowd. Many individuals are firm believers in doing as the Romans do, when in Rome. Many a boy is easily influenced by his companions. His morals are the morals of the crowd with which he happens to be at the moment. This is due to his fear to stand against the crowd. It is again a form of the inferiority complex.

Enter ye in at the strait gate: for wide is the gate, and broad is the way, that leadeth to destruction, and many there be which go in thereat: Because strait is the gate, and narrow is the way, which leadeth unto life, and few there be that find it.—Matthew 7:13-14.

This teaching also has significance for the inferiority complex and is the most discerning of all, in showing the very nature of the reaction. The key to it is in the words, "Many there be which go in thereat." Everyone likes to be with the crowd, or rather, is afraid not to be. Showmen realize that if they can gain the reputation of having a crowded house, the people will come. Likewise, if a church can get the name of being crowded at every service, it will be filled with those who like to be with the crowd. The power of popular opinion is far-reaching. Most individuals are afraid of it and are slaves to its dictates. To have the courage of one's convictions is a very rare virtue. Most of us follow pretty closely the convictions of the multitudes. The theory of democracy that the majority is right probably has its foundation in the fear to go against the principles of the majority, not only because of fear of the wrath of the majority, but because of the lack of faith in one's own opinions when the majority is against them. A man may believe that money is secondary and spiritual values first, but if the whole world seems money-mad he is likely to fall in line with that notion. A student may come to college to gain the best possible education, but if the majority of his friends tell him that such ideals are old-fashioned, he may desert them because of the fear of public opinion. Socially, we are constantly doing things and leaving things undone because of our fear of what others will think.

It is to be noticed that the term is "strait and narrow," not "steep and crooked," as many seem to think. It is hard to find, and hard to follow. Few find it. It is interesting that the word most commonly used by Jesus to refer to sin was one which meant "missing the mark." Thus, the prodigal son "missed his mark." The publican praying said, "Be merciful to me a man who has missed his mark." Again the idea of having a great purpose and going toward that purpose is seen as an essential in Jesus' teaching.

On the other hand, the words are "broad and wide," not "easy and comfortable." There is no indication that one way is any more comfortable or happy than the other. Its chief danger lies in the fact that it is easy to find, and that there are lots of people there. It is doubtful if the weak and diseased personality has any easier time in the world than the strong and healthy one, and probably is much less happy, but he is in the majority. He is following the crowd. He conforms. He is afraid to do otherwise.

Conformity is probably the strongest temptation man faces. He who conforms is socially acceptable. Even in our colleges, when a new course is being considered, the first question asked is whether or not other colleges teach it. The great educators of America have been men who refused to conform. Orthodoxy in religion is easy. The minister who is orthodox has a much easier way than he who does some thinking for himself, and dares to have the courage of his convictions. Yet, it may be said without fear of contradiction, that conformity has not yet made a significant contribution to the spiritual riches of mankind. It is the man who dares to differ with the crowd who advances civilization. This does not mean the childish behavior in which some people obstinately do just the opposite of society. That is quite as unoriginal and more puerile than conformity.

It is a slow path to the achievement of this form of objective attitude. Almost everyone has lived in fear of gossip, and has often done some rather deceitful things to avoid it. Jesus is saying that we must keep our life free from that which is worthy of gossip, and in the end we shall be impervious to whatever may come of it. The inferiority battle of counterplot and deceit will never solve the problem. Many a young graduate student works, not only for his doctor's degree because it is supposed to be done, but also absorbs the all too common graduate school definition of value; that is, salary and advancement in rank. He fears being without either. Although much in love with his subject, he finds it hard to forget these other things, and bury himself in the search for the secrets of nature as studied in his chosen field. Happy is he who can leave alone the "broad way" of conformity and feverish anxiety about salary and rank. One who can gradually get these secondary values out of the dominant place in his thinking, and get back on the "straight way" of high purpose and achievement, will soon find this sort of inferiority complex also disappearing. It has been pointed out that purpose is very essential to mental health. Here is one of the places where its necessity is most apparent.

Fear, even when it is conscious and under our voluntary control, is bad enough. In the forms of anxiety and worry, it is the source of most of our sleepless nights and lack of faith. But when this fear becomes a deep-set feeling that we are inferior, it is much worse, for the desire to be superior is a fundamental one in human nature. Then, when this fear of inferiority is repressed into an unconscious complex, it saps our strength without our knowing it, makes us dangerous to society, prevents us from greater usefulness, and expresses itself in forms of very undesirable behavior.

A complex has been defined as unconscious behavior. As long as the feeling of inferiority is conscious, we are in a position to deal with it relatively easily. We can take an objective attitude and measure it. We can discover in what things we really are inferior, and in what things we have strength. We can then seek our places in those fields for which we have adequate capacities. That is relatively easy.

The feeling of inferiority enters into most of the mental diseases. A mental disease is nothing more than a bad mental-emotional habit or a group of them. The chief characteristic of these abnormal forms of expression is that they are not recognized by the subject as being what they really are. He can usually offer good excuses for them, and does so. This type of behavior we have described already as rationalization. It is typically true of unconscious behavior, which includes most of our mental life. Our conscious reasons are usually rationalizations, and we are unconscious of the repressed drive behind them.

Thus, the gossip, who judges men adversely, does not know that the real reason is because he feels inferior to others, and by this method is trying to drag them down below himself, in order that he may feel more superior. He believes, through a rationalization, that the behavior of the other individual is really reprehensible and worthy of criticism.

The fanatical reformer is akin to the gossip. He believes that he is trying to accomplish a great thing in the world. He actually believes that the salvation of the world depends upon his reforming it. He does not recognize that the reason for his zeal is a fear of his own inferiority, which he wishes to keep from the attention of his neighbor by emphasizing some other virtue in which he has a degree of proficiency.

The individual who is so anxious to have popularity that he is willing to do anything to get it does not realize that in "giving his holiness to the dogs" and "casting his pearls before swine" that he does so because he is afraid of unpopularity. He really thinks he is trying to serve the other person and is willing to pay any price to do so.

The individual who insists that there is no personal God, and that if there were He could not answer prayer, does not realize that his lack of faith is very often based upon an inferiority complex, and that this professed atheism is only a good rationalization for it. This does not mean that there are no sincere atheists. But for every sincere atheist there are a hundred who are using atheism as a compensation for an inferiority complex.

The man who insists upon the unfriendliness of the universe and the meaninglessness of life is hardly aware that his pessimism is an indication of his inferiority feeling. He believes that he is a profound thinker. This rationalization makes possible his cowardly attitude toward life.

The individual who professes to attend to his own business and let others strictly alone does not realize that this attitude is due to a fear of others and a resultant inferiority complex. He believes that this is an admirable attitude to take.

Finally, the individual who does what everybody else is doing because he wishes to be popular, does not realize that he is also compensating for an inferiority complex. Actually, this is only a rationalization for a fear of his own judgment of righteousness. Therefore, he takes the "broad way" of social conformity and "misses the mark" of real achievement.

It seems probable that if we can instill into the mind of the child the great concepts of life which are involved in the Beatitudes, he will not suffer greatly from any of these forms of the inferiority complex. Unfortunately, most of us have come along without such training. We do have inferiority complexes. They do destroy our efficiency.

The psychiatrist traces back the complex to its childhood beginning, but if he is to accomplish any beneficial effect, he must reëducate the individual into a new attitude toward life, which will not have the elements of inferiority in it. Whichever program is tried, the elements of the program of Jesus will have to be employed. Furthermore, the Christian religion has in it the faith in a fatherly God, which is the center of the Christian personality, with its program of fatherly behavior. Such a faith is essential to the strongest personality, and can be found nowhere except in the teachings of Jesus.

Here, then, is the inferiority complex. It is the source of most of our weakness. With Jesus' program of mental hygiene for getting rid of it centering in the Golden Rule, Christians can root it out of themselves. Along with it will go the many other less important forms of undesirable behavior which are also a part of it; such things as extreme sensitiveness, conceit, anger to criticism, shyness and seclusive behavior, expansive response to flattery, grandstand acting, hard losing, pugnacity, profanity, suspicion, standing up for one's own rights, and many others too numerous to mention. If, by sincerely applying these teachings of Jesus in our lives, we can rid our personalities of the inferiority complex and its many by-products, we shall certainly become happier and more wholesome.

Chapter XI

THE CHRISTIAN PERSONALITY

There is still one phase of personality with which we have not dealt in this study of the Christian personality. Every parent recognizes that there is an incurable tendency to hero-worship in the child. For example, here is a man who is having difficulty persuading his son to submit to a diet of spinach. He told him that such a diet was essential to his health and strength. This was all to no avail in the mind of the boy. Then the captain of the college football team whom the boy admired very much was invited to dinner. He ate spinach enthusiastically, and left the impression that the major portion of his football ability was due to his eating spinach. After that, the boy was willing to eat spinach three times a day. Every child develops an ideal which motivates his every act and dream. What is the psychology of the formation of such ideals? Everyone will recognize that the ability to control the formation of them would be very valuable in the development of the child's personality.

Many people think that education in character consists in the formation of codes of conduct, and in preaching these to the child on every occasion possible until he learns them. Children do not always do what they know to be right. Furthermore, if they get an ideal which is non-conforming in its nature, they may even scorn ethical behavior. Many a boy would think that he was a "sissy," if he obeyed all of the commandments. His ideal is non-conformity. It is much more important, then, to give the child an *ideal* that is ethical, than to teach him what *behavior* is ethical. If he has hero-worship for such an ideal, he will come much more nearly developing moral character.

THE CHRISTIAN PERSONALITY

The child can be taught almost any philosophy of life. Due to his love for his parents he will accept from them almost any statement of what is good and bad, strong and weak, pleasurable or unpleasurable, valuable or worthless, noble or ignoble. This development of a philosophy of life is gained both by what the parent says and by what the parent does. It is this concept of life and its values which spells the future of the child. This concept has been variously called the "super-ego," the "guiding fiction," or the "ideal."

It has been pointed out that the fundamental motivation in human life is the desire to be a "complete man." "Be ye therefore perfect" is the most earnest prayer of every individual. The problem arises, however, as to what a complete man is. If we were to ask a number of individuals, each of them would give a different response. Characteristics which seem very admirable to one, are held in indifference or contempt by another. Where does each get his notion of what constitutes a complete man? These questions are very important, and play a large part in the growth and health of the personality involved. The concept of a complete man which an individual gets is described by Adler as the *guiding fiction*. This guiding fiction is in a sense the ideal toward which one strives, which he regards as the essence of manhood. Whence, then, this guiding fiction?

There are two factors which certainly enter into the formation of a guiding fiction. In the first place, the person who has the greatest power in the eyes of the child is likely to be chosen as the complete man, and his characteristics to become the guiding fiction of the child. To the average young child, this is his father. In the second place, it is the person for whom the child develops the greatest admiration and affection, which is usually also the father. Hence, the guiding fiction of the normal child is usually his idea of his father. It may be that his concept of his father is very far from being the true picture of his father. He may imagine, for example, that his father can whip any man in the world, and that he knows everything, and can do anything, and never did anything wrong. But whatever his notion of his father, this comes to be the guiding fiction toward which he strives, consciously or unconsciously. It is this guiding fiction, with whatever modifications come into it, that determines the whole future motivation of his life.

Since the guiding fiction represents the ideal of greatness which will spur the child on to achievement and will guide his behavior, it is very important that the right guiding fiction be found. The most important factor, then, in the beginning of the guiding fiction is the parents. In two ways they set the child's ideal. In the first place, they consciously try to give the child a high ambition. This does not always bring about the desired results, but it does bring about some results. Many a child has some ideal set before him which is far beyond his capacity. He cannot change his heredity, and can reach only such achievements as he has the inherited capacity to achieve. It would be tragic if every mother did make her child believe that he must seek to become President. Many a boy comes to college to prepare for a vocation for which his inherited intelligence makes him unfit. His is certain to be a life of frustration and disappointment. No purpose must be chosen which does not fit the child's capacities. It is quite as common for the opposite to take place. Here is a boy who has outstanding artistic talent. His father assures him that there is no money in art, and urges him to become a business man. Whether he succeeds or not in business, he can never be happy, because he will be always dreaming of lines of achievement which were intended for him in his heredity. He obviously cannot reach the peak of his personality ability, because some of his potential power is never used. His purpose must use all of his ability. Often, the notion that is given the child of the complete man is so unattainable that he retreats into a world of fantasy, and builds success only in daydreams. He may retreat entirely from society and become a victim of that disease we call schizophrenia or dementia præcox. He may be given the ideal of having as good a time as possible. He is told that

THE CHRISTIAN PERSONALITY

he is only young once, and that he should live while he can. He thereby obeys a morality similar to that of the psychopath, runs into all sorts of conflicts, and ends up disillusioned and unhappy. These are only a few of the many possible ways of wrecking personality very early in life by the wrong type of guiding fiction.

But there is another way in which the parents help to form the ideal of the child, which has to do with the second factor in the formation of the guiding fiction. It frequently happens that a child worships a hero whom the parents would never have picked out for him, and certainly whom they do not admire or want their child to emulate. How does this come about? The parents themselves unwittingly bring it about. It will be recalled that the second factor in the guiding fiction is the emulation of one whom the child loves or admires. The child's first love is likely to be his parents. He will then build up a guiding fiction that has the qualities which he sees in his parents: first, those which make him love his parents, and also those which make him admire his parents, especially those which seem powerful. Now, this formed ideal will have a great deal of influence upon his admirations and affections in the future. If he comes to admire some undesirable hero, it is because this hero has the qualities which he learned to attribute to his parents, even though they may have been far from being the important characteristics of the parents. All through his life, every person whom he admires and loves will modify his guiding fiction. Indeed, the only way to change the child's ideal is to win his admiration and affection. No teacher has any permanent effect in the life of his students who does not succeed in doing this. If the parents can be to the child all of the things they want him to be, and if they can elicit from him the type of admiration they want him always to have, they will be forming in him the right guiding fiction. The goal for the Christian personality is to make the child admire the qualities of Jesus, so that Jesus will become his ideal.

Here, then, is a crucial factor in the development of personality. It occurs very early in the child's life and influences his whole future career. It is of supreme importance that the right guiding fiction be formed in him. The possibilities are obvious. The responsibility of fathers and mothers is clearly seen in this concept. In a way, the whole future personality of the child depends upon this. It will be largely responsible for his purposes, his sense of values, his judgments, his notions of what he will call common sense, his concepts of pleasure and pain, indeed even what things he will remember or forget. Life seems worth living on the basis of whether or not progress is being made toward this goal. Fear is engendered if the goal is blocked off. Anger is stimulated when others try to hinder our progress toward it. Ambition is defined by its nature. One to whom wealth is the essence of value in his guiding fiction will have a hard time appreciating cultural things in which there is no practical value. One to whom pleasure is the chief good in his guiding fiction, service is not likely to appeal. One who conceives physical prowess as the greatest achievement will neglect the more spiritual qualities. Such illustrations make the value of the guiding fiction obvious.

But there are many philosophies of life. Almost everyone can speak authoritatively on how life ought to be lived and how children ought to be brought up. There are other religious philosophies than the Christian, whose adherents are quite as sincere as the followers of Jesus. How shall we distinguish between them? Science would say, "Experiment." What does Jesus himself say?

> Beware of false prophets, which come to you in sheep's clothing, but inwardly they are ravening wolves. Ye shall know them by their fruits.—Matthew 7:15.

In the final section of this great sermon, Jesus deals with this problem of choosing a guiding fiction. Perhaps this verse could be modernized to read, "Beware of false guiding fictions." This verse is the first of a series of three descrip-

THE CHRISTIAN PERSONALITY

tions of false prophets. It becomes necessary to distinguish between the true and false prophets, because there are so many who claim to be prophets. Buy a copy of one of the popular journals which profess to disclose the secrets of personality and character. Especially, examine the advertisements. One can find in them promises of anything he wishes. The advertisements use a great many phrases and sentences calculated to catch the unwary. "Become a dynamic personality." "Be so magnetic that you will win men and women with the wave of a finger." These are only a few samples typical of the common claims of these false prophets. Needless to say, such promises cannot be fulfilled. Character is achievement.

But, how shall the uninformed distinguish between the psychology which is real and that which is false? The first test is that the false prophets come in sheep's clothing. What is the significance of this attribute? It should be noted that they do not come in shepherd's clothing. They do not even profess to be leaders. Sheep are followers not leaders. These men come calling themselves representatives of the crowd. They lead revolts of the "masses." They talk about "us plain common people" as opposed to "those autocratic tyrants." You have heard such men. They are at the bottom of a considerable portion of our labor troubles. They profess to be workers. Actually, they are false prophets.

What advantage has this assumed humility, which they use in their prophetic work? Why do they not come out and lead? The real leader who stands out in front and commands the crowd to follow must have certain characteristics. He must especially make them admire him. If he cannot command their affection, his leadership will be short-lived, however just his cause may be. He must, of course, have the qualities of a leader and faith in his cause. He is likely to run counter to the people and needs power to overcome their opposition and convert it into support. The "sheep's clothing" leader, however, appeals not to his own leadership nor his cause, but to the conceit of the people, which is effective because of their sense of inferiority. He makes them feel that they are the leaders, and he simply one of them. Every part of the cause built up is called their cause. Because of their inferiority feelings, which express themselves in conceit, they are pleased with this tickling of their vanity and are much less rational concerning the justice of the cause. It makes them take emotional points of view. The soap-box orator appeals a great deal to the pride of the people and very little to the wisdom of his program. Unfortunately, it is much easier to lead, wearing sheep's clothing than wearing shepherd's clothing. Of none of these men could it be said, "He spoke as one having authority." They carefully avoid any suspicion of having authority.

"But inwardly they are ravening wolves." Such agitators are always "ravening wolves" inwardly, regardless of the justice or injustice of their causes. It has always been an interesting question as to whether the end ever justifies the means. Such reformers always assume that it does, and have not hesitated to use whatever methods are necessary to obtain their ends. The difficulty with the method is that in so doing they destroy personalities, and produce mental diseases. Since personality is the one great value in the world, it may well be asked with respect to their reform, "What shall it profit a man if he gain the whole world and lose his own soul?" Men are made better when they are given higher guiding fictions and have nobler resultant purposes. They are destroyed when their emotional disintegrated lusts are stimulated. When the false prophets thus foster their inferiority complexes by tickling their vanity, and stimulate their emotions by making them hate their so-called oppressors, they are "ravening wolves" tearing out the hearts of these very people whom they profess to serve.

Recognizing the many faults to be found in over-emotional appeals, some men have tried to deify "dignity" in what they have called conservative religion. This is quite as much a "sheep's clothing" type of religion as the other. Great religious leaders have never been conservative. The prophets

THE CHRISTIAN PERSONALITY 341

were continually calling men to repentance. To be sure, they were preaching a fear religion, which is undesirable, but it was certainly far from being conservative. Jesus did not preach fear, yet one will look in vain for any approval of conservatism on his part. He demanded that one man "go sell all he had and give to the poor." He challenged all men to "take up crosses and follow him." He made men leave their homes and work in order to become his disciples. He walked deliberately to certain death for the cause in which he believed. Jesus was not conservative, nor can any adequate application of his teaching result in a conservative religion.

Those who have imagined that Christianity is easy have seen only very diluted forms of it. It requires the best efforts of any man to even approach, much less to become perfect in the teachings of Jesus. Therefore, when ministers and other religious leaders preach a conservative religion, they do so because they want to dodge its responsibility. They want to take it like medicine with as little bad taste as possible. This can only mean that they think religion is distasteful. This in turn indicates that they have emotional urges not in line with religious principles, which they do not wish to sublimate.

When emotions are left out of religion, it does not mean that they have been left out of the individuals who profess that religion. It means that the real drives which characterize their lives are taken out of religion. It means that religion ceases to have any important influence on personality.

We are forced, then, to set up some ideal, some guiding fiction, toward which we set our faces. If we choose the wrong one we shall suffer the results that always come from breaking universal laws. Here is a group of prophets. We now have at hand the data for the elimination of some of them. When they appeal to our vanity, which is an inferiority compensation, we can be certain that because they do stimulate our inferiority they are not sources of power. When they appeal to fear, anger, hate, greed, or suspicion, we may likewise discard them, for experiment has clearly demonstrated that such forces are destructive of mental health and power. We must, then, choose an ideal which challenges the best of our abilities, and is built on the love of men.

In order that it may be clear as to how religious education must take place to become effective in the development of strong character and personality, let us contrast two case histories. The first describes a boy who was subjected to religious education, probably of the verbal type so common in our church schools. The other is an example of education which, while it involved no worded principles at all, actually produced mental health.

John Dillinger is dead, shot by agents of the federal government. The nation is relieved that this "public enemy number one" has reached the end of his career. To begin with, he started life with what America has generally assumed are the "advantages" necessary to insure an honorable and rewarding place in society. His heredity was good; his environment was that of the open country and outdoor life; he was continually, throughout his boyhood and youth, under the influence of the "character-forming agencies" of church, Sunday school and public school. Conditions inside his family circle were good. His mother died while Dillinger was still an infant, but a stepmother won his affection. His affection for his father seems never to have wavered; he recognized and took pride in the respect which the community accorded his family name; his relations with the other members of the family seem to have been uniformly good. As the boy entered his late teens he seems to have become something of a victim of the general aimlessness which sometimes settles on youth in a village. He graduated from high school, rated as a good student and a better athlete, and almost immediately married. On a Saturday night in September, ten years ago, a grocer returning to his store in the darkness was set upon by two indistinguishable figures. The grocer resisted; there was a scuffle; a gun was discharged; the would-be robbers fled; the grocer, unharmed and unrobbed, went on to his store. Dillinger stood self-revealed as a participant in the abortive hold-up. Together with his tough pal—who was ten years his senior—Dillinger was arrested. His father, acting on the moral code which has ruled his life, counseled his son to make a clean breast of the whole affair. Dillinger followed his father's advice. Despite his previous unsullied record, despite his father's standing in the community, the youth was sentenced to from ten to twenty years for assault and battery with attempt to kill, and from two to fourteen years for conspiracy to commit a felony. Dillinger's accomplice pleaded not guilty. After his conviction he was sentenced, in the face of his bad record, to from two to fourteen years. At the end of two years he was paroled. Dillinger was held in prison for nine years. A petition signed by most of the leading citizens of his home town, including the man who had been the victim of his amateurish hold-up, finally secured his parole, the governor being moved to some degree by knowledge of the critical illness of Dillinger's stepmother. A brother was waiting for Dillinger as he stepped out of the prison gates; despite the speed with which they drove home they arrived fifteen minutes after the stepmother's death. From that point on the story is that of an embittered, cynical and desperate man. What moral is to be drawn from such a sorry episode in contemporary American life? In the earlier stages of his career it is almost impossible to evade the conclusion that society's own institutions fell down.[1]

This case history speaks for itself. Whatever may have been the factors that complicate this story, it is evident that John Dillinger was not given sufficient foundation for character by the methods of religious education given him.

Here is an entirely different story. It is clearly illustrative of the sort of religious education and general education which will produce much better results.

A boy of eleven was observed by his teacher when in a fight with another boy. She discovered that he did not get along with any of the boys. He seldom fought them, but rather stayed away from them. He expressed dislike for most of the boys of his class, for the school, and was, in general, very bitter in his attitude. He hated school and his ambition was to get even with the boys who tormented him.

This would seem to be a much worse background than that of John Dillinger. It might well have been if his teacher had confined her efforts to preaching the right and wrong of hating.

[1] Editorial, "Dillinger," *The Christian Century*, 990 f., August 1, 1934.

She discovered that he was an only son of a widowed mother who had been in this country but a few months when he entered school at the age of six. He seemed queer to the other boys, who therefore tormented him. The teacher decided that the cure lay in finding an adjustment for him with the other boys. She therefore contrived to build a friendship between him and one of the other boys whom he hated least. She formed other friendships, and soon the boy's adjustment was complete. How much of a disaster she averted in the life of this boy it is impossible to say, but when we understand that many serious mental maladjustments have just such a beginning we are inclined to believe that such work is of inestimable value.[2]

It is not intellectual assent to a code of ethics that constitutes character education. It is the transformation of the emotional attitudes so that the natural reaction of the individual is in conformity with the code of ethics.

Does the end justify the means? On first coming into the executive side of a certain religious organization, a young man found that there were some very questionable practices in it. False reports of the numbers of adherents were sent out. Reports of the expenditures of the money were not always perfectly true. He was told that all religious organizations do these things, that they are forced to in order to exist. Furthermore, he was assured that the end justifies the means. Propaganda during a war is deliberately exaggerated to get the emotional nature of the people stimulated. The propagandists may be perfectly certain that the means are justified by the end. Sincere people feel that it is perfectly right to fight evil men with evil means. Does the end justify the means? With respect to personality, no psychologist would hesitate to answer, that the means constitute the foundations upon which the end is built and are an integral part of the end. What did Jesus say?

Do men gather grapes of thorns, or figs of thistles? Even so every good tree bringeth forth good fruit; but a corrupt tree

---

[2] Adapted from Morgan, J. J. B., *Psychology of Abnormal Peoples*, 593-595. Longmans, Green and Company, 1928.

THE CHRISTIAN PERSONALITY

bringeth forth evil fruit. A good tree cannot bring forth evil fruit, neither can a corrupt tree bring forth good fruit. Every tree that bringeth not forth good fruit is hewn down, and cast into the fire. Wherefore by their fruits ye shall know them.—Matthew 7:16-20.

It is certain that Jesus was not referring to inheritance qualities in this parable, but to what we have called psychogenic characteristics. Can a strong personality be developed from wrong character education? It may not matter so much for the future of the personality of the child as to who are his parents, but it makes a tremendous difference as to who associates with the child and gives him his social inheritance in his early years. If the "false prophets" are followed, who are themselves "thorns and thistles," it is very likely that their followers will have the same characteristics. When Jesus asks about "gathering grapes and figs of thorns and thistles," he is referring not only to the "false prophets" from whom the good fruits of personality cannot be secured, but also to the followers in whom the good fruits of personality cannot be developed.

What, then, are the characteristics of "thorns and thistles" which distinguish them from "grapes and figs"? How can we by this criterion distinguish between the "false prophets" and false methods of personality development and the correct ones?

It will be observed in the first place that the distinction is not on the basis of looks, size, roots, or leaves, but of "fruit." The Oriental did not believe in raising trees just for looks. If the tree did not bear fruit, it was hewn down. It is curious that the word used for "thorn" in the context refers to a showy and beautiful weed. If looks were the paramount issue, this weed would have been valuable. It did not, however, bear grapes. It was much easier to cultivate. Indeed, it did not have to be cultivated at all. On the other hand, the grape requires a considerable amount of cultivation. It must be watered, pruned, and sprayed, if good grapes are to be forthcoming. Figs especially were much harder to cultivate. Perhaps, we have in these illustrations one of the best methods of determining the false from the true prophets. The pseudo-psychologies promised quick results. Some of them promise instantaneous personal magnetism. Actually, the growth of personality must come with greater difficulty. This contrast between the fast-growing weeds and the slowly developing fruit-bearing trees can be brought out by two illustrations. The first is the copy of an advertisement of one of the pseudo-psychology courses. It reads:

Release your stupendous individuality. Discover this amazing power within you—a power so mighty, so all pervading, so irresistible, that it knows no obstacle. It is a power to materialize your every wish—to bring wealth, dominance, personal magnetism, happiness at your bidding. . . . At last I can help you to realize your greatest desires. . . . I can help you to the top rung of life's most successful ladder. . . . Let me help you to open that wonderful storehouse in your mind and bring out the precious jewels contained therein.[3]

Contrast that with this analogy, which much more nearly describes the difficulty of developing strong personality. It reads:

The rose horticulturist carefully prepares his soil, mingling with it in perfect proportions the fertilizers which centuries of experience have taught to be best. Into this pregnant ground he places with intelligent and patient skill the tender shoots of some rose, the latest child of a long ancestry of genetically guided parentage. Now he bestows upon his acres, with unremitting solicitude, all the attention that the most thoughtful mother could give her children. Day by day he makes over their bed. At night he covers them to protect them from the cold; at dawn he is out to remove their blankets that they may thrive in the warmth of the sun. Day by day he feeds them the life-giving water: not too much—just enough. He prunes, he props, and he sprays. And so there comes a time when the harvest of roses is blown and plucked and carried away to some chemist's laboratory. Then begins another patient and mysterious process; the slow distillation, achieved by a means that generations of distillers and

[3] Valentine, P. F., *The Psychology of Personality*, 354. D. Appleton and Company, 1927. By permission of D. Appleton-Century Company.

the contributions of science have conspired to perfect. And out of the long process, from soil to beaker, draining into a final essence, there comes attar of roses—for every forty thousand roses an ounce; for every eighty roses, a single drop.[3a]

The "corrupt tree" is not necessarily a rotten tree, but a worthless one. Perhaps the figure could be used to describe those folks who are good but not good for anything. This is another emphasis on a point that has been previously stressed. It is to be noted that people are not to be judged by their behavior but by their "fruits." It often happens that people look good on the outside who are "inwardly ravening wolves." A very common notion is that a person of bad character can lay it aside at will like a suit of clothes. Many a Sunday school teacher lives a rather doubtful life during the week, and imagines that he can convey the spirit of Christ to those under his guidance. Unfortunately, the spirit of Christ is best given in lives and not in words. Such "corrupt trees cannot bring forth good fruits."

A tree, then, is to be judged by its fruits. If it does not bring forth good fruit it is certain to be hewn down and cast into the fire. Many a man has followed false prophets into easy and selfish forms of character and personality development, and found himself in the "fire" of unhappiness because of his selfish and often unpopular personality. Again, Jesus does not use simply an emotional appeal but urges the pragmatic test of trying it out. Psychology has amply demonstrated that his methods are right.

Here, then, is another warning about the guiding fiction. Personality is not inherited, but the guiding fiction is formed so early in life that we often think it is. Jesus indicates clearly in this passage that not much can be done with us if our early guiding fiction is of "thorns and thistles." Short cuts are never possible. The man who has attained a high position by short cuts may seem to be successful. He may seem to have a strong personality. Any test, however, will show that he cannot produce strong character and person-

[3a] *Ibid.*, 356.

ality which will stand against trials, unless it has been built solidly. "Good fruit cannot come from corrupt trees."

The most dangerous of the false prophets is he who thinks that he is a Christian. In dealing with mental disorders, the most difficult patients to treat are those who will not admit that they are sick. There is in every hospital for the insane a large number of patients who believe that they have been put there unjustly and are always begging to be let out. In the preaching of Jesus, he changed the lives of many men and women. The ones with whom he had the greatest difficulty were those who believed that they were already righteous. They are the ones whom he described as "rich in spirit." The parents most certain to destroy their children's chances of happiness are those who are sure they instinctively know how to bring up children. They simply mix an abundance of "common sense" (which they are sure they possess in uncommon amount) with good intentions. Unfortunately:

Not everyone that saith unto me, Lord, Lord, shall enter into the kingdom of heaven; but he that doeth the will of my Father which is in heaven. Many will say to me in that day, Lord, Lord, have we not prophesied in thy name? and in thy name have cast out devils? and in thy name done many wonderful works? And then will I profess unto them, I never knew you: depart from me, ye that work iniquity.—Matthew 7:21-23.

The famous description of love in Paul's letter to the church at Corinth is undoubtedly a commentary on this verse. It is an excellent summary of the teachings of Christ on this subject. The findings of modern psychology would corroborate it in almost every detail. Men have tried every available scheme in the range of the imagination to seek "salvation." "False prophets" are as diverse as they are numerous. Paul describes in this chapter on love a number of them, all of whom seem to be very righteous.

There are preachers who are great pulpit orators, and who hope to achieve the salvation of themselves and others by the beauty of their sermons. There are men looking for strong personality who expect that it can be found in the mastery of oratory. They learn public speaking. They train their voices. But this is not the secret of strong personality, as Paul says: "Though I speak with the tongues of men and of angels, and have not love, I am become as sounding brass, or a tinkling cymbal."

Again, there are those who prophesy in the name of Jesus. They study the scriptures, and are well educated. Are they not saved? There are those who read the classics in the hope that strong personality will be found in speaking learnedly. Many men believe with all their hearts in some wrong concept of Christianity; their faith is powerful. Many a man believes that he has found the secret of social and individual achievement. He may believe it so strongly that he converts others to his doctrine. If it is not in accord with the real nature of the spiritual and natural laws, it is worthless. Paul says: "And though I have the gift of prophecy, and understand all mysteries, and all knowledge; and though I have all faith, so that I could remove mountains, and have not love, I am nothing."

Finally, there are those who believe that good works are the secret of salvation. They give generously to the church and to charitable organizations. Then, there are those who expect to win public approval by their gifts. They think they will seem to have stronger personalities by giving. Unfortunately, it is not the gift but the loving character that prompts the gift which makes for power. "And though I bestow all my goods to feed the poor, and though I give my body to be burned, and have not love, it profiteth me nothing."

If one looks at the various pseudo-psychological courses, he will see that they are built on just such principles as the preceding ones. They promise that personality will result from a fine voice. They urge that it be sought in learned and witty conversation. One actually suggests that it consists in walking about with one's chest thrust out. Another tells us that we should learn to look at another person without blinking the eyes. Another insists that we must learn to enlarge the pupil of the eye when looking at anyone whom we wish to influence. "Clothes make the man" is a well-known theory of strong personality. Correct etiquette is often held out as the "open sesame" to happiness. Auto-suggestion has had its day. Dozens of cults arise for a while with their gospels. Yet, when psychology objectively studies human personality in the laboratory and in the clinic, its answer is none of these. Its answer is that the most important things in personality are purpose and social interest.

In religion we have an almost perfectly analogous picture. Some think that they will be saved for their much exclaiming of "Lord, Lord." Others "prophesy." Others "cast our demons." Still others do "mighty works" in the name of Christ. Yet he says that they are "workers of iniquity." The word translated "iniquity" means "lawless." They have not obeyed the spiritual law.

We have been talking about "false prophets," thus far, whom one may or may not follow. Suppose, however, that the "false prophet" is oneself? If such is the case, the fact is seldom recognized by the individual. We have developed such strong capacities for rationalization, that we can find excuses for all of our behavior, however bad it may seem to others. This passage is one of the most tragic of all Jesus' utterances. A tremendous number of people believe themselves to be Christians, even very devout Christians, who actually are not even recognizable by the standards set up by him.

"The road to hell is paved with good intentions," but very few people believe it. "I didn't mean to do it," is quite as futile in the development of personality as in the irrevocable result of injury. A very common question is why a boy can be brought up in a fine Christian family and still live a wasted life. The answer is that he cannot. If he lives a wasted life, it is certain that his family did not obey the whole Christian law. They may have meant well. They may have been devout church members. They may have frequently and earnestly said, "Lord, Lord," but if they did not know the spiritual law, they were "workers of iniquity." The day has just about passed when people blame God for disasters which come to them from breaking the physical laws. It is still common, however, to blame Him for the disasters which result from breaking the spiritual laws.

Many an individual forms a guiding fiction which has only the outward characteristics of his ideal. The futility of outward behavior for inward character development needs no further elaboration. The student who imagines that grades, obtained in any but the most worthwhile manner, are indications of an education, is a case in point. Like the child who puts on his father's clothes and then imagines that he is as big as "daddy," he is living in a world of fantasy. Many individuals are content to follow a God to Whom they ascribe some humanly impossible characteristics, and to Whom they give a verbal allegiance accompanied by some perfunctory gifts. When they say that they love God, they do not really mean it; they use the word *love* in a different sense than they do with respect to their worldly loves. So it is with some of the pseudo-psychologies. They advise their adherents to go through certain forms of behavior which they say are characteristic of those with strong personality; and thus assume that if one exhibits that behavior he will have strong personality. Unfortunately, this does not accomplish any such results.

Here, then, are the "false prophets." They have all been tested by experience and found wanting. It should be especially emphasized that each of them looks good on the surface. None of them are outwardly "ravening wolves." If we are to discover the methods by which we can give our children the right ideals, we find in these verses four important warnings.

The first of them, described as those who "come in sheep's clothing," are the most dangerous. It is not uncommon for parents to try to stimulate their children's ambition by assuring them that they are the cream of the earth. Having ingrained in them the seeds of vanity with its consequent inferiority complex and narrow-mindedness, they become slaves to those who tickle this vanity. This only weakens their personalities and leads them into any cause, just or unjust, so long as it caters to this weakness.

To permit a child to remain fixated at the childhood level of working only for immediate rewards would be fatal to his growth in strong character. Those who promise immediate achievement or changes in personality are stimulating just this sort of behavior. Character is an achievement which requires a lifetime. Personality is not gained overnight. To let a child grow up looking for magical transformations and achievements for which he does not work is to destroy the best in his personality.

Then, there are those parents who put all of their attention on outward behavior. But "not everyone who says, Lord, Lord, shall enter into the kingdom of heaven." Parents are often very much concerned about the external things. They worry over-much about the child's clothes, bodily health, manners, ethical behavior, and social contacts. To persuade a child to emulate an ideal only on the basis of outward appearance will hardly develop strong personality.

What guiding fiction, then, shall we instill in our children? It is the hypothesis of this book that the ideal which will give the child his best personality is Jesus. Obviously, this is more easily said than done. Many parents try very hard to do this very thing and fail. Jesus himself pointed out the reason. "Why callest thou me good? there is none good but one, that is, God." In this reply which Jesus once made to a questioner he is implying that there are final spiritual laws which constitute the will of God. Jesus wanted to know what concept of himself, his questioner held. Unless he saw in Jesus the attributes of God, then he was not in any true sense a follower of his. It is important not only that parents give their children the ideal of Jesus, but that this ideal be the right one. In the spiritual realm, parents expect to perform

THE CHRISTIAN PERSONALITY 353

the extremely difficult tasks of human engineering in the personalities of their children on good intentions and loose vague generalizations. Certainly, we cannot doubt the everlasting mercy of God when we see how little tragedy is caused and how many come out with at least a portion of their inheritance. Who knows what may be accomplished when parents really learn the will of God, the spiritual laws, and teach them to their children with great exactness and thoroughness? The "name of Jesus" has been praised in our hymns, but it will not accomplish much in the life of an individual unless it carries with it all of the principles which constitute the will of God.

It is probable that few people realize how bad a job we are doing with personality development. Most of us plod through life just getting by. We are not sent to mental hospitals. We do not come into conflict with the law. We earn a living, and do not end up in the poorhouse. This, we call a successful life. No wonder men have hoped for a heaven in the hereafter. They have done a pretty poor job of making this life very much like one. Probably not one-tenth of one per cent of the people attain even an approximation of their highest capacity for achievement and happiness. Consider this study of a college class, a highly selected group.

In the effort to discover just how much mental hygiene is needed in the American College, a graduate investigated the careers of his classmates a generation (twenty years) after leaving the institution. Of one-fourth he knew practically nothing, so he left them out of the investigation. Of the three-fourths, whose careers he had been able to follow in detail, he discovered that about forty per cent had since graduation shown signs of neurotic, psychoneurotic, or even psychotic difficulties. Among this number were two-thirds of those who were admitted to Phi Beta Kappa and this group included also the most serious cases of mental and nervous diseases. Of the seventeen per cent that had died, two-thirds gave evidence of some degree of neurotic difficulties. One death was a suicide. There was nothing in the college history of this class to indicate that it was a particularly psychopathic group.[4]

[4] Groves, E. R., and Blanchard, P., *Introduction to Mental Hygiene*, 221. Henry Holt and Company, 1930.

Even this is perhaps a very optimistic statement. Consider again that almost every college student has in him the inherited capacity for greatness. Observe the small percentage of great men, and then see what a large percentage of personality waste there is. When we consider the achievements of these few great men, and picture the social possibilities if even a majority of men were so developed, we understand why the kingdom of heaven can be brought in only by such men. Seeing the losses due to our ignorance and indifference to the spiritual laws of personality, we understand what Jesus meant when he said:

And every one that heareth these sayings of mine, and doeth them not, shall be likened unto a foolish man, which built his house upon the sand: And the rain descended, and the floods came, and the winds blew, and beat upon that house; and it fell: and great was the fall of it.—Matthew 7:26-27.

When one realizes that approximately one-half of all the men and women who graduate from our colleges, carefully chosen, highly endowed, coming from the best families;—when these men and women are unable to withstand the "rains and floods and winds that beat upon them," we see clearly the penalty of disobeying the spiritual law, or even of not mastering it. Is religion the cure for this condition?

Whatever the method of training we must not neglect religion. It represents the main interests in life. We must discern life's values and make a practice of them a habit. Religion is also the source, preserver, and promoter of man's highest ideals. Whenever religion is constructive it deserves support. Whenever it is not, let us lend our influence to make it such. Anything less will be like the folly of a nation trying to establish a monetary system without a substantial gold reserve.[5]

There is a common belief that one can learn the principles of moral conduct and put them into effect whenever he desires. Thus, a boy may believe that he can "sow his wild oats" in youth, and simply "put away childish things" when

[5] Gilliland, A. R., *Genetic Psychology*, 339. The Ronald Press Company, 1933.

he is older. The inability to learn without doing has been thoroughly proved in psychology. A recent animal experiment demonstrates the fact that this is true even in the simplest sort of learning.* "And everyone that heareth these sayings of mine and *doeth them not,* shall be likened unto a foolish man, which built his house upon the sand." It would seem that not only do we learn best by doing, but that that is the only way we learn. No one would expect to learn football, skating, or boxing, by a correspondence course. What reason is there to believe that the teachings of Christ can be learned, if we do not put them into practice? It is a very common notion among people that they can accept the teachings of Jesus intellectually, but that these teachings are too idealistic to be put into effect. Probably ninety per cent of the membership of any church feel that this is true. Let us see just what happens psychologically when one hears without doing, and why this implies a weak foundation for personality.

What is happening when we hear but do not act? Let us assume that the hearer is convinced, that he gives intellectual assent, that he even experiences what we commonly call a conversion. If he does not act on it, what is happening? The fact is that he is acting on another system of values, which he has repressed. We must act on something. When we face a situation, we react to that situation in some way. We may react with fear, or anger, joy, pleasure, or love, depending on what emotional value we have attached to it. Thus, if we actually live by the creed, "Money is God"; we will show fear or even panic when our bank account is threatened. We will show anger when someone blocks our seeking after it. We will show joy when we can secure it. If we profess to follow the teachings of Jesus and still make these same reactions, it is evident that fundamentally we are still worshiping mammon, although we may have repressed that concept. There is no question of whether or not we have a system of

* Harlow, H. F., and Stagner, R., "Effect of Complete Striate Muscle Paralysis upon the Learning Process," *Journal of Experimental Psychology,* 1933, 16, 283-294.

values; it is only a question of what system of values we have. The man who thinks that he is a Christian, but who does not even know what Jesus taught, or if he does, does not act on it, is simply fooling himself. He may act somewhat Christian when things are going well, but when "the rains descend and the floods come and the winds blow," he will fall back on his real concepts of value. His Christianity is only superficial.

Many of us survive mentally only because we are fortunate enough to be spared "the rains and floods and winds." The measure of the strength of one's personality is found when responsibility is placed upon him. Very few people can stand the strain of highly responsible jobs. Many mothers covet for their sons, honor and glory; but they do not give them foundations strong enough to bear the responsibility of glory and honor.

Only he who accepts Jesus as the guiding ideal of his life, and identifies himself with Jesus by his action, can hope to stand against whatever forces try to overwhelm him. There is something pitiful in seeing men and women break under only a slight strain simply because their parents did not give them a strong enough personality foundation. Insanity is usually nothing more than a breakdown when an individual meets a situation to which he has not the power to adjust. For example, every year a large number of women have manic-depressive insanity following the birth of a baby. This is because they have no strength of personality with which to meet this crisis. When the stock market crashed in 1929, many men committed suicide because they had no strength of personality with which to meet such a crisis. However, the birth of the child or the stock market crash did not cause these breakdowns. These were only precipitating causes. The real causes were the poor foundations of personality laid in childhood. Shell shock during the war was nothing more than an indication of a lack of strength which made it impossible for large numbers of men to face that trial.

Perhaps it may be asked why one must necessarily build

personality on Jesus' teachings. Cannot strong foundations be built outside of Christianity? The answer is that Jesus knew the spiritual law. When one obeys the spiritual law, he is strong. To whatever extent other teachings represent the spiritual law, they are sources of power. There have been powerful personalities founded on other religious teachings. Without doubt there are many who refuse to classify themselves as followers of Jesus, who are far more powerful than many who are outspoken and fervent Christians. To the extent that this is true, the former obey the spiritual law more closely than these Christians do, and hence in a basic sense are better Christians.

Psychology is not at all optimistic about changing adult personalities to any very great extent. It is becoming more and more certain that unless the child is educated aright in the first place, his chances of strong personality are very slight.

Jesus met a fine young man one day. He was a splendid young man of influence. He impressed Jesus so much that he loved him. But when he heard Jesus' words, "he went away sorrowing, for he had great possessions." His personality was built upon a weak foundation. He apparently heard Jesus with enthusiasm, but had not the courage to carry out Jesus' teachings. Jesus met another young man, and challenged him to leave his chosen profession and follow him in a very doubtful and dangerous enterprise. That young man was Simon Peter. His personality had a foundation of rock. If let alone, children may just grow. Character does not. There must be built for it a strong foundation. Here is a case history taken from the article previously cited on the history of a college class twenty years after graduation.

> Perhaps the most brilliant member of the class, who subsequently attained to the rank of a college professor. The patient's career in two colleges was terminated by the onset of depressions, the first mild and lasting for only about six months, the second severe and involving two years of treatment in hospitals for nervous and mental diseases. Since the latest episode a few years

ago, the uncongenial profession of teaching, in which success was attained at such immense cost of vitality, has been succeeded by research work, for which this individual is eminently adapted.[7]

Here was an individual who seemed to have all of the requirements of strong personality. But without the right foundation he could not meet the trying circumstances of teaching. Mere intelligence is not enough.

Here is a boy, previously mentioned, with very high intelligence, approaching the level of genius, with a perfect moral character from the viewpoint of negative morality, and with a healthy body. One would think that this would be all that could be required for success in any field. Yet, when he began to face difficulties, he committed suicide. He had no strong foundation with which to withstand the "rains and floods and winds" of trouble.

Certainly, this shows the overwhelming importance of starting right. To say that "an ounce of prevention is worth a pound of cure" is putting it far too conservatively in the realm of personality. Anyone who has tried to undo some of the unhealthy beginnings in his own life or in that of some one else knows the truth of this statement. It is the job of psychoanalysis to do just this thing. But the psychoanalysis of even a very minor symptom requires the patient endeavor of a trained worker for many days, even months. Every psychoanalyst would understand perfectly what Jesus meant when he said that one needs to be "born again." Here is one more case from this same study of the college class.

One of the ablest members of the class, who received not only the highest marks for scholarship, but also the highest office in the gift of the student body. This individual, an only child of New England extraction, was, it appeared later, of a markedly, though long latent, manic-depressive constitution, and after achieving considerable success in a professional field, succumbed some fifteen years after graduation to this increasingly emerging and menacing type of disease. A long course of psychoanalysis resulted in marked improvement and the diminution of the fre-

[7] Anonymous, "Mental Hygiene and the College Student," *Mental Hygiene*, October, 1921, 736-40.

quency and severity of the alternations of the emotional states, but the prognosis has never been considered very favorable by the psychiatrist in charge of the case.[8]

What did Jesus himself think of this problem? Did he believe that anyone could be "saved," even in later life? There are numerous instances where he expressed clearly the difficulty. He pointed out that it is "easier for a camel to go through the eye of a needle than for a rich man to enter the kingdom of heaven." In the parable of the Sower, he pointed out some types of soil in which sowing seed is perfectly useless. He told another that he would have to be "born again" to be saved. Good foundations were needed upon which to build; good soil in which to sow. He spoke of the "kingdom being like a grain of mustard seed" which could grow. This would indicate that he believed that only if there is a good beginning on which to work, can salvation be accomplished.

It was the contention of Jesus, then, that there was only one way in which to build strong personality which would stand against strong trials, and that was through obedience to his teachings. The progress thus far made by psychology can find no flaw in this contention.

It is impossible to build strong structures upon weak foundations, but it is possible to lay strong foundations.

Therefore whosoever heareth these sayings of mine, and doeth them, I will liken him unto a wise man, which built his house upon a rock: And the rain descended, and the floods came and the winds blew, and beat upon that house; and it fell not: for it was founded upon a rock.—Matthew 7:24-25.

Cases of men whose character was set in a strong foundation are not very numerous. Here is a statement of Edward Everett Hale, which shows the power of a good childhood religion.

I was born into a family where the religion is simple and rational. I always knew God loved me, and I was always grateful

[8] *Op. cit.*

to him for the world he placed me in. I can remember perfectly that when I was coming to manhood, the half-philosophical novels of the time had a deal to say about the young men and maidens who were facing the "problem of life." I had no idea whatever what the problem of life was. To live with all my might seemed to me easy; to learn where there was so much to learn seemed pleasant and almost of course; to lend a hand, if one had a chance, natural; and if one did this, why, he enjoyed life because he could not help it, and without proving to himself that he ought to enjoy it. A child who is early taught that he is God's child, that he may live and move and have his being in God, and that he has, therefore, infinite strength at hand for the conquering of any difficulty, will take life more easily, and probably will make more of it, than one who is told that he is born the child of wrath and wholly incapable of good.[9]

When Horace Bushnell first began teaching "that the child is to grow up a Christian, and never know himself as being otherwise," he faced strong opposition from those who believed that a conversion experience was necessary for salvation. But Bushnell was right, both according to the results of psychological research and according to the teachings of Jesus. The conversion experience is always a thrilling one. It is inspiring to see some man who has long lived a worthless life suddenly change the whole course of it for good. But be not deceived, "Whatsoever a man soweth, that shall he also reap." However dramatic and thorough the conversion experience may be, he will never have a personality as strong as if he had not lived the worthless life to begin with. The foundations must be laid before the building is erected. No one can deny the power of conversion where there are foundations upon which to build. But true greatness involves the right foundation. When the wise parent considers these things, he will walk with fear and trembling, wondering what sort of foundation he is laying for the future of his child.

Mental diseases are nothing more than bad mental habits of thinking. If one examines the most common functional mental diseases, he will find that there is a rather small group

[9] Starbuck, E. D., *The Psychology of Religion*, 305-306. Charles Scribner's Sons, 1899.

of pernicious mental habits, which constitute the basic symptoms of almost all of these diseases. Here are the most important and common of them. If we could be rid of these, we should have very little mental disease. It is a bad mental habit to want to live alone and avoid society. It is another bad habit of thinking for one to be always suspicious of others and to believe that they are jealous of him. It is mentally unhealthy to go about with a chip on one's shoulder, always losing his temper. It is not wholesome to be flippantly optimistic, not facing the facts; or on the other hand, to be looking always on the dark side of everything. One should not be fearing constantly that he will fail in whatever he tries to do. One must not pay morbid attention to his own physical shortcomings, especially to those which he only thinks might be present in him. One should not expect to be strong mentally whose whole motto in life is, "I want, what I want, when I want it." One should not dodge reality, or build in fantasy an unreal world. These are a few of the worst habits of mind, which when extreme we call mental diseases. One must form some mental habits. If he is to avoid forming bad ones he must form others which make them impossible. It is possible to discover a group of habits of mind, which if formed, will make impossible any of these. Furthermore, these good habits are sources of strength and character. They are the basis for true greatness. They form the foundations upon which Jesus' teachings can be carried out in great achievements. They are simple and rational. They can be taught every child. Here they are, eight of them.

Give the child the firm belief that there are great spiritual principles, which if discovered would solve the problems of personality and of society. Develop in him a dominant desire to discover these principles. Teach him to believe that whatever happens is in accordance with these laws, and that if he can discover them, he can prevent evil and achieve great happiness for himself and all mankind. Let him make this vision the completely dominating purpose of his life. This is what is implied in Jesus' teaching on experimental faith. Observe that all of these are habits of thinking, not objective behavior.

Then, teach the child that the universe is fatherly. Teach him that this principle of fatherliness is the great spiritual power of the universe. Let him, like a father for his child, become sensitive to the needs of the world. Fill him with the desire to give every man the opportunity to attain the best and happiest life of which he is capable. Make him anxious to solve the conflicts that tear men's minds with fears and angers, hates and suspicions; and solve the conflicts that men have with one another as individuals and as social groups, races, social classes, and nations. Finally, challenge him to be willing to sacrifice his very life, if necessary, for the attainment of these ends. These constitute the essence of Jesus' teaching on fatherly love.

Here are the foundations in Jesus' teachings upon which we can build our personalities without fear of "rains, or floods, or winds." If we give them to our children, we will have released all of théir potentialities. We will have given them their full chance at happiness and achievement. If these attitudes are placed over against the ones described as unhealthy, it will be found that a person having these Christian attitudes absolutely cannot have the others. Other habits might be named to contradict each of the bad ones. But observe that those which Jesus gave do not conflict with one another. It seems probable that no other single group of healthy attitudes could be found, which have both of these requirements for perfect integration.

Many a parent builds the character of the child, habit by habit, with no purpose or unity. Each situation is a unit in itself. If the child is crying, the problem is how to make him stop at that moment, not a problem in the total personality of the child. It is small wonder that his personality when he is an adult seems founded on a sand foundation of countless unrelated habits and desires, which conflict and vacillate with one another, with no apparent direction and no stability against the forces that beat upon the individual.

THE CHRISTIAN PERSONALITY

The whole of the personality must enter into the integrated whole. Any part left out affects the efficiency of every other part. "Every one of these least commandments" must be obeyed. He who "heareth and doeth," will certainly be he who has integrated all his talents into one great purpose which dominates his whole personality and all of its behavior.

If we are to bring up children to identify themselves with Jesus, which is the only real form of conversion, we must cause them to admire and love him. To make him the personification of a set of very disagreeable rules of conduct will leave them perfectly indifferent, and Jesus will become for them like the model boy next door whom they despise but do not emulate. Furthermore, since Jesus cannot appear to them in person to inspire this identification, they can gain it only from those who have already formed such identifications. Only the parent, preacher, and Sunday school teacher who so deeply admires and loves Jesus that he unconsciously emulates him, can hope to convey this identification to the child. The whole process is an unconscious one, and the unconscious is brutally honest. It is incapable of the hypocrisy which characterizes the rationalizations of the conscious. "I live; yet not I, but Christ liveth in me," is a necessary qualification of the true teacher.

Parents and teachers of course will recognize how far short of the stature of Jesus Christ they fall. It was indeed in a fatherly spirit that Paul confessed himself to be "chief of sinners," when he was advising his adopted son, Timothy. When the father has done everything he can to be like Christ what more can he do? A common error of parents is to assume infallibility before their children. "Because I say so," is equivalent to saying, "The king can do no wrong." Parents may well be pointing constantly to Jesus as the supreme guide. The child commonly will assume the same attitude toward Christ that the parent does; not verbally but actually. Just as the children dislike the people whom the parents dislike, and like those whom the parents like; so they will come to truly love Christ, if this is the obvious sentiment of the parents. Let parents be constantly telling the child stories of Jesus, with warmth and enthusiasm; let them be constantly seeking to discover what Jesus would do in the solution of their own problems; let them constantly be showing their faith in him, however trying circumstances may be; and the child in identifying himself with his parents will come to have a genuine affection and faith in Jesus.

We teach our children to thrill at the name of Lincoln and Washington, or the football and baseball hero; but all too frequently not at all to the name of Jesus. We must, by the process of identification, bring it about that Jesus becomes the guiding fiction in the mind of the child.

The second method of laying good foundations for personality has to do with teaching the child the specific mental habits which go to make up the Christian personality. For example, how shall we go about teaching him Christian love? The child will adopt a principle into his innermost character, when it proves by experience to be the source of happiness and achievement. Find for him opportunities for acts of mercy. Let him perform them for people whom he loves. He will get pleasure from this. One such experience will do more toward making him a loving personality than many years of moral teaching about right and wrong. Experience which is accompanied by a sense of achievement is the best teacher.

Among the parables of Buddhism is found a good illustration of this principle. A woman lost an only son. She was grief-stricken out of reason. She went from house to house asking for medicine. Finally she was sent to Buddha. He told her that he could cure the child with a few grains of mustard-seed, if she would bring them to him. They must, however, come from a home in which no one had lost a child, husband, parent, or friend. She went from house to house, but in every case she found that some loved one had been lost. Then she realized that her own grief was not unique. Her thoughts were: "How selfish am I in my grief! Death is common to all; yet in this valley of desolation there is a

THE CHRISTIAN PERSONALITY

path that leads him to immortality who has surrendered all selfishness." This carries us back to the Beatitude: "Happy are they that mourn; for they shall be comforted." He whose sympathy makes him suffer the griefs of all mankind, so strengthens his character that when his own trials come, he is able to make them a path to immortality, and not a destructive force to loss of faith and character.

But the minister wants to know how to change adult personality. He is faced Sunday after Sunday with people who have not the rock foundations of which Jesus spoke. He is painfully aware, as Jesus was, that his auditors hear but do nothing about it for years on end. Is there no way to influence adult personality?

Psychology has never been very optimistic about this possibility. Only the pseudo-psychologies profess to be able to do it easily. But they "say, and do not." It can never be easy. On the other hand, Jesus did transform a great many adults. Psychoanalysis does cure diseases. Conversions do take place. Every minister feels that if he only knew the method, he could change the lives of his people. This is also true of the man who wants to make his own life more Christlike. Let us see what principles can be used.

In former days in theology there was the strong belief that one had to be convicted of sin before he could be saved. This doctrine has been pretty well abandoned, as the ideal of building a Christian personality from infancy has arisen. But there was much in that older notion of the conviction of sin. It is certainly true that it is almost impossible to change a personality which does not feel the need of being changed. The preacher will preach in vain to a self-satisfied congregation, whose members are certain that they are thoroughly Christian and are in no need of further ethical teaching. Unfortunately, this is the condition of most of us. Repentance is out of date. An increased ability for rationalization has replaced it. Ask almost any man to account for his behavior. He can offer plenty of excuses and reasons for it. To admit that he has sinned without any good excuse for it is fairly rare.

Unfortunately, convicting men of sin is no simple task. The reason why we do not like to admit sin is because we are ashamed of it. Actually to convict us of sin, then, requires the use of shame and guilt which is worse than the sin. How, then, can it be done? Let us take an instance from the life of Jesus. Here is a young man who is wasting his talents on fishing. It is his life work. If someone had told him he was sinning, he would have been highly indignant, and might have recited at length on the dignity of the fishing business and the prospects for a brilliant future in it. Jesus made no such plea. "Follow me, and I will make you a fisher of men." Immediately, Peter was convicted of the sin of wasting his life on fishing. He had a new vision. Probably, the most common conviction of sin which comes into modern life is the coming of a child into the family. Here are two young people rather sure that they are perfectly respectable and upright folks. Then a baby arrives. As they face this baffling bit of humanity, they suddenly are seized with an inferiority feeling that is far from being unconscious. They search eagerly for information that will help them meet their new problems. They are instantly aware of their previous short-comings. This is a healthy "conviction of sin." No one will deny that some of the most remarkable transformations of personality that occur in adult life, occur in the lives of young parents, when they suddenly find parental love the dominating purpose of their lives. Here, then, is one of the finest ways of changing adult personality; stimulating a fatherly interest in others. Every minister can profitably spend most of his time picturing the needs of humanity. If he has in his congregation some self-satisfied individual, bring him face to face with someone who needs help badly. Challenge him to meet that need. Suddenly his self-sufficiency will vanish, and in its place will come true humility of spirit. Personality can be perfectly integrated around fatherly love, and only around fatherly love. Find some such purpose for those whose personalities you wish to strengthen. If you are doubtful of your own personality, and if you have no children of your own, become as interested in some child as if he were your own. Try solving his problems. You will soon be seeking eagerly for spiritual guidance. Your own personality will grow in the process.

Jesus told one man that he would have to be "born again," if he were to be saved. This is the cue to the second method of changing adult personalities. It is fundamentally the method of psychoanalysis. It is necessary to trace back in the mind of the man to the beginnings of those motives which now rule his thinking. If this childhood source can be shown to be false, and a new one substituted for it, again personality can be changed. Here is a young college student who refused to study and was in constant conflict with his instructors. He regularly broke the college disciplinary rules. A psychological study revealed the childhood handicap of a tyrannical and severe father. Actually what he was doing now was reacting to his instructors in the way he had learned to react to his father. Being told of this source of his trouble, the trouble soon disappeared. This is a psychological picture of being "born again." Phobias and obsessions yield to this sort of treatment quite frequently, if their original source can be discovered. Much of our adult behavior, which we think of as fundamental, is of this sort. Let the minister study his people. Let him search for the childhood principles which bring about their adult ethics. Thus, he will help them really to be "born again." This, of course, is another form of reconditioning.

Finally, adults are also changed by the process of identification. Whenever someone comes into a man's life whom he admires or loves, his life will be slightly changed by that person. No minister will be effective in the life of any man in whom he does not inspire admiration or affection. This reaches its highest point in the principle of vicarious sacrifice. Jesus chose his twelve disciples and vastly influenced their lives for the time they were with him. He was not successful in completely transforming them. One of them left him entirely. Most of them were cowardly when faced with the persecution of the rulers. Even Peter denied him at the trial. He had not completely changed their lives. Finally, he was crucified for his ideals. This act brought about the final transformation of these men. Read again their rather small behavior at the Last Supper. Then read of their courage during the first days of the Church as recorded in Acts. It hardly sounds like the same group of men. Psychology has found no way to change men so completely. This requires the love of a Christ. When we see the transformation both of men and of social organizations through the vicarious sacrifices of great souls, we understand a little of its power, and why Jesus said that those who were "persecuted for righteousness' sake" would be happy. The only real source of happiness is achievement; and all of the great achievements in history have been made by prophets who were "persecuted for righteousness' sake."

Here, then, is the teaching of Jesus with respect to personality. Many of its elements had been expressed in the teachings of other great religious leaders. Other men seeking to understand the secrets of the soul had made brilliant discoveries, and in trying to learn of God had had partial visions of His will. However much similarity there may be between these sayings of Jesus and those of others before him, he is strikingly unlike them in one important respect, his method.

The world of thinking men has always believed in the power of logic to solve problems. The absurdities of the Jewish laws concerning working on the Sabbath are illustrations of the inevitable results of this method. It has many subordinate parts, but it is essentially that of logical deduction. The great advances in learning of the natural world have come through the method of experiment. This is the method of science. Its results have been little short of miraculous in those fields to which it has been applied. In the biological and social fields it is much more difficult to apply, due to

THE CHRISTIAN PERSONALITY

the intricacy and complexity of the subject matter. Yet Jesus said, "By their fruits ye shall distinguish between true and false prophets." This is the method of experiment. It was totally new to his hearers. It took men almost sixteen hundred years to comprehend its possibilities. Its effect upon them is not surprising.

And it came to pass, when Jesus had ended these sayings, the people were astonished at his doctrine: For he taught them as one having authority, and not as the scribes.—Matthew 7:28-29.

The term "astonishment" carries here the connotation of "being greatly impressed," rather than that of mere "amazement." They were impressed because he taught them as one having an ultimate authority. Here was a man who appealed to the very nature of the thing he taught. Can you imagine a scientist urging us to believe in the laws of gravitation because George Washington or Abraham Lincoln believed in it? Here are laws in which one does not appeal to authority. Jesus had been teaching the same sort of law. He had not urged them to love their neighbors because they ought to, or because it was their duty, or because a number of great religious teachers had advocated the loving of neighbors; but because in the very nature of things, loving one's neighbor is necessary to the development of high character and strong personality. This in turn is essential to the development of any solid and successful social order. "By their fruits, ye shall know them." Try out these spiritual principles and see whether or not they are part of the universal plan of things. It is small wonder that Jesus' hearers were astonished.

There was nothing of irreverence in the way in which Jesus dealt with the past. In the fields of modern science, the young scientist does not hesitate to follow his experimental findings against the pet theories of the greatest of his predecessors. Nor do they expect him to do so. The prophets and religious leaders who had preceded Jesus had sought for the answer to the riddle of personality. They had received many valuable insights. Jesus respected and used whatever was valid in them. However, he followed his own insights into the nature of man and his personality.

That our social structure lacks something of being heavenly, everyone will admit. How it is to be corrected is a subject upon which a vast majority of people can discourse "authoritatively." There are hundreds of absolutely sure panaceas. Some would enlarge the police force. Some would make use of war to wipe out the discordant elements of society. Some would use terror and tyranny. We may imagine that we have outgrown this method, but strike violence, riots, and lynchings are harsh testimony to the contrary. Some would redistribute all of the world's wealth. Some would destroy capitalism. Others would abolish labor unions. No one but a well-trained social scientist ought to try to speak with authority upon such subjects. For one thing, however, there seems to be some foundation; namely, that no solution will ever be found for social problems outside the method of Jesus. Strife and violence can never solve social problems. They have raised and always will raise far more problems than they solve, to say nothing of the vast losses in human personalities. Probably, blood will have to be shed to solve these problems; but it will have to be the blood of the righteous making vicarious sacrifices, and not the blood of the guilty being slaughtered in hate and anger.

On one occasion Jesus challenged the disciples to state their opinion of his message, and responded to Peter's great confession by announcing the foundation of his church upon such faith. At the same time, Jesus tried to tell them of the necessity of suffering for mankind. But Peter had not learned the principle of vicarious sacrifice. He hastened to assure Jesus that sacrifice was unnecessary, because of the protection of his friends. Jesus then answered Peter with the words which above all others we are most sure were his: "For whosoever will save his life shall lose it: and whosoever will lose his life for my sake shall find it." Then he went on to say, "For what shall it profit a man, if he shall gain the whole world, and lose his own soul?"

Men have striven desperately for many centuries to find the answer to this last question. They have been astonishingly little concerned about their souls, and very much interested in gaining the whole world. These centuries of striving after the world have gained but little. A few men have tried to ask the question the other way. "What shall it profit a man if he gain his soul, even though he lose the whole world?" These men have made every advance that civilization has ever made. Wherever social problems have been solved, they have solved them. Wherever happiness is found that can transcend even persecution, it is achieved by these personalities. Wherever men completely master fear, these are the men. Wherever there are great characters who carry the devotion and self-sacrifice of a father to all mankind, they will be of this group. Wherever men see God and gain insights into the spiritual law, it will be these men of vision. When personalities are developed to such heights that Jesus describes them as having the perfection of the Father, it will be the personalities of these men. They understand what Jesus meant when he said of his mission among men: "I am come that they might have life, and that they might have it more abundantly."

BIBLIOGRAPHY

It is impossible to list all of the sources which have contributed to the preparation of this manuscript. Listed in this bibliography are only those books which are either quoted in this book or were very frequently referred to in the preparation of the manuscript. The titles marked with an * are the ones most frequently used.

A. Religion

*Allen, W. C., *Gospel According to St. Matthew,* Charles Scribner's Sons, 1907.
*Bacon, B. W., *The Sermon on the Mount,* The Macmillan Company, 1902.
—— *Studies in Matthew,* Henry Holt and Company, 1930.
*Bewer, J. A., *The Literature of the Old Testament,* Columbia University Press, 1922.
*Brown, C. R., *The Religion of a Layman,* The Macmillan Company, 1920.
*—— *The Art of Preaching,* The Macmillan Company, 1922.
—— *These Twelve,* The Century Company, 1926.
*Branscomb, M. A., *The Teachings of Jesus,* Cokesbury Press, 1931.
Bruce, A. B., *The Synoptic Gospels,* The Expositors Greek Testament; Dodd, Mead and Company, 1897.
Burch, E. W., *The Ethical Teaching of the Gospels,* The Abingdon Press, 1925.
Burton, E. D., *The Teaching of Jesus,* University of Chicago Press, 1923.
Case, S. J., *Jesus,* The University of Chicago Press, 1927.
Castor, G. D., *Matthew's Sayings of Jesus,* The University of Chicago Press, 1918.
*Cadoux, A. T., *The Parables of Jesus,* The Macmillan Company, 1931.
*Douglas, L. C., *These Sayings of Mine,* Charles Scribner's Sons, 1926.

EDERSHEIM, A., *The Life and Times of Jesus the Messiah*, A. D. F. Randolph, 1883.
FARRAR, F. W., *The Life of Christ*, E. P. Dutton and Co., 1893.
*FOSDICK, H. E., *The Meaning of Faith*, Association Press, 1921.
*—— *The Meaning of Prayer*, Association Press, 1922.
*—— *The Modern Use of the Bible*, The Macmillan Company, 1924.
FRIEDLANDER, G., *The Jewish Sources of the Sermon on the Mount*, Bloch Publishing Co., 1911.
*GLOVER, T. R., *The World of the New Testament*, The Macmillan Company, 1931.
*GOGUEL, M., *The Life of Jesus*, The Macmillan Company, 1933.
*GORE, CHARLES, *The Sermon on the Mount*, John Murray, 1925.
HARNACK, A., *The Sayings of Jesus*, G. P. Putnam's Sons, 1908.
HEADLAM, A. C., *The Life and Teaching of Jesus the Christ*, Oxford University Press, 1923.
KENT, C. F., *The Life and Teachings of Jesus*, Charles Scribner's Sons, 1913.
*KING, H. C., *The Ethics of Jesus*, The Macmillan Company, 1910.
*MCNEILE, A. H., *The Gospel According to St. Matthew*, Macmillan and Co., Limited, 1928.
*MANSON, T. W., *The Teachings of Jesus*, Cambridge University Press, 1931.
*MARRIOTT, H., *The Sermon on the Mount*, Society for Promoting Christian Knowledge, 1925.
MATHEWS, S., *The Messianic Hope in the New Testament*, The University of Chicago Press, 1905.
*—— *New Testament Times in Palestine*, The Macmillan Company, 1933.
MICKLEM, P. A., *St. Matthew*, Methuen and Co., 1917.
*MOFFATT, J., *Love in the New Testament*, Richard R. Smith, 1930.
*MORISON, J., *The Gospel According to Matthew*, Hamilton, Adams, and Company, 1873.
*PLUMMER, A., *The Gospel According to St. Matthew*, Robert Scott, 1909.
RENAN, E., *The Life of Jesus*, Carleton, 1870.
RIDDLE, D. W., *Jesus and the Pharisees*, The University of Chicago Press, 1928.

BIBLIOGRAPHY

*ROBERTSON, A. T., *The Gospel According to Matthew*, The Macmillan Company, 1911.
*ROBINSON, B. W., *The Sayings of Jesus*, Harper and Brothers, Publishers, 1930.
*ROBINSON, T. H., *The Gospel of Matthew*, Hodder and Stoughton, 1928.
*SCOTT, E. F., *The Ethical Teaching of Jesus*, The Macmillan Company, 1929.
*—— *The Kingdom of God in the New Testament*, The Macmillan Company, 1931.
SIMKHOVITCH, V. G., *Toward the Understanding of Jesus*, The Macmillan Company, 1921.
SMITH, D., *Matthew*, Doubleday, Doran & Co., 1928.
STEVENS, G. B., *The Teaching of Jesus*, The Macmillan Company, 1923.
STEVENS, W. A., and BURTON, E. W., *A Harmony of the Gospels*, Charles Scribner's Sons, 1905.
TAIT, A., *The Charter of Christianity*, Hodder and Stoughton, 1887.
*THOLUCK, A., *The Sermon on the Mount*, T. and T. Clark, 1869.
WENDT, *The Teachings of Jesus*, Charles Scribner's Sons, 1892.

B. PSYCHOLOGY

*ADLER, A., *The Neurotic Constitution*, Moffat, Yard and Company, 1917.
—— *The Practice and Theory of Individual Psychology*, Harcourt, Brace and Company, Inc., 1924.
*ALLPORT, F. H., *Social Psychology*, Houghton, Mifflin Company, 1924.
*BAGBY, E., *The Psychology of Personality*, Henry Holt and Company, 1928.
*BURNHAM, W. H., *The Normal Mind*, D. Appleton and Company, 1929.
*—— *The Wholesome Personality*, D. Appleton and Company, 1932.
*BUSHNELL, H., *Christian Nurture*, Charles Scribner's Sons, 1916.
*CANNON, W. B., *Bodily Changes in Fear, Anger, Hunger, and Rage* (2nd rev. ed.), D. Appleton and Company, 1929.
CONKLIN, E. S., *Principles of Abnormal Psychology*, Henry Holt and Company, 1927.

―― *The Psychology of Religious Adjustment*, The Macmillan Company, 1929.
DARWIN, CHARLES, *The Expression of the Emotions in Men and Animals*, John Murray, 1872.
DAY, A. E., *Jesus and Human Personality*, The Abingdon Press, 1934.
*FISHER, V. E., *An Introduction to Abnormal Psychology*, The Macmillan Company, 1929.
FLETCHER, M. SCOTT, *The Psychology of the New Testament*, Hodder and Stoughton, 1912.
FREUD, S., *The Interpretation of Dreams*, George Allen and Unwin, Ltd., 1913.
*GILKEY, J. G., *Solving Life's Everyday Problems*, The Macmillan Company, 1931.
*GILLILAND, A. R., *Genetic Psychology*, The Ronald Press Company, 1933.
*GOODENOUGH, F. L., *Anger in Young Children*, University of Minnesota Press, 1931.
*―― *Developmental Psychology*, D. Appleton-Century Company, 1934.
*GROVES, E. R., *Personality and Social Adjustment*, Longmans, Green and Co., 1931.
*―― and BLANCHARD, P., *Introduction to Mental Hygiene*, Henry Holt and Company, 1930.
*HADFIELD, J. A., *Psychology and Morals*, Robert M. McBraide and Company, 1923.
HALL, G. S., *Jesus, the Christ, in the Light of Psychology*, Doubleday, Page and Co., 1917.
*HART, BERNARD, *The Psychology of Insanity*, Cambridge University Press, 1922.
*HART, J. K., *Creative Moments in Education*, Henry Holt and Company, 1931.
*HARTSHORNE, H., and MAY, M. A., *Studies in Deceit*, The Macmillan Company, 1927.
*―― and MALLER, J. B., *Studies in Service and Self-Control*, The Macmillan Company, 1929.
*HARTSHORNE, H., MAY, M. A., and SHUTTLEWORTH, F. K., *Studies in the Organization of Character*, The Macmillan Company, 1930.
HEALY, W., BRONNER, A. F., and BOWERS, A. M., *The Structure and Meaning of Psychoanalysis*, Alfred A. Knopf, 1930.

BIBLIOGRAPHY

*HENDERSON, D. K., and GILLESPIE, R. D., *A Text-Book of Psychiatry*, 3rd ed., Oxford University Press, 1932.
HITCHCOCK, A. W., *The Psychology of Jesus*, The Pilgrim Press, Boston, 1907.
*HOLLINGWORTH, H. L., *Psychology*, D. Appleton and Company, 1928.
*—— *Abnormal Psychology*, The Ronald Press Company, 1930.
HOLT, E. B., *The Freudian Wish*, Henry Holt and Company, 1915.
*JAMES, WM., *Varieties of Religious Experience*, Longmans, Green and Co., 1922.
*JANET, P., *The Major Symptoms of Hysteria*, The Macmillan Company, 1920.
—— *Principles of Psychotherapy*, The Macmillan Company, 1924.
*JUNG, C. G., *Modern Man in Search of a Soul*, Harcourt, Brace and Company, 1933.
*LUND, F. H., *Emotions of Men*, Whittlesey House, 1930.
*MCDOUGALL, WM., *Outline of Abnormal Psychology*, Charles Scribner's Sons, 1926.
*—— *Character and the Conduct of Life*, G. P. Putnam's Sons, 1927.
MCKENZIE, J. G., *Modern Psychology and the Achievement of Christian Personality*, National S. S. Union.
*MENNINGER, K. A., *The Human Mind*, Alfred A. Knopf, 1930.
MOORE, T. V., *Dynamic Psychology*, J. B. Lippincott Company, 1924.
*MORGAN, J. J. B., *Psychology of Abnormal Peoples*, Longmans, Green and Company, 1928.
*—— *Child Psychology*, Revised edition, Farrar and Rinehart, Inc., 1934.
*—— *Keeping a Sound Mind*, The Macmillan Company, 1934.
OLIVER, J. R., *Pastoral Psychiatry and Mental Health*, Charles Scribner's Sons, 1932.
*OVERSTREET, H. A., *About Ourselves*, W. W. Norton and Company, Inc., 1927.
*PIAGET, J., *Judgment and Reasoning in the Child*, Harcourt, Brace and Company, 1928.
*PRINCE, M., *The Dissociation of a Personality*, Longmans, Green and Company, 1908.
*—— *The Unconscious*, The Macmillan Company, 1929.

RIVERS, W. H. R., *Instinct and the Unconscious*, Cambridge University Press, 1922.
ROBINSON, E. S., and ROBINSON, F. R., *Readings in General Psychology*, The University of Chicago Press, 1923.
ROHRBAUGH, L. G., *The Science of Religion*, Henry Holt and Company, 1927.
*ROSANOFF, A. J., *Manual of Psychiatry*, 5th Edition, John Wiley and Sons, Inc., 1920.
*SLOSSON, E. E., "The American Spirit in Education," *The Chronicles of America*, Yale University Press, 1921.
SOUTHARD, E. E. and JARRETT, M. C., *The Kingdom of Evils*, The Macmillan Company, 1922.
*STRATTON, G. M., *Anger: Its Religious and Moral Significance*, The Macmillan Company, 1923.
*SYMONDS, P. M., *Diagnosing Personality and Conduct*, The Century Co., 1931.
THORNDIKE, E. L., *The Original Nature of Man*, Teachers College, Columbia University, 1920.
THOULESS, R. H., *An Introduction to the Psychology of Religion*, The Macmillan Company, 1923.
*VALENTINE, P. F., *The Psychology of Personality*, D. Appleton and Company, 1927.
*VARIOUS, *Wittenberg Symposium on Feelings and Emotions*, Clark University Press, 1928.
WEATHERHEAD, L. D., *Psychology in Service of the Soul*, The Epworth Press, 1929.
*WECHSLER, I. S., *The Neuroses*, W. B. Saunders Company, 1929.
*WEIGLE, L. A., *The Training of Children in the Christian Family*, The Pilgrim Press, 1922.
*WOODWORTH, R. S., *Dynamic Psychology*, Columbia University Press, 1918.
*—— *Psychology*, 3rd ed., Henry Holt and Company, 1934.
YELLOWLEES, DAVID, *Psychology's Defence of the Faith*, Richard R. Smith, 1930.

INDEX

A

Abraham, 69.
Absalom, 23.
Achievement: blocked by fear, 247-248; and concept of guiding fiction, 336; in happiness, 175 f.; inferiority feelings as drive to, 299; and rich in spirit, 34; the desire for, a motivation for vanity, 273-274.
Action, a method of overcoming fear, 251-252.
Adaptation to stimuli in fasting, 171-172.
Adapting to one's vocation, 96.
Adler, A., 25, 296, 297, 335, 375.
Adult behavior, not instinctive, 25.
Adultery and lust, a new definition of, 131.
Adventure, in faith which challenges youth, 249-250.
Akeley, D. J., 249.
Allen, W. C., 373.
Allport, F. H., 77, 375.
Almsgiving, a form of worship: 163-168; emotional tone of, 167 f.; to bring good luck, 165; its value depends on its motivation, 167; and the psychology of personality, 166-168; rewards in personality, 168; importance in religion, 164-165; universality of in religion, 164; to bring social approval, 165 f.; and tithing, 165.
Ambition, and guiding fiction, 336.
Amos, 59, 69, 171.
Anderson, J. E. x.
Anger, the psychology of: 253-294; in animals, 260; begets itself in others, 257; stimuli for, 260, 269; blocked behavior a cause of, 280-281; of ministers, usually blocked behavior, 281; injustice a cause of, 274-279; often brought out by unconscious psychogenic stimuli, 257-258; wounded vanity a cause of, 268-274; "without cause" not authentic, 259; how controlled, 263-264; cannot be controlled by external acts, 262-263; control by repression and suppression, 263; control by sublimation, 263-264; cure of, fundamental principles, 284-287; a method of cure, catharsis, 289-290; a method of cure, listing anger attitudes, 289; Jesus' method of curing blocked behavior, 281-282; and fear, dispelled by "daily bread" petition, 207; not cured by sense of duty, 270; fatherly love as a cure, 283-284; not cured by passive action, 265; a method of cure, reconditioning, 290; a method of cure, reëducation, 289; Christian method of overcoming summarized, 294; danger of, 253; and day dreams, 272-273; not enough emphasized, 253; changes in outward expression of, 272-273; an expression of an inferiority complex, 273; and fear, forms of temptation, 216; and fear, and unhappiness, 28; harmful whether just or unjust, 265; its relation to murder, 258-264; located in old brain, 260-261; and mental disintegration, 261; occasions for, 265; physiological effects, 259-260; apparent power of, 290-291; enemy of strong personality, 253-258; its injury to personality proportional to its intensity, 262; repression, injurious to personality, 261-262; training children with respect to, 255, 271; very unattractive, 256; nothing to be vain about, 273; and law of vicarious sacrifice, 264.
Angier, R. P., x.
Anxiety neurosis, 56.
Appearance, outward, a false guiding fiction, 349-350.
Appetites and meekness, 48 f.

INDEX

Archimedes, 58.
Aristotle, 7.
Asceticism, not taught by Jesus, 84.
Ask, seek, knock, exposition of, 314-315.
Atheism: concepts of God, 196 f.; and pessimism, 197.
Attitudes, emotional: the unit of personality, 13-15; the Beatitudes as healthy ones, 361-362; as motivation to fasting, 172; unhealthy, list of, 361.
Attractiveness: the psychology of, 100-105; anger detrimental to, 256; factors of, 100-105; happiness in, 105; intelligence in, 102-103; and leadership, 100; common wrong notions about, 100; physical, 101-102; physical, Jesus' attitude toward, 101-102; physical, lack of no great handicap, 102; and temperament, 103-105.
Augustine, 186.

B

Bacon, B. W., 373.
Bagby, E., 223, 319, 375.
Beatitudes: as healthy attitudes, 361-362; as traits, 27 f.
Beecher, H. W., 212.
Beethoven, van, Ludwig, 299.
Beggars, and regeneration, 283 f.
Behaviorism and character, 111.
Bewer, J. A., 373.
Blanchard, P., 309, 353, 376.
Blindness: functional, 235-236; not seeing black, 236 f.
Blocked behavior, methods of removing, 286.
Borrowing, and serving, 283.
Bowers, A. M., 376.
"Boys don't cry" philosophy, 69-70.
Branscomb, M. A., 373.
"Bread," not to be taken literally, 204-205.
Bronner, A. F., 376.
Brotherhood of man, in Lord's Prayer, 197.
Brotherly love: and Christianity, 22; with fatherly elements, 266.
Brown, Charles R., x, 67, 373.
Bruce, A. B., 373.
Buddha, Gautama, 8, 49, 171, 364 f.
Buddhism, 364 f.
Burch, E. W., 373, 375.

Burnham, W. H., 14, 241, 245, 249, 318, 375.
Burton, E. D., 373.
Burton, E. W., 375.
Bushnell, Horace, 360, 375.

C

Cadoux, A. T., 373.
Cannon, W. B., 260, 375.
Case, S. J., 373.
Castor, G. D., 373.
Capacities: and happiness, 39; and purpose, 17.
Catharsis, method of curing anger, 289-290.
Chapman, J. C., x.
Character: psychology of, 106-151; development, principle of multiple causation, 117-124; not developed by codes of conduct, 334; strength of and drives, 109 f.; and effeminacy, 107-108; not synonymous with ethics, 106-110; and external behavior, 109 f.; strong, factors in summarized, 150-151; not inherited, 110; inner nature of, 122 f.; inner attitudes, not outward behavior, 351; instinctive basis, 110; relation of to love, 111-112; nature of, 124; not negative ethics, 112; the test of personality, 106; special problems of, 124; and prudishness, 107; psychogenic principle in, 113-117; and solution of social problems, 106; sex in, 124-138; training difficult, 106; and unselfishness, 110, 111.
Child psychology: of anger education, 271; of courage, 70, 87-88; teaching "daily bread" petition, 208; of fatherly love, 266; of fasting, 174-175; of fear, 241-242; fear conditioning, 233; of making Jesus one's guiding fiction, 352-353; of hungering and thirsting for righteousness, 44; of identification with Jesus, 364; and the inferiority complex, 332; of meekness, 50-52; of mercy, 74-75; of mourning, 71-72; of peacemaking, 81-83; of persecution, 86-88; possible to teach child any philosophy of life, 335; of being poor in spirit, 38-40; of prayer, 189; psychogenic principle in,

INDEX

116-117; pure in heart, 59-60; of serving two masters, 240; of training in reverence, 148-149.
Christianity: influencing human behavior, 3; power of, 1.
Christian personality: and happiness, 89-91; preventing mental disease, 90-91; summary of traits, 89-91.
Church: decline in power of, 1; legalism in, 123.
Codes of conduct: not education in character, 334; intellectual assent to, not character, 344; ethical, development of, 144; moral, difficulties in, 89 f.
College, religion in, 52.
College graduates, frequent mental disease among, 354-357.
"Common sense": a false prophet, 348; and inferiority, 306; and poor in spirit, 32; method of studying human nature, 7.
Compensation: for inferiority feelings, 297-298; for inferiority, laziness and lack of ambition, 317; reforming others a form of, 305; for inferiority complex, seeking popularity, 309-312; for inferiority, desire for short cuts, 313-319; snobbishness as a, 327.
Complex: psychological definition of, 224-227; involves fear, 226.
Concentration: and adapting to stimuli, 171-172; absence of distractions, 171; and fasting, 171.
Conditioning: definition of, 37; in anger from blocked behavior, 281; examples in everyday life, 37 f.; fear in children, 233; love of money as, 229.
Conflict: methods of adjustment, 126 f.; of attitudes and divorce, 140-142; and disintegration, 222; with environment, examples of, 48-50; not inevitable in society, 81; mental, and thwarting of instincts, 222; sources of, 16; types of, 77-79.
Confucius, 8.
Conklin, E. S., 375, 376.
Conscience, and repressed fear complexes, 228.
Conservative religion, not Christian, 340-341.
Courage: and faith in God, 152; and loving service, 240; and mechanism, 152; and persecution, 87-88; teaching to children, 70.
Creative thinking, method of, 191-220.
Credulity, form of faith, 19-20.
Criminals, and lack of mourning, 68.
Cross, in Christianity, 83.

D

"Daily bread" petition: child training in, 208; and growth in personality, 208.
Darwin, Charles, 60, 208, 376.
David, 23, 69.
Day, A. E., 376.
Day dreams, anger, 272-273.
Dementia præcox (see Schizophrenia).
Demosthenes, 299.
Dependence, sense of, in overcoming fear, 249-250.
Descartes, René, 7.
Desire: selfish, preventing spiritual thinking, 203; for short cuts, form of compensation for inferiority, 313-319.
Digestion, effects of anger on, 259-260.
Dillinger, John, 342, 343.
Direct action, in overcoming fear, 252.
Direct attack, method of curing inferiority complex, 318-319.
Discovery and happiness, 43.
Disease, fear in, 244.
Disintegration: and anger, 261; and conflict, 222; and fear, 241; lust in, 126; motion pictures causing, 130 f.; in personality, 15; and "petting," 130.
Dissatisfaction: and poor in spirit, 38 f.; and progress, 29.
Dissociation, source of, 222 f.
Divine forgiveness, not supernatural mysticism, 212-213.
Divine providence, faith in, 207, 321-323.
Divorce: problem of, 138-144; problem in Jesus' day, 139; lust and adultery in, 138, 142 f.; psychological causes, 139-141; prevention of, 141-144; psychogenic factors in, 142; Jesus' teaching on, 138-140.

Dodge, Raymond, x.
Douglas, L. C., 373.
Duty, sense of, not a cure for anger, 270.

E

Edersheim, A., 374.
Education: not acquiring of information, 123; legalism in, 123.
Effeminacy: abuse of, 108; potential value of, 108; and strong character, 107-108; and weakness, 107-108.
Elijah, 69, 171.
Eliot, C. W., 56.
Ellery, Edward, x.
Emotional appeals of false prophets, 340.
Emotional attitudes: unit of personality, 13-15; objective attitude toward, 308.
Emotional habits, three groups of, 225.
Emotional mood, in temptation, 215 f.
Emotional power, and dynamic religion, 341.
Emotional tone: of almsgiving, 167 f.; value in habits, 149.
Emotions: nature of, 25 f.; and external circumstances, 31; tendency to beget themselves in others, 210-211; emergency, destructive of intelligence, 209; James-Lange theory of, 19; and the meaning of things, 237.
Enemies, definition of, 288.
Environment and happiness, 27.
Epilepsy, 56.
Esau, 29.
Ethics, relation to character, 106-110.
Evil: Christian method for overcoming, 278; three methods for overcoming, 278; returning good for, examples of, 279-284.
"Evil eye," a Jewish idiom, 236.
Evolutionary nature of Jesus' teaching, 113.
Excel, desire to: basis of inferiority complex, 298; underlying popularity seeking, 312; basis of desire for short cuts, 313 f.
Experiment: the method of in personality, 369-370; in religion, 10.
Experimental faith: description of, 24-62; in a friendly, not mechanical universe, 321; trait of, hungering and thirsting for righteousness, 40-44; Jesus taught, 19-21; trait of, meekness, 44-52; value in personality, 60-62; to replace pessimism, 316; trait of, poor in spirit, 28-40; trait of, pure in heart, 52-60.
Experimental method, and poor in spirit, 32.
Expressionism, bad method of resolving conflict, 126.

F

Faith: adventurous, challenging to youth, 249-250; credulity, 19-20; experimental (see experimental faith); in fatherly God, method of curing inferiority complex, 319-323; intellectual assent, 19; healing, and objective attitude, 307; and love and happiness, 28; in others, 300; in others, objections to answered, 54-55; in others, pure in heart, 52-54; scientific, 20 f.; and spiritual thinking, 203-208; and the presence of suffering, 320; types of, 19-20.
False prophets: and assumed humility, 339; stimulating inferiority complex, 340; of outward behavior, 348-352; and pseudo-psychology, 339; recognition of, 338-344; summary of, 351-352.
Fame: reward of some almsgiving, 166; desire for, example of conditioning, 38; and happiness, 38, 176 f.; apparent source of glory, 219 f.
Farrar, F. W., 374.
Fasting: a form of worship, 168-177; child training in, 174-175; bad effects of forcing children to practice, 174-175; and concentration, 171; as expression of inner attitudes, 172; and deep meditation, 171; motivations for, 169-172; common to Oriental religions, 169; in parental love, 173-174; rewards in personality, 174-177; for social approval, modern examples of, 170, 172-173; and superstition, 170; and vicarious sacrifice, 172; not common to Western mind, 168-169.
Fatalism, pessimism, forms of surrender, 314.

INDEX

Fatherly God, and law of vicarious sacrifice, 321-322.
Fatherly love: (parental love) description of, 63-91; as cure of anger, 283-284; compared with brotherly love, 63; motivating brotherly love, 266; and conviction of sin, 366 f.; motivation for fasting, 173-174; illustrating genuine forgiveness, 212-213; and cure of gossip, 303 f.; and integration, 23; Jesus taught, 21-23; and impossible teachings of Jesus, 23; trait of, mercy, 72-75; trait of, they who mourn, 65-77; trait of, peacemaking, 75-83; trait of, persecution, 83-89; and sustained motivation, 64 f.; to replace vanity, 274; value of, 88-89.
Fatherliness: characteristics of, 63-65; concept of, and mental power, 198; to replace justice, 268; and magnanimity, 264-265.
Favoritism of parents toward children, 111 f.
Fear: the psychology of, 221-252; and anger, dispelled by "daily bread" petition, 207; and anger, temptations, 216; and anger and unhappiness, 28; blocking achievement, 247-248; child training in, 241-242; "common sense" and happiness in marriage, 239; involved in every complex, 226; not synonymous with caution, 233; complexes, expressions of, 227; conditioning in children, 233; of the crowd, a form of inferiority complex, 327-330; detrimental in disease, 244; and distintegration, 241; of germs, 233-234; of gossip, 329-330; and hate, 239-240; and belief in immortality, 232; Jesus' teaching on, practical, 242-243; not overcome with logic, 246; and love of money, 229-235; and loyalty, 239-242; of opinion of others, 312; psychological methods of overcoming, 245-252; action in overcoming, 251-252; overcome by Christianity, 229; overcome by sense of dependence, 249-250; direct action in overcoming, 252; Jesus' teaching on overcoming, 242-252; use of knowledge in overcoming, 248-249; dominating purpose in overcoming, 250-251; objective attitude in overcoming, 248 f.; summary of methods of conquering, 252; not overcome with will power, 244-245; and weak personality, 235-239; physiological effects of, 243-244; and pugnacity, 227; reconditioning of, 246; in religion, 225-226; and repression, 226; relation of selfishness to, 230; and attitude toward society, 238; extensive use of in society, 228 f.; not always thought undesirable, 243; as source of unhappiness, 221-222; unconscious, and unhappiness, 224; unconscious, source of weak personality, 330.
Fears: common, food, drink, and clothes, 247; varieties of, 224.
Feeling and emotion, nature of, 25 f.
Fisher, V. E., 317, 376.
Fletcher, M. S., 376.
Forgiveness: psychology of, 208-214; in creative thinking, 209; mercy, 73; psychology of obtaining, 210-213; of others, 211-213; illustrated in parental love, 212-213; and changing personality, 211-213; sense of need of, in prayer, 209 f.; place of prayer in, 212; is regeneration, 210.
Fosdick, H. E., x, 189, 196, 197, 292, 374.
Francis of Assisi, 60.
Friedlander, G., 374.
Friendliness of the universe, 46.
Freud, Sigmund, iii, ix, 224, 228, 230, 376.

G

Galileo, 208.
Gambling "instinct," nature of, 25.
Gandhi, misinterprets Jesus, 274, 277, 278.
Gilkey, J. G., 156, 376.
Gillespie, R. D., 377.
Gilliland, A. R., 354, 376.
Giving, not always a source of strong personality, 349.
Glover, T. R., 374.
God: atheistic concepts of, 196 f.; fatherly concept of, in fear and anger, 291-293; fatherly concept of, in lawful universe, 292-293;

concept of, in Lord's Prayer, 196-200.
Goguel, M., 374.
Golden Rule: as cure for inferiority complex, 323-327; to man with inferiority complex, 325-326; recognized as core of Jesus' teaching, 323; diverse interpretations of, 324-325; "let alone" interpretation, 325; Jesus' interpretation, 325; retaliation interpretation, 324; and objective attitude, 326 f.; appearance in other religions, 323 f.
Goliath, 70.
Good intentions, a false guiding fiction, 350 f.
Goodenough, F. L., 246, 254, 272, 376.
Gore, Charles, 66, 374.
Gossip: and cure through fatherly love, 303 f.; not to be confused with honest estimate, 302; fear of, 329-330; and hate begets hate, 302; insidious form of inferiority complex, 300; and projection, 301; its failure to achieve superiority, 303.
Grant, U. S., 70.
Gravitation, laws of, 58-59.
Greatness, in inverse proportion to anger, 253 f.
Groves, E. R., 221, 226, 309, 311, 353, 376.
Guiding fiction: concept of, 335; and achievement, 336; and ambition, 336; why necessarily Christian, 357; choice of, 338-344; development of in childhood, 335-352; factors in formation of, 335-338; and identification, 337; Jesus as, 352-353; outward behavior, 348-352; importance of in personality, 337-338; tested by results in personality, 347-348.

H

Habits: value of emotional tone in, 149; small, importance of, 119-124; small, in personality, 119.
Hadfield, J. A., 376.
Haeckel, E. H., 196.
Hale, E. E., 359.
Hall, G. S., 376.
Hallowed, meaning of, 199.
Hallucinations in mysticism, 153.
Hamilton, Alexander, 291.
Happiness: in achievement, 175 f.; attractiveness of, 105; and capacity, 39; traits of Christian personality in, 89-91; and discovery, 43; and the environment, 27; and faith and love, 28; and fame, 38, 176 f.; and kingdom of heaven, 35; importance of, 24; and satisfaction of instincts, 26 f.; and persecution, 85; and personality, 27; and poor in spirit, 34-35; and poverty, 29; and power, 177; and pure in heart, 57 f.
Harlow, H. F., 355.
Harnack, A., 374.
Hart, B., 257, 258, 376.
Hart, J. K., 56, 376.
Harte, Bret, 302.
Hartshorne, H., 119, 376.
Hate and fear, 239-240.
Headlam, A. C., 374.
Healy, W., 376.
Heaven: concept of, 199; and earth, psychological distinction between, 231; kingdom of (see kingdom of heaven); two ways of thinking about, 199.
Hebrews, Epistle to the, 61.
"He-man" philosophy, 69-70.
Henderson, D. K., 377.
Hero-worship: and divine forgiveness, 213; factor in the life of the child, 334; and the influence of parents, 337; in growth of personality, 334-352; in pure in heart, 60.
Hillelites, 139.
Hitchcock, A. W., 377.
Hollingworth, H. L., 238, 296, 377.
Holt, E. B., 377.
Homo-sexuality, natural basis of, 135-136.
Hosea, 59, 60, 69, 72.
Howard, D. T., 222.
Human nature, method of changing, 120 f.
Humility, false, in leading the crowd, 339.
Hungering and thirsting after righteousness: a trait of experimental faith, 40-44; child psychology of, 44; and purpose, 43.

I

Identification: and divine forgiveness, 213; and guiding fiction, 337; with Jesus, how brought

INDEX

about, 363; with Jesus, essential to strong personality, 356; in Lord's Prayer, 207; in changing personality, 193 f.; changing adult personalities with, 367-368.
Immorality and weakness, 109.
Immortality, belief in, and fear, 232.
Incubation, mental: and fasting, 171; and worship, 154-155.
Indifference, nature of, 26.
Individual differences: psychological concept, 156; and worship, 155-156.
Inferiority complex: the psychology of, 295-333; in child training, 332; and "common sense," 306; compensations for, 297; seeking popularity, a form of compensation, 309-312; desire for short cuts, a form of compensation, 313-319; snobbishness as a compensation for, 327; direct attack, method of cure, 318-319; Golden Rule as a cure of, 323-327; faith in fatherly God as a cure of, 319-323; definition of, 296; forms of expression, 295; gossip insidious form of, 300; expressions of, as rationalizations, 331-332; fear of the crowd, 327-330; with fear of one's own righteousness, 326; instinctive basis of, 295; Jesus' teaching on, 295-296; and mental disease, 330-331; neurasthenia a form of, 317; objective attitude toward, 308; elimination of, and strong personality, 332-333; reforming others, 304-309; and repression, 298; summary of, 330-333; surrender reactions to, 316.
Inferiority feelings: as drive to achievement, 299; sources of, 296-297; universality of, 297.
Influence of one's character on others, 347.
Influencing human behavior, wrong methods, 116.
Inhibited personality, 15 f.
Injustice: normal examples which cause anger, 276; a fundamental cause of anger, 275; and mercy, 73; methods of overcoming, 79-81; method of retaliation, 275; recovering wounded sense of, 286.
Inner principles of character, 122 f.
Insanity, based on weak foundations, 356.
Insight: and seeing God, 61; in pure in heart, 58-59; in science, 58-59; into spiritual law, reward of prayer, 187-188.
Instinct, use of term, ix.
Instinctive basis of inferiority complex, 295.
Instinctive drives, thwarting of, causing fear, 222.
Instincts: lists of, 24 f.; social, 75.
Integration: and fatherly love, 23; value in happy marriage, 144; condition of mental health, 14-15; of sex into personality, 129-130; necessary to strong personality, 362; dominating purpose in, 56 f.; sources of, 16.
Integrity, and logic-tight compartments, 150.
Intelligence: in attractiveness, 102-103; destruction by emergency emotions, 209; necessary to scientific discovery, 208 f.
I.Q. (Intelligence quotient), 103.
Isaiah, 59, 69.

J

Jacob, 179, 188.
James-Lange theory, of the emotions, 19.
James, Wm., 153, 377.
Janet, Pierre, 235, 377.
Jarrett, M. C., 378.
Jefferson, Thomas, 291.
Jelliffe, S. E., 226.
Jelliffe, X. Z., 226.
Jeremiah, 59, 60, 69, 103, 171.
Job, 165, 184.
Joel, 247.
Jonah, 66.
Jots and tittles in human behavior, 120.
Judge not, form of inferiority complex, 299-304.
Judges, Book of, 32.
Jung, C. G., 377.
Justice: difficulty of defining, 276; should be motivated by fatherliness, 268; to scoundrels, Jesus' method of dealing, 268-269; an impossible ideal of righteousness, 267-268.

K

Kant, Immanuel, 7.

INDEX

Kent, C. F., 374.
Keuka Lake, 184.
King, H. C., 374.
Kingdom of heaven: concept of, 35-40; external rewards in, 36; consisting of spiritual laws, 36; happiness, 35.
Knowledge, in overcoming fear, 245-249.

L

Laird, D. A., 313.
Latimer, Hugh, 84.
Law, natural, and friendliness of universe, 322-323.
Lawfulness of spiritual universe, 47 f., 118.
Laziness and lack of ambition, compensations, 317.
Leadership: and attractiveness, 100; qualities of, 339-340.
Learning: love of, and happiness, 40 f.; the modification of response mechanisms, 12 f.; satisfactions for instincts, 25 f.
Lee, Robert E., 70.
Legalism: of church, 123; in formal education, 123.
Legislation, futility of in character, 122.
Life work, choice of, 92.
Light, service of, 94 f.
Light of the world, 94-95.
Ligon, E. M.: experiment on attractiveness, 100 f.; investigation of causes of anger, 260, 269-272, 276-277, 280-281.
Ligon, L. W., x.
Lincoln, Abraham, 70, 291, 364, 369.
Logic-tight compartments: definition of, 146; examples of, in life, 149-150; and rationalization, 162; and teaching of reverence, 146-149.
Lord's Prayer: the psychology of the, 191-220; blue-print for spiritual thinking, 192; difficult to pray at times, 195; divisions of, 195 f.; concept of God, 196-200; and spiritual laws, 194; first assumption of spiritual scientist, 198; universal use of, 194.
Love: Jesus compares brotherly and fatherly, 137-138; and character, 111-112; not one drive, at least five, 134; of enemies, discussion of, 287-291; of enemies, the impossible commandment, 287; of enemies, not very common, 254; of enemies, those whom you hate, 288; of enemies, emphasized by Jesus, 254; of enemies, power of, 291; of enemies, psychological principles involved, 288; and faith, and happiness, 28; fatherly (see fatherly love); and lust, confusion of terms, 125 f.; of money, a conditioned response, 229; of money, and fear, 229-235; of members of one's own sex, 135-136; of opposite sex, 136-137; parental, highest stage of, 137-138; of parents, 135; in physical punishment, 112; psychogenic development of, 134-138; of self, 134-135.
Love affair, first, the idealism of, 136-137.
Loyalty and fear, 239-242.
Lund, F. H., 233, 377.
Lust: and adultery, new definition of, 131; and adultery, in divorce, 142 f.; not desire, 129; unintegrated emotion, 126; and love, confusion of terms, 125 f.

M

Macintosh, D. C., x.
McDairmid, E. W., x.
McDougall, Wm., 377.
McKenzie, J. G., 377.
McNeile, A. H., 374.
Magic and science, 5.
Maller, J. B., 376.
Mammon, personification of wealth, 240.
Manic-depressive insanity, 356.
Mann, Horace, 250, 251.
Manson, T. W., 36, 374.
March, John L., x, 19.
Marriage: of Catholics with Protestants, 141; happy, fear and "common sense" in, 239; happy, and integrated personalities, 144; types of love in, 143-144; older women with younger men, 141; sex in, 143-144; temperamental adjustment in, 141-143.
Marriott, H., 374.
Masses, revolt of, and false prophets, 339.
Mathews, S., 374.
May, M. A., 119, 376.

INDEX

Mazda, 94.
Meekness: a trait of experimental faith, 44-52; and appetites, 48 f.; child psychology of, 50-52; definition of, 44-46; Hebrew derivation of word, 46; examples of, 45 f.; not groveling, 45; not repression, 49; rewards of, 50-52; attitude of scientist, 46 f.; lack of in spiritual realm, 47 f.; not surrender, 45; and temptation, 217; testing of, 49.
Menninger, K. A., 256, 377.
Mental disease: foundations of, 360-361; and inferiority complex, 330-331; relation to Christian personality, 90-91; and sex, 125; and social contact, 323.
Mental health: integration in, 14-15; criterion of religion, 10; and sympathy, 71.
Mental hygiene, use of objective attitude in, 306-308.
Mental peace, reward of prayer, 185-186.
Mental power, and concept of fatherliness, 198.
Mental set: meaning of, 188; will of God or selfish desire, 200.
Mercy: a trait of fatherly love, 72-75; child psychology of, 74-75; definition of, 72; regenerative forgiveness, 73; and injustice, 73; not negative trait, 73; difficulty of practicing, 74; and righteousness, 72.
Meyer, Adolph, 17.
Micklem, P. A., 374.
Moffatt, James, 22, 374.
Mohammed, 8, 171.
Moody, Dwight L., 182.
Moore, T. V., 377.
Moral character and sexual purity not synonymous, 124.
Morality and strength of personality, 107-110.
Morgan, J. J. B., 39, 344, 377.
Morison, J., 374.
Moses, 45, 69, 118, 139, 170, 196, 259.
Motes and beams: 304-309; use of figure by Jesus, 304-305.
Motion pictures and disintegration, 130 f.
Motivation: of almsgiving, 167; satisfaction of inherited drives, 12-13; for spiritual thinking, 201 f.; sustained, and parental love, 64 f.; for fasting, 169-172; for prayer, 179.
Motives for worship, 158-159.
Mourning: a trait of fatherly love, 65-72; child psychology, 71-72; Jewish meaning of word, 65; not outward grief, 65; being sensitive to needs of others, 65; and sympathy, 67.
Multiple causation in character development, 117-124.
Murder, its growth from anger, 258-264.
Mysticism, not always healthy, 153.

N

Napoleon Bonaparte, 308.
Natural laws, regularity of, implications of, 292-293.
Nearsightedness and narrowmindedness, 237.
Negative morality in religious education, 11.
Neurasthenia: case history of, 316 f.; description of, 317.
Newton, Isaac, Sir, 58, 208.
Niggardliness and fear, 236.
Non-resistance, not the method of Jesus, 277.

O

Oaths: history of attitudes toward, 145-146; Jesus' teaching on, 144-150.
Objective attitude: discussion of, 306-309; toward our biases, 308; in overcoming fear, 248 f.; toward inferiority complex, 308, 326 f.; a form of mental therapy, 306-308; not morbid introspection, 309; and social conformity, 329; to overcome surrender reaction, 318.
"Old-Maid" adjustment, 102.
Oliver, J. R., 377.
Oratory, a false guiding fiction, 348-349.
Orderliness of universe, assumption of science, 8.
Orientation, in Lord's Prayer, 218.
Overstreet, H. A., 377.

P

Paranoia: interpretation of Golden Rule, 324; reformatory, description of, 305.

INDEX

Parental love (*see* fatherly love).
Parents: inefficiency of, 363-364; using "common sense," 7.
Pasteur, Louis, 60.
Patriotism, psychogenic nature of, 114.
Paul, 60, 70, 83, 84, 95, 103, 167, 171, 192, 199, 230, 247, 301, 348, 363.
Pavlov, I. P., 37.
Peace: courage, 76 f.; negative connotation of, 76; and persecution, 83; and psychogenic attitudes, 82; unpopularity of, 76.
Peacemaking: a trait of fatherly love, 75-83; child psychology of, 81-83; inner conflicts, 77-78; conflicts between man and environment, 78; resolving conflicts, 76; conflicts between large social groups, 78-79.
Pearls and holy things, use of, 312.
Pearls before swine, exposition, 310.
Pennell, Theodore, 81.
Perception: and the emotions, 237; and purpose, 238; and repression, 238.
Perfection: and fatherliness, 293-294; and loving enemies, 293-294.
Persecution, enduring: a trait of fatherly love, 83-89; not a form of asceticism, 84; child psychology of, 86-88; and courage, 87-88; normal examples of, 84; and happiness, 85; and progress, 85; and vicarious sacrifice, 86.
Persistence in spiritual problems, 315.
Personality: aim of book, 1; almsgiving in the development of, 166-168; anger repression injurious to, 261-262; the attractive, 100-105; two methods for changing, 193; Jesus changing, 357; changing, and prayer, 192; changing with psychoanalysis, 367; adult, changing, 365-368; adult, difficulty of changing, 365; not changed by emotional appeal, 193; not changed by logic, 368; not changed by logical reasoning, 192 f.; not changed quickly, 346-347; not changed by repression, 193; the Christian, strength of, 362; the Christian, summary of, 368-371; the Christian, value in civilization, 371; development, not usually well done, 353-359; the emotional attitude as the unit of, 13-15; value of experimental faith in, 60-62; growth of, by "daily bread" petition, 208; growth of, value of praying for, 218; growth of, the reward of prayer, 186-187; necessity of right foundations in, 354-355; impossible to build on weak foundations, 359; importance of guiding fiction in, 337-338; and happiness, 27; hero-worship in the growth of, 334-352; the inhibited, 15 f.; inherited characteristics in, 11 f.; the integrated, 16; integration in, 14-15; potential power not used, 314; psychology of, 11-18; psychogenic nature of, 344-348; the psychopathic, 15; the rewards of almsgiving in, 168; the rewards of fasting in, 174-177; the rewards of prayer in, 184-188; service of mankind in developing, 17; strong, anger an enemy of, 253-258; strong, and forgiveness, 211-213; strong, identification with Jesus in, 356; strong, and acting on impulses, 355-356; strong, and elimination of inferiority complex, 332-333; strong, integration necessary to, 362; strong, solution of social problems, 370; potential strength, 11; value of prayer in, 152-190; pseudo-psychology vs. scientific psychology, 6; dominant purpose in, 17; as criterion of religion, 10; problem of science, 6; types of, 15-16; weak, and conflict, 222; weak, and fear complexes, 235-239; weak, unconscious fear as a source of, 330; law of vicarious sacrifice in, 370.
Pessimism and resultant atheism, 197.
Peter, Simon, 53, 54, 69, 73, 74, 129, 199, 216, 217, 224, 357, 366, 368, 370.
"Petting" and disintegration, 130.
Pharisee and the publican, the parable of the, 31.
Philosophy of life, child can be taught any, 335.

INDEX

Phobia: example of, 223; a repressed fear, 223.
Physical punishment and love of parents, 112.
Physiological effects: of anger, 259-260; of fear, 243-244.
Piaget, J., 377.
Plato, 7.
Pleasure: and sacrifice, 51; and work, 41 f.
Plummer, A., 374.
Poor, who pray for bread, 206.
Poor in spirit: a trait of experimental faith, 28-40; child psychology of, 38-40; and common sense, 32; and "daily bread," 204-205; degrees of, 30; and dissatisfaction, 38 f.; and experimental method, 32; and happiness, 34-35; social approval, 35; who pray for spiritual bread, 206 f.; and temptation, 217; and vision, 29 f.
Popularity seeking: examples of, 311; compensation for inferiority, 309-312.
Poverty and happiness, 29.
Power of evil, apparent, 218-220.
Power and happiness, 177.
Power of righteousness, assumption of, in spiritual thinking, 218-220.
Pragmatism, assumption of science, 9-11.
Prayer: a form of worship, 177-189; delayed answers to, 183; child training in, 189; of determination, 182 f.; does not bring intervention in natural laws, 182; common in Orient, 178-179; motivations for, 179; motivated by fear, 182; of perplexity, 183; problem of, in personality, 152-190; power of, in lives of men, 153-154; psychogenic development of, 181; psychological factor in, 152 f.; vain repetition, nature of, 180; rewards of, 181-184; rewards of, in personality, 184-188; the reward of insight into spiritual law, 187-188; the reward of mental peace, 185-186; the reward of personality growth, 186-187; and scientific reasoning, 191 f.; in secret, the psychology of, 180; for social approval, 180; as spiritual thinking, 191; common types of, compared with Bible types of, 179; unanswered, explanation of, 315; value of, 189.
Prince, M., 377.
Prodigal son, meaning of, 137-138.
Progress: in civilization, the Christian personality in, 371; and the concept of brotherhood, 197; and dissatisfaction, 29; and persecution, 85; and vicarious sacrifice, 213-214.
Projection: 286; and gossip, 301.
Propaganda, the nature of, 79.
Pruett, L., 299.
Pseudo-psychology courses, 313.
Psychoanalysis: and being "born again," 367; investigates foundations, 358.
Psychogenic growth of anger into murder, 258-259.
Psychogenic development of the timid soul, 227.
Psychogenic attitudes and peace, 82.
Psychogenic nature of personality, 344-348, 354-355.
Psychogenic growth of prayer, 181.
Psychogenic principle: in character, 113-117; in child training, 116-117; and influencing behavior, 116; practical implications of, 114-117.
Psychology, pseudo, courses, 313.
Psychopathic personality, 15.
Pugnacity and fear, 227.
Pure in heart: a trait of experimental faith, 52-60; child psychology of, 59-60; having faith in one's fellow men, 52-54; as singleness of purpose, 52 f., 55-57; and happiness, 57 f.
Purpose: and capacities, 17; dominating, in overcoming fear, 250-251; dominant, in healthy personality, 17; dominant, in being pure in heart, 52 f.; and hungering and thirsting for righteousness, 43; and integration, 56 f.; and perception, 238; and poor in spirit, 35; in being pure in heart, 55-57; selfish, and temptation, 216.

R

Rationalization: in anger, 257 f.; how to avoid, 162; in college, 163; and conviction of sin, 365; conscious explanation of inferior-

ity, 331-332; and logic-tight compartments, 162; psychogenic nature of, 160-161; psychology of, 160-163; danger of, in temptation, 215; in worship, 161-163.
Reasoning: will not overcome fear, 246; scientific, and prayer, 191 f.
Reconditioning: method of curing anger, 290; and cure of fear of poverty, 234-235; in overcoming fear, 246; in changing personality, 193 f.; about nature of universe, 321.
Reed, H. L., x, 199, 266, 322.
Reëducation, method of curing anger, 289.
Reformatory paranoia, 304-309.
Reforming others, compared with gossip, 305.
Regeneration, involved in forgiveness, 210.
Religion: in college, 52; experiment in, 10; often involving fear, 225-226; outside scope of science, 7.
Religiosity, a false guiding fiction, 350.
Religious education: failure of, 342-343; healthy, 343-344; not always healthy, 11; negative morality in, 11; the purpose of, 11; repression in, 11; types of, 11.
Religious instinct, nature of, 25.
Renan, E., 374.
Repentance, out of date, 365.
Repression: of anger, injurious to personality, 261; in control of anger, 263; method of resolving conflict, 127; and fear, 226; and the inferiority complex, 298; in inhibited personality, 16; not meekness, 49; morbid expressions of, 127; harmful to personality, 193; and perception, 238; in religious education, 11; shame and guilt in, 228; and lack of sympathy, 68.
Resist not evil, 274-279.
Retaliation interpretation of Golden Rule, 324.
Reverence: child training in, 148-149; teaching of, and logic-tight compartments, 146-149; not outward behavior, 147; psychogenic development of, 148.
Rich in spirit: and achievement, 34; and unhappiness, 33; examples of, 31-34.

Rich young ruler, 68, 357.
Richards, Leyton, 80, 81.
Riddle, D. W., 374.
Ridley, Nicholas, 84.
Righteous indignation: Christian method of showing, 264-268; as a good excuse, 255-256; Jesus' method of showing, 266-267; danger of, in personality, 266-267; a temptation, 216.
Righteousness: Jesus' concept of, 43; Jewish concept of, 42; of justice, an impossible ideal, 267-268; and mercy, 72; nature of, 42-43; power of, a necessary assumption for spiritual thinking, 218-220; of scribes and Pharisees, 121-124.
Rivers, W. H. R., 378.
Robertson, A. T., 375.
Robinson, B. W., 375.
Robinson, E. S., 378.
Robinson, F. R., 378.
Robinson, T. H., 375.
Rohrbaugh, L. G., 378.
Rosanoff, A. J., 378.
Rules of conduct and etiquette, 114.
Russell, B., 292.

S

Sacrifice, and pleasure, 51.
Salt: of the earth, 92-94; history of the use of, 93; vicarious nature of, 93-94.
Samson, 70.
Samuel, 69.
Sanhedrin, 217.
Schizophrenia: shut-in personality, 17, 336 f.; stimulated by anger, 271.
Science: the basic assumptions of, 8-11; orderliness of universe, an assumption of, 8; pragmatism, an assumption of, 9-11; importance of little things in, 120; and magic, 5; and measurement, 5; not applied to religion, 7; value of, to religion, 6.
Scott, E. F., 36, 375.
Seeing God and insight, 61.
Self-discipline, in "daily bread" petition, 206.
Self-exaltation, normal and abnormal forms of, 300-301.
Self-feeling, methods of enhancing, 285.

INDEX

Self-realization: and character, 110; a fundamental drive, 25.
Selfishness: and disease, 237; relation to fear, 230.
Sense organs, effect of the emotions on, 55.
Sermon on the Mount, introduction to, 18-23.
Sermon on the Mount, references to expositions:

Matthew 5:1-2,	18.
:3,	28-40.
:4,	65-72.
:5,	44-52.
:6,	40-44.
:7,	72-75.
:8,	52-60.
:9,	75-83.
:10-12,	83-88.
:13-16,	92-105.
:17,	113-117.
:18,	117-119.
:19,	119-121.
:20,	121-124.
:21-22,	258-264.
:23-24,	264-268.
:25-26,	268-274.
:27-28,	124-131.
:29-30,	131-134.
:31-32,	138-144.
:33-37,	144-150.
:38-39,	274-279.
:40-42,	279-284.
:43-47,	287-291.
:48,	291-294.
6:1,	158-163.
:2-4,	163-168.
:5-8,	177-189.
:9,	194-200.
:10,	200-202.
:11,	203-208.
:12-15,	208-220.
:16-18,	102, 168-177.
:19-21,	229-235.
:22-23,	235-239.
:24,	239-242.
:25-34,	242-252.
7:1-2,	299-304.
:3-5,	304-309.
:6,	309-312.
:7-8,	313-319.
:9-11,	319-323.
:12,	323-327.
:13-14,	327-330.
:15-16a,	338-344.
:16b-20,	344-348.
Matthew :21-23,	348-352.
:24-25,	359-365.
:26-27,	352-359.
:28-29,	368-371.

Service: not appearance, important in personality, 345-346; four forms of, 98; of mankind, in healthy personality, 17; and vocational selection, 98.
Serving two masters, 239-242.
Sex: and distorted personalities, 125; a normal drive in wholesome personality, 129; method of integrating into personality, 129-130; the problem of, 124-138; the problem of, for the unmarried, 133; a form of wealth, 233, 234.
Sexual purity and moral character not synonymous, 124.
Shame and guilt in repression, 228.
Shammaites, 139.
Shaw, Bernard, 159.
Shuttleworth, F. K., 376.
Simkhovitch, V. G., 375.
Sin: the psychology of the conviction of, 365-367; as "missing the mark," 329.
"Single eye," a Jewish idiom, 236.
Slosson, E. E., 251, 378.
Smith, D., 375.
Snobbishness, compensation for inferiority complex, 327.
Social approval: fasting for, modern examples of, 172-173; a motive for prayer, 180; and being poor in spirit, 35.
Social conformity: commonness of, 327-328; and the objective attitude, 329; a temptation, 329.
Social contact and mental disease, 323.
Social inheritance in personality, 345.
Social instinct, the, 75.
Social interest, and spiritual thinking, 203-204.
Social problems, and strong personality, 370.
Socrates, 7, 286.
Southard, E. E., 378.
Spearman, C. E., 300.
Spiritual law: insight into, a reward of prayer, 187-188; Jesus' teachings constitute, 369; unhappiness in the breaking of, 118; in the nature of universe, 8; and the will of God, 200.

INDEX

Spiritual thinking: first assumption for, 198; second guiding principle for, 202; motivating men to do, 201 f.; considering the problem, 203; involves faith in the power of righteousness, 218-220; and knowledge of the will of God, 201.
Sportsmanship: development of, 82; and peacemaking, 82.
Stagner, R., 355.
Starbuck, E. D., 360.
Stealing, psychogenic factors in, 115.
Stevens, G. B., 375.
Stevens, W. A., 375.
Stogdill, Ralph M., 116.
Stratton, G. M., 378.
Sublimation: a method of resolving conflict, 127 f.; in the control of anger, 263-264; is not repression, 128.
Suicide, a symptom of weak foundations, 356.
Superiority, the desire for, 271-272.
Suppression: in the control of anger, 263; a method of resolving conflict, 127; forms of, 132 f.; Jesus' method of, 133-134; the method of, 131-134; necessity for, 131.
Surrender reaction: to inferiority complex, 316-318; objective attitude as a cure, 318.
Symonds, P. M., 7, 378.
Sympathy, value of, 71.

T

Tait, A., 375.
Talents, wasted, 210.
Temperament: in attractiveness, 103-105; description of, 103 f.; not inherited, 104; types of, 104 f.
Temperamental adjustment in marriage, 141-143.
Temper tantrum: inhibiting creative thinking, 209; infantile in nature, 254 f.
Temptation: psychology of, 214-218; and emotional mood, 215 f.; of fear and anger, 216; Jesus' description of, 216; methods of meeting, 217; of selfish purpose, 216; types of, 215.
Temptations of Jesus, the psychology of the, 175-177.
Theathanai, 158.

Thinking: the emotional nature of, 225; spiritual, and prayer, 191.
Tholuck, A., 375.
Thorndike, E. L., 378.
Thouless, R. H., 378.
Timid soul, psychogenic development of the, 227.
Timme, A. R., 115.
Timothy, 363.
Tithing: 122; and almsgiving, 165.
Traits, the nature of, 119.

U

Unanswered prayer, and "daily bread," 205 f.
Unconscious behavior, Jesus aware of the existence of, 128 f.
Unconscious fears: and unhappiness, 224; a source of weak personality, 330.
Unhappiness: caused by fear, 221-222; from fear and anger, 28; and being rich in spirit, 33; and unconscious fears, 224.

V

Valentine, P. F., 302, 313, 346, 378.
Values, and the satisfaction of urges, 13.
Vanity: appeal to and false prophets, 341 f.; caused by the desire for achievement, 273-274; replaced by fatherly love, 274; common in religion, 270 f.; wounded, a cause of anger, 268-274; wounded, examples of, 269-272.
Vicarious sacrifice: law of, and anger, 264; and fasting, 172; law of, and a fatherly God, 321-322; not instinctive, 214; and persecution, 86; law of, in personality, 370; and progress, 213-214; law of, the psychology of, 208-214; law of, and "resist not evil," 279.
Visions: of achievement, blocked by fear, 247-248; wrong method of developing in children, 39; hallucinations and discoveries, 153; and being poor in spirit, 29 f.; and spiritual thinking, 202.
Vocation: adapting to, 96; common criteria for choice of, 96; difficulties in choice of, 96; adjustment to, two-fold nature of, 96; choice of, pure in heart, 60.
Vocational guidance, 92-100.

Vocational selection: service criterion, 98; choice of life work, 98-100; Jesus' method of choice, 98; bad results of common criteria, 97.
Volition, dependent on action, 355-356.

W

Washington, Booker T., 256.
Washington, George, 70, 364, 369.
Watt, James, 58.
Wealth: in itself not evil, 231 f.; health and sex as forms of, 233; influence in the lives of men, 230; love of, an example of conditioning, 37 f.; love of, and poverty, 230-231; an apparent source of power, 219.
Weatherhead, L. D., 378.
Wechsler, I. S., 378.
Weigle, L. A., x, 51, 378.
Welles, K. B., x.
Wendt, 375.
Wesley, John, 60, 279, 280.
Will of God: devotion to, 199-202; and spiritual law, 200.
Will power: dependent on action, 355-356; cannot overcome fear, 244-245.

Woodworth, R. S., 12, 378.
Work and pleasure, 41 f.
Worship: in almsgiving, 163-168; built on the attitudes of the Beatitudes, 157-158; from a sense of duty, 159; education in, 156 f.; fasting in, 168-177; forms of, 153; and individual differences, 155-156; Jesus' teaching on, summarized, 189-190; and mental incubation, 154-155; the motives of, 158-159; a function of personality, 157; a source of power, 158-163; prayer in, 177-189; psychological study, analytical not dynamic, 154; three psychological principles underlying, 154-158; rationalization in, 161-163; rewards of, 159-160; to be seen of men, 158-159.

Y

Yellowlees, D., 378.
"Yellowness" and unconscious fear, 227.
Yerkes, R. M., x.

Z

Zaccheus, 231.
Zoroaster, 8, 94.

1